Professional Savages

Professional Savages

Captive Lives and Western Spectacle

Roslyn Poignant

Yale University Press
New Haven and London

Designed by Sandy Chapman

Printed in China

Library of Congress Cataloging-in-Publication Data

Poignant, Roslyn.
  Professional savages : captive lives and western spectacle / Roslyn Poignant.-- 1st ed.
      p. cm.
  Includes bibliographical references and index.
  ISBN 0-300-10247-X (cl. : alk. paper)
  1. Aboriginal Australians in popular culture--History--19th century. 2. Aboriginal Australians--Public opinion. 3. Circus--History--19th century. 4. Barnum and Bailey--History. 5. Racism in museum exhibits--History--19th century. 6. Racism in anthropology--History--19th century. 7. Museum exhibits--Moral and ethical aspects. 8. Human remains (Archaeology)--Repatriation--Australia. 9. United States--Public opinion. 10. Europe--Public opinion. I. Title.
  GN666.P55 2004
  305.89´915--dc22

                                                                    2004000470

A catalogue record for this book is available from The British Library

Contents

Acknowledgements

Goodwill towards my long-term search for the Aboriginal travellers' story has sustained me over a number of years and journeys. Always I have travelled with Aboriginal friends from North Queensland in mind: Walter Palm Island, his brothers Reg and Alan, and his extended family, Josephine Geia, Maurice Bligh, and the Palm Island community, both Manbarra and Bwagan, Ernest and Enid Grant of the Girringun community, Violet Sirrus and many, many others. I thank them all for their warm encouragement and patient anticipation, and I thank anthropologist Nicolass Heijm, who first introduced me to Walter, and always smoothed my way. I am also very grateful to the Cunningham family for their generosity of spirit and practical assistance in providing access to R. A. Cunningham's book of news cuttings and for opening the family archives to me. The American research in 1993 was partly grant-aided by the British Academy, topped up by the Royal Anthropological Institute and the Tambo Repatriation Committee (which was funded by the Aboriginal and Torres Strait Islander Commission), and in 2000 the British Academy again made possible the German and other European research. Considerable thanks are due to them and to the Australian Institute for Aboriginal and Torres Strait Islander Studies for continuing support of the project, particularly Geoffrey Gray for his critical input. Special thanks to that remarkable institution, the National Library of Australia, Canberra, for providing me with the opportunity – as curator of the exhibition *Captive Lives: Looking for Tambo and his Companions* – to present in an earlier form the ideas and narratives developed in this book; particularly Michael Richards and Irene Turpie of the Exhibition division, Morgyn Phillips, Education, and Linda Groom and Sylvia Carr of the Pictorial division. Research in California and elsewhere in America, and in Scandinavia, Russia and France was gathered in transit as other projects allowed but I could not have done it without the wholehearted participation of the skilful interpreters and translators: in Russia, Dasha Stabnikova; in Germany, Nina Nixdorf, Claudia Schemberg, Mark Schreiber, Martin Ledwon and Hannelore Schüz; and Fiona Dawson of the German Academic Exchange Service, London. I am indebted for the translation of German anthropological texts to Christine Winter and Peter Berger; French anthropological texts,

Monique Burg; Italian texts, Wilfred Beaver; and Russian texts, Sheila McKay. I am grateful to the Department of Anthropology, University College London, for an Honorary Research Fellowship during the writing of this book.

The research for this book has benefited from the skills and patience of the librarians, archivists and curators of many institutions: John Oxley Library, State Library of Queensland and Brian Randall; James Cook University Library; Katherine Frankland and Margaret Read, Department of Family Services, Queensland; Queensland State Archives; Fryer Library, University of Queensland; Queensland Museum; Police Museum, Queensland; South Australian Museum and Philip Jones; New South Wales State Archives; Macleay Museum, University of Sydney; Mitchell Library, State Library of New South Wales; and the National Archives Australia, Canberra, Sydney and Brisbane branches. In the UK: British Library; National Archives, London; Student's Room and Sheila Mackie and staff of Library of Department of Ethnography, British Museum; Photographic Collection, Royal Anthropological Institute, and Arkadius Bentowski; Wellcome Institute Library; Bodleian Library, University of Oxford; Imperial College, London; Lambeth Archives; Crystal Palace Museum. In Paris: Bibliothèque Nationale and Société de Géographie; Photothèque, Musée de l'Homme, particularly Christine Barthe and Jacqueline Dubois; Musée d'Orsay; La Bibliothèque Historique de la Ville de Paris; and twenty Mairies d'Arrondissement. In the USA: Bridgeport Public Library; Department of Rare Books and Special Collections Princeton University Library; Chicago Public Library; Chicago Historical Society; Hertzberg Collection, San Antonio Public Library, and Jill Blake; Library of Congress, Washington; Milner Library Special Collections, Illinois State University, and Steve Gossard; National Anthropological Archives, in the National Museum of Natural History, Smithsonian Institution, Washington DC, and Paula Richardson Fleming, and James Harwood; Smithsonian Institution Archives, William Cox and Libby Glenn; Cleveland Research Center, Cleveland Public Library; Cleveland State University Ohio Library and William Becker; Cuyahoga County Archives, Ohio; Western Reserve Historical Society, Natural History Museum, Cleveland, particularly Esther Bockhoff; Circus World Museum, Baraboo, and Fred Dahlinger and Meg Allen; Maryland Historical Society, Baltimore; Free Library, Philadelphia; Philadelphia Historical Society; Brooklyn Historical Society; Brooklyn Public Library; Westervelt Collection, New York Historical Society; New York Public Library, particularly the Performing Arts Division; New York City Municipal Archives;

American Museum of Natural History; National Archives and Records Administration, Washington, New York and Pacific Sierra Regions; Californian Historical Society; Special Collections, San Francisco Public Library; San Francisco Performing Arts Library; History department, Los Angeles Public Library; San Diego Public Library; San Diego State University Library; Coronado Historical Museum; City of San Diego Archives; California State Library, Sacramento; Oakland Public Library; Oakland Museum; Bancroft Library, University of California; San Bernardino County Library; San Bernardino County Archives; Bernice P. Bishop Museum; Hawaiian State Library; Hawaiian Historical Society; and Hawaii State Archives. In Germany: Stadtarchiv Chemnitz; Uwe Fiedler, Museum für Stadtgeschichte, Chemnitz; Stadt Chemnitz Standesamt; Stadtischer Friedhof, Chemnitz; Stadtbibliothek, Chemnitz; Ulrich Schürer, Zoologischer Garten der Stadt, Wuppertal; Stadtarchiv, Wuppertal; Frau Höfeler, Evang. Kirchengemeinde, Wuppertal; Heidi Koch, Völkerkundliches Museum, Wuppertal; Michael Knieriem, Historisches Zentrum Wuppertal; Historisches Museum, Frankfurt; Hauptstaatarchiv, Wiesbaden; Stadtarchiv Darmstadt; Hessisches Staatsarchiv, Darmstadt; Alter Friedhof, Darmstadt. In Berlin: Konrad Vanja, Museum Europäischer Kulturen; Markus Schindlbeck, Ethnologisches Museum; Birgit Schnabel, Deutsches Historisches Museum; Zentral und Landesbibliothek; Zeitschriften Abteilung, Stadt Bibliothek; Manfred Ades, Museum für Naturkunde; Dr Kreuz, Institut für Anthropologie, Humboldt Universität. In Russia: Arsen L. Purundjan and Helena Godina, Research Institute and Museum of Anthropology, Moscow State University; State Public Library of the History of Russia. Also the Royal Library, Stockholm; the Carolina University Library, Uppsala; and the Royal Library, Copenhagen. Thank you to Kate Darian-Smith and James Walter for encouraging me to write the first paper, to Hilke Thode-Arora for her generous and invaluable contribution to my research. Thank you to my constant readers, Elizabeth Edwards, Helen Fenbury, Lynette Russell, Christine Winter, Christopher Wright and my Scandinavian link, Terry Carlbom, who have sustained me through my moments of doubt; the responsibility for the conclusions drawn is mine alone. For their whole-hearted support, I wish to thank Michael Aird, Niels Barfoed, Jonathan Benthall, Florentina Cadalanova, Robert Dixon, Robert Ørsted Jensen, Sara Joynes, Adrienne Kaeppler, Diane Losche, Julie Marcus, Peter Mesenhöller, Christopher Pinney, Kay Schaffer, Ronald Store, Nicholas Thomas, Paul Turnbull and Michael Williams.

Author's Note

A major concern of this book is an examination of the language of nineteenth-century colonial discourse where words such as 'savage', 'savagery', 'native', 'cannibal', 'Black' or 'black' were used frequently. To avoid sprinkling the text with quotation marks these have been dispensed with, except occasionally on first use of a word, or where there may be any ambiguity. Aborigine and Aboriginal are capitalised except in an original direct quotation. When Indigenous is used as a proper name, inclusive of Aborigines and Torres Strait Islanders, and as an alternative to them, it is also capitalised, similarly with Black and White.

'Illustrirte' is spelt as printed, not modernised.

List of Illustrations

from 1883), long after the Australian Aborigines and other groups had departed. Bridgeport Public Library.

41 'Indian Bushmen from New Holland', woodcut, broadsheet of the Australian Aborigines and a woman from Angola, toured in Germany by Heinrich Hill in the 1830s. National Library of Australia.

42 'Price One Penny: The Growth of City Populations', unidentified news item from Cunningham's cuttings book.

43 Sussy in boots. Photograph: Negretti and Zambra, Crystal Palace, London. National Archives, London.

44 'Pigmy Earthmen at the Royal Aquarium', a Khoisan group led by N/kon N/Qui and his wife, N'arbecy, presented by the showman Farini, Westminster, September 1884. Bodliean Library, University of Oxford.

45 ' "Krao" The "Missing Link," A Living Proof of Darwin's Theory of the Descent of Man'. Broadsheet for show at the Aquarium, Westminster, 23 March 1887. Bodliean Library, University of Oxford.

46 Castan's Panoptikum, Berlin 1884. Landesarchiv Berlin.

47 'Bei den Australnegern', artist Walter Busch, in *Uber Land und Meer. Allgemeine Illustrirte Zietung*, 1885. Toby (centre) and Billy (right) entertain at Castan's Panoptikum Berlin, 1884.

48 Boomerang throwing in Hazenheide, Berlin, artist Georg Koch, in *Illustrirte Zeitung, Leipzig und Berlin*, 1884. Toby and his son in background, Billy, Jimmy and Bob centre, Sussy and Jenny on right.

49 Professor Rudolf Virchow surrounded by skeletal material in the Institute for Pathology,

University of Berlin. Bildarchiv Preussischer Kulturbesitz, Berlin.

50 The boy, Toby, Paris, 1885. Photograph: Prince Roland Bonaparte. Royal Anthropological Institute, London.

51 (L to r) Billy, R. A. Cunningham, Jenny, Toby, his son, Toby, Jimmy, Sussy (seated) and Bob reclining. Photograph: Carl Günther, Berlin, 1884. Société de Géographie and Bibliothèque Nationale, France.

52 Bob. Photograph: Carl Günther, Berlin, 1884. Société de Géographie and Bibliothèque Nationale, France.

53 Note on takings for Mr Cunningham, Kaiserhof Hotel, Halberstadt, Germany, 10 March 1885. From Cunningham's cuttings book.

54 'Australneger in Frankfurt am Main', *Kleine Presse*, 14 May 1885. Centre, Jenny, Billy and Sussy, foreground, Sussy sells photographs, young Toby throws boomerangs, left corner group, Billy, Toby, young Toby and Jenny.

55 Jimmy, Berlin, 1884. Photograph: Carl Günther, Berlin, 1884. Société de Géographie and Bibliothèque Nationale, France.

56 Sussy, Berlin, 1884. Photograph: Carl Günther. Ethnologisches Museum, Berlin.

57 Toby, Berlin, 1884. Photograph: Carl Günther. Société de Géographie and Bibliothèque Nationale, France.

58 Billy, Paris, 1885. Photograph: Prince Roland Bonaparte. Royal Anthropological Institute, London.

59 Jenny, Paris, 1885. Photograph: Prince Roland Bonaparte. Royal Anthropological Institute, London.

For the descendants and kin of the Aboriginal travellers

To recount the odyssey of sorrow of the young man called Tambo, his wife and their companions and of the members of the second group which followed is not to encourage bitterness. Such a recounting is an act of sorrow, acknowledgement and attempted reclamation . . . In Tambo's case, the reclamation had in part occurred when his body was returned to his people in 1993 . . . In truth, however, his reclamation is complete only now the appalling facts of his story are confronted and acknowledged.

Sir William Deane, 3 November 1997

Introduction: The Journey

The world of the journey furnished a symbolic text where each culture read its own intentions.

Paul Carter, *The Road to Botany Bay*, 1987

In October 1993 I was in the United States researching the little-known story of the removal overseas of two groups of Australian Aborigines from neighbouring North Queensland communities, one in 1883 and the other in 1892, by the same showman, Robert. A. Cunningham, when news flashed round the world that the mummified body of a young Aborigine known as Tambo had been found in the basement of a recently closed funeral home in Cleveland, Ohio.

Tambo was one of the first group of nine – six men, two women and a boy – from the Palm Islands and nearby Hinchinbrook Island abducted by Cunningham, who was acting as recruiter for the circus impresario Phineas T. Barnum. During the circus touring season of 1883 Tambo and his companions featured in Barnum's *Ethnological Congress of Strange Savage Tribes*, together with other performing groups of Zulu, Toda, Nubians and Sioux, who had been similarly dispossessed on other colonial frontiers. Then, during the winter of 1883–4, Cunningham toured the dime museums of northern USA with the Aboriginal performers until, in Cleveland, on a bitter winter's day in late February, Tambo was the first to die. Unknown to his companions, he was subjected to a final, terrible indignity: his embalmed body was placed on show in Drew's Dime Museum, and it remained on display there and elsewhere in Cleveland well into the twentieth century.

When Tambo's story broke, although I already knew from a contemporary European account of their story[1] that Tambo, from Palm Island, had died in America, I did not know where. Several months earlier, while in Australia, I had also gone in search of descendants of the Aboriginal travellers and had met Walter Palm Island – whose family name reflects his

1   (L to r) Walter, Alan and Reg Palm Island with their grandfather's sword club, against background of Welcome Home Tambo banner at the *Captive Lives* exhibition, National Library of Australia, Canberra. Photograph: Louis Seselja.

status as a traditional owner.[2] From him I learnt that his family's genealogy, as told to anthropologist N. B. Tindale in 1938 by Walter's grandfather, Dick Palm Island, included the note that Walter's great grandfather had a brother (unnamed) who 'died in the USA/went to America for a show'.[3] When we parted Walter knew I would soon begin my researches in the United States.

By late October my search had brought me to the Hertzberg Circus Collection in San Antonio, Texas, where there was a rare copy of Barnum's route book for 1883, setting out the itinerary of the tour in which the Aboriginal travellers took part. Quite by chance, within minutes of my arrival, a TV reporter telephoned from Cleveland (at the other end of the country), to ask about Aboriginal circus performers, and more specifically: 'Did anybody know who Tambo was?' The enquiry was passed to me. Meanwhile Walter had heard the Reuters news flash and, after consulting with him by phone, I was soon on my way to Cleveland. I stayed in America until December 1993, when the brothers Walter and Reg Palm Island arrived in Cleveland to repatriate the remains of their ancestor. Accompanied by Kitchener Bligh, a senior elder representing the other Aboriginal peoples who make up the present-day Palm Island community, they performed a ceremony to release Tambo's spirit, assisted by a Native American within whose Seneca tribal domain Cleveland is situated. finally, on 23 February 1994, the 110th anniversary of his death, Tambo was ceremonially laid to rest in his own land (chapter 11).

The trauma of Tambo's death bridged time. His 'return' did more than add to the knowable history of these travellers; it restored their humanity and their identities. It enabled not only the family and the community but also the wider Australian public to absorb his story – and by extension, the stories of his companions – into the shifting ground of the present 'history-as-lived'.[4] The event also made instant storytellers of everybody, the Palm Islanders, other Australians, government officials and the media. While the language used by some came dangerously close to repeating the sensational and stereotypic language of the circus, others saw Tambo's return as a redemptive moment that offered the potential for reconciliation between Indigenous and non-Indigenous Australians. One piece of public storytelling took the form of the exhibition *Captive Lives: Looking for Tambo and his Companions*, which I developed for the National Library of Australia, in consultation with Walter Palm Island and other representatives of the North Queensland Aboriginal communities (pls 1 and 2).[5] During the 1990s the exhibition was one of a number of cultural productions that were concerned to recover the suppressed histories of dispossessed Indigenous Australians. A discussion of the key events associated with Tambo's return, and the important issues with which they connected at that time, will be reserved for the final chapter.

Tambo died only one year after Cunningham embarked with the Aboriginal travellers from Sydney, and his story is, then, only one strand of an encompassing narrative that also embraces that of the second group removed by him. In 1892, Cunningham returned to the same district and persuaded another eight Aborigines (six men, two of whom were accompanied by their wives) to go with him, ostensibly to appear in the World's

2   Elders of the Indigenous Australian community in Mackay, Queensland, visit the *Captive Lives* exhibition on tour in their city. Photograph: author.

Columbian Fair in Chicago in 1893 (chapter 10). Although the journeys of the two groups did not overlap, together they spanned sixteen years, threading the show places of the metropolitan and provincial centres of America and Europe. In the course of their travels, they were regarded as objects of curiosity, which by the late nineteenth century was a curiosity blinkered by the preconceptions of an age that saw them as representatives of a type – a 'savage' type – rather than as individuals. But the Aboriginal travellers, so suddenly thrown together and transported to an unimagined world, were the curious ones, and they exercised their curiosity in order to communicate, experience and survive as show people – professional 'savages'. Although their story mainly comes to us through European eyes and voices, and its recovery sometimes takes us to a speculative edge, it is this larger story that is told in this book.

The showman's response to Tambo's death was to move the troupe on as soon as possible, and by the time the reluctant travellers reached England at the beginning of April 1884 another young man was dead or abandoned, leaving only seven survivors. Tambo excelled as a performer, but as the eldest man it was Toby, also a Palm Islander, who was the accepted leader. Cunningham continued to tour the ever diminishing group through Europe until, in November 1885, when Toby died in Paris, there were only three survivors: Toby's wife, Jenny, their son, 'little Toby',[6] and Billy, the eldest of the three men from Hinchinbrook Island. Reputedly a 'medicine' man, Billy's powerful presence is evident throughout their travels and he emerges as the central protagonist in the story of their journey that continued for several more years.

Billy, Jenny and young Toby

I first became aware of a possible narrative over a decade ago when I came across an uncaptioned photograph of the three whom I soon came to know as Billy, Jenny and her son Toby (pl. 3). This disturbing image is one of a set of photographs in the collection of the Royal Anthropological Institute, London, taken by anthropological photographer Prince Roland Bonaparte in Paris in 1885. The Aboriginal appearance of the three, combined with their troubled expressions, immediately conveyed a sense of dislocation. When I first looked at them across time, detached from any identifying text, I saw them not as 'types' but as 'likenesses' of particular people who were once alive and stood in front of the camera.

3   Billy, Jenny and her son, Toby. Paris, November 1885. Photograph: Prince Roland
Bonaparte.

The group has been photographed against a backdrop of a European pastoral scene that suggests a performance space (probably the stage of Folies Bergère) rather than a photographic studio. Their costumes identify them as show people, and the weapons Billy loosely holds have been transformed into props for performance.[7] The anthropological intention is here subverted; the photograph is more like the commercial portraits that were made of such performing groups, the sale of which – together with the sale of artefacts, route books and pamphlets – played such an important part in the economy of their exploitation.[8] Instead, I read the photograph as a 'quotation from experience', a record of a moment of confrontation that disrupts both scientific and commercial scenarios.[9] The body language – Billy's tilt of the head, Toby's apparent dejection, Jenny's tensely raised shoulder and folded hands – conveys an air of resistance to the proceedings.[10] Further, in an already ambiguous image, the point to which the eye is drawn with a horrible fascination is the stuffed dog in the foreground. Symbolic of death and embalmment, it offers a commentary both absurd and insensitive on the three survivors' existential extremity.[11] This cruel visual pun, with its edge of terror, must have had an initiator. Could it have been Cunningham or Bonaparte who placed the stuffed dog in the frame? Drained of factual meaning, the photograph of Billy, Jenny and young Toby is a visualisation that articulates the whole narrative of captive Aboriginal lives. It catches a crystallising moment in which the dynamics of the exchange across cultures is exposed.[12]

Such a photograph demands interrogation. Who were these people? Where were they from? What were they doing there? This perturbing image was the spark that ignited the slow fuse of research, leading me to further documentation both visual and written – from which a fragmentary narrative began to emerge. In particular, the 1884 report made by two anthropologists, E. Houzé and V. Jacques, who examined and interviewed seven of the Aboriginal performers in Brussels, not only established who they were and where they came from but also provided tantalising glimpses of them as individuals. Their report and Bonaparte's photograph together signalled the intersection of the personal stories of these people with another narrative concerning the entanglement of popular culture and anthropology. The language lists, bodily measurements and photographs of the anthropologists' accounts were part of the classificatory project that Stephen J. Gould has described as 'the mismeasurement of man'. Their attitudes reflected the misconceptions of the period, namely that the physical and mental characteristics attributed to Australian Aborigines and other hunter-gatherers consigned them to the lowest position in the scale of human development. And both scientists and laymen attributed the rapid reduction in number of hunter-gatherers, whose lands had been colonised, not so much to policies of dispossession as to their supposedly innate nature that 'doomed' them to extinction. Such dubious social-evolutionary notions[13] similarly provided the rationale for the frequently brutal disregard for the welfare of these touring troupes of indigenous people; they were considered expendable. For the onlookers, their performances also served to neutralise and render the idea of the 'savage' harmless.

The show-space

In the metropolitan centres of America and Europe, Cunningham's Aboriginal troupes, together with other indigenous performers, similarly displaced by frontier conflict and strategies of 'dispersal' on the colonial margins of the world, became enmeshed in Western systems of mass entertainment and education, involving display and performance, which marked the emergence of the modern world as spectacle, as it was configured in the fairgrounds, circuses, exhibition halls, theatres and museum spaces. I call the arena in which this engagement took place the show-space. This term is more than a collective name for the actual show places; rather it defines a cultural space that is both a zone of displacement for the performers and a place of spectacle for the onlookers. It is a chronotopic space, that is to say, a conjunction of time and space, where certain stories can 'take place':[14] where historically specific relations of power between colonisers and colonised were made visible. From the 1860s, the process was most evident in the 'universal' exhibitions, particularly those organised by the rival imperial powers. In these complex show-spaces the ascendancy of the modern nation-state was visualised in displays that emphasised technological progress. For instance, in the 1889 universal exposition in Paris, visitors of European stock could reassure themselves of their superiority by contrasting the Palace of Machines with the reconstructed colonial villages and the performances of 'savages' in the entertainment areas along the perimeter of the grounds (chapter 9).

If the boundary of the world of the Aboriginal performers appeared to be expanded by their travels overseas, their experiences were restricted by their containment in the show-space. Although the performances they gave were grounded in their own cultural practices (see p. 29), Billy, Toby and the others were ensnared in a hall of distorting mirrors. Within their performance roles they were simultaneously themselves and reflections of the 'savages' of Western imagination. While they were on the move, especially when they were with Barnum's circus in America, they were absorbed into the subculture of the travelling shows. Even there, but particularly in Europe, where Cunningham toured them independently, their well-being depended both on retaining a sense of their Aboriginality, and on their adaptability – for instance the rapidity with which they acquired a smattering of European languages, or learnt to keep the too curious at a distance. As cultural theorists have argued, the unyoking of culture from place – the deterritorialisation of culture – is one of the signifying forces of the modern world.[15] I suggest that an early modern expression of it was the indigenous presence in the show-space. For the West's appropriation of colonial spaces in the course of the imperial enterprise was paralleled by the social construction and presentation of savage otherness in the show-space. The metropolitan appetite for the exotic – both human representatives and their productions – was insatiable, and formed part of the living fermentation that produced modernity.

Cast in the role of anonymous savage other to Western civilised self, these nineteenth-century indigenous performers continue to be captive in more recent discourse on the show-space. For instance, the two North Queensland groups tend to be regarded as one,[16] although the anthropologist Rudolf Virchow established this was not so when he compared the body measurements of both groups in his report of 1896.[17] Therefore the narrative thrust of my approach, with its emphasis on the particular – particular lives and events – developed partly as a reaction to much of the recent discourse on the display of indigenous performers in the metropolitan show places and the larger exhibitionary formations such as world fairs and exhibitions. With a few exceptions,[18] there has hardly been a concern for the recovery of the details of the actual lives and experiences. Yet distinguishing between the different groups, and knowing who these Aboriginal performers were and something of their experiences, adds more than substance and texture to the analysis of the social context and cross-cultural elements of their display. In the communities from which the Aboriginal performers came, their recovered history reshapes the present; and the acknowledgement of it within the wider Australian community contributes to the ongoing debate that attends the continuing reformulation of the nation's narrative (chapter 11).[19]

Search for narrative

Early in my investigations I wondered if it would be possible to recover more than disconnected traces of the North Queenslanders' travels. Reasoning that they had been regarded as British subjects, I searched the 'Register of British Deaths Abroad', and there, in a list of anonymous deaths at a likely date, I found a single entry 'Jimmy' – the name of another of the first group. Although it was a long shot, I paid my five pounds and sent away for a copy of the certificate. With its arrival came confirmation: 'Jimmy' had died in Darmstadt, Germany, on 31 May 1885, and his occupation was given as 'Australian Savage' in the Cunningham Company. Although it was never to be as easy again to locate vital records, this minor breakthrough was enough to determine a strategy of research that took me beyond the great repositories of British imperial history back to Australia, then to America and Europe on a series of journeys that paralleled those of the Aboriginal travellers.

Thus, over a number of years, my project has been a search for narrative.[20] Put simply, the search has been for the answers to a number of questions: Who were these people? Where were they from? How could they be taken so easily? What happened to them along the way? How were they able to withstand the disintegrating effects of such a journey? What were the more positive elements of their experience? At the same time, the search has been more than the uncovering of a core narrative; it has been about unravelling the socioeconomic and cultural processes by which Toby, his wife, Jenny, and their companions were reduced to objects and treated as commodities, and real and captive lives were written out of history. To excavate the shards of their narrative we must interrogate the narratives we have told ourselves: the narratives embedded in official documents, settler diaries, and letters, and the narratives given form in the texts and images of anthropological and newspaper reports, circus publicity, frontiersmen's tales and triumphalist histories of nation.[21] My concern, then, is with the entanglement of fact and fiction in these narratives; their constructions are riddled with the ideologically fictional, deploying such potent euphemisms as 'dispersal' instead of slaughter, defining resistance as 'outrage' and those who resisted as 'criminals', and describing indigenous peoples and their cultures in terms of a 'savagery' that by the last quarter of the nineteenth century was rarely projected as 'noble' but rather carried negative connotations. Supposedly, savagery could be read in the features and on the body as a visible sign – as scarification, tattooing and so on – and it was said to be evident in behavioural traits such as 'ranting' (talking gibberish) and cannibalism.

Above all, in late nineteenth-century colonial discourses, 'savage' was synonymous with 'cannibal', and there is one book, *Among Cannibals*, by the naturalist Carl Lumholtz, that (perhaps more than any other) propagated the view of North Queensland Aborigines as uncivilised cannibals whose extinction was imminent. In it Lumholtz described an eleven-month stay, in 1882–3, with the Aborigines on the Herbert River, who were near neighbours to the groups removed by Cunningham. In spite of his book's title, Lumholtz's assertions about the cannibal nature of the 'northern savage' were based on hearsay, and even he concluded that eating human flesh 'is rare' (p. 297). Although he also reported that the Blacks were 'hunted for sport' and 'poisoned', and that 'a war of extermination . . . is being waged in the frontier districts' (Lumholtz 1979, 273, 373), his account of dangers overcome thrilled the public. Even before the book was published in Scandinavia in 1888 – and in an English edition in 1889 – Lumholtz was making lecture tours and publishing articles, for example in the Swedish *Ny Illustrerad Tidning* in November 1886 – which appeared within months of the visit of Billy, Jenny and young Toby to Stockholm. The book was also serialised in the French journal *Le Tour du Monde* through 1888 and 1889, and Bonaparte's portraits of Jenny and Billy (pls 59 and 66) were used as illustrations. Cunningham himself, kept illustrations from *Among Cannibals* in his news cuttings book (p. 13).

Consequently, a cannibal refrain threads its way through this present narrative, ensnaring Billy, Toby and their companions in the most powerful ideological fiction of the period. Whatever the realities of actual cannibal practices (and, in spite of Lumholtz's assertions, they are not well substantiated among these North Queensland clans[22]) the cannibalism invoked in show business publicity and newspaper reports was a product of Western fantasizing; an obsession with the most transgressive human behaviour, the consumption of human flesh, a practice that was identified as marking the boundary between the civilised self and his or her cannibal other. And in imperial discourses the attribution of cannibalism displaced the violence of the colonisers onto the colonised (chapter 2).[23] The cannibal trope is part of colonialism's culture, given expression as much in the centres of empire as on the margins, and the obsession with it in both popular and scientific descriptions of the Aboriginal performers has provided an opportunity to explore its shifting meaning through the responses, ranging from fear to scepticism, that their performances induced in their Western audiences, in America, Britain and continental Europe (particularly chapter 8).[24]

Although the focus of my study is on the late nineteenth century, the removal of indigenous peoples from the margins of the known world to be displayed in European capitals has a long history that shaped the development of Europeans' ideas about both themselves and non-Europeans. The third century mosaic pavements of Piazza Amerina, Sicily, enigmatically depicted a man in a cage among a cargo of animals imported from Africa to be shown in the Roman world. For the first European voyagers to the Americas, living people were also a most desirable trophy for returning travellers. Curiosity led to self-reflection. The presence of Tupis (Tupinamba) from Brazil in Rouen in 1562 inspired Montaigne's essay 'On cannibals' – a reflection on cultural difference, and critique of his own society. By the eighteenth century, encounters between European voyagers and Pacific Islander societies, and the presence in Europe of antipodeans, who were presented to London and Parisian society as well as being exposed to popular curiosity, inspired theatrical performances and generally fostered ideas of the Noble Savage. From the late eighteenth century, how and where indigenous peoples were displayed became progressively more structured and institutionalised, as positivist science formulated a systematised view of the world's land forms, life forms and cultural productions. The natural sciences, particularly those with a biological emphasis, took an anti-humanist turn as the practitioners of the new disciplines of phrenology, physiognomy and anthropology[25] sought to measure, quantify and classify human physical differences to arrive at a typology of race that sought to grade humankind on a scale extending from the savage to the civilised. The treatment of Saartjie Baartmann, brought from South Africa to be exhibited in London and Paris as the 'Hottentot Venus', was indicative of the accompanying shift in the idea of savagery from the noble to the ignoble end of the spectrum. Regarded with pity by some and derision by others, after her death in Paris in 1815 Saartjie was dissected by the French naturalist George Cuvier, and her skeleton and body parts were put on display, together with a cast of her person. It is only now as I write – almost 200 years later – that her remains have at last been returned to South Africa for burial.

During the 1990s, in Australia – as in many decolonising parts of the world – the demand for return of Aboriginal remains from overseas museum collections became such an important issue that, although my research priority was to find out what had happened to the Aboriginal travellers as living people, I had, of course, considered the possibility of finding remains.[26] When it happened, however, the sensational nature of the discovery of Tambo's mummified body put the story into immediate public circulation, and for a while altered the trajectory of my research. Given the enduringly fragmentary nature of the travellers' story, the challenge has been to find a way of telling that lends coherence to the narrative while at the same time acknowledging the gaps and the silences. In due course, other researchers will close some of the gaps, but the silences are more resistant – both the silencing in the frontier space of terror, and the journey's silences that punctuate the narrative when one of the group is left to die and her or his companions are moved on to another show place. There are also the silences derived from mutual unintelligibility across cultures, and the detectable absences or lacunae in an account that serve as 'indicators' that can be 'used as levers to open out the ideology of colonial discourse . . .'[27] Thus the drive has been to excavate the narrative, and to assemble from diverse sources what is in effect a new archive. Although I hope this book will extend the range of a knowable past for the Aboriginal travellers' descendants and communities, no claim is made to it being an Aboriginal history. Rather it is an exploration of a particular encounter across cultures that shifted from the culturally hybrid frontier spaces of North Queensland to be played out in the show places of America and Europe – an encounter in which the central protagonists were the travelling Aboriginal performers and their showman. And theirs is a story that will be retold many times, in both factual and fictional forms.

Sources

Although over the years I had followed the trail of newspaper ads and reports relating to both groups – particularly Billy and his companions in Europe, and the second group, King Bill and his company, in California – whenever and wherever my own travels provided the opportunity, a new phase of research embarked on in late 1999 advanced the recovery of the larger narrative. I was fortunate enough to access Cunningham's own scrapbook of newspaper cuttings that, according to a contemporary report, was one of several 'heavy enough to derail a tramcar'.[28] Cunningham's news cuttings book lends a new dimension to the story, for although it includes a somewhat randomly arranged selection of reports about his long career as a showman, particularly of indigenous performers, there are a number of other cuttings that reveal his awareness of the rapidly changing character of the cities he visited, and that he grasped the relationship between the economic and cultural forces that made his touring enterprise and way of life possible. R. A. Cunningham was a true representative of a self-consciously aware age.

He collected articles giving statistics of the recent rapid growth of urban populations, not only in America but also in Europe (pl. 42), and another on the spread of telegraphic communications throughout the world – also with statistical details. He shared this confidence in 'Progress' with the new urban classes, with money in their pockets, who constituted the audiences for his shows. Without the telegraph his ability to make advance bookings and to plan itineraries would have been severely limited, but the telegrams, surely the most ephemeral of documents, have not survived. On the other hand, the news reports he collected reflect his pride in the international character of his enterprise. As part of the burgeoning entertainment industry, together with other new trades like the salesman or sales-woman and the commercial traveller, he was part of the new commercial culture of cities. As a compulsive traveller, he was the ultimate flâneur,[29] the voyeuristic passer-by, free from social attachments and constraints, moving within the city's crowd but separate from it. No matter in which city they were, he and his travelling troupe of Aboriginal performers became part of the city's perpetually changing spectacle of humanity. Although Billy, Toby and their companions experienced something of Cunningham's freedom within the crowd, as conspicuous strangers they were also part of the spectacle of consumable products on display. As showman, Cunningham sought to satisfy the crowd's insatiable appetite for wonders, so that it was his production and presentation, matched to the crowd's expectations, that framed their performance and shaped their experiences.

Among the most numerous of the clippings are cannibal tales that – no doubt – were added to his repertoire of anecdotes used in the lectures the showman gave to accompany the performances. His talents as an entertaining and informative speaker were remarked on in several biographical pieces, while others were less than complimentary. That he kept the latter is indicative of the self-image the showman cultivated. The knowable Cunningham is a creature of his own making. His projection of himself as 'manhunter' and 'freak-catcher' in his publicity gave him a bad press, and fellow showmen as well as commentators censured his behaviour towards his charges.

There is one such report in his cuttings book that Cunningham himself must have had translated from the German. In August 1885 in Münster, Germany, a Professor Landois wrote about the four remaining North Queenslanders, asserting that Cunningham 'would show these savages, till the last breath had gone out of them, and that he would never send them back to their country'. In sketching Cunningham's demeanour, Landois wrote (as translated): 'In the dress of an English reverend, and with a steel cane covered in rinocerous [*sic*] skin in his hand, he has the appearance from head to foot of a genuine American slave-driver.'[30]

I had regarded the showman as an ambiguous, even sinister, figure but had not previously thought of him as a 'slaver'. Although it is not quite what Landois had in mind, master/slave is an apt enough description of a relationship – both unequal and intimate – that, particularly in the case of Billy, Jenny and young Toby, lasted between five and six years. Over time, showman and performers appear to have reached an accommodation of sorts. In December 1885, Cunningham apparently planned to send the three survivors home to Australia from Liverpool. Instead they chose to embark with him on a second continental journey from Dublin to Constantinople, by way of Scandinavia and Russia – returning across Europe through Austria and Italy. For this journey there is at last sufficient narrative continuity to form an impression of the relationship between the showman and the Aboriginal performers in terms more subtle than victim and villain or even master/slave (chapter 8). Nevertheless, when thinking about the generally compliant behaviour of the Aboriginal travellers (of both the first and the second group) it should be seen as of the same order as the compliance of the defeated and colonised in the North Queensland contact zone where the disciplinary function of terror prevailed. Although, in the course of the journey, their fears were mediated by the occasional distractions of travel, the attractions of show life, their own confident performances and the money earned, the North Queenslanders' responses to the white man, as shaped on the frontier before departure, were always ready to reassert themselves.[31] It is difficult to assess what monies they actually received. In spite of the complaints they are reported to have made about no or inadequate payment they were also compliant in this regard. They did as they were told, and accepted the recompense offered.[32]

Apart from the particular insights provided by the selection of cuttings in the scrapbook, these also helped to fill in some of the missing pieces in the narrative jigsaw. From early in my research the gathering of news items has been important in establishing each group's itinerary, and has sometimes provided the only information about particular incidents, as well as about the public's responses and attitudes. But newspapers can also be a treacherous source, confusing names, and even numbers in the group. So it is through the *accumulation* of the news reports that trails have been followed and details confirmed, but it is also in the accumulation that we can see how constant repetition of the same written and visual representations of indigenous groups such as the North Queenslanders reinforced the savage stereotype. The news reports are important not only for what they say but also for their way of telling it. Most importantly, news reports alone cannot provide access to the story. Before the seven survivors of the first group reached Europe in 1884 only three of the nine received anything more than passing mention by name in the many news reports about them: once when Billy and Jimmy attempted to escape from Cunningham in Sydney, and again when Tambo died in America. It is only in Europe, where several comprehensive accounts based on interviews were set down by Belgian, German and French anthropologists and a number of photographs were made, that a satisfactory point of entry into the story becomes evident, and it becomes possible to identify the Aboriginal travellers both by name and appearance.

1   *Meet the Travellers*

When it came to photographing . . . we had asked them to remove as much as possible of their rags; but our savages, who had already admired themselves in their dress, in the photographs executed in London, didn't intend at all to allow themselves be photographed again without posing with all their finery.

E. Houzé and V. Jacques, 'Communication . . . sur les Australiens du Musée du Nord', 1884

When Cunningham arrived in London early in April 1884 with the seven Aboriginal survivors of the American tour, he immediately busied himself with the preparations for their first engagement at the Crystal Palace in south London for the week of 19–20 April. He had an English edition printed of his pamphlet *History of R. A. Cunningham's Australian Aborigines, Tattooed Cannibals, Black Trackers and Boomerang Throwers*, and on 10 April he registered copyright in it at the Stationers Hall – thus ensuring that copies survived.

It is evident that the London printing (pl. 8) is a reprint of an American edition of the pamphlet. Although the inside text lists the Aboriginal names of the original nine of the group, a new back cover announces the presentation of 'Seven Australian Boomerang Throwers, Queensland Black Trackers and Ranting Man Eaters'.[1] As, to date, this is the only record of the Aboriginal names of all nine it is regrettable that Cunningham did not correlate them with their English given names. It is only possible to do this for the seven survivors who were interviewed by European anthropologists. Ambiguity remains concerning the Aboriginal names of Tambo and the other young man who died shortly after him. The accompanying table (1.1) lists the names, and estimated ages of the members of the troupe, according to three sources, so that the transliteration of the Aboriginal names comes to us through the screen of each recorder's own language – Irish-American for Cunningham, French for the Belgian anthropologists

Houzé and Jacques, and German for Rudolf Virchow. I regard the spelling of the names in the French rendering as probably the closest to the Aboriginal pronunciation because Houzé and Jacques collected word lists and also supplied a guide to pronunciation. They were also critical of Cunningham's spelling of Aboriginal names.

On 28 April 1884, after the show was over, Cunningham registered copyright in a set of seven photographs,[2] which also survive in the copyright files. An analysis of this set in conjunction with the anthropologists' texts and other portraits enables us to arrive at identifications that link names and appearances not only of each of the seven survivors but also of each of the original nine.

First, let us meet the seven survivors of the American tour (pl. 4). Using the English names by which they will be known in this narrative, they are, from left to right: Billy, Jenny, her son Toby, her husband Toby, Sussy, Jimmy and Bob – who is reclining on his forearm in front of the others. It is possible to arrive at these identifications by relating the appearance of each to the body measurements and descriptions of scars and other identifying features made of each of the group members by Houzé and Jacques, as well as to named photographs of several of the group, published in their report of 1884. This group portrait of the seven is perhaps the best known of the many photographs taken of them. It is found in collections in Britain, Australia and France,[3] bearing the copyright stamp of the photographic firm Negretti and Zambra, Crystal Palace, South London. It and two portraits of Sussy, who is also identified on the form by her show name, Tagarah, were undoubtedly made during the week the group was showing at the Crystal Palace (pl. 43). It was conveniently done, because Negretti and Zambra had their studio within the south nave of the Crystal Palace itself. Yet, apparently without notifying the photographers, Cunningham registered copyright in these photographs two days after the show closed. On one of the forms the name of Emilie Zambra has actually been crossed out, and for all of the Crystal Palace photographs the photographer is recorded as William Robinson of Sydenham. It is difficult to understand why Cunningham made these changes, because as commissioner of the photographs he would have been entitled to claim copyright.

At the same time, one of the prints Cunningham registered copyright in is another group portrait of nine Aborigines (pl. 5), showing the seven in plate 4 and two others. The photographer is named as William Davis

4   The seven survivors to reach Europe were (l to r): Billy, Jenny, her son Toby, her husband Toby, Sussy, Jimmy and Bob (reclining). Negretti and Zambra, Crystal Palace, London, claimed the copyright, although, in fact, R. A. Cunningham registered copyright in his name, 1884.

of 415, The Strand – one of the two temporary London addresses the showman also gave for himself. However, this photograph could not have been taken in London, as it must have been taken before Tambo and the other young man died. It was almost certainly taken in the United States, probably commissioned either for Barnum's circus publicity or for Cunningham's later tour of the dime museums (chapter 4).[4] The calfskin show-clothes they wear are similar but not the same as those in the Crystal Palace photos. And contrasted with photographs taken before they left Australia (pls 22 and 23, chapter 3), their wild hair, which is part of the savage look cultivated for performance, would have taken time to grow.

5   The nine North Queenslanders removed by R. A. Cunningham in 1883. The accompanying sketch identifies the names and language groups. Place and photographer unknown. Jenny, young Toby and Toby (seated l); Tambo and Sussy (seated r); Bob, ?Wangong, Billy and Jimmy (standing l to r).

One of the two men who are not in the Negretti and Zambra portrait of the seven is standing second from the left, between Bob and Billy; the other is seated second from the right, next to Sussy. Which one is Tambo?

Jenny, her son and her husband are seated as a family group on the left, and the arrangement therefore suggests that the couple seated on the right are Tambo and Sussy. But there are other means of confirming that the seated man is Tambo. According to Tambo's autopsy report, he was only $59\frac{1}{2}$ inches (1,513 mm) in height. According to the measurements made by Houzé and Jacques, Billy (standing third from the left), who was the shortest member of the group at 1,510 mm, was about the same height.

The unknown young man standing on Billy's right is not only taller than Billy, he is one of the tallest in the group. Like the men on either side of him, his body is scarred by a number of horizontal cicatrices. As it is known that Tambo did not have this type of scarring, the tall young man cannot be Tambo.[5] From left to right, the four men standing are Bob, a man whose name may be Wangong, Billy and Jimmy. Although married (according to Houzé and Jacques), none is accompanied by his wife or family. It is understandable that the others did not mention the death of the second man to Houzé and Jacques, because of the Aboriginal restriction on naming the dead. Tambo's death was probably disclosed only when the question of Sussy's marital status was raised. And perhaps it is not surprising that Cunningham did not want to draw attention to this second death so soon after the first.

In the culture area from which these people came there was a reluctance about 'telling the names',[6] and therefore it is possible that some of the Aboriginal names collected were not personal but other forms of address denoting either kinship, class (skin) affiliations or local group names. This could explain why the name Wangong is attributed to Toby by Houzé and Jacques, and to Tambo by Cunningham (see the table 1.1).[7] Throughout the region, the suffix -bara or -barra means 'belonging to' and is usually linked with the name of a place, thus Yorembera (Jenny) may denote a place name. Houzé and Jacques also provided long word lists for two of the Aboriginal languages spoken by different members of the group, and noted dialectical variations. The analysis of these by the linguist R. M. W. Dixon established that the two groups spoke distinct but related languages.

Where were they from?

The majority of the seven identified themselves as from the Palm Islands, which they called Borkoman. Dixon identifies the Palm Islanders' language group as Manbarra, two dialects of which, Mulgu and Buluguyban, were spoken on Great Palm Island. Several other dialects were spoken on nearby Magnetic Island and along the coastal strip, from the environs of Townsville to Rollingstone on Halifax Bay. Today, the language embracing all these dialects is referred to as Wulguru (pl. 6).[8] North of these clans, on Halifax Bay, were the Nyawaygi clans[9] from which most of the second

Table 1.1 The names and estimated ages of the travellers in the first group, 1883–1888, by source

Cunningham's pamphlet (1884) (English)	Houzé and Jacques (1884) (recorded in French)	Virchow (recorded in German (1884))	Other
1 *Tagarah	Sussy/Tagara, 18–20 yrs	Tagarah (Princess), 16–18 yrs	Susi Dakara (variant spelling in Germany)
2 *Yorembera	Jenny/Yarembera, 30–40 yrs	Jenny/Yemberi/ Yorembera, 20 yrs	
3 *Telegorah	'Little' Toby/ Kottiganden, 7–8 yrs	Telegorah, 7 yrs	After the death of the father, Toby, the son is called Tom (Ireland), (B)Denni (Northern Europe)[6]
4 Dianarah	*Tambo?		Johnny? (*Pittsburg Critic*, Feb. 1884) Unknown man
5 *Corgarah	Toby/Wangong, 40–50 yrs	Toby/ Koddigandal/ Kuttegandal, 40 yrs	
6 Warchsinbin	Billy/ Warutchsenben, 30–35 yrs	Warrisimbol/ Warchsinbin, 28 yrs	
7 Wangong			Tambo? (*Cleveland Herald*, 27 Feb 1884)
8 Orininben	Bob/ Oritchnenben, 20–25 yrs	Orininben/ Orininden, 20 yrs	Bob, death certificate
9 *Tinendal	Jimmy/James/ Tinendal, 20–25 yrs	James/Teninder/ Tininder/ Tinendal, 20 yrs	Jimmy (German newspapers, death certificate)

Starred names denote the six from Palm Islands. The other three men were from Hinchinbrook Island. See pp. 20–2. The Aboriginal names are set out in the order listed in Cunningham's pamphlet. When considered in conjunction with plate 5, the first five listed are seated. Nos. 1 to 3 are the two wives (younger and older) and the boy. Then I suggest nos. 4 and 5 are the two husbands (younger and older). Nos 6 to 9 are the four unaccompanied men whose identities can be confirmed by other means (see pp. 19–20).

group were taken by Cunningham in 1892. Jenny was also said to have spoken a different language, but from the few words recorded it is not possible to be certain whether it was a separate language or a dialect. As Yoembara was the name of a Nyawaygi camping place, her name Yorembera suggests she may have been Nyawaygi. On the other hand she may have spoken a deferential or avoidance language, spoken when a potential or actual in-law relationship existed between persons.[10] The Belgian anthropologists gave a confusing description of avoidance behaviour by the two women, Jenny and Sussy (Tambo's wife), that suggests such a relationship may have existed between them. On the other hand, Sussy seems to have stood in the right marriage relationship to Jimmy – but other aspects of the group's relationships remain elusive.

Bob and Billy referred to Hinchinbrook Island as Pouandaï (pl. 6). Although they were both Biyaygirri, they spoke different dialects of Biyay: Billy used that of Hinchinbrook Island and the environs of Cardwell, and Bob spoke the dialect of the mainland adjacent to the southern end of the island. Their dialects were very closely related to that spoken by the Warrgamay-speaking clans who lived a little further inland along both banks of the Herbert River. From first contact, these three groups were together known as the Rockingham Bay tribes, considered by some to be the most powerful 'tribe' in North Queensland.[11] Their closely related northerly neighbours, speakers of the Girramay language, whose territory extended from the tableland rainforests along the Murray River to the coast of Rockingham Bay, just north of Cardwell, were also considered to be a Rockingham Bay 'tribe' by the first white settlers in the area. Although boundaries between language groups were undoubtedly fluid, involving dispute and negotiation, according to Dixon the close affinities between all these neighbouring languages suggest they had been contiguous over a long period of time.

The pattern of Aboriginal land occupation was more sedentary in this relatively densely populated area than in many other regions of Australia – a point noted by Houzé and Jacques, who could only have learned it from the travellers themselves. While language was a way of marking group differences, intermarriage and the sharing of resources of particular habitats contributed to intergroup dynamics. The basic hearth-unit of, say, ten to twenty people who lived and moved around together would have been multilingual.[12] Thus the mix of languages and dialects spoken by the

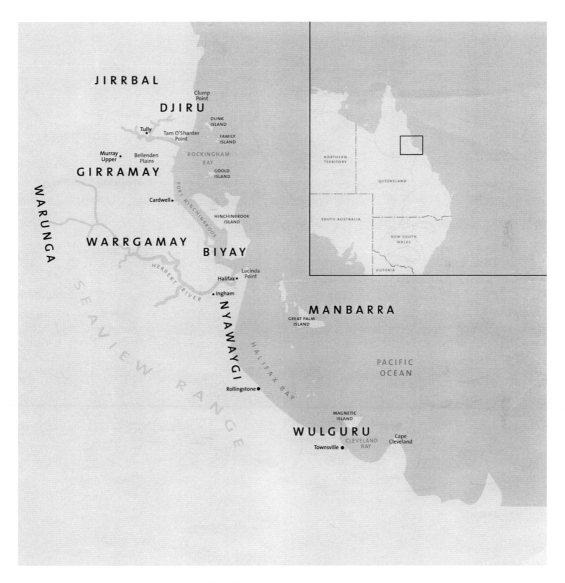

6   Map of the area indicating the distribution of the language groups to which the Aboriginal travellers and their neighbours belonged in North Queensland. Based on H. Brayshaw (1990) and R. M. W. Dixon (1979 and 1983).

7   Hinchinbrook Channel, Queensland, black and white engraving, artist unknown.

group was not a consequence of Cunningham's random selection of them when he picked them up; rather it reflected the multilingual character of the communities from which they came. The most distinctive of the weapons carried by the men, the shield and the wooden sword, were also typical of this area.[13]

With the photograph of all nine original members (pl. 5) available for what was largely forensic analysis, suddenly the grouping in it yielded new meaning. Until I located this photograph of the nine I had assumed that the 'unknown' man was Manbarra – from Palm Islands. But the photograph shows that his horizontal body marks match those of Bob and Billy who, from the linguistic evidence, were both Biyaygirri. It therefore appears that all three men standing together – Bob, the unknown man and Billy – were Biyaygirri, while, to the right, Jimmy, who was Manbarra, stands a little apart. It suggests that the grouping in the photograph is not arbitrary or imposed; rather it movingly reveals that the North Queenslanders are standing together according to their own family and clan affiliations. Of course this may have been coincidental, but the formality of the pose suggests otherwise. Their intergroup behaviour, particularly as reported by Houzé and Jacques, also confirms that Billy and his companions continued to relate to each other while abroad according to their own cultural practices.

English names

At the same time, the troupe's survival also depended on their ability to adapt, and their use of English names, whether given or adopted, rates as an important strategy. Their use simultaneously protected their personal names, and therefore their Aboriginal selves, while providing them with cloaks for new personae, and a form of address that could be used when they referred to each other, and were referred to by others, in the company of non-Aborigines, in the foreign – deterritorialised – world to which they had been transported. By the time they arrived in Europe there was some constancy in the names adopted, so that the combination of English names and the photographs has given us a way of knowing Billy and his companions, and speaking about them. Uncertainty remains, however, as to what their names were before they left Australia and I want to unsettle matters a little by looking more closely at the Aboriginal practice of using English names, either adopted or given, on the North Queensland frontier, in that period.

At least in the case of Tambo, he was not given this name until after arriving in San Francisco. Although Cunningham was reported as saying that Tambo was a 'modification' of Banjo, it is worth noting that Tambo and Bones were the names given to the 'end players' in an American 'blackface' minstrel show who, positioned at either end, provided the rhythm by shaking the tambourine and 'clapping' bones.[14] More than that, in American popular culture, in books and in performances, the Black American character Sambo/Tambo represented the non-threatening savage, childish and comical, slave and servant, and a natural entertainer. According to Cunningham, Tambo had 'style' and he enjoyed public performance, so he may well have taken such a lead position. He already spoke a little English, learnt while he and Sussy had worked with the pearling fleets off North-Eastern Australia, in 1882. There he would have been called by an English name. So far, the only clue as to what that may have been comes from an interview Cunningham gave to the Pittsburg Critic in February 1884,[15] when he said that the only two of the group who spoke a little English before they left Australia were Johnny and Toby. Because of this, he added, he had been dependent on these two men reassuring the Australian authorities that all of them were prepared to go abroad with him. Toby, who at forty was the oldest member of the group, was said to have spent some time with the Black Police.[16] Although the rest of the group apparently spoke no English, they too had very probably had contacts with 'whitefellas'– in spite of Cunningham's claims for their being 'wild'.

At the time of Cunningham's short visit to the Townsville district, the Norwegian naturalist Carl Lumholtz was staying for a much longer time a little further north, along the valley of the Herbert River, in Warrgamaygan territory. Among the things Lumholtz had to say about the impact of white settlement on the Warrgamaygan was the frequency with which he was asked 'to give them European names', which they saw as a prerequisite to moving down to the coast to work for the white man, and as a first step in accessing the white man's goods. And as Lumholtz also noted, 'they are constantly called by it among their comrades.'[17] English names were, then, an indicator of the developing hybrid society – unequal, but none-the-less hybrid. Names were sometimes exchanged; names of station owners or 'bosses' were adopted sometimes because of a biological connection, or at other times as a substitute for a place name. For instance, many of the Nyawaygi ancestors of the second group removed by Cunningham took the name of Cassady, because James Cassady was the owner of the station, Mungalla, that was the heartland of their territory. For many years, three important 'Black' camps remained on the property; so the land continued to be shared in spatial – though economically unequal – terms. Continuities of knowledge about land ownership were retained partly through adopted English names, so that recently this knowledge has facilitated the return of Mungalla to the traditional owners. In other cases, descendants knew if there was a kin connection, and the information was frequently inscribed on the genealogies collected in the area by anthropologists and missionaries. The family name of Palm Island is a clear example of the adoption of a European place name to maintain a continuity of knowledge of the ownership of land – that by the turn of the century has at last been acknowledged in a historic agreement between the Manbarra traditional owners and the 'historical' people, the Bwgcolman.[18] The collective name of the people who were sent to Palm Island after the establishment of the government settlement in 1918. This is not to deny that the lack of fixity in the choice of English names, particularly in the early days of contact, has made for difficulties in establishing genealogical continuities. Sometimes more than one name attached to a person depending on where he or she was, and the circumstances. Frequently names were shared, as in the case of the second group, three of whom were called William. Over time, in this area, personal names such as Rose and Dennis – which, at first, were the only name – became surnames.

The small travelling community of Toby, Tambo, Billy and their companions therefore projected an already culturally hybrid identity, through a mix of traditional cultural traits, such as body scarification, piercing of the nasal septum and kinship behaviour, and innovative features such as the use of non-Aboriginal names.

During their short stay in London, Cunningham assembled various promotional materials, such as the pamphlet and photographs that he was to continue to use throughout the European tour. For Billy and his companions, the cover illustration of the pamphlet (pl. 8) played a powerful part in shaping the public perceptions about them. It was not based on a photograph, although by the 1880s photographs were used as reference by artists and block-makers. Instead, the Aborigines were pictured as generic savages of the late nineteenth-century Western imagination who, in this instance, were depicted as vaguely Fijian-looking. Whatever their supposed 'racial' origins, they were said to be characterised by 'ferocity' and 'treachery'; they practised self-mutilation, lacked language and ate people. In the cover picture these traits are signalled by the depiction of a cannibal scene on the seashore – a graphic representation of encounter that is iconographically related to a number of other images, both earlier and contemporary with it, with which it shares a mix of pictorial motifs (pls 32 and 36). The ship (or shipwreck) in the bay, a rush of natives on the

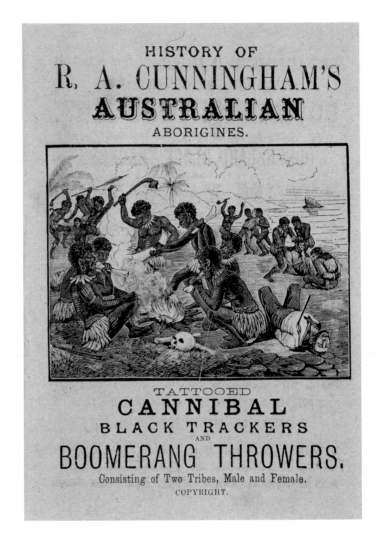

8   Cover of English edition of the pamphlet '*R. A. Cunningham's. Australian Aborigines*', 1884.

shore, massacre and a cannibal feast evoked the terror of being cast away, cut adrift from the civilised world and being physically overwhelmed, if not obliterated. By the 1880s the Aboriginal performers were represented by a well-established stereotype of savagery.[19]

On the other hand, although the photographs taken of the troupe were also socially constructed, tending to conform either to a commercial or an anthropological representational regime, the stereotypic elements in their construction do not prejudice their value as evidence. The identifications would not have been possible without them. In the group portrait (pl. 4) the seven who survived to reach Europe face the camera with a sombre yet confident gaze. After a year of travel and exposure to circus crowds in America, and the loss of two of their number, they have the look of experienced show people. Although the fur pelts or tails the men wear at the waist may be from the Tullah possum of the North Queensland rainforest, the weapons they hold – the shield, sword club, boomerangs and fighting stick – are the only possessions that we can be certain were brought with them from their homeland.[20] This representation of them as professional savages, in their fanciful performance costumes, is undoubtedly one of the set of photographs they spoke of with delight when interviewed by Houzé and Jacques in Brussels a month later (see chapter epigraph).

The appearance of the face, supplemented by gait and gesture, is important to identifications; thus portraiture has always played an important part not only in the representation of self to others but also in self-identification, an aspect that gained much wider currency throughout Western society in the nineteenth century with the proliferation of inexpensive photographic portraits. 'How we appear to ourselves plays an important part in self-imaging and self-presentation':[21] so that for Toby, Billy and the others, being photographed frequently, as well as handling photographs of themselves on an almost daily basis (when selling them to the public), gave them access to a new self-awareness – a professionalism – that they projected into their performances and that helped them to withstand the disintegrating aspects of their experiences. A flavour of what I mean is present in Houzé and Jacques's account of Toby's performance of a war dance (1884, 142):

> Many times we have had the occasion to observe Toby's war dance more at our leisure. He commences with a series of jumps on the spot, his body bent in half; he takes in his left hand his shield, looking to cover himself with it, and in the other hand his club – he looks always directly ahead. Suddenly he mimes the throwing of the spear, before delivering to his enemy an imaginary blow with the club, and uttering a cry. Always, there is a very curious trembling movement in his legs, bent in

9   Toby, photographed by Carl Günther, Berlin, 1884.

half under him: this movement is carried out with increasing rapidity, interrupted from time to time with jumps and great blows from the club, and always with the 'Han! Han!' gutteral sound. He performs like this, in a strong manner, for a quarter of an hour, a half an hour if he wishes; and terminates it with a series of disordered movements and savage cries. Afterwards [it has to be seen] that Toby promenades with a majestic air and noble deportment (for in truth these savages have, as they say, an elegant deportment). He appears to receive the felicitations of the audience, a man convinced of his importance and his superiority.

Toby was the undoubted leader of the group, both on account of his seniority and his personal authority, and this description of his performance conveys a trace and an echo of his presence. The photograph of him, seated with an arm resting on his knee, in a relaxed pose (taken by Carl Günther in Berlin some months later) conveys the same self-assured, but relaxed, personality (pl. 9). From these combined written and visual sources, a picture emerges of Toby, culturally centred in his performance, yet at the same time conscious of the image he is projecting across cultures. To some degree, they tell us what the journey was sometimes like for him – and also for his companions.

2 'Now Enough'

The first and chief cause of their disappearance is their being killed, in districts newly occupied by Europeans. Sometimes this is styled 'war', although mere disparity of forces, especially of weapons, and the helplessness of the blacks in such a contest suggests 'massacre' as a more appropriate term.

Rev. Duncan McNab to Minister of Lands, 1876

There are many humorous things in the world; among them the white man's notion that he is less of a savage than the other savages.

Mark Twain, Following the Equator, 1907

The events that propelled Billy, Toby, his wife, Jenny, their son and their companions onto a world stage had their epicentre in their North Queensland homelands. As I stood on the beach of Great Palm Island, one morning in 1997, looking towards the mainland, the thoughts passing through my mind were of the multiple histories belonging to the land and seascape before me: foundational Aboriginal narratives, themselves multi-layered; and stories from the shifting frontiers of North Queensland of the profound rupture of pre-invasion Aboriginal society, stories of resistance and survival; and the present history-as-lived of Aboriginal social and cultural renewal.

The Creative Being whose journeys had shaped the now familiar landscape of coastline, rivers, channels and islands was the Carpet Snake. He had also established social order in the Aboriginal communities whose territories were traversed by his songline. But the land spoke also to the invaders. In 1864, George Elphinstone Dalrymple, the founder of Cardwell, had seen the reverse view to mine when he stood at the top of the Cardwell Range: 'the [Herbert] river winding far below like a silver snake out of the gorge of its uplands birthplace . . . the Palm Island far to the seaward; all softened and mellowed by the gauze-like summer-heat haze of the declining day . . . and the setting sunbeams shining deep purple on the . . . peaks of Hinchinbrook . . .' (pl. 7).[1]

10   View from Goold
Island, 1843,
watercolour, Edwin
Augustus Porcher, artist
aboard HMS *Fly* (titled
by artist 'Australia,
wigwams at Gould [*sic*]
Island').

It is a powerful and assertive landscape.

From the beach I was also looking out on the bay where Cook's *End-eavour* had anchored close inshore in June 1770. The party who went ashore at dusk heard some of the inhabitants but did not see them, although they had certainly themselves been seen. Cook's bestowal of English names on the prominent headlands, bays and islands of the region – Cape Cleveland, Halifax Bay, Rockingham Bay, the Family Isles, Magnetic Island and Palm Isles – began the process of naming and claiming that, after 1788, was continued by a succession of British survey voyages, some of which gave the local Aborigines their first contact – and conflict – with white people. For the first half of the nineteenth century, however, there were few recorded close encounters along these beaches. Aborigines watched from the edge of the scrub, sent smoke signals to their neighbours and sometimes threw a shower of stones or spears at the white men who were fishing without permission.

The clans of Rockingham Bay had their first extended encounter with the British when HMS *Rattlesnake* anchored off Tam O'Shanter Point (at the northern end of the bay) in 1848. Although the local clans preferred

'Hal being painted'

'the whites to keep their distance', there was sufficient interaction for the scientist Thomas Huxley to have his face painted, and to note in his diary: 'I fancy we were a source of great amusement to one another' (pl. 11). Other early encounters, which were frequently devastating, were with the first irregular exploiters of the products of the reefs, the sea and the shore, particularly the bêche de mer (a sea slug, regarded as a delicacy by the Chinese), pearl-shell, sandalwood and cedar. The Palm Islanders seem to have developed a strategy early for dealing with random aggression. In 1849, the visiting *Will o' Wisp*, belonging to a sandalwood cutter called Roach, was attacked by about thirty Islanders. 'The cause', said Roach, 'was the iron they had seen aboard, earlier in the day', but it was probably also in retaliation for the abuse of women. The islanders' skilful tactics, which were adaptations of their hunting techniques, involved throwing bark torches down the hatchway into the cabin – revealing a familiarity with the boat's layout – but they were finally repulsed by the shot from a small swivel gun.[2]

11 'Hal being painted', pencil sketch probably by T. H. Huxley, unsigned and undated, annotated later by his wife.

Landtakers

From the early 1860s the full thrust of invasion, both overland and from the sea, was felt in the area. The landtakers moved in to occupy the newly designated Kennedy District, the area drained by the Burdekin and Herbert Rivers. Bowen on Port Denison became a springboard for the advance northward, and in 1864 the establishment of the ports of Townsville on Cleveland Bay and Cardwell on Rockingham Bay provided bridgeheads to the pastoral and mineral wealth of the interior, and bases

'Our Father'

/abu ngali/	Our Father
/nginda wandu galin nhi-na/	You are in heaven
/milgin nginu ngura-ngga/	Your name is praised
/yamalma nginu gayi-ngga	Your will is done among your people
bambarra ngunbar gundana/	on earth
/yila-urha-la galin nganging iriya-y/	
/uga buril gajin ngaling/	Just as it is fulfilled in heaven
buwan nginda ariya ngali/	Give bread to us
yila warha ngali ngaw bu-ma danura/	Do not take revenge upon us
/urha wirra bambarra nginu	As we do not kill others
ngali bula dararu/	
/anu nginu milgin mulgan du/	Now lead us rightly to where your
	praise is great
/ilgura garay mana/	The people shall not be taken
/mira ganggay arra gina margan/	Why has there long been bloodshed?
/dalmara yugi/	Sleep easily
/urha bayra/	Now enough

Charles Price 'Language of the Townsville Area (Coonambela')', in the Royal Commonwealth Society Collection, Cambridge University Library.

    The above phonemic transcription and translation is by Nicolaas Heijm and Walter Palm Island. Coonambella is a dialect, closely related to the two dialects spoken by the Manbarra of the Palm Islands, of what is now called the Wulguru language (see Heijm 1997).

    An alternative translation of line 4 is 'Your will is done in your rightful domain of people on earth'.

    Little is known about Charles Price, a Townsville draper, who over some sixteen years studied local dialects, particularly of the people who lived on the coastal plain between the Ross and Black rivers on the northern side of Townsville. In his preamble to the Lord's Prayer he regretted that, being bound to the town, he had not had the opportunity to make more extensive language records. He also regretted that it had not been done by others 'who have had the "native" constantly in their company'.

for the more intensive exploitation of the resources of the sea, reefs and coasts further north. The coastal frontline of this theatre of invasion, the territories of the clans bordering Cleveland, Halifax and Rockingham bays, nearby Hinchinbrook Island, adjacent small islands and the neighbouring Palm Islands, was the homeland of the Aboriginal protagonists of our story. Cleveland Bay was a favoured camp site for the local clans; in 1860 three large camps were sighted there, consisting of 'forty warriors' and their dependants – an estimated 200 people.[3] The initial impact on the coastal populations came from the laying out of the towns themselves and involved immediate displacement from the town environs and destruction of resources. Timber cut for the construction of Townsville lead to the rapid drying up of the coastal lagoons to the north of the town,[4] while the site chosen for Cardwell meant that the local clans were cut off from valuable freshwater wells. In due course other enterprises – the taking up of land for sugar, and the development of the bêche de mer and pearl-shell fisheries – were to play a greater part in the reduction of these clans than any other. The violence of the displacement and destruction of the indigenous inhabitants was bound together with the economy of landtaking and exploitation of the resources of the area that, for two decades, made this frontier a space of terror. The evidence is extensive, though one-sided, because almost no Aboriginal voice reaches us from these years.

A localised version of the Lord's Prayer (opposite[5]) which was translated into Wulguru and written down some time before 1885 (here also translated back into English), directly addresses the terror that powered the conflict between Black and White, at its peak during the 1860s and 1870s, on the coastal frontier. An Aboriginal voice of protest at the slaughter is heard in the concluding words, 'Now enough'. At the same time, there is a compassionate and enabling complicity that saturates the flow of words between languages, making it possible for the Aboriginal voice to bridge time and let us know how it was for the mainland Wulguru-speaking clans displaced by the establishment of Townsville. Although the Manbarra of the Palm Islands were spared the immediate displacement suffered by their Wulguru kin, they continued to be exposed to random visits and assaults.

In the early 1860s, the Palm Islander Toby, the oldest of the group, would have been a young man of twenty, and Tambo and his wife, Sussy, would have been infants. Some of Toby's experiences were apparently of working on the mainland with settlers and perhaps as a tracker in the Black Police. By the early 1870s Billy would have been a young man and the other two Biyaygirri men would have still been children when a succession of punitive drives on Hinchinbrook Island and the mainland opposite reduced their people to a handful of survivors. In 1882 Tambo and Sussy had been recruited to work in the pearling fleets in northern waters, where Tambo learnt some English. Both the men and women in the group bore body scarifications that were associated with initiated status. Jimmy, alone of the Manbarra men, had vertical cicatrices on one shoulder only, and said he was unwilling to go through the operation on his other shoulder.[6] All the men except Bob wore bones through their pierced nasal septums.[7]

Although before 1860 interlanguage group gatherings of as many as a thousand apparently took place at regular intervals to perform ceremonies, settle disputes and trade, in the early 1880s gatherings of as many as two hundred were still taking place in the mountain fastnesses of the Warrgamaygan and the Girramaygan.[8] And Archibald Meston later recalled that in 1881 he had encountered a group of fifty Palm Islanders who had landed at Cape Pallarenda, on the northern side of Townsville, and were on their way to initiation ceremonies at the southern end of Halifax Bay.[9] That these practices persisted and ceremonial gatherings were still known to take place indicates there was still a degree of social cohesion in these communities. Bear in mind, as you read the following account of Black–White relations in this area, that Toby, Tambo, Billy and their kin were almost certainly involved in many of the incidents described, that close kin – maybe brothers, sisters, cousins, parents and children – would have been reckoned among those 'natives randomly dispersed'.

Happenings on the North Queensland frontier were shaped by attitudes forged not only on earlier Australian frontiers but also in other theatres of empire.[10] The continuities were acknowledged: 'We are pursuing the same policy as in Zululand and Afghanistan . . . on a more barbarous scale,' wrote 'Nevernever' to the *Queenslander*.[11] Among the first to take up land in the district were men who had seen service in Ceylon (George E. Dalrymple) and India (Robert Gray and his brother), or were familiar with the plantation economy of the West Indies (John Ewen Davidson). Although Dalrymple's partner, the pastoralist Arthur J. Scott, who was one of the landing party at Cardwell, was immediately sensitive to 'the fact

[that] occupying their country is at once a declaration of war with the blacks',[12] by and large their displacement was considered justified by what was regarded as unproductive occupation of land. The dominant – but not universal – attitude towards the 'natives' was that they were expendable. The landtakers were preconditioned. As one later reminisced: 'In Melbourne we looked on North Queensland as a terra incognita inhabited by fierce tribes of cannibals and all sorts' (Rowe 1931). The diaries, letters and settlers' accounts from this frontier (as from earlier Australian frontiers) reveal the fear and anxiety engendered by the 'invisibility of the natives', and their unpredictability, attributed to their 'treacherous' nature. There is a circularity here, for the cultural representations (in visual and textual forms) of Aborigines as treacherous, conceived on earlier frontiers, when transferred to North Queensland are reinforced and reinscribed in published frontier tales of this place and time.[13] In turn, these texts, so popular in Europe, framed the presentation of Billy and his companions by R. A. Cunningham, and contributed to their reception as 'savages'.

In actuality, however, on this frontier, as on other frontiers, the well-established 'cultural representations of Aborigines . . . as treacherous beings . . . in effect authorized and inspired greater acts of terror'.[14] The space of terror became the locus for a series of retaliatory acts; the supposed savagery of the 'native' could be extinguished only by a greater savagery perpetrated in the name of civilisation.[15] The fearful instrument of terror was the mobile force of the Native Mounted Police, mainly made up of young men from distant areas, free of the restraining presence of kin. The randomness and opportunism of attacks, by both Black and White – either aggressive, or in retaliation or resistance – also made the frontier a space of chaos. Much has been written about conflict on the shifting frontiers of North Queensland, so I have drawn on only those incidents from which can be gleaned something of how it was for the clans from which the Aboriginal travellers came.[16]

What happened at Rockingham Bay in 1864 when George Dalrymple's small invading force landed on the beach had its beginnings in earlier events, further south. When the castaway James Murrell (Morrill) 'came in' to Bowen in 1863, after living for seventeen years with clans around Mount Eliott and Cape Cleveland (just south of Townsville), he became a transmitter of information both ways across the frontier. He recounted how one of his Aboriginal friends had been killed, and another wounded, when they tried to tell members of the exploring party of Dalrymple's HMS *Spitfire* of the presence of Murrell nearby. Then fifteen members of a fishing party were killed near Cape Upstart. Before Murrell returned to colonial society he had warned his Aboriginal friends 'for their own good' to avoid the white men, saying:

> they had plenty of guns, and that if they went near them they would be killed. I told them that they had come to take possession of their land. . . . So believing me, and bowing at once to the force of might, they requested me to ask the white men to let them retain all the land to the north of the Burdekin, also to allow them to fish in the rivers; also to let them have the low and swampy grounds near the sea-coast, where they retained most of their root food, and which would not be so useful to white people.[17]

Cardwell

There is no evidence that Dalrymple heeded (or even noted) the Aboriginal proposal for coexistence. On the other hand, Aboriginal knowledge of his aggression against the clans south of Townsville would certainly have travelled ahead of him to cast a shadow across events in Rockingham Bay (pls 12 and 13). It is probable that the clans there would also have been willing to work out a realistic accommodation with the invading white man. But when the *Policeman* anchored at the northern end of the bay in January 1864, Dalrymple discouraged the Aborigines from coming alongside, and in spite of the availability of Murrell as a go-between, he made no attempt to negotiate. Instead, landing on a small sandy beach where the land's owners were assembled, he pointed to the site of the present-day Cardwell and told them, through Murrell, that 'we were going to settle there, and possess it.'

The blacks 'seemed much astonished that Murrell could converse with them' and 'they hoped that we were not going to war with them'.

To which Dalrymple replied: ' "No: that we did not wish to hurt them, but that we wished to be left alone; that if they would keep off and not molest us, we would not injure or interfere with them in any way." They seemed to understand the ultimatum and retired slowly into the mangroves.'

12   *Boatmen of Rockingham Bay*, woodcut, Harden S. Melville, artist aboard HMS *Fly, c.* 1843, engraved by H. Newsom Woods for *Curiosities of Savage Life* by James Greenwood, 1864. These small canoes were a feature of this area.

Murrell also told them to pass on the message to neighbouring tribes. Dalrymple's arrogant assumption was that the presence of Murrell as interpreter had avoided bloodshed because the blacks learnt 'what the white men require of them . . . having always required heretofore to be taught them by the rifle and the revolver.'[18]

In practice, however, displacement continued to be underpinned by force. In January 1865, Cardwell's Police Magistrate, R. B. Leefe, wrote to the Colonial Secretary that in keeping the 'blacks' away from Cardwell and nearby Muenga Creek where gardens were being established, he was following 'the policy throughout – which [Dalrymple] commenced on his first landing here'. He was making a formal complaint against Lieutenant Charles Blakeney, who was in charge of a contingent of nine Native Police. He considered that Blakeney had challenged his authority when he (Leefe) asked for police support in the 'duty' of destroying 'a black's camp'.

13   View of
Rockingham Bay, North
Queensland. The
recently established
port of Cardwell in
foreground; and (l to r)
Tam O'Shanter Point,
the Family Islands,
Goold Island and
northern end of
Hinchinbrook Island.

In refusing, Blakeney had said: 'I should have to use violent measures which for the present would be unwise and lead to making the natives retaliate. . .' Further, Blakeney's assertion that the Aborigines 'only use that portion of the country as a passage down from the range to the sea on fishing excursions' suggests they were following a strategy of avoidance – especially as a large camp site and bora (ceremonial) ground was located on the high ground above the creek. When the Colonial Secretary reviewed the matter, however, he supported Leefe's right 'to make the suggestions which Mr Blakeney refused to carry out'. Soon after, Blakeney was replaced by Inspector John Murray, who held the post until 1870 and routinely carried out dispersal patrols.[19]

Davidson at Bellenden Plains

As land beyond the settlement was taken up, the pressures on the local clans increased exponentially (pl. 14). John Ewen Davidson was the first to attempt cultivation of sugar cane at 'The Plains',[20] only twenty miles north of Cardwell. But more important for the movement of machinery, it was accessible from the Murray River.[21] The sugar-planter's unpublished diary records the processes of displacement and dispersal over a twenty-month period, and there is not a single entry that refers to an attempt at a rapprochement.[22] From the first he received back-up from the Native Mounted Police 'to clear out the blacks'. For instance, 'Sub-Inspector Uhr and six black police' accompanied his party on a reconnaissance in January 1866, about which Davidson wrote (7 Jan.):

> Some blacks were seen, pursued and shot down; it was a strange and painful sight to see a human being running for his life and see the black police galloping after him and hear the crack of the carbines; the gins [women] and the children all hid in the grass . . . one little girl took refuge under my horses belly and would not move: of course I took no part in these proceedings, that being the duty of the police: it is the only way of ensuring the lives of white men to show that they cannot be attacked with impunity.

But this was not a response to an attack: it was a pre-emptive strike. Later the same day the party discovered another 'wild black's camp', and 'secured

14 'A Brush with the Blacks', frontispiece to *My Wife and I in Queensland*, by Charles. H. Eden, 1872. 'We determined to have a day after the blacks,' wrote Eden, about an incident at Bellenden Plains sugar plantation.

their dinner – fish prawns, and scrub hen's eggs, all cooked to a nicety'. It was common practice to remove or destroy food, weapons and articles of manufacture utterly regardless of the loss inflicted on their owners.[23]

Davidson's diary reveals his capacity to compartmentalise, because he also noted his church attendances, and saw himself as a Christian gentleman.[24] Maybe the planter also received more than usual support from the Native Mounted Police, for he was a man of experience and influence who, when he went south to purchase stores, arrange agents and hire labour, was welcome at Governor Bowen's table in Brisbane, and in Sydney he dined with Captain Towns, financial backer of the settlement on Cleveland Bay, Townsville. A few months later, when he returned to set up the plantation, he was again accompanied by five troopers and Cardwell's Police Magistrate, Leefe, in one boat, and Sub-Inspector Urh and two more troopers in another. Again they made a pre-emptive strike. Some 'blacks' were pursued and 'no end of dilly bags, fish baskets, spears etc. were brought back' (30 March). Davidson and his men cleared the ground for a garden, fenced it and built huts. Over the next few months the 'blacks' attacked the place twice. On the second occasion he and his men managed to get behind them and 'pitched in freely', gathering up 'two dozen swords and shields for firewood'. Shortly after each attack, Murray and his Black Troopers arrived 'to clear out the blacks' – mostly without finding any. The explanation, thought Murray, was that recently 'they had dispersed two mobs of about 60 fighting men near the coast'. Murray promised to return in a week or ten days 'and clear out the neighbourhood'.[25]

By August, Davidson had a small quantity of canes planted. But 'fear of the blacks' had 'unhinged' his partner, and he and some of the workers left. When Murray returned to clear out the 'blacks', he found only a camp of 'gins' – the lack of men was not surprising after a series of such raids. At Christmas 1866, Davidson was washed out by a great storm and flood, and with insufficient capital and labour to carry on, he came to an arrangement with the sugar company Trevillian & Co. He planted fresh canes and stayed only until 'his future partner, H. F. Morgan' arrived in June 1867. Although he retained an interest in Bellenden for a while, he shifted his main operation to the town of Mackay, further south. His parting gesture to the Cardwell community was to join a retaliatory action against the 'Goold Island niggers', who 'showed up and struck their swords on their shields challenging us to fight'. After dislodging them from a high hill on the island, the party 'sailed back to Cardwell with a string of canoes'.

Apparently Davidson did not use all his Rockingham Bay trophies for fire-wood, for in 1872, on a visit to London, he gave the British Museum a shield, a sword, two baskets, a cylindrical fish-trap and a 'pearly' shell necklace of ovoid plates strung on cord; sad relics of a destroyed people and culture (pl. 15).[26]

Some time between 1868 and 1870 an even more devastating assault was made on the clans in the vicinity of Bellenden Plains. Having resigned from the Native Mounted Police, Robert Johnstone had taken over the management of the plantation for Trevillian & Co. In his memoir he recorded how several clashes between the twenty imported South Sea Islanders who worked the cane and the local clans culminated in a concerted attack by about one hundred 'blacks', whose shields formed 'a movable barricade'. But bullets from his Enfield rifle penetrated their shields and they broke ranks. Next day, Sub-Inspector Murray arrived with his troopers and together they 'thoroughly patrolled the valley', through which the Murray and the Mackay (now called the Tully) rivers run in close parallel, enabling them to hem in and drive the Aborigines towards the coast, 'as far as Tam O' Shanter Point'. Johnstone's memoir also provides some idea of what he meant by 'thoroughly': 'I never approached an island or the mainland, or ascended a river, but each rifle was loaded and ready for action . . .'[27] At a conservative estimate – and without any loss of white lives – the numbers killed in the recorded engagements against these clans just inland from Cardwell, during the first four years, must have been well over a hundred – mostly men. Even more were displaced, putting pressure on the resources of their neighbours. Random events on the coast and the

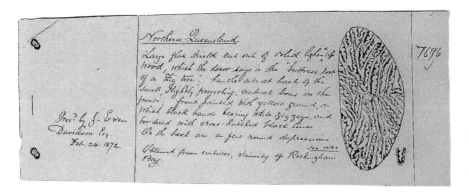

15 'Large flat shield . . . obtained from natives, vicinity of Rockingham Bay', presented by J. Ewen Davidson, 24 February 1872. Accession sheet, British Museum.

islands also placed additional pressure on them. Hinchinbrook, separated from the mainland only by a narrow channel fringed by mangroves, and with its near impenetrable forested slopes and rocky gorges, was both a place of refuge for the Aborigines and a site of anxiety for the white settlers. On one occasion, these anxieties generated a massive search and 'sweeping' of the island.

Sweeping Hinchinbrook

The interport steamer *Eva* disappeared in a tropical storm in March 1867. Months later, four white people, including a woman, were supposedly sighted on Hinchinbrook by a passing steamer. Three search parties set out: one from Bowen led by Police Magistrate Pinnock, on *Louisa Marie*, accompanied by several volunteers, including the mayor, Korah Wills, sub-inspectors Marlow and Thompson and troopers; a long boat from Townsville; and another party from Cardwell, led by Murray and his troopers. There are three accounts, Pinnock's official report, published in the *Port Denison Times* on 9 November 1867, an unpublished memoir by Korah Wills[28] and a second-hand account by Charles Eden, published in a series of *Illustrated Travels* from many parts of the world.

Korah Wills was at various times a butcher, miner or pub-keeper by occupation, and an adventurer and politician by inclination, having been one-time mayor of both Bowen (in 1867) and Mackay (in 1876–7). His recollections of 'troublesome times' on the frontier, written down in 1896, for all his exaggeration – 'in my time we dispersed by hundreds if not thousands' – come across as uninhibited truth-telling. As he observed: 'Many are the curiosities I have picked up in the camps of the Natives' who 'were perfectly rude and cannibles [*sic*] into the bargain' (memoir, p. 109). In his case 'trophies' included human beings – living and dead. On one occasion (pp. 113–17) he brought back to Bowen both a little girl he had kidnapped and 'certain limbs and head of a black fellow' whom he had 'anatomised' in front of his mates. He later exhibited the skull and arms and legs covered by the Union Jack, which had to be raised for the viewing (p. 131). 'Volunteers', Wills explained, 'were men whom [the commanding officer of the Native Mounted Police] thought he could trust for *pluck* and a quiet *tongue* after all was over, who he could solicit to join him and his one or two troopers and go out and disperse the mob' (p. 106; emphasis is in the original).

As things turned out – according to Pinnock – the Bowen and Townsville contingents found only two or three deserted camp sites, and failed to make contact with any of the islanders. Eden, however, speaks of how the search party patrolled the channel to prevent the passage of the natives between the island and the mainland, and how canoes were seized (pl. 16). It is not surprising that Eden was captivated by the story of the sweeping of Hinchinbrook in search of the survivors of the *Eva*, for the ship on which he was travelling south, *away* from Cardwell, was caught by the tail-end of the same cyclone that wrecked her. It was a case of what might have been; although he did not take part he later wrote 'An Australian search party',[29] a highly elaborated version, with much detail about the incident – including a pseudonymous Abiram Hills (Korah Wills) – that he could have learnt only from others. He would have had the opportunity to hear the much-told tale when he returned to Cardwell to become Police Magistrate 1868–70. This government post (which he does not mention in his writings) would not only have given him access to this

16   'Escape of the Black Fellow', from *An Australian Search Party* by Charles H. Eden, in partworks *Illustrated Travels*, ed. H. W. Bates, vol. 6 (1869–72). This image was recycled in other tales of imperial adventure.

and other 'camp-fire tales' but also given him experiences of his own of other similar incidents, and of life in the bush.

Aborigines appear in the story as either the elusive locals or as troopers recruited in New South Wales. Fictionalised, they are characterised as the standard characters of the Clown, the Fool and the Knave, that is, treacherous and thieving, yet comical.[30] Yet enmeshed in this fictional word-spinning there are flashes of insight into how it was between Black and White; the accommodations the former made to survive, and the interdependency that was beginning, particularly for Aboriginal women. For instance, 'Lizzie', a young woman of about fourteen from Hinchinbrook, has been seized by one of the troopers, 'Ferdinand', on an earlier raid on the island, and although her English is presented as comical – particularly her mastery of expletives – she is recognisably based on a real person who has quickly mastered the language sufficiently to act as scout and interpreter. Eden misinterprets her supposed readiness to betray her own people as savagery, not as a survival strategy.[31] Even so, the main relevance of Eden's account is more as an expression of white attitudes than a source of information about cross-cultural exchanges. It is part of an ever growing collection of colonial adventures that, according to Governor Bowen, were marked by a 'tinge of danger . . . fascinating to many minds'. These frontiersmen's tales sought to justify the harassment and casual slaughter as an inevitable outcome of the 'colonization among savage races';[32] they also reinforced derogatory attitudes towards the indigenous.

Wreck of the Maria

In late February 1872, the wreck of 'the crazy old bring *Maria*' on Bramble Reef, thirty miles east of Cardwell, was regarded as one such colonial adventure.[33] She was bound for New Guinea, and of the seventy-five gold prospectors and crew aboard, half survived, while at least twenty-one of those who did not were drowned. The tragedy was due to bad planning, the rottenness of the ship and the incompetence and cowardice of the captain who, in his determination to be first away from the ship, cast off with only six aboard the whaleboat that was able to hold twenty-five.[34] They landed ten miles north of Tam O'Shanter Point, where he and two others were killed by the 'natives'. Two escaped and made their way the short distance to Cardwell where they raised the alarm. Within a few days two more of the captain's party came in, and twenty-eight men reached Cardwell in other boats. Others had left the wreck on two make-shift rafts, and over the following days the search for survivors along the coasts to the north of the town was to have terrible repercussions for the local clans, particularly the Biyaygirri and the Girramaygan, bearing in mind that they were already reduced in number and displaced by the Cardwell settlement.

At the time, HMS *Basilisk*, under the command of Captain John Moresby, was surveying the nearby coasts, but some of the crew who were ashore were prevailed on by the Police Magistrate Brinsley Sheridan to try to recover the Captain's remains and his boat. When Moresby returned to port with the *Basilisk* he found the town in a panic because the recovery party had been repulsed 'by about 120 natives' near Tam O' Shanter Point – regarded as uncomfortably close to the settlement. Reluctantly, Moresby acceded to Sheridan's request that his men take part in a punitive raid in order 'to secure the safety of Cardwell itself,' and he dispatched a boat manned by three naval officers and twelve seamen under Lieutenant Francis Hayter. They were accompanied by a party of 'black troopers and their officers', under Robert Johnstone. According to Hayter, the troopers destroyed a large camp on 13 March, and, afterwards, when he 'stopped at the burn-out camp' he gathered up the only survivor, a frightened small boy he found lying among the slaughtered, and took him back to Cardwell. Hayter arranged for the boy's adoption and he travelled aboard the *Basilisk* to England – where he died three years later. In summing up the attack on the camp, Captain Moresby wrote that the 'blacks' were shot down by the troopers with 'an unrestrained ferocity that disgusted our officers'.[35] Although officers like Hayter avoided taking part in actual 'dispersals' they were implicated by being there. The ferocity of the attack was not forgotten by local clans, who said the troopers cut the blacks off at Tam O' Shanter Point and 'drove them out to sea and shot women and kids and all' – only five old men survived.[36]

Meanwhile, Moresby had sailed north in the *Basilisk* and located eight castaways who had made landfall from the larger raft near Point Cooper, about fifty miles north of Cardwell, where they were looked after by the Aborigines. Three bodies from the second raft were also found a short distance to the south. The moving story of the eight survivors, however, is usually neglected for that of another eight who were also cast ashore from the smaller raft, whose bodies were found by the official search party.

On 15 March the *Governor Blackall*, under the command of Lieutenant J. T. Gowlland, arrived in the area with the official party of forty-eight volunteers, a crew of water police from Sydney, and 'a supply by Govt. of 20 Snyder Rifles & 4,000 rounds of ammunition.' (Gowlland's unpublished journal, 1872, 1.) They were joined in Cardwell by more volunteers, one officer from the *Basilisk* and 'a party of Native Police' under Sub-Inspector Johnstone. Gowlland divided the searchers into four separate boat-parties and he records in gruesome detail the state of the eight bodies they found scattered along the beaches. He lists by name a total of fourteen men whose deaths he attributes to the 'Blacks', three being from the captain's boat near Tam O' Shanter Point, and eleven from the second raft (Gowlland's journal 1872, 23). In his accompanying detailed account, however, he suggests several of the dead found by the boat-parties from the *Blackall* may have died from exhaustion. As two bodies were also not recovered, this reduces the number of certain deaths at the hands of the Aborigines to nine (Gowlland's journal 1872, 8–24.)

Gowlland not only records the burning of canoes and 'native houses' along the length of the coast, on 21 March he reports specifically that Mr Johnstone's trackers accounted for sixteen men, and the following day they surprised 'a large Camp of Natives where they found remnants of pairs of trousers' and other belongings of one of the miners from the *Maria* and they 'shot 27 of the Blacks in the Camp'. In his unpublished journal, Gowlland's tone in recording the indiscriminate slaughter is matter-of-fact:

> As these are undoubtedly the tribes who have committed all the murders Mr. Johnston(sic) purposes to punish them, or 'disperse them in the usual manner'; the phrase he adopts when making his reports to Govt. after a raid of this kind on their camps – This boat brought with them several curiosities of native ingenuity such as wicker baskets . . . (entry 18 March)

His published report, however, omits the numbers of Aborigines killed on the raid, and Johnstone's euphemism 'punished' is substituted.

At the time, the townsfolk credited Johnstone with having 'avenged the massacre by the blacks' – and presented him with a testimonial. Others reviled him for having 'punished the innocent together with the guilty', and anonymous accusations made against him in the southern press led to an enquiry by Chief Magistrate Sheridan.[37] The Colonial Secretary dismissed the charges as slanderous.[38] But the accusations were repeated by Charles Heydon[39] (one of the volunteers from Sydney aboard the *Governor Blackall*) and in 1874 they reached the desk of Lord Carnarvon, Secretary of State, in London. Heydon particularly attacked the role of the Black Police, and claimed 'he had heard white men talk openly of the share they had taken in slaughtering whole camps, not only of men, but of women and children'. Although he did not directly name Johnstone, he referred to an officer who seemed 'animated by intense hatred for the natives, and positively craved for the opportunity of killing them'. Lord Normanby, Governor of Queensland, dismissed these accusations, on the grounds that 'the natives in the North . . . are numerous, savage, treacherous, and very commonly cannibals . . .' He also enclosed the report by Commissioner of Police, David Seymour, on the 'alleged outrages' in which Seymour asserted that 'the little isolated settlement was greatly excited against the Aborigines, in consequence of the massacre of *the greater part of the crew and passengers of the Maria*' (my emphasis). This claim was, of course, outrageously inaccurate and arrogantly dismissive of the testimony of a man who, while he was not in the same boat-party as Johnstone, would have been aware of what Gowlland was told when Johnstone's party returned to the *Blackall* after a raid.[40]

The retaliatory actions that followed the wreck of the *Maria* were the culmination of the long war of attrition against the Rockingham Bay clans and their near-northern neighbours. Although Gowlland alleged that 'every native camp between Cardwell and Point Cooper' had been visited, the brunt of the attacks fell on the camps found along the twenty miles of coast from Tam O' Shanter Point northward. In 1874 Reverend Fuller attempted to set up a mission first on Hinchinbrook Island and then at Bellenden Plains; each in turn was abandoned because of the lack of Aborigines.[41] After the *Maria*, Aboriginal resistance also seemed to become more reckless and the more northerly Aboriginal clans became more hostile to intruding Aborigines and white men alike.

Pearl-shell and bêche de mer

The pearl-shell and bêche de mer fisheries which were well established by the 1870s in these more northerly waters were unregulated. Small luggers were used for collecting the bêche de mer, working either separately or in groups, serviced by a tender to convey the catch to the curing station on land. The industry was particularly dependent on cheap labour. Chinese, Malays, South Sea Islanders and Aborigines were employed. The most an Aboriginal worker received for either gathering or processing the edible sea slug was 10 shillings to £1 a month, if paid at all.[42] The industry attracted 'the lowest class of white man', and decoying and kidnapping of Aborigines, men, women and children, from the islands and mainland was prevalent. In 1873 the *Goodwill* from Townsville shanghaied some Palm Islanders who murdered all but one of their abductors and made off with the cutter, only to be murdered in turn when they reached the mainland. This was only one of several similar incidents involving Palm Islanders and others, and Loos has recorded that 'a surprisingly large number of non-Aboriginal deaths' – twenty-five in the 1870s – occurred in these industries as a result of Aboriginal resistance.[43]

Gradually the Manbarra learned to seek redress. In 1880 Mickey, a clan elder, crossed to the mainland to report the abduction of several women from Palm Island and the wounding of a man called Jimmy. (Was he the same 'Jimmy' taken abroad, and could this be the incident when he lost his eye?) To accompany Mickey's 'statement', Johnstone wrote that 'on several occasions in which I have officially visited these Islands, the Blacks have always mustered and reported themselves to me.' The musters that took place on the beach may well have included Tambo, Toby and Jimmy, for Mickey was Tambo's brother and Walter's great-grandfather. Johnstone urged that such abductions would lead to 'massacres', to which Seymour, Commissioner of Police, appended his agreement but also his observation that 'there was no Act bearing on the subject' that could redress the situation.[44] Yet, these relatively small island populations were not able to withstand the trauma of these random seizures. By the turn of the century the Palm Islanders were variously reported to be twelve or twenty-five in number.

Although Aboriginal labour was regulated by the Pearl-Shell and Bêche-de-Mer Fishery Act, 1881, decoying and kidnappings continued to create social chaos. Families were arbitrarily divided, workers were transferred from one boat to another, time-expired workers who were dumped on the mainland, and absconders, attempted to make their way home along the beaches. In February 1882 a particularly brutal incident was recorded by B. Fahey, the Sub-Collector of Customs at Cooktown, that involved the rape of 'a mere girl of eleven'. She was one of eighteen Aborigines of both sexes, ranging in age from nine to forty, who had been procured by the crews of the *Reindeer* and *The Pride of the Logan*, 'in suspicious circumstances', from Hinchinbrook and Dunk Islands and the vicinity of Johnstone River, in what was euphemistically called 'a recruiting drive'. Fahey wrote that they were then divided into two groups of nine, of mixed sexes, 'after the manner of sheep . . . without reference to the inclinations or feelings naturally induced by the filial or friendly instincts of the parties concerned, some of whom, I know manifested a strong aversion to their separation'. Steve Barry, the mate of the *Reindeer*, had seized the child and, dragging her through the main street of the town, he 'secreted her in a public house'. Fahey instructed the local Inspector of Police to recover her, and as she had no kin among the kidnapped group, the Police Magistrate ordered that she be returned to Hinchinbrook. Again, Police Commissioner David Seymour made a marginal note on the documents sent to the Colonial Secretary: 'This forcible carrying away of gins is cause of much ill feeling existing towards whites but I do not know any way of preventing it.'[45]

The Seamen's Engagement Book lists the names of the remaining seventeen who were signed on to the *Reindeer* and the *Pride of the Logan* – Dick, Johnny, Billy, Rosie, Jinny, Margie and so on. When their time expired the following year, ship's mate Steve Barry attempted to take revenge on Fahey, by laying a complaint that the Collector of Customs, Fahey, had knowingly permitted their re-engagement for a second term.[46] This was not the only recorded case where the new law did not offer much protection to those recruited. Of twenty-two persons from the Cardwell district signed on to the schooner *Prompt* in June 1882, twelve men successfully made their escape, while three other men, five women and two children were recaptured just south of Cooktown and charged under the new Act as deserters. These were related to some of the escapees. In a decision worthy of Solomon, Fahey decided that unaccompanied women should not be classed as 'seamen', and that only the two who were still together with their men could be signed on. The other three women and their children, whose menfolk had absconded, were discharged, and detained, pending their return south on the weekly steamer.[47] When and where would these families have ever been reunited?

Certainly most of the women and children involved in these several incidents would have been known to Billy, Bob and their Biyaygirri kinsman, and some may have been the missing wives and children they spoke of to Houzé and Jacques. For the survivors of such incidents to go with a stranger like Cunningham would have seemed hardly more dangerous than their recent life experiences.

'The Way We Civilise'

The North Queensland frontier was a very public one, and white voices were raised against what a representative in the Queensland Legislative Assembly called 'a history of horrors' (pl. 17).[48] Each year throughout the 1870s and into the 1880s the treatment meted out to the Aborigines became a matter for debate when the vote for the financing of the Native Mounted Police was taken. Then, in 1880, Gresley Lukin, the editor of the *Queenslander*, provided the forum for a public debate, later published as a pamphlet, *The Way We Civilise*. Many of the incidents referred to in these letters to the editor took place in the Kennedy and the more northerly Cook districts during the 1870s, and it is notable that most of those who put their names and not pseudonyms to their letters were also those who spoke out against what was happening.

Visitors to the district as different from each other as Carrington, 'a university man' (1871), Moresby, the captain of HMS *Basilisk* (1876), Carl Lumholtz, the Norwegian naturalist and author of *Among Cannibals* (1888),[49] and A. Vogan, the journalist who wrote a novel called *The Black Police* (1890), all witnessed the aftermath of killings where numbers of Aborigines had been left to die (pl. 18). Although today they read as reliable witnesses, there is a terrible anonymity about these accounts, whereas the story of 'Kassey', who was shot down and burnt 'near the public road, Lower Herbert [River]', exposes the intimacy of the enmity as the interdependency of Aborigines and settlers increased. Her story was mentioned in a letter to the *Queenslander*, 26 June 1880, from the property-owner James Cassady. It was refuted by W. E. Armit, ex-officer of the Native Mounted Police in a subsequent letter. 'No,' he said, 'Cassy' was hit

17   'Queensland Squatters "Dispersing" Aborigines', frontispiece to Arthur J. Vogan's novel, *The Black Police*, 1890.

by a bullet meant for her man, an absconding trooper called Alex. 'It was purely an accident.' He also added that it caused the Black Police much time and trouble before they caught up with him.[50] Cassady fired another salvo in a letter to the *Brisbane Courier*, 7 October 1880: 'Very plausible story indeed!' Apparently Kassey had been shot '*in the breast*' by Sub-Inspector Shairpe, who himself had been his informant, and who had later been dismissed from the service for the outrage.[51]

Working for the white man was no security against attack. In another letter, published on 7 August, Cassady mentioned the 'dispersal' of three 'station boys', Tommy, Charley and Billy, 'well known' to him. 'I conscientiously believe', he wrote, 'that one and all of the victims were wantonly murdered, and on each occasion by the orders of a different officer or individual.' In reply Armit castigated Cassady for carrying 'his sympathy rather too far'. He accused him of first allowing 'blacks' to be dispersed on his

18   'Native Police Dispersing Blacks. Sketch after a description given to me on the spot.' Engraving, *Among Cannibals* by Carl Lumholtz, 1889.

property, Fairview, on the Lower Herbert in 1873, and then constituting 'himself as black protector, for his own interests, and to the detriment of his neighbours' property'. Further, he accused Cassady of giving 'shelter to *the* ringleader in the double murder in 1875 of Mr and Mrs Conn', a couple who had a small selection about twelve miles north of Cardwell.[52] Again Cassady refuted Armit's claims in a letter of 7 October, giving a detailed account of the actions he had taken to have 'Dicky', the reputed murderer, apprehended. But the revenge for the Conn killings was swift, terrible – and indiscriminate.[53]

The remaining coastal lands, including Nyawaygi territory on Halifax Bay, had been taken up for sugar-growing from the beginning of the decade. In 1877 the Legislative Council debated the establishment of an Aboriginal Reserve in the district that would include the Palm Islands, Dunk Island and nearby small islands, and a block of land, north of Cardwell, to be funded by land sales; but funds were never allocated.[54] It had been said that wanting food and blankets was a motive for the Conn murder. There were other indications of hunger among the survivors of the local clans, and they were becoming dependent on pastoralists like James Cassady and William Craig who were prepared to 'let them in'.[55] On the other hand, Armit spoke for many other frontiersmen when he wrote 'the destiny' of the 'Blackman' is 'extinction'.[56] Above all, the letters republished in *The Way We Civilise* exposed the relentless pressure on the local clans and the chaos of the contact zone.[57]

How is the evidence from these largely anecdotal sources to be assessed? In these post-Holocaust and post-Bosnian times perhaps the processes of denial are better understood. The code of the Native Mounted Police was one of secrecy, and denial was built into the official reporting on their activities.[58] As one of their officers wrote, it was 'forbidden to publish any information which could give the public even the slightest glimpse of the doings of the Native Police'.[59] These were the silences of the frontier.

Conservative estimates of the pre-invasion populations for each of the language groups in the area was about 500, except for the Manbarra of Palm Island who were said never to have been more than about 200.[60] It is difficult to arrive at figures for the survivors of each language group in the area by the 1880s. By then, 'the system of continual war . . . to utter extermination'[61] was almost over. Along the coasts Wulguru-speaking clans of Cleveland Bay and the clans of Rockingham Bay were greatly reduced in number. In 1881 a visitor to Hinchinbrook sighted only seven people, three of whom were men.[62] A year later Cunningham took three Biyaygirri men from the district. According to Lumholtz, even the inland Warrgamaygan and Girramaygan were probably no more than 200 to 250 in number. According to the pastoralist William Craig, however, by 1898 they too were reduced to 'about 80 . . . who have not yet gone down to the coast'.[63]

From 1882 the pastoralist James Cassady and Sub-Inspector Johnstone became close neighbours, Cassady on Mungalla station and Johnstone at the police camp at Molonga, both in Nyawaygi territory on Halifax Bay (pl. 19).[64] Molonga means 'devil' and for many years the place continued to be regarded with fear by the local Aborigines. Both men supplied information about the Halifax Bay clans (Nyawaygi) for E. M. Curr's book, *The Australian Race* (1886–7), and perhaps their figures are the most accurate for the period. In 1865, said Cassady, there were about 500 persons. By 1880 these were reduced to '200 souls' of whom there were about 40 men, 30 boys over ten years, 100 women and girls over ten years, and 30 children of both sexes under ten years. Both the decrease in numbers and the excess of females over males Cassady attributed to 'the brutality of the Native Mounted Police and some of the settlers, who, in the beginning, relentlessly hunted down and shot as many of the males of the tribe as possible'. For his part, Sub-Inspector Johnstone asserted that the tribe had been diminished during fifteen years of settlement 'by measles, consumption and drink'.[65] In his 1903 memoir, *Spinifex and Wattle*, however, Johnstone's reflections were more ambiguous. 'In fact,' he wrote, 'the whites I know have a lot to answer for. Though it is too late now to try to undo the harm that has been committed, the only thing is to make it pleasant and comfortable for the doomed remnant.' Thus, in old age, when he reflected on

19   'Native troopers dispersing a camp', from *Australia's First Hundred Years* by Hank P. Mahony, 1888.

the defeated clans, he permitted himself to acknowledge his admiration of 'the fine, wiry, athletic men at a bora fifty years ago . . . whose every movement was graceful, each muscle playing under the ebony skin'.[66] Desire and dread were close companions.

In a report of 1883, British officialdom condemned the Queensland settler society as being unfit to play any part in the governance of the neighbouring newly colonised New Guinea, on the grounds that 'even among the most enlightened and humane of their number, the native is regarded simply as an encumbrance on the soil'.[67] The 'mechanisms of forgetfulness'[68] began early. Governor Bowen saw the settlement of North Queensland as 'the triumph of peaceful progress . . . conquest not over man, but over nature, not for this generation, but for all posterity, not for England, but for all mankind'.[69]

At the same time as Cunningham's removal of the North Queenslanders – which was of such small concern to Queensland's Police Commissioner, David Seymour – an account by A. A. Hull, designed to attract new migrants, described the coastal districts north of Cardwell as being, until recently,

a natural wilderness . . . where the sound of an axe in the virgin forest was a thing unknown; where the cooee of the wild natives was answered by the booming of the cassowary, and the roar of the alligator alone broke the stillness of the deep and sluggish rivers as they wound through miles of dense tropical scrub . . . And now what will you see there? Steamers lying at large commodious wharves, towns in which thousands of white people ply a busy trade, where . . . the rivers are highways to large and flourishing plantations, where the shrill steam whistle of the sugar-mill startles the denizens of the still standing scrub . . . and life, energy, and busy trade, have changed this wilderness into the home of the refined and cultivated race for whom it was no doubt created.[70]

The ideological underpinnings of Bowen's confident assertions, and of the blinkered observations of Alfred Hull's lush prose, were that the Aborigines had forfeited their rights to the land because they had failed to make productive use of it. More than that, it was seen as a reflection on their place in the human social order. The idea that the industrious and the rational were the natural inheritors of the land had deep roots in European Enlightenment thought – particularly that of John Locke – and it had already been used in the earlier American colonies to justify the separation of the land from its original inhabitants. It was argued that such appropriation was justified because the more rational use of the land benefited 'the public good'. By extension, the dependence of the savage 'on the spontaneous hand of nature' for sustenance denied the savage rationality. In his *Two Treatises of Government* (1690) Locke argued that those who opposed men of reason exposed themselves to being treated as 'Beasts of Prey'. Such ideas were based on a deep misapprehension of Aboriginal life and relationship to the land. They also denied the reality of the Snyder rifle. As Peter Hulme has observed, here was 'the language in which all colonial wars . . . have been justified'.[71] From the late nineteenth century such ideas were given a rigidly hierarchical gloss. On the North Queensland frontier they were ruthlessly applied and the slaughter of the land's owners was cloaked in the language of denial, for were not the Aborigines 'doomed to disappear'?

Bridgeport Conn. August 9th 1882.
U.S. America

Dear Sir,

I desire to carry out as far as possible an idea I have long entertained, of forming a collection, in pairs or otherwise of all the uncivilized races in existance [sic] and my present object is to ask your kindness to render me what assistance is in your power to acquire any specimens of these uncivilized peoples.

My aim is to <u>exhibit</u> to the American public, not only <u>human beings of different races</u>, but also where practicable, those who possess extraordinary peculiarities such as giants, dwarfs, singular disfigurements of the person, dexterity in the use of weapons, dancing, singing, juggling, unusual feats of strength or agility etc. With this object in view I should be glad to receive from you descriptions of as many of such specimens as you could obtain and photographs as far as possible, and if it is necessary to send an agent into the area for this purpose. The remuneration of these people in addition to their board and travelling expenses is usually nominal. I shall see that they are presented with fancy articles such as are acceptable and a small allowance monthly.

In any case a group of 3 to 6 or even 10 would be as novel. I should probably take them but I must study money, inasmuch as I propose to add this 'Congress of Nations' to my other attractions in our great show for no extra charge – if interpreters should be absolutely necessary please inform me what would be the cost which must be moderate.

For yourself I should be glad to reimburse you for any outlay, and to give you a reasonable compensation for trouble which you may take in this matter.

If necessary I might send a special agent to your country for any specimens which you may bring under my notice, provided they appear to me to warrant such additional outlay. If you would meet with any living animals or reptiles of a special nature or in any sense rare or unusual I should be glad to receive and to refund to you the cost of a photograph and full description of the same, but inanimate objects I do not desire. As it is my wish to get at least a portion of this collection together by January or February 1883 I wish to thank you kindly to favour me with an early reply as convenient.

Yours faithfully,

P. T. Barnum [signed]

Note: The underlining is in the original document. Barnum wrote to several hundred American consulates and other agencies throughout the world. In Australia, in this period, there was a consul in Townsville as well as in the southern capital cities – probably because of the nearby goldfields. Letter in Permanent Administrative Files, Smithsonian Institution Archives.

3   Colonial Circuits

The history of European settlements in America, Africa and Australia, presents everywhere the same general features – a wide and sweeping destruction of native races by the uncontrolled violence of individuals, if not of colonial authorities, followed by tardy attempts on the part of governments to repair the acknowledged crime.

Herman Merivale, *Lectures on Colonization and Colonies*, 1841

The two groups of North Queenslanders removed overseas by R. A. Cunningham in the late nineteenth century were part of 'the circuits of ideas and people, colonizers and colonized, within and among empires'.[1] The itinerant showman, who was an active agent in their exploitation, was himself part of the European migratory movement to America and the colonies. The pursuit of his show business career took him to Australia, and resulted in his encounter with Toby, Billy, Tambo and the others. Together, the showman and Aboriginal performers of first one group and then another toured the show places of the metropolitan and provincial centres in both America and Europe, from Barnum's circus and the American dime museums, in 1884, to the Crystal Palace in England, Folies Bergère in Paris, Berlin's Panoptikum, St Petersburg's 'Arcadia' and the court of the Turkish Empire, the Universal Exposition in Paris, 1889, the 'Midway Plaisance' of the Columbian World's Fair in Chicago in 1893, and Coney Island in its heyday. These sites were arenas for the representation of cultural difference, which paralleled the development of ideas about the classification of human types – ideas that served to define and maintain cultural differences and distance within colonialism's cultures.

The showman

In the last quarter of the nineteenth century, a number of showmen regarded P. T. Barnum as a role model – especially those who worked for his circus organisation, for even a short period, and R. A. Cunningham was one such independent impresario. According to his own account of the 'strange history' of the North Queenslanders' capture, he was in Melbourne 'on 16 November, 1882', when 'he received orders from P. T. Barnum's agent to proceed at once, and if possible, secure a number of the finest specimens of Australian Aborigines.' The 'agent' was J. B. Gaylord who, according to an item in the entertainment industries' journal, the *New York Clipper*, had been dispatched by Barnum in September 'to Australia, New Zealand and various other countries . . . to obtain several special attractions' for presentation in an *Ethnological Congress of Savage Tribes* proposed for the following season. Gaylord and another trusted agent, J. R. Davis, had been issued with money and credits to the extent of $20,000 for the purpose.[2]

Although it seems that Gaylord may not have made it to Australia at that time, it is possible that Cunningham was in touch with him telegraphically. Nevertheless, the word 'orders' implies a more substantial connection than probably existed between him and men who worked directly for Barnum. There was an alternative source. At that time, there were American consuls in Melbourne, Sydney and Townsville, and Cunningham could have heard of Barnum's request from a circular letter, one of the several hundred handwritten copies, devotedly made by Barnum's niece, addressed to American representatives abroad. In this P. T. detailed his desire to acquire 'specimens' of 'all the uncivilized races in existence . . . to exhibit to the American public' – and his expectation that they could be acquired for a 'nominal' sum. As the success of such an enterprise depended on suppliers such as Cunningham, I shall begin by probing the background of the elusive Mr Cunningham, returning to the subject of Barnum's long-time involvement in the display of indigenous people, and its culmination in the *Ethnological Congress*, in a subsequent chapter. For an itinerant entertainer such as Cunningham, Barnum's request must have seemed an opportunity not to be missed. He already had several years' experience behind him of 'travelling through the colonies of Australia, New Zealand and Tasmania' with his 'own company of Theatricals'. Already in his late forties, this may well have been the show business break he had been waiting for.

American entertainers – particularly circus and variety performers – found Australian cities and towns lucrative places to visit. During this period two great American circuses toured Australia. In 1877–8, Cooper, Bailey & Company's Great International Allied Shows had toured five states, travelling as far north as Rockhampton in Queensland,[3] but Cunningham is not listed as being on the payroll[4] – although after it became amalgamated with Barnum and Coup's to form The Greatest Show on Earth, this was the company that Cunningham and his Australian troupe were to join. Moreover, for these years Cunningham is listed in San Francisco directories as being resident there. Nor does he appear to have accompanied William Washington Cole's highly successful circus tour of New Zealand, Victoria and New South Wales in 1880–1, among the attractions of which was a troupe of Native Americans.[5] Nevertheless, it was in Australia as well as in America that he honed his skills as an advance agent for circuses and variety shows, travelling ahead of the company and making all the necessary arrangements for the coming show.

Cunningham arrived in Sydney in July 1879 as business manager to the Taylor Family Troupe, the star of which was the ten-year-old daughter, Mattie. He had previously been on tour with the Taylors in Arizona, New Mexico and California. In San Francisco (June 1878) they were billed at Platt's Hall together with Otto, the son of Nez-Percés Chief 'Joseph' – 'the only opportunity to see these accomplished young people, the little lady going to Australia and the "young chief" to the Paris Exposition as a representative of our American Indian'. This combination of acts is typical of the mix that made up variety performances of the period, and of the role indigenous performers frequently played in them. In Australia, while Mattie's impressions were rated 'amusing' and 'talented' by some, *Town and Country* wrote: 'a more dismal performance than the banjo-playing and character sketching given by them has seldom been imported – even from America.'

At the same time as organising the Taylors' tour of New South Wales country towns, or soon after, Cunningham seems to have operated as a theatrical agent for other touring performers, arranging a tour of the towns of southern New South Wales and northern Victoria for Professor Menton, 'Phrenologist and Champion Ventriloquist of the World', exponent of magic and 'exposer of spiritualism thrown in'. In December 1880, Cunningham was back in California, where he paid up two years of back dues to the Columbia Lodge, no. 28; so, in his travels, the showman could also call on the brotherhood of Freemasons. Returning to Australia, he acted as advance agent for the British American Circus – a metamorphosis of Burton's Great Circus – then for The Great American Circus, also known as Valhalla and Barlows Great American Circus, which toured the country towns of New South Wales and Victoria through 1881.[6] Cunningham's own skills as a musician increased the opportunities available to him. During 1881 he joined with another showman to form 'Messrs Cunningham and Cameron's Great London Gaiety Company' that, by arrangement with Burton's Royal Australian Circus, gave 'A Grand Concert and Minstrel Entertainment' after the circus performance was over. By February 1882, Wilson's Millionaire Confederation, incorporating Wilson's Great World Circus, with which Cunningham was associated in some way, reached Melbourne. Closer to the November 1882 date which places him in Melbourne, The Great American Circus, one of the shows with which he is known to have been associated, was seen at Prahan, a suburb of Melbourne.[7]

Cunningham was, therefore, part of the American – particularly Californian – influence of variety and minstrelsy on popular culture in Australia that flourished in the 1870s and on into the 1880s, which has been well documented by Richard Waterhouse (1990). Both St Leon (1983; 1992) and Waterhouse (1990) stress the role of itinerant, popular performers as shapers of Australian popular culture – and more. St Leon describes 'Australia's show-people' as early 'binding threads' in the weave of Australian identity.[8] Waterhouse notes that 'despite the distinguishing traits which marked the American, British and Australian minstrel shows, the international popularity of minstrelsy suggests that there were common reasons for its appeal: those who enjoyed this form of popular theatre in North America, the British Isles and Australasia lived in comparable modern industrial environments, which generated similar cultural values'.[9] Values that Waterhouse sees as being underpinned by the prevailing imperialist ideology linked with contemporary theories of a hierarchy of races. Grounded in these same notions, the corollary to these imported shows was Cunningham's export of groups of Australian Aborigines to perform as 'savages' in the show-spaces of America and Europe.

Cunningham belonged to a coterie of itinerant showmen who stood outside conventional society yet could be described as belonging to a cosmopolitan, even international, culture of show people who were versatile, worldly and attached to the travelling way of life. His boast was that he had 'never spent two New Year's days in the same city or locality in thirty years'.[10] At the same time, he was instrumental in drawing the North Queenslanders into the same extraterritorial space in which they coexisted with other show people – without necessarily intermingling.

The most constant trace Cunningham left in the records, such as shipping lists, show advertisements, official documents and newspaper reports, is his use of the initials, R. A. 'R' stands for Robert. Like other showmen, he was possibly emulating P. T. Barnum's use of personal name initials, but his preference for R. A. appears also to have been a long-standing practice, a marker that set him apart from the other Roberts of the extensive and far-flung Cunningham clan. Moreover, he deployed the 'A' more ambiguously. For instance, on the pamphlet copyright forms he used 'Anderson', and several days later on the photographic copyright forms he used 'Andrew' (pp. 16–17). Much later, in 1892, he was referred to as Alexander. As the narrative unfolds it is clear that Cunningham played by his own rules, secure in the knowledge that he would soon be moving on. As a showman, Cunningham operated at the margins of society; on the other hand, as part of the Scotch-Irish diaspora, he enjoyed a sense of belonging, independent of place. Being a Cunningham, he said, provided him with relatives and namesakes in Canada, Australia and Britain, as well as America.

For a time, Cunningham's itinerant habits and his solitariness made it difficult to establish which branch of the Cunningham family he belonged to, and details of his early life prior to his notoriety as an impresario of indigenous performers, such as the Aborigines and the Samoans, have been just as hard to accumulate. The first break came while I was researching his 1892–3 tour of the second group of North Queensland Aborigines in California, and found he was hailed in the press as a cornet-playing 'old Californian' from Tuolumne County, who had been well-known in theatrical circles for over forty years.[11] Given his actual age, it was an exaggeration that was hardly complimentary!

Robert was born on 27 July 1837 to Margaret Emberson, wife of Andrew Cunningham, farmer, in Godmanchester (near Huntingdon), Quebec province, Canada. The first member of this branch of Cunninghams to arrive in Huntingdon from Londonderry County, Northern Ireland, was Andrew's brother, William, in 1826. The following year, Andrew and their father, Robert, and other family members arrived. Andrew married Margaret Emberson in Montreal in 1830, and Robert was one of a number

20   R. A. Cunningham.
Photograph: Cramer, San
Francisco.

of children.[12] The Cunninghams were part of the chain of Scottish-Irish nonconformist emigrants who came to North America from the late eighteenth century on. Many – including other branches of Cunninghams – settled in Pennsylvania because of the civic and religious freedom afforded them there, and that state was also a dispersal point from which different branches of Cunninghams spread first to neighbouring Virginia, then to Ohio and further west. Young R. A. is recorded as arriving in Columbia, Tuolumne County, California, in January 1856 from Pennsylvania.[13] He was part of a migration of over 300,000 people who came overland, and by way of Panama – from all parts of the world – for two decades after 1849, drawn to California by the rich gold deposits of the Sierras. His stated occupation: miner. Weren't they all? He was eighteen years old. The state of California – proclaimed after the defeat of the Mexicans – was barely a decade old, therefore 'old Californian' is a relative term.

Columbia had been founded in 1849, at the beginning of the gold rush. The population soon swelled to 8,000, and it remained a prosperous mining town for several decades. Only Americans and those of European descent were allowed to mine in the district. All other foreigners had to declare their intent, and Chinese and South Sea Islanders were excluded. The few remaining Miwok Indians both mined for themselves and hired themselves out to others. The newspapers that soon flourished reported the frequent visits of singers and other theatrical performers, gamblers and the circus. When gold lost its appeal for the cornet-playing Cunningham, departing entertainers may well have offered him an escape route – and a new occupation (pl. 20).[14]

By 1864 Cunningham was in San Francisco, where, in August, he was mustered in Company D of the Sixth Regiment of Californian Infantry. During the Civil War some 6,000 Californian men were mustered in several regiments and battalions mostly to mop up pockets of confederates. Some regiments saw active service against hostile Indians, but no service records have survived for Cunningham's Company D. The Indians were beyond the Sierras and along the Mexican borderlands – by then the local Indians, contemptuously referred to as 'diggers' on account of their food-gathering lifestyle, had been almost wiped out. An estimated 300,000 Californian Indians were reduced to 25,000–30,000 by 1865. Hubert Howe Bancroft, writing in 1884, condemned their extermination as 'one of the last human hunts of civilisation, and the basest and most brutal of them all'.[15] These were words that could have applied equally to the slaughter that was taking place in North Queensland at about the same time – a north Australian frontier that was soon to be visited by Cunningham.

The city of San Francisco was booming when Cunningham was discharged from the army in December 1865. The 1870 census records his residence there in a hotel and that he was thirty-five years old (he was in fact thirty-three), a musician, worth $1,000, with no real estate. It confirms his Irish parentage – but also says erroneously that he was born in Ireland. During the next decade he turns up on Californian coastal shipping lists and appears intermittently in San Francisco directories until 1879, as a musician, living at different addresses in the theatre district. The only other years he is listed as resident in San Francisco are 1889, 1890 and 1891,[16] dates that tally with his recorded movements beyond California. While he may have arrived in Australia earlier than 1879, when he was with the Taylors, the ease with which he set about his search for a group of Aboriginal performers in late 1882 confirms his familiarity with circus and minstrelsy circles and circuits, and with travel in the Australian colonies beyond the southern state capitals.

In spite of the considerable differences, there are interesting similarities between the Californian frontier experienced by Cunningham and the North Queensland frontier he visited a couple of decades later. The first Spanish settlements in California had coalesced around defensive and missionary outposts. By 1840, as America's westward expansion quickened pace, California became simultaneously part of the Spanish borderlands and an American western frontier, a situation that was only resolved by the Mexican War. Richard Slotkin, among others, has interpreted the dynamics of this American frontier as being powered by an internal colonialism, in which the developing political economy of the metropolitan cities in the east regulated the demand for the resources of the western frontier territories.[17] Similarly, after 1859, although the newly established state of Queensland was formally a British colony, the opening up of the districts beyond Bowen, first North Kennedy and then Cook district, was also powered by an internal colonialism, mainly capitalised by the financial centres of Sydney and Melbourne,[18] although it also attracted investors and settlers directly from Britain.

Cunningham would have been familiar with the cultural attitudes he encountered in North Queensland, especially those regarding the

Aborigines. They were much the same as those he would have experienced on the Californian frontier towards the Native Americans; they were grounded in a similar ideology, linked with a similar socioeconomic formation. Thus the male camaraderie of a pub in Townsville – and the frontier tales exchanged there – would have been much the same as in a saloon bar in San Francisco. So much so that he remarked in his pamphlet of 1884 how 'strange' it was that the colonial government considered the removal of 'the blacks' 'without legal permission . . . came under the head of kidnapping'. In his pamphlet the dangers of 'the capture' were aimed at titillating the reader. The same rhetoric was employed in Barnum's advertising of the *Ethnological Congress* in which Billy and his companions took part.

> The public can form no adequate idea of the enormous costs and difficulties involved; of the dangers braved, the privations endured, the obstacles overcome, the disappointments sustained, and the disheartening losses incurred, in collecting this greatest and best of Object Teaching Schools from the desert-environed wilds of Africa, the remote and pathless jungles of Asia, the dreadful and unexplored solitudes of Australia, the interior of Brazil and Central America, and the mysterious islands of the southern seas.[19]

Although, in his pamphlet, Cunningham offers his account of 'a few difficulties in obtaining them' as a measure of the authenticity of his 'rare' and 'savage' charges, it can be taken as a broad guide to what happened, because his movements are also traceable from other sources. In the event, the success of his enterprise partly depended on his opportunistic adaptability; and a preparedness to move on that flowed from his lack of personal ties or attachment to place.

Capture

> *At last I succeeded in getting those that accompanied me.*
> R. A. Cunningham, 1884

It seems R. A.'s plan was to connect with Barnum's agent J. B. Gaylord in 'Singapore where a special steamer had been chartered for San Francisco'. Taking the SS *Euxine*, one of G. R. Stevens & Co.'s steamers that plied between Singapore and Australia's eastern ports, he arrived in Port Darwin on 10 December 1882 in search of Aborigines to go with him. He describes how he was preparing to embark on the steamer with 'five fine specimens'[20] with the agreement of the Resident Governor, Mr Price, when the local Police Inspector 'frustrated my intentions. He made known to the blacks they would never return, which utterly scared them, and they immediately fled into the bush.' Thus, eight days after his arrival in Darwin, he departed on the SS *Hungarian* on its southward voyage from Singapore to Sydney.[21] Aboard were fifty 'Malays' who had been signed on in Singapore to work in the pearl-shell and bêche de mer fisheries. Recent legislation had for the first time regulated the use of Aboriginal labour in these industries, but the Malaysians were favoured for this employment because there was no legal compulsion to pay for their return home.[22] They were disembarked on Thursday Island, and Cunningham himself left the ship in Townsville on 26 December, in the middle of the holiday season.

He found Townsville – with about 4,000 residents – to be a town of substance with the beginnings of a public transport system, a Chamber of Commerce, a Turf Club, cricket clubs and Masonic Lodges. Linked to the mining hinterland by rail, it had telegraphic links and flourishing newspapers, and was already the principal centre in the region. Residents had formed a Separation League advocating that it become a future capital of a separate state. Several of the town's best hotels – particularly Queens Hotel – were situated along the Strand and were places where visitors encountered not only the townsfolk, the shopkeepers and government officials, but also the squatters from inland properties who came to do business, collect supplies and take a break by the sea. There were also rougher elements, the miners from Charters Towers and the masters of the bêche de mer and pearl-shell fishing boats, who contributed to the town's reputation for an absence of sobriety. The hotels were also places where visiting entertainers performed and Cunningham would have found such company congenial and perhaps helpful to his project.

As Cunningham tells it in the pamphlet he later published, he first hired 'a cutter of ten tons burden' (about the size of a bêche de mer boat); he endured hardships at sea, paddled up creeks in canoes, 'and attempted to offer the creatures on shore all inducements such as tobacco, red handkerchiefs etc', but without success. 'At last,' he concluded, 'I succeeded in getting those that accompanied me.' What details of his encounter with the Aborigines who finally went with him did this bland statement hide? What would he have been able to achieve in the about three weeks he spent in the environs of Townsville before embarking for Sydney on the *Quiraing* on 22 January 1883[23] with Billy, Jenny and Toby, and their companions?

The place Cunningham most frequently mentions in later accounts is Cardwell, a settlement just north of Townsville, and he certainly could have taken the small coastal steamer there and back. Similarly, he could have made the journey by cutter to the Palm Islands, to which residents of Townsville were beginning to make short excursions from the 1870s on. But if he had picked up the members of the group from different places he would have found it difficult to keep them together – as was to be the case later in Sydney. If he had found a seaman willing to assist him in such an enterprise, it is reasonable to surmise that they would have been met with caution, as there was much fear of abduction among the inhabitants of the offshore islands, because it was one of the commonest means of acquiring labourers for the fisheries industries. It is difficult to imagine that he could have operated in the town without the knowledge and support of the police magistrate, and later, in Sydney, it was confirmed that the Queensland authorities knew of the showman's activities. It was also implied that he had found Billy and the others in a 'blacks' camp', which is

21   'Camp of Natives, near Townsville' from *Sketches of Life in Queensland*, engraving, *Illustrated London News*, 19 Jan. 1884.

the most likely scenario. There Cunningham would have had time to reconnoitre the camp, make return visits and find Aborigines who spoke a little English. To travel south with the Aborigines he would have had to dress them in decent clothes, for those mostly available to the local inhabitants were the cast-offs of the white people. Carl Lumholtz tells how a well-worn shirt, a tattered hat and a clay pipe were frequently among the first attributes of civilisation to be acquired by those who worked for the white man; but 'civilised blacks . . . like to wear clothes, and they like to have their clothes fit nicely.'[24] Thus for Toby, Jenny and the others the offer of a complete set of clothes would have been a persuasive factor.

There were many reasons why the different members of the party taken by Cunningham might have come together by chance in Townsville. In spite of dispossession and dispersal – and the consequent rupture of traditional life – groups of Aborigines continued to gather at different centres in the district for ceremonies at about that time of year (p. 35). Townsville was also a supply centre for the bêche de mer fisheries, and Aborigines working in the industry were often discharged and picked up there; so that some of the group may have turned up there at the end of a contract or in search of missing family members. Aborigines also had a presence within the town, where some found casual employment. There was a large 'blacks' camp' at Hermit Park, near the racecourse, and others at Rowe's Beach and Mt Marlow, on the northern side of the town, where those in transit for one reason or another gathered. Although the detailed circumstances of the life-changing encounter with Cunningham of Billy, Toby and the others remain speculative, that they could be removed so easily is understandable – the events narrated in the preceding chapter show how precarious life had become for the people in the environs of Townsville, whose lands bordered Halifax and Rockingham bays and the offshore islands of Hinchinbrook and Palm.

Sydney escape and recapture

Whatever the difficulties, 'Mr Cunningham finally got his Aborigines to Sydney with the intention of transferring them to the San Francisco steamer.'[25] As the next one, the SS *City of Sydney*, was not due to depart until 22 February, he established himself in the centre of the city at the Carlton Club Hotel, Elizabeth Street, where the North Queenslanders were accommodated in an out-house at the rear. Within a few days, two of them escaped, and on 12 February Cunningham put out a public notice announcing: 'Two Aborigines strayed'.

The escapees managed to reach Manly, on the northern side of the harbour, where, six days later, they were reported as wandering in the bush, 'utterly wild', one naked and the other wearing only a shirt. When the local Senior Constable Leplaw found them, he signed to them that he would give them food and clothing if they would go with him, but the man in the shirt bolted, and when the constable caught up with him he drew a knife from under the shirt and stabbed Leplaw in the hand. The man was restrained and 'bundled like a pig' onto the Manly ferry. Back in Sydney he and his companion were confined in Darlinghurst Gaol, and the following morning – Monday, 20 February – they were brought before Mr Marsh, the magistrate at the Water Police Court.

'Barnum's agent, Mr Cunningham . . . who appeared in court told his story with a charming insouciance and seemed much surprised when Mr Marsh said it looked like kidnapping.' Marsh then instructed the police to enquire from Queensland into the circumstances of the Aborigines' removal and 'the case' was placed before the Attorney-General. George Thornton, Chairman of Aboriginal Protection Board in New South Wales,[26] also tabled the matter in the New South Wales Legislative Council, where he declared that 'these poor creatures are evidently in great terror, and want to run away from their employer; if taken away, or even separated, they would fret to death or destroy themselves', and he asks for them either to be returned home or found employment in the Sydney area.

When W. Camphin, Inspector of Detectives, found that these two, who were now referred to as Billy and Jimmy (or Jemmy), were travelling with seven more (four men, two women and a child) who were held in an out-house at the back of the Carlton before 'being taken to America as a speculation', it caused a furore. 'It will never do', trumpeted the *Evening News*, 'to have Sydney made the entrepôt of a kidnapping trade.' Camphin reported back to Fosbery, the Inspector-General of Police, that 'two of the males spoke English and say they were willing to go to America. The others do not appear to know where they are going to [but] Mr Cunningham . . . appears to pay attention to their wants . . .'

It was all over in a few days. Billy was released into Cunningham's 'care' on 22 February, while Jimmy was remanded on a charge of wounding

Leplaw. A telegram from Queensland's Chief Inspector of Police, David Seymour, said: 'have ascertained they went willingly understanding their destination and terms of absence. There is no objection to their going under such circumstances.' Upon which the *Sydney Morning Herald* commented that although 'they left Queensland with the cognisance of the government of that colony . . . this telegram gives no information as to the tribe to which these men belong, nor is it clear how it was ascertained they went willingly. This is certain that they are very unwilling to proceed beyond Sydney . . .' Then, on 23 February, the charge against Jimmy was dropped on the contradictory grounds that nobody could be found 'to interpret the language spoken by the accused' nor was it possible 'to make the accused understand the nature of the offence with which he had been charged'. Jimmy was discharged – but too late for the group to take the SS *City of Sydney*, which had sailed for San Francisco the very same day. So Cunningham did what he was almost always to do in later crises – he moved the group on immediately, embarking with them on the *Barrabool* for Melbourne, arriving there 26 February, where they remained until, on 9 March, he sailed with them on the *Wairarapa* for Auckland, New Zealand.[27] There they gave their first performances and also demonstrations of boomerang throwing at Takapuna racecourse on the North Shore,[28] while waiting for the SS *Australia* to arrive from Sydney and take them on to San Francisco.

What sense can be made of the events in Sydney in 1883?

There is an element of raw truth in the observations of *Figaro*'s reporter, writing in San Francisco two months later:

Powerful influence was brought to bear in Mr Cunningham's favour, as he is well-known in the Colonies, in as much as two of the blacks who could make themselves understood in English, acknowledged their willingness to go with him to America. Although the others were not able to express themselves clearly as to the inducement held out to them, further proceedings were abandoned for the time being, and Mr. Cunningham again secured full control of the blacks, but the press called upon the Colonial Secretary to set in motion every engine of the law to prevent their removal from Sydney. The Colonial officials, however, were not a match for Barnum's agent, and here he is blacks and all. (26 April 1883)

I have the advantage here, in knowing how this early attempt at telling the story of 'The capture', conveyed in *Figaro*'s report, metamorphosed into the version in Cunningham's pamphlet, and was to become part of the showman's repertoire of self-promotion, and to be quoted endlessly in newspapers in many languages, over the years.

Although Cunningham was later to say that the two men who were instrumental in his being able to remove the group were Johnny (identified as probably being Tambo, see p. 103) and Toby, the degree of their understanding and their ability to convey what they knew to the others remains doubtful, and the idea that a degree of coercion as well as cajoling was involved cannot be dismissed. For instance, why were Billy and Jimmy found in Manly with only a shirt between the two of them? Did Cunningham remove the Aborigines' clothes while at the Carlton to prevent them from running away?

There is another question: were Billy and Jimmy the same persons as the two men known by those names later on the journey? The man called Billy seems to have been a constant, but the Jimmy described in the interviews in Brussels by Houzé and Jacques (and by others later) had a very distinctive physical injury – made by a boomerang that had blinded his right eye (pl. 55). Yet none of the Sydney reports mentions this as an identifying feature of the runaway Jimmy. Moreover, Inspector Camphin noted that 'the two in our charge' appeared to be of the same tribe – and different from the others confined at the Carlton. But Billy was Biyaygirri and the man later known as Jimmy was Manbarra; they had different body marks and probably spoke differently. While Camphin cannot be considered a reliable witness in matters of language, it does seem more probable that the two escapees would have been from the same group. They also spoke no English.

Even more confusingly, the account given by Houzé and Jacques (1884) – who seem otherwise to be such reliable witnesses – asserts that Tambo was the man who wounded the policeman 'in Melbourne'. But I dismiss this version as garbled because it is well established that the incident took place in Sydney and that Tambo and Toby were the two English-speakers.[29] Moreover, both Tambo and Toby had their womenfolk with them and I doubt they would have deserted them to make their way back home alone. All the other men – the three Biyaygirri and Jimmy – had left wives and children behind, a good enough reason to try to escape. My conclusion is that the two escapees were Billy and the other Biyaygirri man whose name is not yet known for certain. (He is the man standing next to Billy in plate 5.)

There is also other evidence relating to events before the departure from Australia – a set of photographs, probably the first made of Billy and others in the group, were taken in the studio of Cunningham's friend William Nutting Tuttle, a fellow Californian. At that time Tuttle had studios in both Melbourne and Sydney, so it is not possible to be certain if the photographs were taken before or after the escape and recapture.[30] I first located two of them in the American collection of Joseph T. McCaddon, business manager of Barnum and Bailey, and brother-in-law to Bailey.[31] They were archived together with the photographs of the other indigenous groups – the Todar (*sic*), Zulu and Nubians – who were shown alongside the Aborigines (chapter 4). They had presumably been sent in response to Barnum's request for photographs to be forwarded as an indication of the product he was expecting to receive, maybe by the SS *City of Sydney* whose departure the group had missed.

While the commissioning of the photographs by Cunningham was part of the marketing of the group, they were taken before the transformation of Billy and the others into performers. Their appearance – expressed again through their pose, clothes and expressions – is evocative of the hybrid nature of the colonial space. They don't look like 'savages'; they look attractive and marketable. Billy (pl. 22), standing with his sword club held horizontally behind him – his weapon (representing his savage nature) neutralised – and his hair neatly cut, is a picture of an amenable and employable 'native'. Looked at another way the photograph could also suggest a more active participation by Billy, eager to play a new social role defined by European clothes and goods. On the other hand, the photograph of Sussy, Jenny and her son, Toby (pl. 23), has a disturbingly out-of-character, pastoral quality. Their dress, though simple enough, is much finer than would have been worn customarily in the fringe camps of Townsville or Cardwell. At the same time as being themselves, there is an air of self-conscious mimicry in their pose – maybe encouraged by Tuttle and Cunningham – so that the representation has an edge of caricature to it. There is also a subdued sexual charge.

Very much later I found another photograph in a Berlin collection, taken on the same occasion, displayed alongside portraits very similar to those discussed above. It is much more voyeuristic in tone, and when seen

22   Billy, Sydney,
1883. Photograph:
Tuttle & Co.

in juxtaposition with the portraits of Billy and the women, it emphasises the manipulative character of this particular moment in Tuttle's photographic studio.[32]

In this crudely constructed photograph, Jenny, Sussy and Toby are arranged as a tableau representing a European narrative of savagery. Toby is standing in the foreground, brandishing a spear in a threatening manner in the direction of the women, who have been stripped to the waist so that their upper garments are hanging loosely down. Violence is implied both by the arrangement of the figures and the exposure of their scarified torsos, presented as the visible embodiment of savagery underneath the civilising clothing. Today, the implied contempt and suppressed violence of the representation is palpable.

A German visitor to Australia had purchased a set of the Tuttle photographs in 1884. And, by chance, these representations of Billy, Sussy, Toby,

23   Sussy (standing), Jenny and her son, Toby, in Sydney in 1883. Photograph: Tuttle & Co.

his wife, Jenny, and their son had independently made a journey parallel to that of their Aboriginal subjects, arriving in Berlin in the same year, thus demonstrating very well what Appadurai has called 'the social lives of things'. In the case of the photographic print, tracing the processes of consumption, particularly the networks of exchange between collectors and institutions, as well as the processes of production, exposes how meanings are transformed as the print physically enters different associations.[33] Even photographs such as these, which were produced for a commercial purpose, were perceived as somehow 'anthropological' and entered the scientific discourse. Thus the crude visual allusion to savagery played its part in the formation and consolidation of racial stereotypes both by way of the academy and in popular circulation.[34]

   After making their first public appearance as performers in Auckland, New Zealand, Billy and his companions spent the next three weeks aboard

24   Message stick carved by Tambo, said to record the voyage across the Pacific, as illustrated in the account of E. Houzé and V. Jacques.

the SS *Australia* on route for America, perhaps giving them their first opportunity to get to know R. A. under more relaxed – but none the less confined – circumstances. Later Bob was to talk to the Belgian anthropologists E. Houzé and V. Jacques about the journey, and an incident that impressed them most occurred when the *Australia* had taken on provisions of sugar from another ship. Billy drew the ship for them, in what we would now describe as X-ray style, and he filled the hull with 'little rounds'. When asked what these signified, he replied: 'That is a boat full of sugar, and these are the balls of sugar.' Tambo also made a message stick, which the Belgian anthropologists reported 'they were made to understand' was about the crossing from Australia to America (pl. 24).[35]

In San Francisco Cunningham installed the group in the New Continental Hotel on Mission Street, where he awaited 'telegraphic advices' as to whether he should delay travelling east until the arrival of the steamer from Singapore with other consignments for Barnum. There was time to prepare costumes and perhaps to have photographs taken. San Francisco was where Tambo acquired his American name.

The impression Billy and his companions gave *Figaro*'s reporter in San Francisco was that they appeared 'perfectly contented with their present surroundings, and displayed the greatest confidence in Mr Cunningham, whose experience in acquiring them sounds more like a thrilling romance than anything else' (26 April 1883). While such observations on the part of reporters were no doubt shaped by previously acquired assumptions, the voyage must have provided some respite for the North Queenslanders, and certainly the recorded fragments of their own response to it suggests the journey was experienced as an adventure. Towards the end of the year Barnum's agent J. B. Gaylord wrote in a similar vein to friends: 'The native aboriginals which Cunningham got are the best feature of the show [Barnum's circus]. They like the life, get good warm clothing, and plenty of good food – in fact just the same as the white men get.'[36]

Those were early days. Almost always the experiences of Billy and his companions are filtered through the accounts of others, and only slowly does a more complex picture emerge of their experiences in America.

4 American Spectacle: 'Attractions of Wonder'

According to the Australian census returns, the number of aborigines still existing in the Australian colonies, exclusive of New Zealand, is only 31,700 . . . In Victoria, at the recent census, the number returned was 780, as against 1330 at the former one. This indicates such a rapid extinction, as to justify the conclusion that the Australian Cannibals exhibited in our Ethnological Congress of Savage Tribes are not only the first, but the last, of their race that we of America will ever behold. **Now or never is the time to see them.**

Advance Courier, P. T. Barnum's Greatest Show on Earth, 1884

A number of factors coalesced to draw Billy, Toby, Tambo and their companions into the orbit of the circus world. Displacement and dispossession in the colonies, chance and curiosity, Barnum's initiatives, Cunningham's agency and the metropolitan public's insatiable appetite for new, strange and exotic attractions of wonder upon which they could project a range of white fantasies and fears. Within this 'world as spectacle', which in America was epitomised by the circus, they were presented as living pictures of savagery, and the processes of circus promotion, presentation and performance served to 'fix' these ideas. Billy and his companions became commodities to be packaged and promoted, and the use of statistics in the press notice in the epigraph above, which was headed 'The last of the Cannibals', was part of the rhetoric of authentication.[1] Figures presented as facts were meant to confirm the inevitability of the imminent extinction of the Aborigines and, at the same time, to guarantee that those on exhibition were indeed 'the last'. To be categorised as 'the last' emphasised both their exotic difference and their distance, their being other than the onlookers' civilised selves. As part of the interrogation of these processes of representation, we must take a closer look at how the spectacularly varied yet highly organised American circus was constituted, and the central role Barnum played in its development, especially his interest in the display of living people.

The circus

By the time Cunningham and his troupers arrived in San Francisco the circus season had already begun in New York, with a three-week run at Madison Square Gardens. Barnum's Greatest Show on Earth had opened with a most spectacular Grand Torchlight Parade that stretched for over a mile, led by the mighty elephant, Jumbo, acquired the year before from London's Zoological Gardens. 'The night was clear and cold. The streets were densely packed. Brooklyn, Jersey City, Staten Island and the outlying suburbs poured out their vast crowds to swell the immense masses of the Metropolis . . . the press with one accord styled it "The Crowning Triumph of Barnum's Career". These words, written either by Barnum himself or his publicist, introducing *My Diary or Route Book* of 1883, identify the grand parade as much more than an appetiser before the main event, a publicity stunt. It was a circus spectacle that melded with the greater spectacle of the city – and the assembled onlookers saw themselves as part of the show. By the 1880s in America the circus had become an entertainment institution where the key elements were professional presentation and promotion to a paying public. The circus drew greater crowds than major sporting fixtures or visiting potentates. The day the circus came to town was declared a public holiday.

The season of 1883 was the third since the 'consolidation' of the three great circuses of P. T. Barnum, J. A. Bailey and J. L. Hutchinson – an amalgamation that was indicative of the transformation of the travelling circus into an industrialised form of mass entertainment. The merger was represented by the introduction of a third ring under the big top, and one of the rings contained an elevated stage.[2] Within these three arenas and an encircling track the action was ceaseless and simultaneous, so that the attention of the spectators switched back and forth from trapeze artists to acrobats, jugglers and clowns; to parades of trick stallions or the 'Marvels from the Museum', and tableaux of great historical moments (pl. 25). During the performance strategically placed comic turns also erupted among the spectators. There was a separate tent for the Menagerie and another for the Museum, where the 'specimens of Savage Tribes' were exhibited. All this

25 Title page of
Advance Courier,
distributed in Jackson,
28 August 1884.

was to be had for 50 cents an adult and 25 cents a child. For Barnum it
could all be quantified: the distances travelled, the amount of rolling stock,
the persons employed, the salaries paid, the number of elephants and so
on. Then there were the running costs – for 1883 these were declared to be
$4,800 a day. The gross receipts for the preceding year, 1882, 'for a season
of 186 days, had been about a million and three-quarters dollars', which
were, said Barnum, 'more than the combined receipts of any three travelling shows in the world'. His cavalier use of statistics characterised
Barnum's style of publicity.[3] Although his name was given precedence in
publications and press releases he no longer played an active part in the
day-to-day running of the circus, and the success of the Greatest Show on
Earth owed much to the business acumen and organising skills of the
much younger James Bailey, 'who gave his entire personal attention to its

management'.[4] All the same, Barnum remained the presiding genius of circus ballyhoo.

An important development of the circus had taken place a decade earlier. In 1868, after Barnum's American Museum in New York had been destroyed by fire (for the second time), Barnum joined forces with W. C. Coup, who, in 1872, was responsible for putting their new entertainment operation, The Great Travelling World's Fair, on rails. They made use of the recently integrated and expanding railway network to penetrate the largest and most profitable centres on the northern East Coast and Midwest, depending mainly on one-day stands, with longer stays of several days reserved for the larger industrial cities. The route provided the structure (pl. 26). In the 1883 season the cities that were the nodal points in the itinerary were old cities of the east, New York, Baltimore, Philadelphia and Washington, and the major western metropolitan centres, Chicago, Cincinnati, St Louis, Milwaukee, Cleveland, 'a system of cities' that could be regarded as a metropolitan corridor that linked the older eastern cities of capital with new investment destinations in the metropoles of the west, each one the hub of its own region.[5] In spite of ethnic and class differences, these cities shared a metropolitan culture that was essentially middle class. Although the circus was for everybody, Barnum's target public was the new urban classes, the middle class and their 'respectable' working-class allies with money to spend and leisure to do so. His stated aim in 1875 was 'to bring rational, moral and instructive entertainment, combined with attractions of wonder . . . to within the reach of the masses and the possibilities of the slenderest purse, and to make them subservient to Christianity and enlightenment, and the auxiliaries of our Public Schools'.[6] Putting principles into practice, he admitted clergymen for free – understanding well the publicity value of the goodwill generated.

Negotiations with the railway companies and the development of specialised rolling stock were crucial. Dismountable carriages made the show highly mobile. An army of circus hands – over 600 in the 1883 season – went swiftly into action. Duplicate sets of canvas (introduced in 1884) reduced the time lost between show places, and guaranteed the show would go on in spite of accidents. The success of the operation depended on capturing the attention of whole communities, a cast of many hundreds seen by tens of thousands, very often in the course of a single day. Illustrated newspaper advertisements, promotional publications called

26 Illinois Central Regional Railroad poster.

Advance Couriers, posters and billboards summoned the crowds from the surrounding districts, often from up to forty miles away, and excursion trains brought them in, at what was aptly termed the Special Barnum Tariff. In America the expansion of communications – both transportation and informational systems – underpinned most other developments, even that of the great entertainment institution, the circus.

In the 1830s – almost as soon as it was technologically possible – travelling shows pioneered the use of illustrated newspaper ads, beginning with Hackaliah Bailey, who publicised the exhibition of an elephant. By the 1880s two-column-width illustrated circus ads, the length of the page, were commonplace. It is said that the special contribution of the circus to 'the American economy and way of life' was the development of the black and white style of press art and advertising.[7] Its influence was literally visible on the days before and just after a Barnum show hit town: department store ads increased in size and announced 'Jumbo Sales' and proclaimed their store to be 'The Greatest Store on Earth'. Similarly the circus played an important part in developing outdoor advertising – both the letterpress broadsides and handbills, and, by the late 1860s, the coloured lithographic posters. In 1883 Barnum's circus operated five advance publicity cars, staffed by about sixty men. These were moveable workshops as well as transporters, where date strips and local information were overprinted on handbills, couriers and posters, where the paste was prepared and where the billposters sorted their supplies according to size: single sheets and half-sheets for shop windows, double sheets for fences, sheds and barns, and the occasional monster poster.[8] Between 6,000 and 10,000 sheets were posted in a day. The area to be covered was mapped out, and each day bill-posting teams spread out from the cars, the specialist banner-men carrying ladders to hang the muslin banners on high. They worked a district up to three weeks in advance, with a follow-up visit in the week before the show.[9] Before the movies, the circus was probably the most influential instrument of mass culture in shaping public attitudes, through an extraordinary range of linked representational activities associated with publication and performance.

Living curiosities

Long before his circus years, Barnum's successful career as a showman was closely bound up with the display of living people for commercial gain. It took off with the exhibition of Joice Heth, allegedly 161 years old, and one-time nurse to George Washington, whom he took on tour for a few months before her death in February 1836. The public response to this tiny, blind, toothless old woman, with claw-like nails on her paralysed limbs, was divided between gullibility and hostile disbelief. For in this pre-Civil War American society – split over the issue of slavery – the power of Heth's performance to attract and hold the attention of the crowd lay in the combination of a disturbing foundation story about a slave's nurturing of the future Father of the Nation and the appearance of the storyteller. After her death, a public autopsy – attended by 1,500 people who paid Barnum 50 cents apiece – established her body was that of an eighty-year-old.[10]

Later, Barnum gave several discrepant accounts of his part in the Heth hoax, without ever showing concern for his humiliating treatment of her. In the last version, given in his autobiography, *Struggles and Triumphs*, in 1869,[11] he presented himself as the one who had been deceived – and from

Benjamin Reiss's recovery of Joice Heth's story, it seems there may be some truth in that. For Heth, by the time she met Barnum, was too old to have newly learnt a story that she apparently performed without ever slipping out of character. Riess establishes rather convincingly Joice's association with the family of a William Heth, a revolutionary war captain, who had his own repertoire of George Washington stories that, he suggests, she appropriated and made her own through many performances. As Benjamin Reiss proposes, 'the story fits the cultural dynamics of slavery and the larger rhythms of American popular culture', which was so much a product of cultural hybridisation, of the appropriations and reappropriations between blacks and whites.[12] But complicit or not, Heth was not in control of her life because of her age and infirmity.

As the Heth–Barnum relationship suggests, white Americans (for most of the nineteenth century) saw the slaves of African origin as domesticated 'other',[13] and attributions of savagery tended to be reserved for Native Americans. In 1842, however, Barnum's attempts to procure Vendovi, a 'Fijian Cannibal Chief', for exhibition at his American Museum in New York, although thwarted by Vendovi's death, signalled a shift of interest to imports of exotic living curiosities from overseas.[14] Vendovi had been 'arrested' and removed to the United States by Charles Wilkes, the commander of the United States Exploring Expedition of 1838–42, for the murder of several of the crew of a shipwrecked American schooner seven years earlier.[15] Vendovi died of consumption within days of his arrival in New York, and within a few more days was transformed from captive cannibal to scientific specimen. Vendovi's skull was included in the official display of the ethnographic collections from the Wilkes expedition in the great hall of the Patent Office in Washington (now the National Portrait Gallery), along with Fijian clubs, cloth and other artefacts. Alongside it was another skull, 'with marks of having been roasted in the fire' still upon it.[16] This head had been 'purchased with a fathom of cloth' when brought aboard one of the expedition's ships, the *Peacock*, in July 1840. Wilkes and his officers saw this incident as confirming the Fijian cannibal nature, and it led Wilkes to categorise the Fijians as 'degraded beyond the conception of civilised people'.[17] Although the derogatory views of the Fijians were not universally accepted, they prevailed overwhelmingly in popular accounts, helping to construct the Fijian as archetypal cannibal. They also influenced debates in anthropological circles in support of the polygenist ideas about the multiple origins of humankind propounded in America by the followers of S. G. Morton, and in England in an influential paper on 'Cannibalism in relation to ethnology' by the polygenist John Crawfurd.[18]

In turn, some of these ideas about race and origins found vulgar expression in a range of fabricated show characters such as the Missing Link, the Circassian Beauty, and a variety of Wild Men, who all survived on the show circuit for a remarkably long time. What were presented to the public as freaks of nature were instead freaks of culture.[19] From about 1860, an African-American named William Henry Johnson, who was microcephalic (referred to as a 'pinhead'), was exhibited by Barnum in his American Museum as 'What is it?' (pl. 27). His fake identity involved a narrative of exotic origin. Allegedly he had been found on the banks of the River Gambia where – so it was said – his captors recognised at once that he represented the missing link between 'wild native African and the brute creation'. Later known as Zip, Johnson survived as a successful performer on the museum and circus circuits until his death in 1926.[20] On the entertainment circuits of America and Europe, Cunningham's Aboriginal troupe crossed paths with both Johnson and other rivals to the title of Missing Link such as Krao. While Barnum was not alone in propagating the idea that geographical marginality equated with the social marginality of the physically and mentally impaired, the size of his operation gave it considerable popular currency. Not only were the congenitally impaired shown together with the exotic indigenous, the latter were described in the language of impairment – as 'deformed', with 'distorted' features, and lacking proper speech. The exhibition of imported living exotics alongside the fake highlights how the representations of the former were no less fantastic than the latter.[21]

The opportunity to show 'Living Fiji Cannibals' came at last in 1872 when among the

27   'Living Curiosities' at Barnum's Museum, *Harper's Weekly*, 15 December 1860

DECEMBER 15, 1860.]   HARPER'S

Living Curiosities at Barnum's Museum.

Since Mr. P. T. BARNUM re-purchased the Museum last Spring, it has become more than ever a popular place of resort for Ladies, Children and Families, and the energies of this world-renowned "Prince of Showmen," seem to increase in a corresponding ratio with his patronage. Our artist has sketched the above from a host of other curiosities now on exhibition in the Museum at all hours, day and evening.

The two centre figures in the foreground of the above cut represent the celebrated AZTEC CHILDREN, found in one of the long lost cities of Central America. It will be observed that their cast of features, and very small heads, bear a striking resemblance to the sculpture found in those cities by Stephens and other travelers, which fact seems to indicate that the race of men to which they belong were the original type of these sculptures.

The figure on the right represents a creature, found in the wilds of Africa, and is supposed to be a mixture of the wild native African and the Orang Outang, a kind of Man-Monkey, but for want of a positive name is called "WHAT IS IT?"   The two WHITE FIGURES represent two ALBINO GIRLS, and the black ones their black father and sister. These Girls, though of black parentage, are a PURE WHITE, WITH WHITE WOOL AND PINK EYES, but with every other feature and characteristic of the real African. No one can look upon them without feeling the conviction that they are beyond all doubt WHITE NEGROES. All these extraordinary living wonders are on exhibition at

Barnum's American Museum,

In this city, where everything novel and curious is sure to be found. In addition to the above, the Museum presents a combination of wonders and curiosities, unequaled in any part of the world. The GRAND AQUARIA alone constitutes an attraction which well repays a visit. Here, in miniature Oceans, are to be found almost every variety of living Fish and other aquatic animals disporting in their native element, from a noble specimen of a living Seal, down to the tiny Stickleback, which builds its nest on the rocks and in the weeds. The HAPPY FAMILY, consists of beasts and birds of opposite natures, as Dogs, Cats, Rats, Hawks, Chickens, Pigeons, &c., &c., all living in peace and harmony, and the whole made amusing and interesting by a number of lively and playful Monkeys, which always keep spectators in capital humor by their inimitable sports. A monster den of mammoth Serpents, 30 in number, has just been added to the

850,000 Other Interesting Curiosities

contained in this wonderful Museum. How so much can be afforded for the low price of twenty-five cents admission is only explained by the fact that an average of nearly four thousand persons visit the Museum daily; on holidays the number of visitors frequently exceeds twenty thousand.

28   'P. T. Barnum's The World in Contribution', *Harper's Weekly*, 29 March 1873. The Fijians are bottom left.

varied 'contributions' Barnum offered an expectant public in his *Travelling World's Fair* were three men – and their 'Christianised female companion' (pl. 28). The men had been removed from Fiji by W. C. Gardenhire in 1871 and exhibited together with an assorted display of Fijian and New Zealand artefacts and objects – including the 'hand of the late Lovoni Rebel King' – first in Hawaii and then in America, in the 'Principal Cities of the Pacific Slope', before proceeding east to join Barnum. 'General Ra Biau, the Dwarf' – who qualified both on account of his foreignness and his anomalous body – was billed as the fiercest of them. The story was that as prisoners of King Thokambau they were destined to be killed and eaten, but once they were taken on by Barnum, he insisted that he would rather forfeit the $15,000 bond paid as guarantee of their return than allow them to go back to such a fate. So it was that Barnum 'met with quite a loss' when the little general died while the show was playing in York, Pennsylvania, on

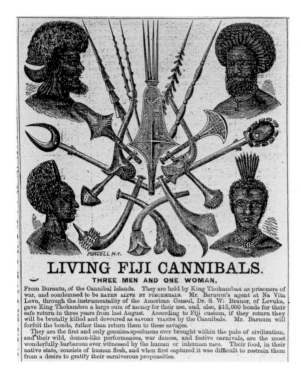

LIVING FIJI CANNIBALS.

THREE MEN AND ONE WOMAN,

From Burauta, of the Cannibal Islands. They are held by King Thokambau as prisoners of war, and condemned to be EATEN ALIVE BY PIECEMEALS. Mr. Barnum's agent at Na Vita Levu, through the instrumentality of the American Consul, Dr. S. W. Brauer, of Levuka, gave King Thokambau a large sum of money for their use, and, also, $15,000 bonds for their safe return in three years from last August. According to Fiji custom, if they return they will be brutally killed and devoured as SAVORY VIANDS by the Cannibals. Mr. Barnum will forfeit the bonds, rather than return them to these savages.

They are the first and only genuine specimens ever brought within the pale of civilization, and their wild, demon-like performances, war dances, and festive carnivals, are the most wonderfully barbarous ever witnessed by the human or inhuman race. Their food, in their native state, consists of human flesh, and when first captured it was difficult to restrain them from a desire to gratify their carnivorous propensities.

29   'Living Fijian Cannibals', *Advance Courier*, 1873, advertising a group that was no longer on show.

14 May 1872. According to newspaper reports, his male companions attempted to revert to their cannibal habits, but the body was recovered and buried in a Potter's Field (paupers' graveyard). A few days later, the *York Dispatch* discredited the story of cannibal rites as a hoax perpetrated by the management to bring in the crowds to see the General's companions. (Apparently attendances exceeded 5,000.) In addition, an ex-resident of Fiji insisted that the Fijians were now Christians, and that the woman was not Fijian at all, but from Virginia. In 1897 developers acquired Potter's Field and when some 500 bodies were exhumed for reburial the little general's was not among them (only his coffin lid). It seems the local doctor had disinterred the 'wild man', dissected him and kept his 'neatly articulated' skeleton.[22]

Although Barnum's attempts to introduce 'savage curiosities' had faltered, he continued to advertise the Fijians in the Advance Courier for the following season – regardless of their absence. He had an investment to recoup. An analysis of the design of the associated ad, displaying – in the manner of trophies – an arrangement of Fijian clubs together with four Fijian heads, each with a different hair style (pl. 29), is not only revealing about objectifying representational processes but also about the transnational flow of ideas. For the engraver copied the heads from a plate in an English book, published several years earlier, *Origin of Civilisation and the Primitive Condition of Man*, by Sir John Lubbock. It is irrelevant that Lubbock believed in the unity of humankind, for it is a magpie borrowing of images only. Although the decorative symmetry of the design does no more than hint at anthropology's classificatory impulse, the neutrality of the image is undermined by an accompanying text that stigmatises the Fijians as 'an inhuman race', right off the scale of human development. In America, popular representations of Fijians as prototype 'cannibal savages' provided a model for graphic repre-

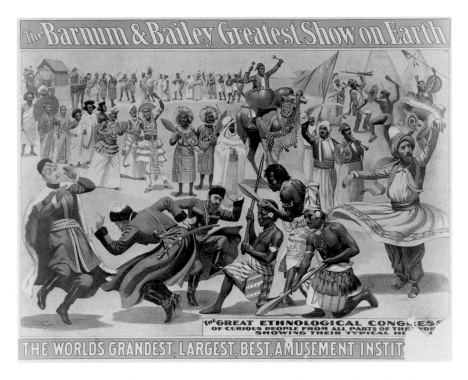

30   The Barnum and Bailey Greatest Show on Earth, poster advertising the *Great Ethnological Congress.*

sentations of Billy and his companions in Cunningham's pamphlet and in newspaper ads.

When, towards the end of the successful 1882 season of the Greatest Show on Earth, Barnum announced an *Ethnological Congress of Strange and Savage Tribes* as the star attraction for the following year, it was the culmination of 'an idea he had long entertained' (pl. 30). As well as sending a circular letter to American consuls and dispatching agents throughout the world to bring back 'a collection, in pairs or otherwise, of all the uncivilised races in existence . . . to astonish, interest and instruct' the American public, Barnum solicited support from the emerging anthropological institutions.[23] He wrote to Spencer Baird, secretary of the recently established Smithsonian Institution, asking for a testimonial. The reason

31   Zalumma Agra, 'The Star of the East', one of the many personifiers of the Circassian beauty.

he gave Baird was that the authorities in the Dutch colonies, and also in New Zealand and Sydney, were very reluctant to let people go 'unless they are first satisfied that the party taking them is responsible'. Although Baird commended the showman's enterprise, he could not give it official endorsement as he was 'hampered somewhat by the regulations of the Institution'. Nevertheless, in his reply he added his hopes that 'my official letter herewith will answer all the purposes. You, of course, can use your own discretion as to the mode of employing it.'[24]

In the event, the only indigenous groups Barnum acquired for his 1883 *Congress* were the Nubians, Todas, Zulu, Sioux and the Australian Aborigines, but since many of the other artists in the show were of different nationalities, they were simply listed as part of the *Congress*, including the entirely bogus Wild Men of Borneo, who were two brothers of small stature,[25] and the Circassian Beauty. The latter, a show character first enacted by 'Zalumma Agra' in 1864 at Barnum's American Museum, represented the embodiment of white racial purity, as a kind of counternarrative to the black exoticism represented by other show types (pl. 31). At the same time, her specially frizzed hair and provocative clothing signalled her own exotic sexuality. Supposedly, she was a Circassian from the Caucasus, rescued from captivity in a Turkish harem. This racialist fantasy, presented as a titillating captivity narrative, claimed its 'scientific' authority from Professor Friedrich Blumenbach's designation of the white races as Caucasian.[26] Usually an immigrant girl from New York enacted the Circassian Beauty – every show had to have one.

Although there was not much fraternising among the different groups of performers,[27] the show-space where they came together was also a point of intersection with the onlookers. And there the public responses to the mix of the make-believe with the strange but real ranged from the gullible to cynical rejection. This was the circus world into which Billy, Toby and the others were absorbed.

'P. T. Barnum's Last Sensation!'

Billed as Barnum's 'last sensation' – in the sense of 'latest' – the arrival of the Aborigines was announced in the *Baltimore Morning Herald* of 7 May 1883:

The Australian cannibals

To-day their first appearance in Public in a Civilised Country

This strange group arrived in Baltimore yesterday in the charge of one of Mr Barnum's agents direct from Northern Australia. They were captured in the wilds of that desolate region and while on route from San Francisco, have attracted more attention than any human beings ever before seen in civilisation.

The piece of advertising copy was geared to stir curiosity but not to satisfy. By hinting at a narrative of capture it aimed both to thrill and to authenticate the Aborigines' savage presence, while at the same time providing a reassuring reverse image of the spectators' civilised selves. Looked at from the perspective of the antipodean travellers, what did they make of this world of spectacle in which they became immersed?

Think about the shock of their first train journey across deserts, plains and mountains of America; their experience of the sweeping panoramic view and the blur of speed from the carriage window, and their encounters with fellow passengers. For several days and nights Toby and his companions travelled, ate and slept in the swaying, rattling, jolting belly of a monster. No other single experience had such power to change their perception of the world about them. Just as the Europeans and Americans had been transformed by rapid technological change throughout the century, the journey across America would have dramatically inducted the Aboriginal travellers into the modern world. The change in consciousness it wrought only becomes evident slowly as the narrative of their journey unfolds.[28] Similarly, the tensions of their experiences, the constant travel and exposure to a succession of strangers, may well have contributed to their lack of resistance to illness, particularly to tuberculosis.

As it was a Sunday when the Aboriginal travellers arrived in Baltimore, there was no performance, but the circus was being installed. Think of their sensory immersion in the sights, sounds and smells of the circus. They watched as the flapping canvas of the big top was raised in Newington Park baseball grounds, and they gazed in wonder at camels and elephants. Goats roamed about and there was even a kangaroo grazing alongside a llama. They were startled by the concatenation of howls, roars, whistles, chattering and cawing. They watched as the hippopotamus was forced to take a constitutional and the snakes were tipped into an empty wagon so their glass cages could be cleaned. In a field beyond the tented area they saw some of the circus-hands sitting around camp fires on which were balanced the pots for boiling their clothes, while curious bystanders, mostly men and boys, stood about, spellbound. Later they ate supper in a dining tent with others in the company.

At 8.30 next morning the Aboriginal troupe led the Grand Parade, with Jumbo the elephant, through the streets of Baltimore. Toby, Billy, Bob and Tambo danced while the others sang and clapped pairs of boomerangs together in accompaniment. And while they performed, the Zulu hissed them. According to the press reports, 'the Nubians, and Indians, and Zulus looked with disgust at the crowds that stood open-mouthed before the new arrivals.'[29] Later, there were two performances of the circus, one at 2 pm and the other at 7.30 pm, when, as well as parading under the Big Top, the Aborigines were exhibited in the Museum tent. There Cunningham was in charge; he was the lecturer or 'talker' who attracted the crowds and then held their attention by 'talking up' such features of his performers as their body scarifications, nose-bones and 'wild' appearance. He introduced Sussy as 'Princess Tagarah, daughter of the Cannibal King of North Queensland', and embellished his stories of their capture, of their skills as trackers and of their cannibal appetites. On the first day 30,000 people saw them. Even before the end of the evening performance the Menagerie was being loaded, and the grounds gradually cleared so that once the crowds had gone there were only the canvases to lower and transport. The whole operation was performed with 'quiet precision'. Only the managers and leading performers were placed in hotel accommodation or had a railway carriage, or a section of one, for their exclusive use. Billy and his companions almost certainly travelled and slept in a shared railway carriage, fitted with bunks, which became their home.

Although this was to be the routine every day except Sunday for the six months they were with the circus, occasionally it was varied when an open

32   Page 7 of *Advance Courier*, 'Australian cannibals', 1883.

space or vacant lot was found where Toby, Billy and Bob demonstrated the skill of throwing the boomerang. These three were the star boomerang-throwers: 'when hurled from their hand it soars like a bird through the air,' wrote the *Chicago Tribune* reporter on 6 June, 'describing a circle about 300 feet in diameter, and descends in a spiral line to the feet of the thrower . . . In their hands it becomes a deadly weapon.'[30]

Throughout the season, Cunningham's group received more column inches and more subheads than any of the other circus acts except Jumbo, but always these reports referred to Cunningham's account of their capture, and their savage appearance, rather than to any particular incident or performance – except for boomerang throwing. For instance, their slight build and 'lack of muscle in the calf' was attributed to the belief that 'they

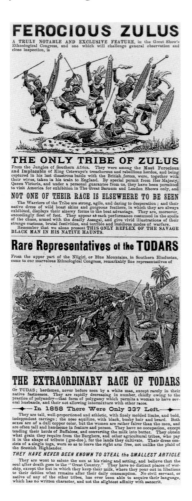

have never done anything more than was necessary for mere subsistence in a torrid climate' (*St Louis Daily Globe-Democrat*, 1 June 1883) – the inference being that they were not as highly developed as the rest of humanity. The source of these fanciful reports was Barnum's circus publicity, with its constant reiteration, both in words and images, of the troupe's supposedly cannibal nature. The graphic representations, particularly, drew on the already well-established visual stereotype of cannibal savagery (pl. 32) in which the captured Aborigines are depicted as captors. The explicitly racist language of the accompanying letterpress was also borrowed in the newspaper reports of the performances, and it is very difficult to gain any idea

33 (*facing page, left*) Page 10 of *Advance Courier*, 'Ferocious Zulus and Extraordinary Todars [*sic*]', 1883.

34 (*facing page, right*) Zulu Warriors, *c.* 1883. Photograph: Charles Eisenmann.

35 Toda (from the subcontinent of India) *c.* 1883. Photograph: Charles Eisenmann.

of how Toby, Billy, Tambo and the others were perceived by the public, except through the screen of circus publicity.

On another page of the Advance Courier, graphic representations of the 'Ferocious Zulu' and the 'Extraordinary Todars' (*sic*) were paired (pl. 33), but when these stereotypic illustrations are compared with the photographs of these performers the contrast is stark, and the photographs appear to show what they are like as people (pls 34 and 35). In the case of the Toda, however, the photograph, with its emphasis on their dress, also suggests their supposedly 'biblical' connections more strongly than the graphic.[31] Photographs also have their own stereotypic elements, and

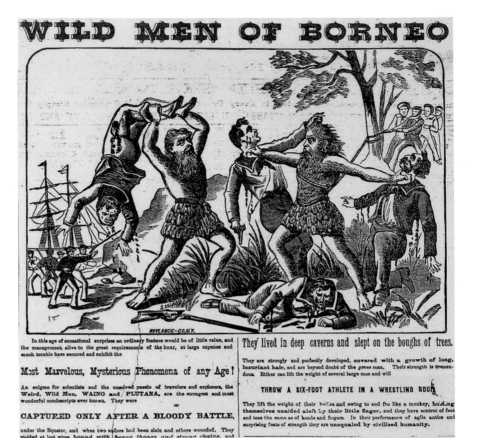

WILD MEN OF BORNEO

ROYLANCE—CO.N.Y.

In this age of sensational surprises an ordinary feature would be of little value, and the management, alive to the great requirements of the hour, at large expense and much trouble have secured and exhibit the

Most Marvelous, Mysterious Phenomena of any Age !

An enigma for scientists and the unsolved puzzle of travelers and explorers, the Weird, Wild Men, **WAINO** and **PLUTANA**, are the strongest and most wonderful nondescripts ever known. They were

CAPTURED ONLY AFTER A BLOODY BATTLE,

under the Equator, and when two sailors had been slain and others wounded. They yielded at last when *bound with heavy thongs and strong chains*, and

They lived in deep caverns and slept on the boughs of trees.

They are strongly and perfectly developed, covered with a growth of long, luxuriant hair, and are beyond doubt of the *genus* man. Their strength is tremendous. Either can lift the weight of several large men and will

THROW A SIX-FOOT ATHLETE IN A WRESTLING BOUT.

They lift the weight of their bodies and swing to and fro like a monkey, holding themselves unaided aloft by their little finger, and they have control of feet and toes the same as of hands and fingers. In their performance of agile antics and surprising feats of strength they are unequaled by civilised humanity.

36   Wild Men of Borneo, Roylance & co. Advertisement in *Advance Courier*.

sometimes there is more similarity between the photographs of the different groups. Compare the similar pose and dress of the Zulu group and the Aboriginal group (pls 34 and 4) that identify both groups as professional show people. In spite of the commercial motivation behind the construction of the photographs of the Toda, Zulu and Nubians, however, they still offer ethnographic information, and also the possibility of the recovery of their subjects' personal histories, as in the case of the Aboriginal group.[32] By contrast, the stereotypic nature of the graphic representations is accentuated when, in the same circus season of 1884, a woodblock of the fake Wild Men of Borneo (pl. 36) in an Advance Courier and an advertisement for the Australian Boomerang Throwers in the *Cleveland Plain Dealer* of 23 February employ the same elements of visual narrative – the wrecked ship in the bay and the cannibal feast on the shore. In fact, the advertisement appears to be from the same block as the cover illustration to Cunningham's pamphlet of that year (pl. 8).[33] Central to the effectiveness of this representational regime is the relationship between fixity of form and fixity of ideas that is implied by the duel meaning of the words 'stereotype' and 'cliché', both initially terms for repetitive printing processes.[34] Graphic stereotyping as a process gave form, and therefore substance, to the image of the savage, and the constant recycling of the same pictorial elements, and sometimes the same block, imprinted it in the minds of the readers.

In spite of the derogatory views disseminated by the press, the troupe's facility with languages was frequently commented on. Even before I began the American research I understood from Houzé and Jacques that all of the group learnt to speak English while they were with the circus in America, although not surprisingly – because of their association with Cunningham – it was said to be with an Irish accent. After all, they had new needs and new desires, wanting to talk about all manner of practical things related to the journey such as food, clothing, bedding and feeling unwell, as well as about pleasurable things such as beer, sweets, tobacco and trinkets.[35]

Cunningham maintained that in the beginning he had to teach them European manners, and they learnt quickly. 'Now they pick up all the ideas of civilization very readily.' To the questions of how he was able to manage them, he explained: 'I have gained control over them by a system of kind, but firm treatment, and they now understand and obey my slightest command. They have every confidence in me as their protector, as well they may. They realise fully that their good behaviour will be duly appreciated and properly rewarded by me and as they know I am the only one who can restore them in safety to their native wilds they act accordingly.' As an experienced showman Cunningham was aware of the profitable partnerships that existed between performers like Zip and the Wild Men of Borneo and their managers, built on fair treatment and trust, and of the value in emulating them. In matters relating to daily life, the group also demonstrated a degree of independent action that suggested they were confident and comfortable in their surroundings. While the pressures of constant travel and performance were relentless, they were to a certain extent looked after. When it came to food they were quick to express their preferences for 'a variety of foods, especially tropical fruits, fish, oysters . . .

and if permitted to eat everything raw, much prefer that style'. Cunningham related that 'they are extremely fond of making small purchases of gaudy handkerchiefs, bright trinkets, etc., and value all they buy far more highly than if I should buy and present to them articles of much greater value.'[36] Sussy and Jenny acquired the heavy copper necklaces and jewellery they loved to wear. And in Chicago Sussy was reported as performing in pink knickerbockers. The men were as susceptible to fashion as the women and, while with the circus, Toby, Billy and Bob replaced their nose ornaments with ivory nose-bones of which they were very proud.

Although later in the winter, while travelling the dime museum circuit, they would be involved in stressful incidents, we know (reading back from Houzé and Jacques) that in general they were cheerful in behaviour and affectionate towards each other, and that Toby and Jenny were loving parents, playing, teasing, sharing food, comforting and instructing their young son. The impression they created belied the press handouts about their savagery. As a reporter from the *Pittsburg Critic* wrote: 'A careful inspection of their features and person made it hard to realise that they were all given to cannibalism but a few months since.' Others were more openly sceptical of the cannibal tag.

In spite of these deductions about how the antipodean travellers faired, what they actually *thought* about their experiences in the circus is more difficult to access. In conversation with the press, Barnum and Hutchinson asserted that the indigenous performers were 'awed, terrified and mystified' by the circus. Hutchinson volunteered that he 'would give $1,000 to be a Nubian for two hours . . . [to enter] their thoughts and feelings!' More direct conversational methods seem not to have been tried.[37] For Billy and his companions the world of the travelling circus must have seemed a world of the fantastic, of tricksters and magic. A surfeit of wonders. Yet a view that they responded to the world around them only in magical terms would characterise the Aborigines (and other indigenous performers) as childlike and irrational, whereas their survival in the show-space depended on their ability to adapt and make rational responses, as well as on the inner strengths derived from their own culture, which they carried with them. Thus it is significant that they displayed a capacity for total absorption in their performances, which would also have helped relieve the tensions generated within the show-space. Even as the troupe were in the process of becoming professional performers, learning nuanced responses to culturally different, and often uncomprehending, audiences, while they were actually performing they were most themselves, in touch with the certainties of their own culture.

While it is difficult to recover much about the North Queenslanders' individual experiences, there were a number of experiences shared with the rest of the company that would have made a profound impression on them. Just a few days after leaving Baltimore, in the town of Wheeling, a severe storm occurred in the middle of a performance. The rain 'beat with a dull roar on the canvas' and drowned out the sound of the bands. Elephants trumpeted and birds whistled. Then a mighty wind struck; the huge canvas surged up and down, the tent poles swayed dangerously, and people ran for the exits. The stagehands leapt into action, the big lights were lowered in an instant and the trapeze came down in a rush. Ropes were tightened, poles replaced and people went back to their seats. Afterwards the mud was ankle deep, and lowering the sodden tents was a Herculean task.

A few weeks later in Chicago, in the early hours of the morning, all the edges of the big tent were seen to be fringed with fire, and although the blaze was contained, after twenty minutes all that remained was 'an immense amphitheatre of lurid embers'. Next morning Barnum himself was on hand to reassure the public that although the losses were great – they were $15,000 at the outside – they could be sustained. And Jumbo and all the other animals and performers were safe. Last season's canvas was raised and the show went on in the evening 'as though nothing had occurred'. For a number of the following performances, however, side canvases only were used.[38] These and other memorable incidents, such as a derailing of the cages of the Big Cats, would have helped Billy to commit to memory the places in North America visited on their journey (see p. 164).

The Barnum's circus was not without competition. In St Louis the advertisement for Sacket Dime Museum, in the *Globe-Democrat*, 27 May, challenged its arrival under the banner line 'Jumbo Justly Jealous'. 'A band of genuine Apache' had been brought 'direct from Hermosillo Mexico, the seat of the present Indian War' to perform 'scalping scenes and battle dances'. The 'cultural work' of this spectacle of a less remote savagery was, perhaps, that it provided a more localised, and therefore more apposite, contrast to their own urban society.[39] Nevertheless, if Barnum is to be believed, the 1883 circus season that ended in late October had been 'the most successful season ever known in show business', perhaps attributable more to Jumbo than to the *Ethnological Congress*. Business manager Joseph

McCaddon's tabulation of finances from 1881 to 1897 also confirms that a peak was reached in that year, with takings of $1,419,498. In spite of numerous mishaps, and 45 days of rain out of 180, in the eleven days in Chicago alone the takings had amounted to $119,172.30. But the two main years of recruiting for the *Ethnological Congress*, 1883 and 1884, also produced the highest expenses, and in 1884 the dividend of $277,000 was only half that declared in 1883. Although only a skeleton staff was kept on at the winter quarters in Bridgeport, Connecticut, to look after the equipment and stock and to prepare for the coming season, the overwintering costs were high – for instance in the winter of 1881/2 they amounted to $225,000.[40] Consequently only a handful of leading artists were retained, and the rest of the company had to find other employment. It was a time of crisis for some like Alice Smith, otherwise known as Zuleika the Circassian, who on 21 January 1884 was arraigned on a charge of attempted suicide – the cause was said to be destitution and dispair.[41] But as one astute pressman noted: 'The Dime Museum has been a Godsend to natural curiosities. Now [it] affords them a congenial means of earning an honest dollar in the season of blizzards . . . where once fat women, skeletons, Albinos and Circassians would work for their board during the winter.'[42]

I have not been able to ascertain precisely what Barnum paid Cunningham and the North Queenslanders, but his stated policy was to pay indigenous performers like them a 'nominal' sum only, above their board and travelling expenses (see his letter, p. 58). On the dime museum circuit they, and Cunningham, would do better.

Entrance – a dime

As the circus reached a peak of popularity in the 1880s and 1890s the dime museums 'of curiosities' also entered their heyday throughout the cities of North America. Taking Barnum's American Museum as a model, they were essentially places of entertainment, open until 10 pm, and able to flourish alongside the new national and provincial museums of science and natural history. For instance, Stanhope and Epstean's New Dime Museum in Chicago listed among its attractions on five floors an art gallery, a salon of wax statuary, a menagerie, an aquarium, Indian relics and mechanical marvels, as well as Doctor Schafhirt's Anatomical Collection, which included 'Left Foot of Human Female,

AN ALL-COMPRISING COLLECTION OF NATURE'S HUMAN WONDERS.

Irish' and 'Right Hand of Human Female, *Negro*', Foot of Grizzly Bear, and so on.[43] Although the avowed aim was instructive family entertainment for 'the better class of person', such displays of macabre specimens of human remains were popular. For the Victorians believed that the difference between peoples could be 'read' in the size, colour and shape of the body – even of its individual parts. The main attractions, however, were to be found on what was called the 'freak platform', where live platform appearances of human 'oddities' and touring exotic curiosities took place (pl. 37). More elaborate presentations also took place in the 'lecture room' – so-called to lend an aura of respectability to the theatre – where performances by the curiosities were rotated with vaudeville acts and such stock dramatic performances as *Uncle Tom's Cabin*. In the Midwestern and East Coast cities there were dime museum chains, some run by ex-employees of Barnum. One of the largest chains on the Aborigines' itinerary was Middleton and Kohl, with branches in New York, Chicago and about six more cities. It was George Middleton, who at one

37 Broadsheet: 'An All-comprising Collection of Nature's Human Wonders', Morgan Print Co. Live platform appearances were part of the dime museum's repetoire.

time had been the star press agent for Barnum, who was said to have inaugurated the florid adjective-sprinkled style of press advertisement that announced many of these entertainments, and that remained a Barnum trademark.[44]

In the winter season of 1883/4 the performers from the *Ethnological Congress* – the Nubians, Toda, Zulu and the Australian 'Bushmen' – joined other attractions controlled by Barnum – the Elastic-Skinned man, General Dot, Chang the Chinese Giant and the Wild Men of Borneo – on the dime museum circuit, earning a percentage for him. Billed as 'P. T. Barnum's Last Sensation!', the Australian troupe's fee was $300 a week (about a quarter of a policeman's average wage per annum), which compared well with the $500 a week paid Mrs Tom Thumb, who was a well-established performer. The Elastic-Skinned man received only $200, the Skeleton Man $100, while the Circassians earned between $15 and $50 a week. The minimum pay was roughly four times the mininum for a female servant girl in a big city.[45] The Barnum connection no doubt ensured the bookings, but the management and costs – including for hotel accommodation – of touring ten people and their baggage were down to Cunningham. Performers frequently stayed in attic accommodation above the Museum, fitted with sleeping cubicles and a common dining room, but Cunningham seems to have provided hotel accommodation.

Apparently the Aboriginal performers kept the proceeds of the booklets and photographs they sold directly to the public, but I have not established what proportion of their earnings they received. They did have money in their pockets because they were 'ready to buy . . . everything pretty and flashy they [saw] in the show windows, such as a red undershirt . . . an accordion or trombone, or a musical instrument of some sort', which, Cunningham said, they usually dismantled to see what was inside. Travelling as a smaller unit, they had more freedom and opportunity to shop, and Cunningham declared: 'I carry more baggage now, the property of these fellows, than I know what to do with.'[46] When they were not performing in the circus, Billy and his companions mingled with the crowds and became absorbed into the spectacle of the city streets, markets and department stores. Their presence rendered the exotic familiar and they, in turn, became part of that cultural mix that characterised urban modernity. Who would deny the Aboriginal group the same degree of anonymity and intimacy as was experienced by others moving within the city crowd?

During the months of touring the dime museums the reporting about Toby, Billy and their companions is more personal, and for the first time we come a little closer to them. The season began for them in Philadelphia, only two weeks after the close of the circus tour, and already they were in serious trouble. On 9 November the *Evening News* carried the headline 'The Brightest of the Australian Cannibals Likely to Die of the Climate Here'. Although they called her 'Princess Tinendara', this was an error because she was also identified as the sixteen-year-old 'child-wife' and therefore must have been Sussy, otherwise known as 'Princess Tagarah'. She was, they said, 'wasting away with a pulmonary disease that will eventually result in consumption'. Seeing this was so, 'the members of the troupe 'are constantly upbraiding their manager, Mr Cunningham. They reproach him for bringing them away to die in a strange country.' For his part, Cunningham stated that 'he did not know what to do should the girl die' because he thought 'it would be impossible to control the rest.' Sussy was everybody's favourite; she was very cheerful and bright, and smiled and chatted 'with her companions in spite of her physical suffering'. She received 'the best medical attendance' and recovered sufficiently to move on to the city of Providence with her companions. By the time the troupe arrived in Baltimore at the beginning of December, Sussy's husband, Tambo, and 'two others' had contracted severe colds and were 'more or less seriously troubled with illness' thereafter. Although Sussy was still unwell, the two others referred to were the boy, Toby, and the other Biyaygirri man whose name remains in doubt. Although Cunningham later asserted that he had been 'obliged to be in constant attendance upon them' and everywhere they went he 'had large doctors bills to pay', apparently 'the doctors in all cities had been at a loss as to the method of treating them.'[47]

Baltimore remembered their earlier visit and decided that 'The Australian Bushmen still seem to have the spice of novelty . . . for all day yesterday the Dime Museum . . . was crowded.' In spite of illness, 'they performed their grotesque dancing, strange boomerang-throwing and other sports to the delight of all.'[48] In this instance, the block for the advertisement bears a closer relationship to the group photograph than to the characteristic graphic representation used elsewhere (pl. 40). Next, in Chicago, in an engagement that spanned the holiday season of 1883–4, the 'Australians' pleased the crowds at Kohl and Middleton's South Side and West Side establishments, while the Zulu entertained the public at the

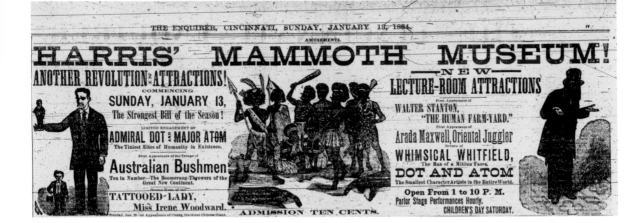

38 (*above*) The Australian Bushmen, newspaper advertisement, *Cincinnati Enquirer*, 13 January, 1884

39 (*right*) Australian Bushmen, newspaper advertisement in the *Baltimore Eagle*, 2 December 1883. The Baltimore and Cincinnati papers seem to have risen to the challenge of representing the new performers, the 'Australian Bushmen', with their own blocks

Great Chicago Museum. In Cincinnati the troupe had a three-week engagement through January into February at Harris's Mammoth Museum, where they performed for the largest crowd yet assembled there, and were hailed by the press as the best engagement of the season. Again, the advertisement in the *Enquirer* (13 Jan. 1884) has a more photographic quality, although a crude headless figure is positioned in the foreground. The 'Australian Bushmen' were on the same bill as Admiral Dot and Major Atom (pl. 38), and towards the end of their run they were joined by the ever popular Chang the Chinese Giant. Although it was mid-January, the weather was 'uncommonly propitious', and the sun shining in a cloudless sky made it a day for boomerang-throwing.

At Harris's Museum in Pittsburgh, mid-February brought a change in the weather: blizzards and floods. The troupe was staying at the St Clair hotel, where a *Pittsburg Critic* reporter found Cunningham administering 'a nauseous dose of medicine to an inoffensive and submissive looking Australian cannibal' called Johnny (Tambo). The showman confided that 'it just breaks my heart to be dosing these poor creatures with medicine from morning to night.' He went on to explain that 'all have more or less some sort of lung infection. In the summer they get on all right but in the winter it is all I can do to keep them alive.' In spite of the inevitable superficiality of the *Pittsburg Critic*'s article, the interview conveys something of the closeness of the relationship that had developed between R. A. and his charges, as well as the tensions of the situation. For Johnny's illness reminds Cunningham that it is only because of the 'testimony of Johnny and Toby . . . and their willingness to go with me . . . that I am here with them to-day.' For their part, Johnny and Toby seemed to take illness in their stride because they voluntarily embarked on a graphic tale from North Queensland, a description of a 'fierce battle' in 'defence of the wife and children of their employer'. This is one of the few occasions in America when they are directly interviewed. The reporter concludes that 'Cunningham takes a pardonable pride' in the success of his venture and hopes to ward off the evil effects of the cold and exposure by careful attention and medical treatment – the unspoken suggestion being that otherwise his investment is in jeopardy.[49]

It was also in Pittsburgh that Billy, who it seems was a 'medicine man', exercised his powers to circumvent death. The seven-year-old Toby had been taken ill and in anticipation of his death 'the physicians made a request to hold a post-mortem examination', which Cunningham refused.[50] The story – attributed to Cunningham on several later occasions in Germany – was that

> the doctors declared the case hopeless, and indeed the boy seemed to breathe no longer . . . and was, one would have sworn, a dead cannibal. But there was one person among the Aborigines who had a high reputation as a doctor among his companions. His name was Warchsinbin [Billy] and the Australians absolutely trusted his words and his advice. The doctors had already put pressure on Mr Cunningham to give them the corpse of young Toby for scientific purposes, but after a short examination of the boy, Warchsinbin declared that Little Toby was not dead but possessed by an evil spirit called *Bawwa* whom he would expel. He blew into the nose, mouth and ears of the boy, rubbed his limbs, and finally caught the *Bawwa* by sucking it out of the boy's mouth and spitting it into a small bag, which he tied very thoroughly and put into a suitcase. The same evening he carried the case to the river, made it heavy with a stone, and drowned the bad spirit in the deep water. The little patient recovered more and more every day and he became completely healthy again . . . a very lively proof of the healing art of Warchsinbin.'[51]

The North Queenslanders were later to tell Houzé and Jacques that a bad spirit was the cause of illness or death, either a spirit of the dead or a nature spirit. They are everywhere they said, 'in the trees, in the rocks, and also in the air'.[52] The techniques used by Billy to extract the spirit were recognisably in line with the practice in the area from which Billy and his companions came. Medicine men, however, could cause mischief as well as cure, serving as a vehicle for the conveyance of the evil spirit. Thus all death directly or indirectly involved human agency, and after death, a medicine man's skills were enlisted to determine the cause.[53] The Aborigines also practised other healing skills such as herbal cures, massage and smoking of the patient, so that they recognised the white man's medicine for what it was – another method of healing. The exercise of Billy's healing skills in Pittsburgh remains a most powerful evocation of their own cultural practices within the deterritorialized space within which they found themselves.

On their last day in Pittsburgh Toby and Bob gave an outdoor demonstration in boomerang-throwing at the Allegheny baseball grounds for assembled reporters and special guests of the manager of the dime museum, Mr Starr. 'It is thrown with a force that is wonderful,' one newsman wrote, 'but instead of going forward it slowly rises in the air, whirling around and around with a whizzing noise, circling like a chicken hawk in its upward flight, and alighting within a short distance of the thrower' (*Pittsburg Leader*, 22 Feb. 1884).

For me, constantly reading of their skills at boomerang-throwing, the boomerang becomes a metaphor for their journey, always travelling but always caught within the orbit of the show-space.

Death of Tambo

The following day, Saturday 23 February 1884, Cunningham shepherded the travellers onto the Erie railroad to Cleveland, Ohio, for their next engagement. Frank Drew, the proprietor of the dime museum on Superior Street, met them at the station and escorted them to the New England Hotel on Water Street (now West Ninth street). The weather was appalling and the area was flooded. On arrival at the hotel Tambo collapsed and a doctor was called, but it was of no avail and at 11 pm the young man died. He was only about twenty-one years of age, was not quite five feet in height and weighed not more than 100 lb. Years later Drew recalled that (in spite of their brief acquaintance) he had been impressed by Tambo's bearing and flair for clothes. What happened after his death can be reconstructed from a number of short news items in Cleveland's newspapers, particularly the *Penny Press* and *Plain Dealer*, where the events were recorded with little or no compassion.[54]

Immediately, in spite of the surroundings, his kin and companions attempted to carry out the customary funerary procedures, folding and tying his body so that his knees were drawn up under his chin, and his arms folded across his chest, but Cunningham intervened and stopped them. Then they attempted to suspend the body from a tree in the yard, and plaster it with mud, but again they were prevented. They also gathered together Tambo's weapons and personal belongings, including his top hat and cane, preparing to burn them, as was their custom.[55] It was also the custom for the place of death to be abandoned, or even burnt, after the funerary ceremonies, and as Tambo's kin and companions did not have control over their own movements, it is possible that they found it less disturbing when the body was removed. For Drew later claimed that he finally prevailed on them to give him the corpse, and it was removed to Hogan and Harris, the undertakers. Even though they were never to see Tambo again, they 'lamented the deceased loudly in broken English' and their own tongue, 'and acted much as Christians would under similar circumstances' (*Penny Press*, 25 Feb.). According to the official record of Cuyahoga County, Ohio, the cause of Tambo's death was said to be inflammation of the lungs – that, in the opinion of a reporter, was 'a disease that was hastened in this instant unquestionably by the exposed manner in which he was compelled to sit all day' (*Cleveland Evening News*, 26 Feb.). In fact, the 'Abstract' provided by the physician, Herman Bock, stated the cause was Phthisis (tuberculosis).[56]

On the Monday, unbeknown to the group, 'scores of people' called during the day to examine the corpse at the establishment of Hogan and Harris, several blocks away, while the despondent survivors sat in a row on the bench in the dime museum and 'refused to perform their usual tricks'. The *Plain Dealer* reported that 'the medical colleges would like to get possession of this subject', but Drew and Cunningham had other plans. (This was the second, but not the last time, Cunningham showed himself reluctant to allow an Aboriginal body to go for dissection.)

Drew also owned dime museums in Providence, Columbus and Indianapolis and had spent ten years working as assistant to Merritt Young, who was in charge of Barnum's human curiosities, so he took the initiative in contacting the circus for permission to have the body embalmed.[57] Telegrams were exchanged with Barnum, who authorised the embalmment – in case the Australian authorities demanded its return – and as early as Tuesday, 26 February, Drew revealed to the *Penny Press* that after the embalmment he planned to exhibit Tambo behind glass in his museum. When on the following day Cunningham told the troupe that Tambo had already been buried, they finally became resigned to it (*Cleveland Herald*, 27 Feb.). Newspaper reports calling the Aborigines 'Moody Man-eaters' and hinting at 'Cannibal rites'[58] attracted the crowds, and the troupe performed to packed houses for the rest of the two-week season. Cunningham congratulated Drew on having 'the best and most comfortable museum in the country'. By the end of the run it was announced that 'if the Dime Museum was trice as large it would still be too small to hold those who flock to see the Australian Boomerang Throwers, the giants and dwarfs . . . and so on'.

Meanwhile Tambo's kin and companions had to deal with the trauma not only of his death but also of the removal of the body before they had performed the proper ritual, and it is reasonable to suppose that when they sang their songs and danced before an uncomprehending public, they mourned their loss, and the separation from their homeland. Sussy mourned for many days and 'refused to lift or touch food'. Weeks later, in Europe, according to Houzé and Jacques, she and her companions continued to show much sadness at Tambo's death as they performed their mourning dances.

Cunningham told the *Plain Dealer*'s reporter that he had 'great trouble with the creatures and wishes they were off his hands . . . and Tambo was the worst of the lot'. The reason he gave was Tambo's refusal to take the medicine, 'just out of cussedness and stubbornness'. The defensiveness of Cunningham's reply suggests an underlying desperation at the failure of his treatment, rather than shifting the blame to his charges. Yet lung infections were a well-known hazard among travelling performers, and given the change in climate the North Queenslanders had experienced, the crowded living conditions and the relentless public exposure, whatever the weather, they were very predictable afflictions for the Aboriginal travellers. The bacillus that caused tuberculosis had only been discovered in 1882, and both the public and general medical practitioners were still treating pulmonary ailments with a variety of patent medicines. Cunningham was no exception, as several news items on patent medicines in his cuttings book testify; and we can only hope he did not resort to the remedy based on wood creosote recommended there.[59] Although the disposal of Tambo's body to Drew was without doubt the ultimate in callous commodification, embalmment as an American funerary practice was not unusual, particularly in the west where a stranger's body would be preserved in case it might be reclaimed. Nor was the display of a mummified body unusual. Tambo remained on display at first in the dime museum and then at Hogan and Harris and elsewhere in Cleveland, together with other mummified bodies, well into the twentieth century.

Several days before their departure from Cleveland it was reported (*Cleveland Leader*, 3 March) that 'another of the number is seriously ill', and that again 'the patient' was reluctant to take the medicine Cunningham administered. Tambo's death was a very public one, but silence surrounds the death of the second young man, whose English name remains unknown. Was he left behind in Cleveland or somewhere on the route to die? Silence suited Cunningham better; it was less disturbing both for the other members of the group and for his own reputation as a showman. For the survivors, 'moving on' approximated to a certain degree the abandonment of the camp site after a death and was probably the less traumatic option. Later, in Europe, as others in the group became ill and were near death, Cunningham always moved on, leaving them in care in a hospital, and sometimes it was several weeks before they died. According to Aboriginal custom the names of the dead were not mentioned. Tambo's name was only mentioned to the European anthropologists because Sussy's status as a widow had to be explained, but the other young man is never mentioned again.

The troupe was due to rejoin Barnum's *Ethnological Congress* for the 1884 circus season. The opening was set for 15 March at Madison Square Gardens, New York. Instead, a few weeks later, in the first week of April, Cunningham arrived in England with the seven survivors. He was later to claim that he moved them to Europe to avoid the harsh American winter, but it was early spring and they had sure employment with Barnum, who also had a policy of hospitalising the sick and injured – which would have relieved Cunningham of the responsibility of care. Because of illness, expenses had been heavy during the dime museum tour; to move them to Europe, however, meant that Cunningham could establish his independence from Barnum and continue to exploit the Aboriginal performers for his own profit.

Cunningham had earlier voiced his fears about how he would manage the troupe if any of them died, because they could not really be held except by persuasion, but it seems that the trauma of death bound the group more closely to him. In America, under the leadership of Toby and Tambo, the two English-speakers, the group had become performers – professional savages. The curious flesh-coloured body stockings, worn under their calf-skin garments, reflected the double vision of their situation. When wearing them, they appeared to the white spectators to be naked savages, without offending a sense of decency. For their part, they saw their show clothes as marking their status as performers, and they frequently expressed their liking for them. Whatever the traumas experienced in Cleveland, and during their last days in America, and in spite of the reproaches they heaped on Cunningham for removing them from their

40   'Australian
Cannibals', *Advance
Courier*, distributed in
Jackson, 28 August 1884
(recycled from 1883), long
after the Australian
Aborigines and other
groups had departed.

homelands, their independence of spirit was too demonstrable for
Cunningham to have compelled them to move on against their will. They
had forged new identities for themselves: they were professional performers, and this was what they now did.

And what of Barnum's *Ethnological Congress*? The same Advance
Courier in which 'Bestial Australian Cannibals' were given top billing, and
illustrated by the same representation of a cannibal feast on the beach, was
recycled during the touring season of 1884, even though Cunningham's
group was no longer with the circus.[60] In fact, neither were they listed in
Barnum's *My Diary or Route Book* for 1884. And if they were not there, who
among the others listed in the Advance Courier advertisement (pl. 40) –
'the Mysterious Aztecs, Big-Lipped Botocudoes, Wild Nubians, Ferocious
Zulus, Ishmaelitish Todars, Buddhists Monks, Invincible Afghans,
Ethiopians, Circassians, Polynesians, Tasmanians, Tartars; Patans Etc.' were
actually there? Some – like the so-called Aztecs and the Circassians – were,
of course, fakes, who were easily replaced. Admiral Dot and Major Atom

joined the *Congress* as 'Distinguished Lilliputians'. Others, such as the Nubians, were constantly reduced in numbers; when first mentioned by Barnum in October 1882 there were twenty-five, in 1883 there were fifteen, then twelve, and in 1884 there were only eight. There were still some Sioux, Zulu and Toda. In Europe, later in the year, the North Queenslanders crossed tracks with the same group of Zulu, while a large troupe of Sioux travelling the German show circuit may have included some they had performed alongside in the *Congress* of 1883.[61] It seems Zulu were also replaceable because Zulu became the generic name for black American circus workers who dressed as Africans.[62] Anyway, Barnum's expectations were that indigenous performers possessed some other physical attribute or skill, and it was the art of boomerang-throwing that distinguished Billy and his companions from the other professional savages. Even so, did it matter whether or not the indigenous performers were fake or real, or what skills they had, when the circus crowds regarded them all as 'savages'? For as I have said earlier, it was the way in which they were represented through performance and in the accompanying promotional literature and other popular accounts that masked their identities and frustrates attempts to reconstruct more than a fragmentary account of what actually happened to most of them.

5   European Spectacle

If the fundamental cultural fact of the nineteenth century was understood to be the development of great cities, the representative modern subjectivity was understood to be that of the city dweller, the passive yet compulsive consumer of a rapidly and perpetually changing spectacle.

Dana Brand, *The Spectator and the City in Nineteenth Century American Literature*, 1991

As early as the 1830s a showman, Heinrich Hill, distributed a broadsheet in Berlin advertising 'Bushmen from New Holland' – a male forty-three years old, a female of twenty-seven who was part European, and a child – on display daily from 9 am to 8 pm, together with an African woman, during the period of the wool market.

Exhibiting human oddities had long been part of the entertainment provided at European fairs and markets,[1] but Hill, who also owned a cabinet of wax figures, attempted to give his new speculation a scientific respectability. He had his living exhibits 'authenticated' by none other than Professor Blumenbach, of Göttingen, and other professors 'famous because of their knowledge in matters of race, differences and main branches of the human family' (pl. 41).[2] How Hill's 'Bushmen' came to be in Europe or what was their ultimate fate is unknown but it was certainly an outcome of their dispossession. Further, as in the case of Saartjie Baartman, who was known pejoratively as the Hottentot Venus, and who became the object of the anatomist George Cuvier's investigations, the conjunction of popular and scientific interests in such displays was to characterise their future presentation. By mid-century, as the fallout from the many colonial wars swelled the numbers of exotic 'others' removed overseas to be exhibited, the growing contempt for them – engendered by their treatment in the colonies and their demeaning presentation abroad – was given popular expression in England by Charles Dickens in an essay deriding 'The Noble Savage'. Dickens, in his earliest literary incarnation as

41   'Indian Bushmen from New Holland', woodcut, broadsheet of the Australian Aborigines and a woman from Angola, toured in Germany by Heinrich Hill in the 1830s.

Boz, claimed to 'read' the urban spectacle for his public. When, later, as part of that spectacle he encountered the 'Noble Strangers' in the persons of 'Mr Catlin's Ojibbeway Indians', the 'Earthmen Bushmen' and, most recently, 'the party of Zulu Kaffirs' at the St George's Gallery, Hyde Park Corner, he decided 'a savage is something highly desirable to be civilised off the face of the earth.' In performance, Dickens wrote, they were 'miserable', 'wretched', 'odiferous' and so on, and he unambiguously concluded that while there was 'no justification for being cruel . . . the world will be all the better when his place knows him no more.'[3]

During the last decades of the nineteenth century, at the confident high-point in the colonial enterprise, the displacement and dispossession of indigenous peoples further increased the supply, and Billy and his companions – and other groups like them – made their appearance on the stage of the spectacle of the world as it was configured in the fairgrounds, circuses, museums, zoos, theatres, exhibition halls and other entertainment spaces of metropolitan North America and Europe. All were sites that privileged the visual mode of experience. In Europe – as in America – the same broad economic forces of industrialisation and urbanisation were accompanied by dramatic sociocultural changes that transformed the way in which life was experienced. In addition to large-scale emigration of Europeans to the colonies and the Americas, the movement of people was also to the cities, and by 1880 many European cities had populations of over a million and that of London was approaching 4 million (pl. 42). The cities were in a perpetual state of transformation. In Paris great boulevards cut through and obliterated old quarters, in London the inner sections of the Underground were under construction, in all the capitals the improvement of artificial illumination continued, and everywhere light entered through the glass and iron constructions that arched over railway stations, exhibition spaces, shopping arcades and the glass windows of the department stores, where the massed displays of goods stimulated desire. 'The immense and perpetually renewing spectacle of commodities and images' provoked a restlessness of spirit, and produced new forms of imaginative expression that Charles Baudelaire had earlier identified as 'modernity'.[4]

Modes of transport also changed the way the world was experienced – for instance the panoramic view from a train. By the late nineteenth century, communication systems (transport and telegraphic) were global. Steamship networks linked continents and rail networks crossed them in a matter of days and weeks rather than months, connecting cities and industrial centres within national boundaries and across them. When Cunningham crossed the Pacific in 1883 with his Aboriginal troupe the Pacific Mail Steamship Co. were offering passages from Sydney through to London and Paris, via any railroad route in North America – 'unlimited stopovers allowed' – for £66, steerage £20. In October the same year the first Oriental Express sleeping carriages reached Constantinople, and other grand European rail expresses had as their destinations all main

PRICE ONE PENNY

THE GROWTH OF CITY POPU-LATIONS.

(Appleton's Popular Science Monthly.)

The sudden growth of great cities is the first result of the phenomenon of immigration which we have to note. We think of this as essentially an American problem. We comfort ourselves in our failures of municipal administration with that thought. It is a grievous deception. Most of the European cities have increased in population more rapidly than in America. Shaw has emphasized the same fact in his brilliant work on "Municipal Government in Europe." This is particularly true of great German urban centres. Berlin has outgrown our own metropolis, New York, in less than a generation, having in 25 years added as many actual new residents as Chicago, and twice as many as Philadelphia. Hamburg has gained twice as many population since 1875 as Boston; Leipsic has distanced St. Louis. The same demographic outburst has occurred in the smaller German cities as well. Cologne has gained the lead over Cleveland. Buffalo and Pittsburg, although in 1880 it was the smallest of the four. Magdeburg has grown faster than Providence in the last 10 years. Dusseldorf has likewise outgrown St. Paul. Beyond the confines of the German empire, from Norway to Italy, the same is true. Stockholm has doubled its population; Copenhagen has increased two and one-half times; Christiania has trebled its numbers in a generation. Rome has increased from 148,000 in 1860 to 450,000 in 1894. Vienna, including its suburbs, has grown three times over within the same period. Paris from 1881 to 1891 absorbed four-fifths of the total increase of population for all of France within the same period.

42 'Price One Penny: The Growth of City Populations', unidentified news item from Cunningham's cuttings book

Western and Central European cities.[5] And Cunningham made use of this network.

Fast mail services also brought delivery of newspapers and journals, with their reportage, entertainment and advertisements, to the rural districts and intercity. Developments in print technology and the press in the course of the century flowed from – and at the same time were implicated in – the formation of the industrialised, urbanised and largely literate societies emerging in Europe and America, and the popular pictorial press has come to be regarded as the cultural production that best characterised the age.[6] It developed in response to the increased purchasing power and time for leisure of the new urban classes (both middle and working class), with their insatiable appetite for news, commodities and self-improvement. Although much emphasis has been placed on the democratising force of the process, the social values expressed were those of the dominant white, male-oriented, middle classes. As the century advanced, the various national mass circulation newspapers and the illustrated journals mirrored for their consumers the modern world of spectacle in which they were themselves immersed. It was a world not only of home events but also of foreign ventures, especially colonial wars, which were presented in terms of civilisation's triumph over savagery. The positive self-imaging of what Benedict Anderson calls 'imagined communities' of nations involved a dialectical opposite – and the defeated indigenous inhabitants of the colonies constituted the 'other' ideologically relevant to this narrative.[7] In the teaming cities, surrounded by an anonymous underclass, there was always the fear of falling off the ladder of progress, or the growing threat to the social order of anarchic revolution, but the projection of these fears onto a 'savage other' allowed the threat to civility to be externalised. The touring shows of indigenous peoples became, as it were, a savage presence in the midst of urban life, and the integration of visual, written, oral and performance techniques in the production of these shows provided a powerful platform for the popular expression of ideas about difference between peoples in terms of inferiority and superiority, endowing the spectacle with a disciplinary function.

The large-scale shows of indigenous people that characterised the period were promoted mainly, though not entirely, within those European countries that had imperial ambitions and whose economic development was linked with overseas trade and exploitation of colonial resources and markets – and they were frequently promoted transnationally. Carl Hagenbeck, animal trader, trainer and showman, was well situated for the trade, based as he was in Hamburg, Germany's major port, and he pioneered the process in 1874 when he imported a group of geographically proximate others, some 'Lapplanders' (Saami), three men, two women and two children. He described his show as 'zoological and anthropological' because the 'Lapps' did not perform, they simply lived as they did at home – with their animals, sleds and implements – in the zoo grounds behind his house. The experience, he later wrote, 'taught me that ethnographic exhibitions would prove lucrative' and he followed their visit with 'other wild men': in 1876 a Nubian caravan from the Sudan, and in 1877–8 a party of 'Eskimo' (Inuit) from Greenland.[8] The public came in thousands. Hagenbeck not only toured the Nubians and the Greenlanders to several other German cities, he also made them available to the Jardin d'Acclimatation in the Bois de Boulogne, Paris,[9] where their performances produced a spectacular attendance figure for the year 1877 of over 800,000, an increase of over 200,000 over the previous highest figure, which, in turn, provided a clear profit of 57,963 French francs. Although they were to change in character over the years, these large-scale shows of indigenous people remained a feature of Parisian life, both at the Jardin and elsewhere, for the rest of the century.

From the beginning, a characteristic of the shows had been the professional interest the members of the Anthropological Society had shown in them. But in the 1880s in Paris there was a shift in attitude among the anthropological fraternity as to the scientific value of such displays; doubts were raised about their authenticity and, in spite of their immense popularity, they were temporarily discontinued in 1880, 1884 and 1885. Faced with a fall-off in attendance during those three years, the Jardin's director, Geoffroy Saint-Hilaire, seized the opportunity to achieve more legal independence from the Zoological Society for the Jardin, so that he could reintroduce these shows, 'Zoo humains', without interference from the scientific community. Although the emphasis shifted to choosing companies such as the 'Singalese dancers' or the 'Ashanti Warriors' for their entertainment value rather than their ethnographic interest, and the anthropologists ceased to report these shows in their official journals,[10] they continued to visit, and report on, similar touring shows held at other venues such as Folies Bergère (see chapter 7).

Meanwhile, in Germany, Hagenbeck experienced a similar crisis of confidence in these shows of indigenous people, or Völkerschauen. First an entire party of Inuit from Labrador in Canada, who had been procured by Johan Adrian Jacobsen in 1880 in spite of the protests of the Moravian Mission, died of smallpox.[11] Then six of a party of eleven from Tierra del Fuego, the most southerly tip of South America, billed as Feuerländers (Fire-landers), died.[12] The circumstances surrounding their removal from the Magellan Straits in 1881 were suspiciously unclear; suggesting a degree of coercion was involved. On arrival in Europe, they were already in bad shape and a toddler died during their first engagement at Jardin d'Acclimatation, Paris. Nevertheless, they drew crowds totalling half a million visitors in the six weeks they were there, and Hagenbeck wrote to his colleague Johan Adrian Jacobsen, 'Things have changed for me thank god since I have the fire-land people.'[13] Then another died on the journey between Nürnberg and Zürich, and four more died in Zürich in quick succession, from a combination of illnesses – while their companions continued to perform for four and a half hours instead of the usual ten. A Dr Johannes Seiz, who was treating them, notified the police, who closed their show at the Platten Theatre, and Hagenbeck undertook to send the survivors home. He wrote again to Jacobsen, that the affair 'took away all resolve to get involved further with shows of humans'. It seems he did not like reading disagreeable things about himself in the Stuttgart and Zürich papers. But, he continued, 'I cannot tell you how much I regret that our daring plans all at once are shattered . . .'[14] Hagenbeck soon overcame his scruples, and while his organisation continued to promote Völkerschauen well into the twentieth century, in his own book, *Beasts and Men*, he chose to omit from his list of shows the disastrous Tierra del Fuego show of 1881–2. Generally speaking, it was accepted that members of the indigenous groups died while on tour in Europe and 'on that account', as Professor

Rudolph Virchow pointed out, they 'were more especially noticed' scientifically.[15]

Virchow, who was Professor of Pathological Anatomy at the University of Berlin, and had played a leading part in the founding of the Berliner Gesellschaft für Anthropologie, Ethnologie und Urgeschichte (Society for Anthropology, Ethnology and Prehistory) in 1869, was also an influential politician of left-liberal persuasion. He had enough connections, for instance, to be able to enlist government support in seeking Chilean permission for obtaining examples of 'racial types' for Hagenbeck's shows.[16] He also intervened to smooth Jacobsen's path with the Danish government in acquiring the Greenland 'Eskimos'. For their part, government officials saw their intervention as supporting both German science and business. The shows, which were sometimes visited by the Kaiser, were also thought to stimulate interest in German colonial aspirations (see p. 148). The connections between the showmen and the anthropologists were close. Jean Charles Louis Castan, owner of show places in Berlin, Köln and Brussels, was a founding member of the Berlin Society, and Hagenbeck was also made an honorary member. Over the years, Virchow examined representatives of the different Völkerschauen in Berlin, including the three Aborigines from Fraser Island, Queensland, in 1883, and both the first and second groups from North Queensland toured by Cunningham in 1884 and 1896. In his published reports he defended the practice, and the special presentation meetings organised by the Society for Anthropology attracted press notice and drew large crowds. As well as being a public relations exercise and providing entertainment for a privileged coterie, the scientists saw the society as the disseminator of new knowledge gathered in the laboratory and presented in the society's sessions. The society's journals were distributed abroad and German anthropology was also a major influence in Europe's German-speaking communities and in the neighbouring Netherlands, the Balkans and Scandinavia.[17]

German anthropology was also highly regarded in the Anglo-American scientific world and France. The exchange of photographs, particularly photographs of members of the touring troupes of indigenous people, formed an important part of this transnational network of exchange of new anthropological knowledge.[18] For instance, the photographs of Toby and his companions, taken by Carl Günther in Berlin, are to be found not only there but also in the collection of Prince Roland Bonaparte in Paris, together with photographs of them taken in London, while Bonaparte's own photographs of the Australians were sent by him to the Royal Anthropological Institute, in London. And in each archive they are to be found in association with photographs of the members of other touring troupes and with photographs gathered in the colonies. Because photographs were considered to be 'facts' in themselves, they were frequently deposited without supporting documentation. Thus, they have provided a lingering presence in the archive of the long-since departed travelling performers, where they have become available to present-day anthropological discourse – and through further reproduction and dissemination, to the recovery of indigenous identities and histories.

Gabi Eissenberger (1996) has investigated the Fuegians' story in great detail, and I shall refer to it again because her work, with its concern for the particular, provides a broader context for consideration of the Aboriginal group's experiences and treatment. It seems that the scientists' attitude of callous indifference to the plight of the members of these indigenous shows was matched, by and large, by similar public attitudes. For instance, Hilke Thode-Arora, in her review of sixty years of the papers of one city, Hamburg, from 1874 on, did not find any condemnation of the exhibition of exotic peoples in that city. And, except for the unfavourable reports after the deaths of the Fuegians in Zürich, Gabi Eissenberger, in researching reports on a number of South American shows, found only one other report, in the *Magdeburger Zeitung* of October 1880, that contained a contribution that condemned Völkerschauen. The anonymous writer declared: 'We have had Nubian, Negro, Lapplander [Saami], Patagonian shows and other interesting people will no doubt be sent, or rather our animal-trader on his extended travels will know how to find some "human beings" who will let themselves be influenced to participate.' He went on to observe the melancholy of some Eskimo-women (Inuit) on display, and wondered what they thought of their 'highly educated European brothers', concluding that 'exhibiting humans is shameful, especially in zoos. Scientists measure and put into tables everything, without difference – but what is gained from this?'[19] In defence of the classificatory project, Virchow responded that it was about the most important and biggest questions, 'how man fits into nature'.

Specific exchanges between showmen and scientists were not isolated incidents; they were indicative of the interlayering of these two spheres of operation – popular and scientific. For instance, Cunningham obtained 'certificates as to their [the Aborigines] being what they are represented' from eminent 'Professors' throughout Europe.[20] Most anthropologists regarded the showmen's initiative in touring groups of indigenous performers as advantageous for their special field of study, and most instructive for the general public.

In the many cities where the Aboriginal troupe performed, the journalists mainly regurgitated the press releases that emphasised the sensational, although, particularly in the provinces, they occasionally reported more perceptively and critically. Similarly, although some of the anthropologists who interviewed the Aborigines also acknowledged that death would be the probable end to their European exposure, in sum, the frequency of news reports about these shows of indigenous people played their part in consolidating derogatory attitudes towards non-Europeans. For instance a scanning of just the *Illustrirte Zeitung* from 1882 to 1885 revealed articles on a number of Völkerschauen in Germany such as the Kalmucks, Singalese, Araukarians, Australian Aborigines (1882 and 1884), Sioux, Samojedan, Zulu and Tierra del Fuegians, as well as coverage on colonial life in Papua New Guinea, New Britain and West Africa, on the Maori, and on popular anthropology – Krao, physiognomy and tattooing.[21] A scan of the *Illustrated London News*, and French illustrated journals, particularly *Le Tour du Monde* (from 1885) and *Le Nature*, show a similar interest in colonial affairs and exotic people. By the 1880s many more Europeans also had firsthand experience of the defeated indigenous inhabitants of the colonies or had read geographical accounts and travellers' tales that fostered stereotypic attitudes. Moreover, all these forms of representation were influenced by the language formulated by the new science, anthropology, that shaped the discourse about the differences between human types, ranking them on a ladder of cultural stages that placed the hunter-gatherer societies like the 'Patagonians, Eskimos, Bushmen, Veddas, Laplanders, Australians' at the lowest level of human development (discussed by Virchow in the epigraph to the next chapter).

By the time Cunningham arrived in Europe with his Australian troupe, the public appetite for displays of indigenous people was well established, and he, like a number of other independent impresarios, was able to take advantage of the situation. In America, although the mass spectacle of the circus provided a contrast to the more intimate surroundings of the dime museum, both institutions were part of the same entertainment economy, in which the relationship between the performers and the public was marked by a distancing that fostered stereotypic attitudes. By contrast, in Europe, while many touring groups – particularly those managed by Hagenbeck – were shown in zoos and other large-scale venues where audiences were also rated in the thousands, they provided popular rather than mass entertainment. Cunningham's Australians were only sometimes shown in such places. Their extensive European tour was mainly of smaller places of entertainment where the audience was reckoned in hundreds or even fewer. In such show places, they were hardly separated from the public. Often there was no more than a light rail between them and the onlookers and, in the cabaret setting of some of the show places in Germany and Scandinavia, there was not even that – marking a shift from distance to an intimacy of sorts in the cross-cultural encounter that made for variation in response. While they were in America, Toby, Billy and the others had been transformed into professional show people; in Europe they honed their performance skills. To be successful they had to entertain.

6   Palaces of Illusion and Scientific Discipline

Patagonians, Eskimos, Bushmen, Veddas, Laplanders, Australians, Polynesians, Melanesians; about many of them we really know more than of European nations . . . All these uncivilised nations, which stand so low in their mental development, are becoming known to us. Of most of them we have in Europe good typical examples, concerning whom the most exact observations in respect of their whole organisation have been made. Not a few of these died in Europe, and on that account were more specially noticed. We possess greater knowledge concerning the brains of a Patagonian than about the brains of the civilised nations of Asia.

Rudolf Virchow, 'Anthropology in the last twenty years', 1889

Cunningham's departure from America in the spring of 1884 with his troupe of North Queenslanders appears to have been precipitate but whether or not it was forced on him by the circumstances of the two deaths among them, or was a planned decision, his arrival in England marked the beginning of his independent enterprise. The title of the English edition of his pamphlet, *History of R. A. Cunningham's Australian Aborigines* – printed in time for the group's first engagement at Crystal Palace, South London – made clear his proprietorial claims.[1] He announced that the theatrical agent, S. A. de Parravicini of 49, Duke Street, St James, was organising a continental tour for him. While in London, he also enlisted the services of an agent and secretary, James Pettitt, who assisted his registration of copyright in both his pamphlet and the photographs he commissioned from Negretti and Zambra (for example, pl. 43) while the group were performing at the Crystal Palace (pp. 16–18). When he toured the continent Cunningham continued to hire assistance from time to time, but he also exercised his own skills as an advance agent, and in public relations.

For Billy and his companions, the vast and glittering spaces of the Crystal Palace replaced the tented arena of the American circus. Gone was

43   Sussy in boots. Photograph: Negretti and Zambra, Crystal Palace, London. Another photograph of Sussy wearing shoes was taken at the same session.

the smell of sawdust and animals. Here was the scent of acacias and towering Australian blue gums that were planted the length of the central nave. The week they spent within the warm Winter Garden of the Crystal Palace, surrounded by the giant tree ferns of their homeland, would have provided some respite from the rigours of their winter tour of the tawdry dime museums of North America. Outside, in an English spring, in the parklands of the great palace of glass where they demonstrated their skills with the boomerang, they glimpsed the silent statues of dinosaurs standing on an island in the lake. Perhaps they went into the nearby drum of the rotunda, and stood surrounded by the panoramic depiction of *The Battle of Tel-el Kbir* – in which the British had routed the Egyptians. Between the painted canvas curve of the panorama and the spectators on their central viewing platform there were arranged 'the real tents, weapons, broken carriages, helmets and other impedimenta that provided a lifelike and thrilling representation of some of the horrors of war'.[2] Billy and his companions were caught within Europe's surreal mirroring of distant pasts and foreign spaces. For the onlookers, they were part of the spectacle.

After their close contact in America with other performing groups such as the Nubians and Zulu, who had been similarly displaced by colonial wars, doubtless they were filled with foreboding when they saw the lifelike, but lifeless, modelled figures of tribal people like themselves in the southern transept, 'so arranged as to afford the visitor an opportunity of comparing the physical and social peculiarities of each branch of the great human family'.[3] In this silent company living examples were expendable.

A visit to Crystal Palace was a great day out for all the family: only one shilling on Monday, Tuesday and Thursday; on Wednesday it was seven shillings and sixpence (Wednesday was half-day for the service industries); and on Saturday, a normal working day, it was two shillings and sixpence. For those in search of self-improvement a variety of events competed for their attention. On Monday afternoons, 'ladies' could attend lectures in prehistory, archaeology and anthropology that reached a popular constituency across lines of class and gender that scientific anthropology did not reach. In the entertainment court the main attraction was a 'giant electric microscope' used to show, among other things, samples of different kinds and colours of human skin. The English liked to contextualise their displays of indigenous peoples. The comment of the *London Standard* (28 April 1884) on the group's performance of 'their funeral dances' and 'accomplished boomerang throwing' was that 'although they are described as the lowest type of humanity, [they] seem fairly intelligent.' While the reporter can hardly be said to have confronted his prejudices, he pinpointed an unsettling tension between expectations and appearances that was frequently to characterise other European responses to the Aboriginal performers. First-hand observation competed with stereotypic assumptions.

44 (*above left*) 'Pigmy Earthmen at the Royal Aquarium', a Khoisan group led by N/kon N/Qui and his wife, N'arbecy, presented by the showman Farini, Westminster Aquarium, September 1884.

Competition also came from the show-spaces of central London such as the Westminster Aquarium,[4] where, for the last quarter of the nineteenth century, exotic living curiosities from the colonies were a frequent attraction. Later the same year a family of six 'Bushmen' (Khoisan) were recommended to both 'the pleasure-seeker and the student' (pl. 44). 'These little people from the Kalahari', South Africa, who mimed the hunting of ostrich and leopard, were exhibited by the showman Farini (William Leonard Hunt), who a year earlier had introduced Krao to the British public.[5] As the programme (7 May 1883) for Krao (pl. 45) proclaimed: 'There stood the fair Farini, he had done with an agent and tourist ticket, in a few months, more than poor Darwin had achieved in a lifetime', for she was billed as the Hairy Girl, the 'perfect specimen of the step between man and monkey, supposedly discovered in Laos by the distinguished traveller Carl Bock'.[6] In the last quarter of the nineteenth century, in Europe, as in America, the show-space became a site where science and popular culture were entangled, and where a potent mix of stereotypic ideas about race was brewed. Although the 'anthropological levee' continued to be a form of entertainment until the end of the century, it no longer attracted the British crowds in the numbers that were still drawn to such exotic human exhibitions on the continent. The British expected something more by way of structured entertainment than voyeuristic displays of physical and cultural difference, and in 1887 it came in the form of Buffalo Bill's Wild West Show.

Brussels

Compared with America, on the continent the pace of Cunningham's tour changed; there were seldom performances for one night only and frequently engagements lasted a week or more. Their stay in Brussels, where the Aboriginal performers spent May 1884, gave them their first long respite from constant travelling. The weather was warm, and they gave regular displays of boomerang throwing in Leopold Park. According to Parravicini, they attracted thousands to their daily performances in the Musée du Nord (Cunningham's press cutting, no date or source). During their month's stay, Billy and his companions were in regular contact with two French-speaking anthropologists, E. Houzé and V. Jacques, whose 'minute study' of them, and remarkable report for the Société d'Anthropologie de Bruxelles, tells us so much about them – as individuals, as well as about their names, origins, languages and travel experiences – that I have already drawn on in this account. The anthropologists also noticed that although the Aborigines displayed an independence of spirit, Cunningham seemed to command a 'passive obedience'. Jacques wrote:

> In our first meetings with the Australians it was the same fear and passive submission that was most evident with them; but after a while they displayed more trust and when we parted our relationship had become almost cordial, if I may say. It is right to add that offering little presents contributed greatly to that result; bracelets for the women, cigars and cigar holders for the men, and from time to time a glass of beer to one or other.[7]

The encounter between the anthropologists and the Aborigines, however, went beyond the reciprocal exchange of presents for information and was advanced by the fluency in English of Toby and his companions. Soon they

45 (*facing page, right*) '"Krao" The "Missing Link," A Living Proof of Darwin's Theory of the Descent of Man', broadsheet for show at the Aquarium, Westminster, 23 March 1887.

were adding French words to their vocabulary. Their linguistic competence also underlay a confidence in dealing with inquisitive Europeans. For instance, Jimmy countered a lady's question as to why he wore a nose-bone with the question: 'Why do you have holes in your ears?' But the breakthrough in their relationship with Houzé and Jacques came when they realised the two white men wanted to learn *their* languages. 'The savages lend themselves rather well to that . . .' commented Jacques. 'If for a while we stopped questioning them,' he wrote, 'they would, of their own volition, look for a new object to name for us. They designated it first in English and then in their own language. The whole was accompanied with gestures aimed at making us understand better what they meant.' And, of course, they made it clear that Toby and Jimmy spoke a different language from Billy and Bob (see pp. 20–4). The respect of the anthropologists grew: 'When we did not understand after two, three or four times, they would bend towards us and repeat the word several times quietly in the ear. We quote this fact as a proof of their intelligence and as a way of their reasoning.'[8]

By speaking directly into the ears of the white men the Aborigines were returning the compliment, for according to Walter Roth's ethnographic record of practices in their home-place in Queensland, the Aborigines also regarded the ear as the site of intelligence.[9] Unfortunately, no sooner were Houzé and Jacques beginning 'to grasp the first elements' of how Billy and Toby ' built their sentences' in their different languages, the troupe departed for Germany. 'We are pointing out this lack in our research', they wrote, 'to those who will have the opportunity to see these individuals in one city or another where they will be exhibited.' Regrettably, their scientific colleagues in other countries seem not to have taken up the challenge, although several acknowledged the valuable contribution made by Houzé and Jacques, whose report they had read.

The ease of relationship that grew between the two parties was all the more remarkable when one realises that this was also the first occasion when Billy and his companions were subjected to the 'bizarre instruments' and measuring devices of the anthropological laboratory. At first, wrote Houzé and Jacques, Cunningham tried to persuade them 'that we wanted to write a beautiful big book about them, such as they had already seen', but they only resigned 'themselves to be touched' after Cunningham allowed his own head to be measured with the callipers. They also refused to have any but their upper garments removed for the photographs taken by M. A. de Blochouse, for 'they did admire themselves in their dress.'[10]

On the other hand, the physical examinations they were given resulted in a clear account of the state of health of each of them. 'Listening and tapping', the scientists wrote, 'revealed to us the presence of tubercules among several of them.' Only Billy and Jimmy had normal breathing and respiratory movements. Bob showed signs of 'dullness' at the top right of the chest, and of 'wet sub-crackling rattles under the clavicle'. He also complained of chest pains and produced infected mucous – as did Jenny. Sussy's breathing was very rough, and the child appeared to be the most infected of all. Their conclusion was that 'most of them are infected with pulmonary tuberculosis of diverse degrees'.[11] They also knew from Cunningham that Sussy's husband, Tambo, had also 'died of a chest infection'. Although as early as 1865 a French army surgeon, Jean-Antoine Villemin, had discovered that tuberculosis was transmittable in animals, and the bacillus had been identified in 1882, it was still thought of as a hereditary rather than a communicable disease, whereas in fact it was highly contagious. Although as trained medical men Houzé and Jacques understood the implications of their diagnosis – that it was almost always fatal – they would have assumed there was little to be done. Like AIDS today, TB was identified with death itself. At the same time, the scientists ensured that the Queenslanders were vaccinated against smallpox, as there was a small outbreak of it in the city.

Although Toby and the others grumbled to the anthropologists that Cunningham did not give them the money they earned, they did not ask for help to be free of him or say that they wanted to go home. The usual observation made was that the Aborigines did not understand the value of money, and that when they had it they only spent it on grog and baubles that they carelessly gave away. Their behaviour, Houzé and Jacques suggested, was because Aborigines 'live unconscious of time' and think only of the day.[12] To venture this opinion, even while the anthropologists recognised they did not have a shared language to explore such ideas, betrayed their own limitations in understanding. Nevertheless, something of the way in which Billy and his companions adjusted to the experiences they were having, and sustained themselves from the depths of their own culture, can be abstracted from between the lines of this detailed report on their physical characteristics, bodily measurements, languages and cultural practices, by which positivist science attempted to explain and contain them. So that from the Belgians' report a picture emerges of a group of Aboriginal performers whose responses were indeed focused in the present; who were dignified in their deportment, confident in the performance of new skills as well as traditional ones, happy in each other's company, and proud of their show clothes, and new possessions – which they mostly seem to have purchased for themselves.

While Houzé and Jacques referred to other commentators on the Aborigines, such as missionaries, travellers and their own colleagues, and were keen to interpret their data in support of the polygenetic theories they espoused, at the same time they stressed that their 'ethnographic account' – as distinct from their anthropological measurements – was not meant to be definitive, as they wished only 'to describe some individuals whom chance made available to us. We are happy [they wrote] if we have contributed to making known these unhappy tribes who will live tomorrow only in our books'.[13] In spite of the Belgian anthropologists' responsiveness, in the final analysis their interest was not in the group as individuals but as representatives of their type. Although they had diagnosed the fragile state of the group's health, they did not make it their concern, for was not the whole race condemned to extinction? The presentation of their data to the society lasted ten hours.

In Brussels a favourite fairground pastime was to play a game the locals called Massacre of the Innocents, which involved aiming balls at a row of dolls to make them fall. According to Houzé and Jacques, Toby was so adept at this that he was able to hit each of the twenty-four dolls six times in succession without missing a shot. He marshalled old skills in accuracy of aim and speed of response to win new rewards, but these were only exercised *within* the extraterritorial show-space: they provided no escape from it. The troupe's new life brought new experiences and rewards as well as sorrows and uncertainties that mediated their memories of life before departure.

Castan's Panoptikum, Köln and Berlin

Cunningham was already known in German show circles, and the group's first German engagement was in Köln, an important city in a region that was rapidly being transformed by the development of iron and steel industries. They performed at Castan's Panoptikum, and at the nearby Brauweiler restaurant. As the adoption of the name implied, the panop-

46   Castan's Panoptikum,
Berlin 1884.

tikum (panopticon) aimed at providing an all-embracing view of the
spectacle of life, in the form of exhibitions, dioramas, panoramas, live performances and particularly in tableaux of wax figures.[14] The gruesome
illustration used on the cover of Cunningham's pamphlet was reproduced
as part of the press advertisement, and while in Köln the showman also
had a German edition of the pamphlet printed.[15] He updated it by including more recent news cuttings from the *London Standard* and from the
Kölnische Zeitung, 26 June 1884,[16] where it was reported that Toby, Billy,
Bob and Jimmy gave enthusiastic displays of boomerang-throwing for
huge crowds gathered on 'Müllerheimer Heide'. A heathland that 'has seen
so many other military exercises in the past', wrote the reporter, 'was now
to witness one as performed by the "bushmen" in the deep forests of
Australia'. The event had considerable exotic appeal.

By July, Cunningham's troupe had reached Berlin, which since 1871 had
become the thriving capital of a Germany united under Wilhelm I, with
new machine, textile, electrical and chemical industries and a growing
proletariat. The Queenslanders were to spend the next three months on
show at the Berlin Castan's Panoptikum (pl. 46). Situated in the heart of

the entertainment and shopping district around Friedrichstrasse, a district of showy shops, cafés and bars, it had been established in 1871 by Jean Charles Louis Castan as an anatomical museum. It was a palace of illusion, where representation replaced reality, where the glowing wax figures of the famous and infamous attracted a public longing to be amazed, delighted – and informed – for the price of 50 pfennig for adults, and 25 pfennig for children. Wax was used in earlier centuries to preserve the bodies of saints and other Christian reliques; as Marina Warner has observed, 'its preserving qualities and inner luminosity symbolically challenge the corruption of the flesh and seem to overcome death . . . The illusion induces the dread shiver of wonder.'[17] There was the fictional figure of the consumptive 'Lady of the Camellias', romantically reclining on a couch. The figures of both Bismark and Virchow were there – as was 'Pichocho', one of the three Patagonians procured by Hagenbeck in 1879.[18] The figure of Chang the Chinese giant – whom the Aborigines would have recognised from the American dime museum circuit – was on display, in the clothes worn by Chang himself when exhibited in Berlin in 1883. In nineteenth-century waxworks, the use of real hair, glass eyes (first made in Germany) and items of personal clothing were markers of authenticity.[19] There were also displays of artefacts, and stuffed animals from the newly established colony in the Cameroons, West Africa. Positioned in these surroundings the troupe became the objects of a panoptic gaze that performed a totalising function, through the marking of 'dissymmetry, disequilibrium, difference'.[20] At the same time there seems to have been a space for cross-cultural engagement.

In a series of panoramic sketches of Castan's Panoptikum in *Über Land und Meer* (no. 17, 1884), the artist, Walter Busch, captures both the ambiance of the waxworks and the lively atmosphere of the beer-hall with its elegant clientele. Toby charges glasses with a prosperous Berliner while a lady seizes the moment to steal a lock of his hair from the back of his head, watched by a curious small girl. In the background Billy carves a small circle for himself among the retreating onlookers by swinging his sword club above his head as he whirls about (pl. 47). The panoramic form of the sketch emphasises the seduction of the spectacle. As well as registering the exchange of gaze between performers and onlookers, Busch catches the physicality of their presence, naked to the waist among the fashionably dressed Wilhelmine bourgeoisie – for the summer warmth

47 'Bei den Australnegern', Walter Busch, in *Über Land und Meer. Allgemeine Illustrirte Zietung*, 1885. Toby (centre) and Billy (right) entertain at Castan's Panoptikum Berlin, 1884.

allowed them to shed their restricting body stockings. And by so doing he exposes the subversive element in their presence. Their performances at Castan's attracted a sophisticated audience throughout the long summer season. Professor Rudolf Virchow, who also visited their outdoor exhibition of boomerang-throwing on heathland at Hazenheide (pl. 48) was equally impressed by the 'magnificent gymnastic spectacle' they presented there and the 'absolutely miraculous' flight of the boomerangs – while Cunningham looked on, in relaxed but proprietorial mode, resting on his stick. Toby, Bob, Billy and Jimmy threw their weapons with such enthusiasm until, one day, a boomerang hit a bystander, and the displays were stopped.

Virchow's examination of Cunningham's troupe was their second experience of an anthropological laboratory and, this time, they were more relaxed.[21] Jimmy appointed himself the professor's assistant and positioned each of his companions in turn against the measuring stick. Virchow called him the clown of the group, because he made faces and constantly thought up new gestures and positions. Was he perhaps sending up the illustrious professor? He also busied himself with making drawings of his companions' various body marks. Virchow also observed that he constantly courted the 'Princess' – Sussy, who was 'always dignified'.

48 Boomerang-throwing in Hazenheide, Berlin, artist Georg Koch, in *Illustrirte Zeitung Leipzig und Berlin*, 1884. Toby and his son in background, Billy, Jimmy and Bob centre, Sussy and Jenny on right.

Although the women refused to undress for the professor, they did so for the photographer, Carl Günther, who made the photographs available to the scientist. Sussy, said Virchow, 'could be considered a beauty'. And the women's 'movements are unforced and natural to the highest degree, executed in an even gracious way . . . as if they had gone to the best schools in European society'.

On the other hand, the professor found Billy apathetic and Bob shy, although he admired his 'big gleaming eyes'. As for Toby, whom he described as 'a wild looking strong man', he noted that, although reticent, he 'makes an effort to tell us about life and customs of his homeland' and 'in a moment of familiarity he boasts how many men he has killed', although he says 'he didn't eat them'. Unlike Houzé and Jacques, apart from several anecdotal observations, Virchow did not record ethnographic details, and he made no attempt to extend his colleagues' valuable linguistic enquiries. His concern was to make cranial and body measurements that would contribute data to his classificatory project, and to develop a comparative physiognomy that would establish a range of physical – and perhaps racial – types. It involved close scrutiny of significant parts of the body such as the nose, forehead and chin – to establish correspondences between external features and inner skeletal structures. In practice, physiognomic observation was a highly subjective exercise in which physical attributes were read as indicative of character, class and race, and practised as much in the streets and drawing rooms of the European metropoles as in their laboratories.[22] Virchow's reading was that although Toby's family exhibits a 'lightheartedness', in a moment 'the facial expression is completely changed, even changed to the sinister.' His conclusion was that 'one cannot overcome the thought that between us and those people, complete trust is difficult to achieve'.[23] Again, there is a tension between his observations and his scientific views. Thus, although he did not propose a hierarchy of races, Virchow's own cultural assumptions about European superiority led him to use expressions such as 'low mental development' and 'lower races'. At the same time he believed absolutely in the unity of humankind and the universal capacity for mental development, and rejected the attempts of others to 'animalise the savage'. Of the Aboriginal performers examined by him he wrote: 'I can only say with full conviction that anybody who has observed the comings and goings of these people could not possibly come to the conclusion that they are nearer the apes than us . . . they are definitely true humans.' In referring briefly to the treatment of Aborigines in the Australian colonies he added 'I am convinced this race has been denied the initiative for independent development.'[24]

In thanking Herr Castan for the opportunity to look at 'these rare strangers', Virchow made an unequivocal defence of Völkerschauen that was in line with his earlier response to the *Magdeburger Zeitung*'s unfavourable criticism of the practice in 1880 (see p. 118).

> The persistence of members of the public who make daily pilgrimage to see the Australians is a visible sign of appreciation. It proves that those who condemn exhibitions are not right when they state that these only serve curiosity. It surely will further the understanding of nature and history of the people and will become the duty of science to have more understanding and for deeper questions to be asked concerning the Australian Aborigines in order to inform a wider public.[25]

To be blunt, Virchow's commitment to empirical techniques of survey and measurement depended on a supply of bones and bodies (alive and dead) (pl. 49). And the contradiction between the humanitarian feelings

49   Professor Rudolf
Virchow surrounded by
skeletal material in the
Institute for Pathology,
University of Berlin.

he expressed and the 'callous scientific ultilitarianism' he and his colleagues practised exposes the ambiguity of his position.[26] Soon, in German
scientific circles, Virchow's humanitarian liberalism and the scientific
sterility of his methodology were both to be displaced by the growing
ascendancy of the Darwinian paradigm, with its emphasis on the struggle
for life and natural selection, so that the differences between 'savage' and
'civilised' were seen as an outcome of a proposed hierarchical structure of
human development. This ideology had not only shaped much scientific
endeavour elsewhere, it had also already found expression in colonial
aggression towards the indigenous, and underwrote the popular cultural
attitudes to class and race that belonged to the social formation of late
nineteenth-century capitalism. In due course such ideas opened the way to
'scientific racism'.[27]

The presentation of the 'Australians from Queensland' made at a sitting
of the Berlin Society for Anthropology, Ethnology and Prehistory on 19
July was well attended and given coverage in a number of Berlin papers. It
was a scientific spectacle that paralleled the spectacle of the show-space,

and formed part of the same totalising regime. The Berlin press also provided a rare glimpse of the off-stage life of Toby and the group, which the reporter found 'not less interesting than watching them at their show' (*Berliner Börsen-Courier*, 8 Aug. 1884). Revealing in its descriptive detail, the article raises a number of issues relating to the Aborigines' treatment, their relationship with Cunningham, and German attitudes towards them, and to Völkerschauen generally, that demand further investigation. For the sake of clarity I have paraphrased while adhering as close as possible to the German text:

Mr Cunningham, who is described as 'the leader, friend and protector of the seven minors', invites the journalists back to the flat of the 'cannibals' after their morning show. It is a porter's flat, partly below street level, which has a window onto the passage so that all who come and go can be seen. When the journalists arrive the Australians are already seated at a table, covered with a white cloth, being waited on by a servant. It seems 'they are not delighted at all by the intrusion. They put down forks and knifes with a gesture of obvious indignation and protest in their own language against the violation of their privacy.' Speaking in English, Cunningham prevails on them to allow 'the gentlemen of the press' to join their 'distinguished company', and when his 'nice words' are supplemented by a 'generous distribution of tobacco' these 'basically very good-natured creatures' calm down.

The reporter then describes their meal of rice, meat and water, and their use of cutlery, which he suggests is because of Cunningham's presence, for surely they would prefer to use their fingers. He compares the food with their diet in their home country of wild fruits, roots and every large and small animal that they could catch – including 'the grilled meat of the enemies they killed'. He gains the impression from Cunningham 'who has studied these savage people for already thirty years' that as long as there is a enough food 'next to his bed' the savage won't bother to hunt.

After dinner, all except Toby and Bob rest on mattresses covered with white sheets, and light up their pipes. Sussy and Jenny particularly praise the new tobacco. Toby and Bob go into the neighbouring room, used as a storeroom for the Panoptikum, and begin to carve boomerangs, 'with eagerness and earnestness', using the wood of the birch tree. Toby uses a little axe, which he grasps not by the handle but by the blade, to shape the form of the boomerang. Then he carves it with pieces of glass from a broken bottle. The two men are seated next to each other on the floor, and hum with enjoyment a monotonous melody. They reject the 'proper' tools, which would make their work easier. They say that there is no better tool than broken glass, and that even in their homeland they use pieces of glass. The reporter adds: 'You will find old bottles all over the world, even in places where the white man never set foot. Bottles were washed ashore on the tide, and for the savages they are the most useful product of the sea. The Aboriginals from Australia to Alaska, from Patagonia to the Tonga-Islands use the glass of broken bottles as a tool, as a knife, as arrowheads.'

After working for an hour, two boomerangs are finished. It seems that Billy has joined the other two because the reporter writes that 'we observed how Billy and big Toby, while working, took up some shavings and blew on them. Old Toby told us that this is an absolutely necessary procedure, otherwise the boomerangs would not return to the thrower.'

Although the *Börsen-Courier*'s report contained a not unexpected mix of confident misinformation (supplied by Cunningham) and reporter's misapprehension about Aboriginal customs, it refreshingly eschewed the usual savage clichés. The group were described as 'cannibals', but there is only a passing reference to the grilled meat of their enemies – a much more restrained mention than in the many other news reports, whose references to cannibalism were calculated to titillate. And contrary to their categorisation as being childlike ('minors'), the article demonstrates that Toby, Billy and the others learnt to assert their rights to privacy and to determine how they would use their free time. Throughout their travels, Toby and Jenny have shown themselves to be nurturing parents, shielding their son from adult demands. Yet even young Toby has learnt to protect himself, and to retaliate when put upon (pl. 50). According to the *Berliner Tagblatt* (undated cutting), when the young servant girl, Henriette, pours kitchen water over him, and he stabs her arm with a kitchen knife, causing her to be taken to hospital, apparently he is not rebuked.

The *Börsen-Courier*'s article also heightens our awareness of the adjustments the group had made to their new life and work, while at the same

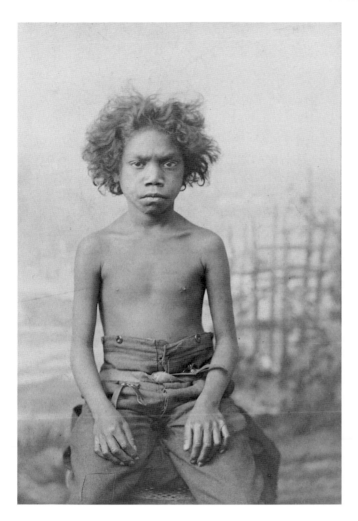

50   The boy, Toby, Paris, 1885. Photograph: Prince Roland Bonaparte.

time integrating traditional pursuits into their activities. Their exchange of words with Cunningham suggests they had arrived at a state of easy communication and mutual understanding. But the news item also raises questions about when they began to manufacture boomerangs, and how they came by the birch wood? Were the weapons made for use or for sale as souvenirs? If for sale, did they keep the money – as they did with the sale of the pamphlets and photographs? From Carl Günther's photographs, it

51   (L to r) Billy, R. A. Cunningham, Jenny, Toby, his son, Toby, Jimmy, Sussy (seated) and Bob reclining. Photograph: Carl Günther, Berlin, 1884.

seems they may have also manufactured their own spears while in Germany, and somewhere in German ethnographic collections there may be examples of their work (pl. 51).[28] Certainly their demonstrations of the art of boomerang-throwing created a craze in Germany. A few years later in California, Cunningham clipped a news item from the *Daily Alta* referring to Weimar manufacturers of 11,000 toy boomerangs (26 Feb. 1888).

Apart from providing the journalists with interesting copy, Cunningham may well have had his own agenda for inviting them to see his troupe's living conditions. While his exploitation of them is not in question, for his style of enterprise to succeed he needed their collaboration and to that end – and also it seems his own inclinations – he treated them as professional entertainers. Although their show clothes were outward signs of their role as performers, it was these clothes that caused some people, particularly in Germany, to question their authenticity. For instance, Virchow prefaced the account of his examination of the Australians by stating that Cunningham's 'elaborations... have to be ignored because of the fantastic costumes worn by the group', and also on account of the presentation of Tagarah (Sussy) 'as princess and daughter of the King of North Queensland [when] every knowledgeable person knows what is to be believed regarding that King'. That is to say, the claim was a fiction. Although the professor discounted Cunningham as an informant, he went on to establish the troupe's Aboriginal authenticity to his own satisfaction, by his own scientific methods.

Carl Hagenbeck's approach was very different. He sought to show Völkerschauen in a culturally 'uncontaminated' state, and when they were hunter-gatherers like the Aborigines, Fuegians or the Inuit, the effect within a zoo environment was dehumanising. For instance, in the case of the eleven Kaweshkar Fuegians (in 1881–2), it meant that they were shown in the skins they customarily wore, except that the men were issued with swimming trunks for the sake of decency. As the showmen could not communicate verbally with the group, they named them arbitrarily – two of the younger children being offensively called 'Frosch' (frog) and 'Dickkopf' (thick-head). Although Hagenbeck may not have intended to be cruel – for he described himself as a 'philanthropist' with regard to Völkerschauen – in practice the treatment the Kaweshkar received at the hands of the man he employed as their manager, Herr Terne, was most inhuman. After their successful Paris season, he dispatched them by freight-wagon on a twenty-seven-hour journey to Berlin, with 60 kilograms of half-rare beef, 40 litres of mussels and some water to sustain them. On arrival they were housed in the ostrich house at the Berlin zoo, where they cooked the beef left over from the trip. The news reports of them ripping the meat apart were so sensational that over two weeks the crowds increased until – on one day – they peaked at 37,000 plus. The 'fire-landers' retreated into their inner room; mayhem ensued, and the police had to restore order before they would reappear.[29] Surely, it is not surprising that when they departed from Berlin in early December, five already displayed respiratory symptoms. Regardless of their ill health, the tour continued via Leipzig, München, Stuttgart and Nürnberg to Zürich, where death, followed by dissection, was to be their fate.[30] It is more likely than not that this scandalous incident was discussed widely in show circles and therefore was known to Cunningham, who may have wanted to make known his different attitudes.

Without more detailed biographical work on the different indigenous touring groups, it would be difficult to assess the part ill-treatment – as distinct from their vulnerability to European diseases – played in the deaths of so many. As in the appalling case of the Karweshkar Fuegians – some of whom already had tuberculosis when they contracted measles in Zürich – bad treatment must have frequently increased the likelihood of succumbing to infection. One case that should be mentioned, however, is that recorded by Abraham, one of a party of 'Eskimo' (Inuit from Labrador, Canada) in 1880, who seems to have been the only member of an indigenous touring group to keep a diary. In it he tells how Jacobsen beat one of his companions, Tobias, with a dog whip for refusing to do what he was asked. Jacobsen also failed to have the Inuit vaccinated for smallpox until three of them had died of it. Then he had the remaining five vaccinated, but it was too late; they also died, including Abraham, whose Inuit-language diary survived.[31]

Although the Aboriginal travellers were not physically ill-treated, there were other experiences that were bound to cause them anxiety. According to another report in the *Berliner Börsen-Courier*, on 8 August 1884, Billy and Jimmy made a visit to the ethnological department of Berlin's Royal Museum at the suggestion of Professor Bastian. There they took 'apparent delight' in identifying various Aboriginal artefacts in the collection – boomerangs, clubs, message sticks, fire-making implements and bowls – for Dr Grünwedel and Dr Grube, until they were abruptly brought to a halt by the sight of a mummified Aborigine, folded, with knees drawn up to the chin – in a manner sometimes practised in their own districts – and wrapped in matting and bark. Apparently, the collector had 'found' it hanging on a tree in Queensland. It is not surprising that Billy and Jimmy were 'petrified' by it: they would have been fearful that the spirit was still in attendance, for all deaths were caused either by nature-spirits or spirits of the dead, who could be invoked by name, especially by medicine men.[32] Surely, for them, nothing could have been more convincing proof of the long reach of Europeans, and their power. It was also a reminder of the recent deaths of two of their number in America. If Cunningham was with them – as he almost certainly was – and saw their reaction, he would surely have been reminded of the mummified Tambo. According to press reports, Bob – who was not with them – was already ill with an inflammation of the lungs and pleurisy, although he was said to be getting better. The summer season in Berlin was over and it was time to move on.

I am reminded again of the Brussels fairground game, the Massacre of the Innocents, at which Toby was so adept. In European art and literature, the portrayal of King Herod's Massacre of the Innocents has great metaphoric power that is surely as applicable to the destruction of Toby's kin in North Queensland as to the destruction of the Flemish peasants by the Spaniards in Pieter Bruegel the elder's great painting. Yet, in a disconcerting reversal, Toby's skill in knocking down the dolls – the Innocents – identifies him with the slaughterers. Trapped in this extraterritorial show-space, he and his companions are the 'savages' and 'cannibals', enacting European fantasies in a performance that is destroying them.

7   'Rare Strangers'

They converse with ease with strangers and adapt to alien conditions with
interest, they observe the new surroundings and people and form an opin-
ion about them which they clearly show with their behaviour and partly by
uttering remarks in pidgin English.

Rudolf Virchow, 'Australier von Queensland', 1884

In September–October 2000 I made a journey through Germany by train,
centred in turn on each of three cities where one of Cunningham's troupe
died: Bob in Chemnitz, Jimmy in Darmstadt and Sussy in Sonnborn
(Wuppertal). Travelling from west to east, I thus came to Chemnitz last,
although Bob had been the first of the group to die in Germany. I knew
Bob had died there because Professor Rudolf Virchow had mentioned it in
a footnote to his scientific paper, 'Australier von Queensland'. Apparently
he had been able to add the bare detail before the 1884 volume of the Berlin
Society for Anthropology went to press.

I arrived in Chemnitz in early autumn, as did the group almost 120 years
earlier. As the countryside flashed past I wrote in my diary:

These travelling days I am thinking again about parallel journeys – theirs
and mine – surrounded by speakers of other languages, learning to com-
municate multi-lingually. Sustained by my own thoughts and goals, I am
haunted too by what I have just learnt about the deaths of Jimmy and
Sussy, and know those thoughts will shape my questions about Bob.

In the first days of October 1884 the *Chemnitzer Tageblatt* announced the
troupe's arrival in ads two columns in width. Sharing the billing with two
African-American clowns and other vaudeville turns, they were to be seen
for the next fortnight at the Mosella Hall, twice daily, morning and afternoon, and again in the evening in a show place called the Tunnel – a total
of eight hours. At 25 pfennig, the entrance was half the price of Berlin. This
was the provinces. In spite of the group's customary categorisation as

Austral Ureinwohner (Aborigines) and Menschenfresser (man-eaters) in the ads, the newspaper's reports (between 4 and 22 October) were moderate in tone rather than sensational. The public were rather mildly recommended to see 'these most uncultivated people . . . here in Chemnitz whom we have never had before.' The reasons given were 'their ethnographic rarity' and the show's educational value. At the same time the reporter found it hard to reconcile their attractive appearance and manners with 'something appalling in the lives of these savages', namely their cannibalism. Especially as 'they have also already learnt some German words, which they use very often and with great liking.' There is often a raw honesty about these German provincial reports, where, although much of the language used is still stereotypic, appearances are seen to challenge received prejudices.

Chemnitz, with a population of about 100,000 at that time, was a manufacturing city and the economic hub of Saxony. Although most of the population were piece-workers in the cloth manufacturing industry who worked at home, there were also outlanders: Russians, Jews and Macedonians who were traders and linen and cotton merchants. There was no high culture; the middle classes joined gourmet clubs and the Freemasons. For light entertainment, they patronised the Mosella Hall, which was part of a property development in Hauptpoststrasse undertaken by a Herr Bayreuther who had made his money in mining in the Ore Mountains south of the city. The site has long since been obliterated by road development, but many similar buildings from the period – consisting of four or five floors around a central courtyard – characterise Chemnitz today. To make the hall, Bayreuther had the courtyard roofed with cast iron and glass, transforming it into an elegant space surrounded by galleries on two floors and a stage at one end. Again it was a space where the public and performers were in close contact.

Death in Chemnitz

On 14 October the morning performance was cancelled to enable 'a number of local doctors' headed by the Royal District Doctor, Maximilian Flinzer,[1] Professor of Medicine, to examine Toby and his troupe. From the news report published two days later, it seems the doctors had wanted to include in their extensive measurements the testing of muscle strength and

52   Bob. Photograph: Carl Günther, Berlin, 1884.

lung capacity, because they were amazed by the Aborigines' lack of calf and arm muscle. But the Aborigines refused. The reporter surmised that these 'absolutely harmless people were frightened and, at the same time, the doctors were afraid of being attacked by them' (*Chemnitzer Tageblatt*).

What was different about this session as compared with the previous examinations by Houzé and Jacques and Virchow? Although there are recorded instances of other indigenous people being terrorised by the anthropologists' measuring instruments, a contributory factor was usually the lack of verbal or any other form of communication.[2] For their part, Toby and the group were experienced, able to communicate and quite prepared to make their objections clear. Because on this occasion they were described as 'absolutely harmless', it seems unlikely that their refusal was enough to frighten the doctors. The most likely scenario is that Bob (pl. 52), who six months earlier in Brussels had presented the most advanced symptoms of tuberculosis, was by then seriously ill, and had either been or was about to be hospitalised. Given their earlier encounter in Berlin with the mummified body, and Aboriginal beliefs about the causes of death, it does not require a great leap of the imagination to recognise the tensions that would have been generated by the Chemnitz doctors' attentions. It was eight months since Tambo's death in America, and the excitement of the intervening months had probably helped them to put thoughts of it behind them. Unfortunately, Chemnitz news reports of any detail cease after that date, except for the mention on 22 October that the Aboriginal season will be continued 'by special request' – though it does not say for how long. Silence descends. Although Bob dies on 7 November, the *Chemnitzer Tageblatt*'s listing of local deaths between 2 and 8 November, published on the 11th, does not include Bob's death. Nor does it appear in later listings.

As with the second death in America eight months earlier, the trail goes cold. The next date and place I have for the group is nine weeks later in January 1885.

In September 2000, in search of Bob's story, I meet the Chemnitz Director of Cemeteries, who, in anticipation of my coming, has a photocopy of the registration of Bob's death.[3] In translation, item 3070 reads:

Chemnitz, 8 November 1884.

The undersigned officer of the Registry Office today received from the
local City Hospital the written confirmation that
the Nigger Bob,
said to have been 32 years old, of heathen religion,
and temporarily resident in Chemnitz,
born in Queensland, Australia – whether married or not is unknown
died in Chemnitz City Hospital
on 7 November 1884, 10.15 am.

See also Collected Records page 69, Vol. IV

Registry Officer: 'Weiss'[signed][4]

It seems no other documentation has survived, because the cemetery records were destroyed in the Second World War. But the director gives me a map showing the plot where the pauper burials took place between 1883 and 1885. Then he drives my interpreter and me to section 3 of the cemetery. It is a pleasant spot, a small stretch of uneven grass that is no longer used for burials. He explains that when the cemetery was established in 1873 soil tests were made, and it was decided that reburial could take place on the same plot after intervals of twenty years, by which time the remains, including bones, would have been absorbed into the ground. But the rate decreases with successive burials, and after three uses this plot was closed.[5] He has his Polaroid camera with him and he provides me with an instant print of the plot. I sense this is something he has done many times before. Certainly his reassuring manner would ease the pain for most people in search of the remains of their loved ones and ancestors. I hesitate to unsettle him by suggesting that his explanation leaves too many questions unanswered. He is a practical man of good will, but without the confirmation of cemetery records or other documentation, doubts about

Bob's interment must remain. Later, I return to the plot on my own and sit in the late afternoon sunshine thinking about what happened to Tambo, and about the scientists' appropriation of other indigenous bodies, particularly those of the Fuegians only several years earlier – and about the German propensity to keep careful records.

Next day I returned to the Registry Office in search of the death certificate. As I had already learnt that the records in some other German cities had a column where alternative methods of disposal of the body could be registered, I was keen to see what was on page 69. But it seemed the volume had not survived and anyway, I was told, it would have no more information because of the assertion that 'this document conforms to the main register'. If it had survived, what might it have said?

Every hospital kept a register of persons admitted which recorded the name, age and condition of each, as well as noting religious belief and dwelling place for the last two years. It also noted who transferred the patient to hospital and who paid the expenses (relative, master or poor chest), date of admission, character of illness, date of discharge or death. As only some of these details were included on Bob's death certificate, I hoped the health records would supply them. But apparently the relevant health records have not survived either.[6]

In fact, management of public health in Germany was centralised and professionalised progressively from the mid-nineteenth century on, and although after 1871 it continued to be mainly the responsibility of the constituent federal states, the Reich Health Office had a limited monitoring and coordinating role. From 1883 on, Bismark introduced legislation for the establishment of sickness and accident funds to provide treatment for the working classes, which gradually set the pattern for state-regulated social welfare. Nevertheless, hospitals were open to all – paupers, Jews, heathens[7]. Among the practices that were systematised early was the supply of bodies – of the unclaimed poor from the hospitals, dying prisoners, suicides, 'common' women (prostitutes) and the otherwise institutionalised – to the anatomy theatres for dissection, so that the grave-robbing so prevalent in English-speaking countries was almost unknown.[8] The interest in Bob's body, however, would have been for scientific rather than practical medical reasons.

The Royal District Doctor, Flinzer, was a medical official of some standing whose duties included the promotion of public health, the initiation of measures against epidemics and oversight of the relief of the sick and the poor[9]. In fact, Flinzer had acquired an international reputation for his statistical analysis of a smallpox epidemic in Chemnitz in 1871–2,[10] so it is to be supposed that he was equally alert to the latest information about tuberculosis, whose cause had been so recently established by his compatriot Robert Koch. Flinzer certainly had the authority to make a request for Bob's body, but I have not found evidence that he did so. If he had, presumably he would have wished to add to his medical reputation by publishing the results. The medical fraternity were not reticent about such matters. For instance, when the Kaweshkar Fuegians, toured by Hagenbeck (see chapter 5) died in Zürich in 1882 there was a circulation of the body parts among the scientists. Professor H. V. Meyer dissected two of the women in Zürich, and then sent the reproductive organs and other parts to Professor Bischoff of the Bavarian Academy who specialised in women's anatomy – and who had been particularly frustrated when the Fuegian women had refused to allow him to examine the genitals of themselves or their small children while they were in München earlier. In death they could not oppose him. At Virchow's suggestion, Bischoff also examined the woman's digestive organs in search of adaptations to their 'animalistic' methods of feeding. Later, pieces of their skin were exchanged in search of evidence of adaptations to the harsh climate. Finally the skeletons were deposited with Zürich University. It seems that because of the distribution of the body parts a grave was not deemed necessary or feasible.[11] The Fuegians were disposed of as if they were animals. At the time, none of this activity on the part of the scientists would have been considered a reason for opposing the shows of indigenous people, any more than fear of public dissection of bodies in anatomy theatres would have prevented the practice in those instances where the procurement was sanctioned by law. Indeed, the increasing activity of burial societies in Germany was later to create a shortage of bodies.[12]

In the light of these instances it is perhaps significant that Virchow's footnote to his account of the Australians refers only to Bob's death in Chemnitz and makes no mention of any acquisition of the body. The professor's reputation was such that, as the examiner of the living Bob, he would have had the first scientific claim on his body. Later, in Berlin, I see the most recent list of remaining holdings of Australian skeletal remains in the collection of the Anthropological Institute, Humbolt University, that incorporates the Virchow collection of the Berlin Society for Anthropology. The professor received his 'specimens' from collectors in

Australia, and there are none that can be identified as having belonged to any of the Aborigines taken on tour in Europe, by Cunningham or others.[13] Similarly, there are no skeletal or body part remains in the Museum für Naturkunde, Chemnitz.

The weight of probabilities begins to support the proposition that Bob was buried, and rested undisturbed, in Chemnitz, but without more conclusive evidence the case must remain open. I am also haunted by other unanswered questions. Did Cunningham allow Bob's companions to stay on with him until he died, or did Bob die alone?

When Cunningham's troupe arrived in Breslau, some distance to the north-east, more than two months had passed. I have searched for them closer to Chemnitz, particularly Dresden, but Hagenbeck had shown the Fraser Island Aborigines at Dresden Zoo only the year before, in 1883, and it was his territory. In spite of the uncertainty about their whereabouts, they must have performed somewhere over the Christmas season, and there were still six of the group alive when the *Breslauer Morgen-Zeitung* of 20 January 1885 greeted the 'Urbewohner' (indigenous) from Australia at the Victoria Theatre as 'our black neighbours'. They were so called because only a few days earlier 'the German flag was raised on New Britain and New Ireland' to Australia's north-east, and 'the question of the colonies is the main topic everywhere.' The writer was disinclined to believe that the Aboriginal performers were cannibals because they were 'calm, modest, even cautious, and nobody needs to be afraid of them'. Nor should it be thought, he advised, that their performance is immoral or offensive to women. Don't miss the opportunity to see these 'rare strangers'.

In February Cunningham's troupe turned south again, to Halle, in Saxony-Anhalt, a small city with a renowned medical faculty, where another anthropological inspection was carried out by Professor Alfred Kirchhoff, from whom Cunningham extracted yet another letter of authentication. For the following two months Cunningham toured a number of small towns and cities that provided access to recreational activities in the Harz mountains: Nordhausen, Halberstadt, Magdeburg, Quedinburg, Aschersleben and Sangerhausen in Saxony-Anhalt, and Gotha, Erfurt, Eisenach and Mühlhausen with access to the wooded Thüringer Wald resorts. They arrived at Göttingen in Lower Saxony in April. More than any other part of the German tour this section was a sig-

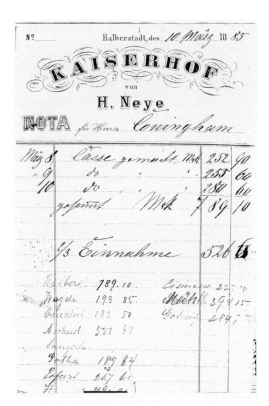

53   Note on takings for Mr
Cunningham, Kaiserhof Hotel,
Halberstadt, Germany, 10
March 1885. From
Cunningham's cuttings book.

nificant indication of Cunningham's touring skills and style. The average
engagement was two or three days and the venues were mostly restaurants
or small places of entertainment. For instance in Nordhausen, Toby and
his troupe performed at the 'Zum Dom' to a 'huge audience' and supplemented their performance there with a display of boomerang-throwing
round one of the town's chimneys – apparently with the encouragement
of Professor Kirchhoff, who was with them.[14]

Some of the evidence for this part of the tour comes from a singular
document in Cunningham's scrapbook (pl. 53), a fragmentary and roughly
annotated account from 'Kaiserhof', Halberstadt, dated 10 March 1885, listing the takings for three days of performance as totalling 789.10 marks. On
the next line is written '2/3 of the takings, 526.0 marks'. As it is addressed
to Cunningham, presumably two-thirds represents his share of the tak-

ings. Beneath that is another rough list of the towns mentioned above, again headed by Halberstadt, and against all but one is a figure representing the total takings. Without knowing the admission charge it is difficult to make much of these figures, but assuming it was the provincial rate of 25 pfennig, this represents an average audience of just over a 1,000 for each of the Halberstadt days. Without knowing the number of days covered by each of the other figures it is not possible to arrive at average audience sizes. 'Huge' is obviously a relative term, but given the relatively small sizes of these communities it seems applicable. An accompanying sheet bears the scribbled information:

Annonc. (advertisement) 12 mks.,
Saal (hall) 20 mks.,
Casse (ticket office) 6 mks.,
Leiter (master of ceremonies) 6 mks.

Compared with the box office receipts at zoos or large entertainment establishments, these takings are modest amounts which, as well as covering the itemised expenses, also had to cover daily accommodation, sustenance and care, travel and advance planning, assistance, and any other personal expenditure by Cunningham and his troupe of six. It is so difficult to recover the details of earnings that I have included these figures in spite of their fragmentary nature – and in spite of the difficulty of using them comparatively because of the variability of German statistics for wages and prices of the period.[15] How much went directly to the performers is unknown.

Death in Darmstadt

It was a wonderfully hot day and we walked through the cemetery until we came to the section III J. The letters were inscribed on metal plates situated at each corner of the field. Quite beautiful. So somewhere in this field Jimmy was laid to rest – the laughing and joking had stopped for him – maybe it had been a day much like this, for it had been summertime. I sat and thought about Jimmy and the others; Jimmy who had started it all when I found the record of his death in the British Registry Office.

(Author's diary, 15 Sept. 2000, Darmstadt)

The arrival of Cunningham's troupe in Darmstadt, capital of Hesse, did not create much of a stir among the cultivated Hessians, for they were used to more celebrated visitors. Queen Victoria's daughter Alice was married to the Grand Duke, and on that same day the Queen arrived for her grandson's confirmation. Billy and his companions performed for ten days in the Music Hall of the 'Saalbau' and gave several demonstrations of boomerang-throwing at the Festplatz, a parade ground and site for fairs on the main route to Frankfurt. On 5 May 1885 Queen Victoria departed, and the same day the troupe moved to Frankfurt, leaving Jimmy behind in the city hospital. Frankfurt is only 35 kilometres away and there are several indications that Cunningham kept in close touch, perhaps even by telephone, which was beginning to be installed in Darmstadt that month.

In Frankfurt the troupe had their first engagement in a zoological gardens. The *Frankfurter Zeitung* (6 May) decided they were more primitive and less interesting than a much larger party of 'Singalese' dancers who had recently visited, and the *Kleine Presse* (10 May) noted that the Aborigines were reduced to five as one was in hospital. The Frankfurters were also surprised by their linguistic skills, and condescended that, remarkably, 'they had retained something of their original customs' despite the years since they left home (*Frankfurter Zeitung*, 13 May). The *Kleine Presse* followed up the next day with 'A bit of fakery [Mumpitz] is always present, and therefore these English-speaking Queensland cannibals probably know as little about what human flesh tastes like as we do.' The reporter also noted a certain reluctance in their manner: 'cowering under a woollen blanket on the podium, they gave the impression that our month of May is very unpleasant for them', until they stood up to show the weals on their bare torsos, 'with bowed heads'. 'Willi' (Billy) alone is 'livelier' and 'answers questions put to him in English . . . each time saying reassuringly, "I do know"'. In the accompanying sketches of them, the ironic tone of the report tilts towards caricature (pl. 54). In the central grouping, Billy, Sussy and Jenny – who is wearing a matronly hat – look very glum, and in another Sussy holds up photographs for sale,[16] while the others huddle, wrapped in coats, clapping pairs of boomerangs together as they sing. On the day that their Frankfurt engagement is extended to 27 May, the *Darmstädter Tagblatt* (21 May) reports that they have heard the Aborigines were too drunk to perform. Not surprisingly, they are no

54 'Australneger in Frankfurt am Main', *Kleine Presse*, 14 May 1885. Centre, Jenny, Billy and Sussy, foreground, Sussy sells photographs, young Toby throws boomerangs, left corner group, Billy, Toby, young Toby and Jenny.

longer the ebullient performers of earlier occasions; Jimmy is dying in hospital and Sussy is growing weaker.

They move on again. Their next six-day engagement is in nearby Wiesbaden, at the popular entertainment place, Saalbau Nerothal, and while they are there they learn of Jimmy's death in Darmstadt. The *Wiesbadener Tagblatt* (1 June) grumbles: 'As always in such shows the best example was not present. In this case the "Princess" was not on show. Her husband [meaning Jimmy] died and since then she suffers from melancholy.' As Jimmy had died only the previous day, his companions must have been informed immediately. Yet there could have been no direct contact because, within a couple of days, they were on the move again to Mannheim, and then Elberfeld.

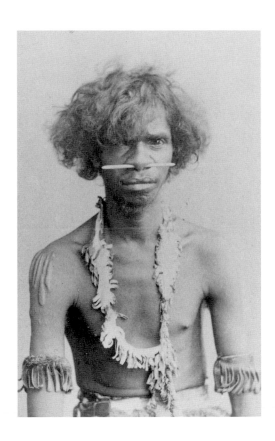

55   Jimmy, Berlin, 1884.
Photograph: Carl Günther.

I first located a copy of Jimmy's British death certificate in 1991 in the records of British deaths abroad. The information, which had been supplied by the Hesse government, stated that Jimmy, an 'Australian savage in the Cunningham Company', twenty-three years old, died in the City Hospital. The British Chargé d'Affaires, Mr Nassau Jocelyn, did not register it until 29 July. Across the accompanying letter he scribbled 'death cert. of "Jimmy"!!'[17] The cause of death was not given. Nor was it given in the brief reference in the *Darmstädter Tagblatt* (4 June), where mention was made of his burial 'yesterday morning in our cemetery'. On the following day the paper included notice of Jimmy's death on 31 May in the official report from the Registry Office of deaths in Darmstadt for the period.

Fortunately the relevant cemetery record has also survived, and item 383 indicates that on 3 June, 'Jimmy (Jacobsen) Australian black in the Cunningham company from Queensland', an adult, was buried in the new cemetery, III J (the area), 3 (the row) and 1 (the plot). Today, the New Cemetery has become the Old Cemetery, with great mature trees and beautiful planting, and although the cemetery director was able to show me the area III J, over the years, as plots were reused, the direction of the rows had been altered and it was no longer possible to establish the position of row 3, plot 1 in 1885. Only a few headstones from that time remain in their original positions because they have been maintained by families. But I am convinced by the documentation that Jimmy is buried there. A year earlier in Brussels, Jimmy and Billy were the only ones to show no symptoms of tuberculosis when they were examined, so what did Jimmy die of? Given their shared living quarters, and his relationship with Sussy, he could have contracted the disease, and sometimes consumption develops a rampant form.

The additional valuable information in this record was the bracketing of the name 'Jacobsen' after 'Jimmy'. It was almost certainly the name of Cunningham's assistant, who was attending to the burial and who kept Cunningham informed. Jacobsen was the name of a Norwegian family, some of whose members, particularly the much travelled Johan Adrian Jacobsen, were associated with the promotion of Völkerschauen and with Hagenbeck – but then Jacobsen is a fairly common name and this connection seems unlikely.[18]

There were now five survivors: Billy, Toby, Jenny, young Toby, and Sussy.

Death in Sonnborn

> *Thus sayeth the Lord: Stand ye in the ways, and see, and ask for the old paths where is the good way, and walk therein, and ye shall find rest for your souls.*
>
> Jeremiah 6: 16, from the Evangelical Lutheran church,
> Wuppertal-Sonnborn

Today, the suspension railway zips along the narrow valley of the River Wupper, just above the water, linking the districts of Wuppertal that were, until the early twentieth century, the separate towns of Barmen and Elberfeld, and several other smaller communities. Built at the turn of the nineteenth century, the suspension railway's construction was the crowning achievement of a century's industrialisation. But the price was high. Friedrich Engels, who was born in Barmen, wrote in 1839 of the pollution of the river by the textile works along its banks and of the grinding poverty, widespread disease – particularly consumption – and the high death rate among the factory workers. He wrote too about the strength of pietist influence in the community, and the narrow-mindedness and meanness of pietist employers. Pietism had its roots in the Protestant reformist movement dating back to the spiritual chaos that attended the Thirty Years' War in the seventeenth century. The Wupper area was sometimes referred to as 'Traktätchen-Tal', the valley of the tracts. There was an Elberfelder Bible – a very literal translation – used for the textual interpretation so central to pietist belief and practice. Among the pietists there was also a strong sense of social mission, for feeding the poor, caring for the sick and education. In the early nineteenth century mission activities were extended overseas by the Rheinischer Missionsgesellschaft, even before Germany's acquisition of colonies.[19] The model of a black man was often to be found in the churches, wearing a placard with the words 'I am the son of a poor heathen'. The figure was known as 'nickneger' because it nodded its head when money was placed in it.

Earlier in the century overseas trading firms such as Godeffroy of Hamburg had raised awareness of the South Seas and other foreign parts. In the 1880s the foundation of colonial societies, Deutscher Kolonialverein in 1882, Gesellschaft für deutsche Kolonisation in 1888, and their amalgamation in 1887, led the push for colonies, and the new colonialism created a nationalistic and patriotic mood that fuelled a more intolerant attitude to 'other races'.

Announcement of the Australians' coming appeared from 13 June, but the 'wild men' (savages) were not presented to the public at the Zoological Gardens, Elberfeld, until the 17th, because they were 'resting from the strain of their journey in their quarters in Sonnborn'. Nevertheless the public was assured of their genuineness, guaranteed by Virchow's examination of them in Berlin.[20] But the real reason for their non-appearance was explained by the following day's announcement that there were 'only four to perform their tribal dances in the small hall of the restaurant building' because 'a fifth specimen, a black princess, has been taken ill suddenly' (*Täglicher Anzeiger für Berg und Mark*, nos 140 and 141, 18 June).

At the end of their first performance, to the astonishment and amusement of the audience, Billy, Toby, and Jenny 'jump from the stage and mingle with the audience'. The reporter tells what happened next with the characteristic mix of observation and received prejudices:

> The blacks even know some German expressions; they are quite familiar with German money and seem to know its value. They charge 'half a mark' or 'fifty Pfennig' for a photograph; for a pamphlet they take 25 pfennig. They already show a touch of our reserved European politeness; when they are offered a cigar or the like they reply with a polite 'Thank you'. For the remaining part, however, their mental abilities are at a very low stage of development. (*Täglicher Anzeiger*, no. 142, 19 June)

The following day's issue of the same paper reported that more than a thousand schoolchildren and others paid 'the black guests a visit'. And that they had moved from Sonnborn, a pleasant village across the river from the zoo, because they were being pestered by the crowds. The *Elberfelder Zeitung* (19 June) reported the incident in ironic vein, at the same time giving a more frank account of their fellow citizen's prejudices under the heading 'Savage Australians and Tame Europeans':

> The idea that 'savages are the better people' has again, the day before yesterday, shown itself to be true. The 'cannibals' from the Zoo, yesterday on the way home to Sonnborn, where they had rooms, were not only surrounded by a crowd of more than a hundred curious people, but actually attacked so that their clothes were almost ripped from their bodies. A policeman saw no other solution than to regard the 'savages' as disturbers of peace, and took down the names of Mr Cunningham as well as the interpreter. We ask ourselves what the penalty will be, as the Australians were dressed in European clothes, and throughout could not have influenced the riot except through their skin colour, so that they at the most can be penalised for unauthorised wearing of darker skin. This sign of a high degree of civilisation had by the way annoyed the savages so much yesterday that they only calmed down after new accommodation had been arranged at the Zoo.

A few days later the same paper (no. 172, Wednesday, 24 June) reported in language that was personal and respectful, eschewing words like savage, cannibal, blacks:

There is deep mourning among the brown guests of the Zoological Gardens because of the seventeen-year-old girl, the adornment of the group, who outshines her companions very much as regards her fine body and the beauty of her face, and who is called 'princess' because she is the daughter of an indigenous chief, who, yesterday, unexpectedly followed her other companions who died on foreign earth during the journey. [She] was already ill when she arrived . . . and didn't even have the opportunity to perform here. She was confined to her bed from whence she was collected by death.

Sussy's death on the 23 June was reported in all the Elberfeld and Barmen papers. The fiction of her title, Princess Tagarah, daughter of the King of the North Queensland blacks, was maintained, though in some papers her name was rendered as Dagarah or Sussi Dakara (*Täglicher Anzeiger*, no. 147, 25 June). Sussy's death had reminded Cunningham of her earlier illness in Pittsburgh, and of the occasion when Warchsinbin (Billy) had saved young Toby's life (a story that I have already told, pp. 103–104). Recalled by Cunningham, it provided the German journalists with good copy. On the following day the *Barmen Zeitung* (no. 146) and several other papers announced that the cause of her death was 'lung consumption and anaemia', and that she was buried at 6 pm in the Protestant graveyard in Sonnborn. It was regretted that her life could not be saved 'despite the intensive care of some nurses at the children's hospital . . . and the medical help of Dr Tischler'.[21] Consumption was an illness with which they were very familiar.

As opposed to the loud crying after the death of a companion in their Australian homeland, the survivors here accepted the new loss with resignation; the liveliest expression of pain was shown by a young man who was about as old as the dead girl . . . The savages did not show much interest in the burial yesterday; the only person who accompanied the stretcher was Mr Cunningham's manager; the gentleman also took care of the sparse decoration of the fresh grave in Sonnborn graveyard.

Although the death 'clearly subdued the troupe's spirit', the news of it attracted the crowds in even greater numbers, from Elberfeld, Barmen and communities up and down the valley. Three classes from a Nützenberg school, an entire girls' school in Oberbarmen, and a thousand pupils from Lennep and a local secondary school paid a visit (*Täglicher Anzeiger* no. 148, 27 June). Entrance to the zoo was 50 pfennig for adults and 25 pfennig for children, but non-members had to pay an additional 20 pfennig to see the performance of the Australian blacks. On the 29th 'the weather was brilliant and tropical, so hot that the sweat was running down the skins of the naked black people. There was hardly space for the crowd. There were a few thousand people in the smaller hall where they were exhibited' (*Barmen Zeitung*). On the following day, Sunday, the crowds reached 'well over 3,600, of which 1,800 paid the 20 pfennig entrance fee to the hall' (*Täglicher Anzeiger*, no. 151, 30 June). And performances continued through to 6 July, with demonstrations of boomerang-throwing on the lawns, adjacent to the restaurant buildings.

The announcement of Sussy's death was accompanied by an ironically critical comment by one of the press on the townsfolk's reception of the Aboriginal performers (*Elberfelder Zeitung*, 30 June):

> It seems that the Australian blacks are making fun of the uncivilised curiosity of the enlightened Europeans. Somebody who is supposed to know their language quite well listened to them when they spoke freely with each other. This was the conversation:
>
> '*Hotoi rena tanti marca leina*'   If only we had enough money, so that we did not have to see these people any longer.
>
> '*Vena ripu estai peto care dakrueis*'   I have to say their stupidity is very amusing.
>
> '*Queti-ti diable li tans la te qui ca tire li*'   The Devil! These idiots stare at us as if they are savages, they touch our arms as if they are cannibals.
>
> '*Queista tusan tekton lare Soneborne leita*'   Recently in Sonnborn I really feared they would grill us and eat us.
>
> '*Quede li tans te qui tire loni Albuma reti sona patri austra – Bumerang*'   We should sell the idiots the pictures for their albums and boomerang back to Australia.
>
> One Australian spotted the listener and took up his boomerang. The 'son of Wuppertown' fled, convinced that these blacks were not as stupid as they were described, or as their looks might suggest. The Australians will not forget Elberfeld easily; they have to leave one of the party here as a corpse. A seventeen-year-old black girl was buried at the cemetery of Sonnborn.

I began my visit to Elberfeld at the zoo, where the director, with whom I had been corresponding, showed me the area where the boomerang-throwing had taken place. The halls of the restaurant building had been completely reorganised and it was not possible to identify the building where the troupe would have stayed. Nor were there surviving records of the Australians' visit. The newspapers provide the only estimates of the size of the audiences. At least from 26 June they seem to have attracted between 1,000 and 2,000 per day, for let us say, ten days. What proportion of the takings went to Cunningham and the troupe is unknown, but it surely would have been a percentage of the 20 pfennig entrance to the hall. Taking the only reliable figure of 1,800 visitors who paid the entrance fee of 20 pfennig, the takings for that day would have been 7,200 marks. Whatever Cunningham's share (10 per cent, 50 per cent, 60 per cent?), it would have been much more than the takings in the smaller places of entertainment usually frequented by the troupe.

For instance, a few months later in Münster, Cunningham showed Professor Landois 'entries in his book of five and six hundred marks that he had taken in other towns in one day', whereas in Münster he had taken only 1,459 marks in six days, an average of 248 per day (*Mescheder Zeitung*, 8 Aug. 1885). Compared with the figures quoted above for the Harz mountains, this figure seems a much more typical average for a day's takings. How any of these figures compare with the takings of other groups is also impossible to estimate with any accuracy, although later Völkerschauen, in larger, professionally organised groups, attracted much greater crowds. Unlike Hagenbeck's Hamburg zoo, Elberfeld Zoo was run by a stock company, answerable to shareholders. The present-day director could only show me records of visits of Völkerschauen to the zoo for the five years from 1896 to 1900, and these formed part of a report on the losses incurred in running the zoo during those years. That there were losses was surprising because in the 1890s the Samoans raised 10,000 marks and the Dahomey 13,000 marks. As a consequence of the enquiry, Völkerschauen were discontinued. The report shows that the reasons were financial; there was no indication of any moral dilemma associated with the exhibition of human beings.

In spite of the numerous press reports of the details of Sussy's death and burial, I was assured there was no supporting documentation in the church archives. But through the careful mediation of my young interpreter we persuaded the archivist to show us the actual register, and there at the correct date was an entry for Susi Dakara. It had not at first been recognised because they had been searching for Sussy or Tagarah, the names I had sent them earlier. Susi Dakara was a transposition I had not encountered until our search of local newspapers on the previous day. In the index to deaths between 1882 and 1970 she was listed under D for Dakara on 23 June 1885, with a reference to item 48 in the Register of the Deceased in the Evangelical Reformed Church for Sonnborn in Kirchhofstrasse from 1 January 1884 to 1904 inclusive. The headed columns spread across two pages.

> *First name and surname*: Susi Dakara
> *Status*: [blank]
> *Hometown*: Australian black (female)
> *Age*: 17 years
> *Month, day and hour of death*: 23/6
> *Cause of death*: Anaemia
> *Month and day of burial*: 24/6
> *If the burial was peaceful and quiet*: [blank]
> *If there was a speech*: [a mark interpreted as affirmative]
> *If there was a sermon*: [blank]
> *Annotations [such as if the person was not buried in the cemetery, or not by a priest, or was not a member of the evangelical church, or any other note]*: 4, 11–6

These final numbers – the only information in the last column – identified the gravesite. The priest joined our discussion, and my questions about the reliability of the record were taken very seriously and discussed at length. The church officers explained that the numbers were a clear indication that Sussy had indeed been buried in the cemetery, for if her body had been taken for medical purposes it would have been noted in this column. They were interested that she had been buried within twenty-four hours instead of the more usual three days, but I reminded them that according to the newspaper reports there had been a heatwave and she was suffering from an infectious disease. Moved by what we had found, the church official picked up a current copy of the parish magazine, remarking on what she considered the appropriateness of the text from Jeremiah: *ask for the old paths where is the good way, and walk therein and ye shall find rest for your souls* (see above). It was a sign, she said, that now

Sussy was found there would be rest, not only for Sussy's spirit but also for her living kin, and all those involved. I replied that for Sussy's Manbarra kin, I thought the knowledge of her burial would help with the healing process.

The archivist hunted for a plan of the graveyard as it was in 1885. To locate area 4, he had to relate it to the present layout of the graveyard in relation to the building we were in. Slowly he worked it out, and we climbed to the graveyard and walked the rows until we came to the plot 6 – which was not at present occupied. The grave would have been across the plot, in the opposite direction to the graves today. He checked the records for the number of occupations down the years and learnt that it was not occupied again until 1925. Although the rule in this cemetery was that the ground could be reused after twenty-five years, Sussy had been left undisturbed for forty years.[22]

Local opinion was that the description of Sussy being carried on a 'stretcher' indicated she was buried in a shroud without a coffin, and that the decoration on the grave would have been flowers, as a headstone would have been too expensive. But I thought of how Sussy's personal possessions would have been destroyed or abandoned by her companions, and wondered if any of them, especially her much-loved copper necklace, had been placed in or on the grave instead (pl. 56). At the time, the greatest local misunderstanding was the assumption that her companions 'did not take much interest in the burial'. But, for them, withdrawal was the only way to deal with being prevented from conducting the funerary ritual according to their own customs. At least when they mourned Sussy in their songs during their performances, they were protected from intrusion by the white people's ignorance of their language.

In reviewing the three deaths in Germany, the evidence that an assistant of Cunningham was present at the burial of both Sussy and Jimmy indicates that the showman met his obligations to meet the costs of hospitalisation and burial in both these instances. Although the documentary evidence is inadequate for Bob, it is reasonable to assume that Cunningham did the same for him. In spite of the treatment of Tambo's body – and remember that the dime museum manager, Frank Drew, claimed he had initiated the mummification (pp. 105–6) – there is evidence that Cunningham refused to allow the bodies of other members of the troupe to go to the scientists. In America, when young Toby was very

56   Sussy, Berlin, 1884.
Photograph: Carl Günther.

ill and thought to be dying the showman is on record as having refused his body to the scientists *(Cleveland Leader and the Plain Dealer*, both 25 Feb. 1884). He also refused to allow Tambo's body to 'go for dissection . . . in fear of public opinion and the English government' *(Cleveland Herald*, 27 Feb.), and he was to do so again, when Toby, the father, died in Paris (see below).

Without Cunningham taking the responsibility for the costs, the bodies of Bob, Sussy and Jimmy would have been designated as unclaimed, and the method of disposal would have been a matter for the German authorities. Although the religion of each was stated to be 'heathen' on their death records, this was no hindrance to their burial. Both Jimmy and Bob were buried in cemeteries maintained by the city. In the case of Sussy, in the absence of a state (public) cemetery, the church was obliged to accept the body for burial in their cemetery, even if the person was not Christian.

Although their deaths were lonely, their final burials were conducted with dignity, kindness and respect by the local authorities. Until I visited the German archives, the knowledge that Aboriginal performers had even visited their cities – let alone died there – had been forgotten. The Olympic Games (held in Sydney, Australia) were on German television screens daily during my stay, and the name of the Aboriginal athlete Cathy Freeman was constantly mentioned. She had raised the threshold of German awareness of Aboriginal matters, and prompted many questions. Everybody I met was very interested to learn that there were living kin of the Aboriginal performers for whom the outcome of my researches was relevant.

In spite of her consumptive state, Sussy constantly displayed great zest for life, not the capacity to will herself to death that Aborigines supposedly had. The last stages of TB can be gruesome and frightening, and by the time she was described as 'melancholy' she was already close to death from loss of blood. She was so much loved by her companions that Cunningham had said, when she was ill in America, that he did not know how he would manage the others if she died. Eighteen months later she and four of her companions were dead, and both the survivors and Cunningham seem to have accepted the deaths. Toby, Billy and Jenny could not have been forced to perform after her death, yet perform they did. Cunningham would have understood death from consumption to be inevitable, and no doubt it eased his conscience that he took responsibility for the medical care.

Yet ambiguities dog attempts to interpret his actions. Among his own personal papers is the translation he had made of the article that Professor Landois wrote for *Mescheder Zeitung* only six weeks after Sussy's death, accusing him of being intent on cold-bloodedly exhibiting Toby and his companions until they dropped, so that he 'would remain the laughing heir to their earnings'. The implication is that Landois saw Cunningham as the cannibal, who would consume them utterly. But that is too simplistic a view, for it was surely more financially advantageous for him to keep them alive as long as possible, that is, to consume their labour but not their lives. It ignores the relationship that grew between the showman and the Aboriginal performers as they lived and travelled together in such close proximity, and it also denies Toby and his companions any agency in the formation of the well-disciplined company of performers they had become. So why did Cunningham keep the translation? It matched the image he projected of himself elsewhere, for this is the same Cunningham whose self-image in his pamphlet – and therefore for press consumption everywhere – is as an intrepid manhunter. Did he not care what the professor said, or did he keep it to reproach himself? Cunningham only seems to have kept newspaper accounts of two deaths, Tambo's and Sussy's. In fact, these were the only deaths that received much newspaper coverage, because in every other instance he managed to move the group on, leaving the dying person behind. Without a performance to publicise, the interest of the press soon waned.

As I follow the troupe's itinerary after Sussy's death, scanning the news cuttings, there seems nothing more to learn from their journey through Holland and the north of France– except to collect the national variations on the endlessly repeated cannibal joke. For instance, in Paris, *Gil Blas* (22 Oct. 1885) insists the 'Australians' prefer their cooked flesh 'à point'.

Death in Paris

In Paris the performance took place at Folies Bergère because shows of indigenous people had been suspended at the Jardin d'Acclimatation (see chapter 5), but on Saturday, 14 November, the director, Geoffroy Saint-Hilaire, gave special permission for 'Billy to display his talents in the art of boomerang-throwing' on the lawn of the Jardin so that the anthropological fraternity, including Topinard and Prince Roland Bonaparte, could attend (*Du Cri du Peuple*, 19 Nov. 1885).[23]

Jenny's husband, Toby (pl. 57), had died several days earlier of 'pulmonarie phthisie' (tuberculosis) in a Paris hospital and, as Topinard explained, although he had done what he could for the body to be sent to the Broca laboratory for dissection, he had been unsuccessful. Topinard's examination of the three survivors took place in his laboratory on 19 November 1885, and he records a moment when his questions about the notion of time prompts Billy to begin reciting the names and places he and his companions had visited since their removal from their North Queensland home almost three years earlier.[24]

Topinard's bare description of Billy's response misses its significance. Billy was retracing the songline of the incredible journey they had made from Australia across the Pacific, through more than a hundred towns and cities of America's North-West and on, with Cunningham, to the bustling

57   Toby, Berlin, 1884.
Photograph: Carl
Günther.

provincial towns and great metropolitan centres of Europe. Billy's litany of names transformed and extended an Aboriginal way of conceptualising space – by memorising the lie of the land and the stages of a journey – to encompass their world-journey. For theirs was an epic journey to rank with the dreamtime journeys of the Creative Beings who had made the sacred landscape of Billy's homeland of sea, reef, beach and rainforest. When interrupted (Topinard noted), Billy started again 'with the preceding town'. Although the order was important, Billy's great feat of memory was more than a mnemonic key to the route they had travelled: each place name had the potential for evoking a story. But the anthropologist wore his own cultural blinkers, and dismissed Billy's prodigious memory as of 'an automatic kind'.[25]

For Billy, recollection through re-enactment was both a system for incorporating knowledge about his vastly extended world and a way of

58   Billy, Paris, 1885.
Photograph: Prince
Roland Bonaparte.

telling; perhaps it was also for knowing – even willing – his way back home. Billy's predicament becomes our predicament: we want to hear what Billy has to tell. Instead, Topinard's culturally bound interpretation ensures that we have to settle for no more than a tantalising hint of Billy's story. Once again the actual voices of Billy and his companions are overwhelmed by the clamour of late nineteenth-century colonial discourses, popular and scientific, about savagery. Topinard failed to grasp the significance of Billy's accomplishment because his concerns were not with Billy as an individual but with the type – the racial type. In his report, he discussed the physical characteristics of Billy, Jenny and her son, Toby, in relation to his earlier findings in *Instructions sur les races indigènes de l'Australie* assembled for the society in 1872. This work drew not on direct observations of living people such as Billy but on travellers' descriptions, as well as

59 Jenny,
Paris, 1885.
Photograph:
Prince Roland
Bonaparte.

on the examination of skeletal material and '11 Australian busts' (casts) lodged in the Paris museum. In this topsy-turvydom, Topinard, as the recognised 'authority', declared the three visitors to be 'authentic' Aborigines, and he wrote a testimonial to that effect for their impresario, R. A. Cunningham, in which he also urged that 'these Curious examples of Man must be seen as their Race is fast dying away'.[26]

Topinard's palpable lack of sympathy – and imagination – led him to misread the Aboriginal performers' non-cooperative behaviour. He rejected the idea that Billy's reserve, even coldness of manner, and Jenny's indifference to the proceedings were a response to the trauma of Toby's death – even though there 'seemed to be a kind of sadness in her that could be related to that'. Again, when he offered Billy several sous (coins of small value) he interpreted Billy's rejection of the derisory gesture, and his invitation to give them to the child, as not understanding the value of money. But, as Cunningham well knew, Billy did understand the value of money – and much else. Topinard wrote that Cunningham confirmed his low opinion of the Aborigines' intelligence, whereas surely it was a matter of the showman agreeing with the eminent professor whose letter of authorisation meant so much to him commercially.

Although Topinard failed to comprehend the depth of the mourners' grief, his descriptions of Jenny's 'sadness' and the uncommunicative state of the three of them, together with the photographs taken by Bonaparte (pls 3, 59 and 60) are witness to their profound unhappiness and psychologically disturbed state. Toby's preparedness, several years earlier, to leave Australia with Cunningham, his strong sense of self and his cultural groundedness had always sustained him, and he had held the group together throughout their American and European journeys. His death in Paris seemed the end of the road, and indeed the professor mentioned that Billy, Jenny and her son were 'on the point of leaving' Paris. Following his usual strategy after a death, Cunningham moved the survivors on, and by the beginning of December 1885 they were in Liverpool, England, waiting for a ship to Australia.

In the early 1990s, I search Parisian institutions and district record offices for Toby's hospital and death records without success.

8   To Constantinople and Back

Apropos of eating, we have asked of our Australians if they have sometimes practised cannibalism, like many of their compatriots; but we have never obtained a precise response: it would seem that they try to evade an embarrassing question. Mr Cunningham assures as that cannibalism is practised in certain circumstances . . . but he does not believe the custom has survived.

E. Houzé and V. Jacques, 'Communication . . . sur les
Australiens du Musée du Nord', 1884

I consider it more barbarous to eat a man alive than to eat him dead.

Michel de Montaigne, 'On Cannibals', 1958

Liverpool, England: three years and six deaths since the group have left their North Queensland home, and Billy, Jenny and her son are reported to be 'on their way to their native land' (*Daily Albion*, 1 Dec. 1885). But the embarkation does not take place. Instead, this smaller, unlikely troupe of a man, a woman and a boy, who superficially look like a family but are not, begin another eighteen months of touring. Maybe it was the chance offer of a season at the Rotunda in Dublin, Ireland – surely irresistible to Cunningham because of his Irish origins – that started them off on their travels again. At first it is not clear how extensive the tour is meant to be, for the *Belfast Newsletter* of 16 January 1886 reports that the Aboriginal performers at St George's Hall are homeward bound for Australia. Instead, a bitterly cold February finds them in Glasgow, Scotland, where, billed as 'bone fide cannibals', they appear for a month at Crouch's Variety Theatre in Argyle Street. Billy gives an exhibition of boomerang-throwing on Glasgow Green near Nelson's Column – 'wrapped up' against the cold and transported there and back in a cab. The Reverend Robert Thomson makes the visitors the subject of his sermon: 'Lord, what is a man'. As the Reverend was a great admirer of Billy's skill with the boomerang, it is

60   Billy, Jenny and her son Toby in Paris in November 1885. Photograph: Prince Roland Bonaparte.

unfortunate the text does not seem to have survived, but it apparently involved a comparison with 'nigger Nero' in Bridewell prison. After examining the Aboriginal performers, John Glaister MD presents them to the Philosophical Society of Glasgow, whose secretary, John McKendrick, writes a letter of authentication for Cunningham.[1] Glaister also notes that the boy is suffering from 'incipient tubercular disease of the lungs'. Apparently Billy retains his immunity, and Jenny also continues to be free of symptoms.

Two months later, in a Copenhagen spring, it is announced that the Aboriginal troupe's Scandinavian tour will be extended to Odense and Arhus (in Denmark), then north to Göteborg (Sweden), Christiania (now Oslo, Norway), Stockholm (Sweden), Helsingfors (now Helsinki, Finland) and St Petersburg, Russia. 'If ever they get as far . . . because they cannot endure the cold.' But it seems that 'they do not want to go back to their own country. The man wishes, as far as he is concerned, to retire to New York, where he has accumulated a fortune' (*Dags-Avisen*, Copenhagen, 1 May 1886). What seems to have begun as several opportune engagements has developed into an organised tour through Scandinavia and Russia – a Grand Tour that eventually will take the showman and his Aboriginal travelling companions to Constantinople and back.

Although all the Scandinavian capitals then had populations of under half a million, they were experiencing the same forces of industrialisation and urbanisation as the rest of Europe. Christiania, Stockholm and Copenhagen were busy ports and vibrant metropolitan centres; they had lively intelligentsias, restless working classes and strong radical political parties. In spite of pan-Scandinavian sentiments, the prevailing temper within each country was nationalistic, linked with an active folklore movement. In Sweden it was promoted by Artur Hazelius whose wax tableaux of scenes from folk-life featured in the Nordic (Nordiska) Museum, founded by him in 1873, and were shown at the world exhibitions in Philadelphia in 1876 and Paris in 1878.[2] In Copenhagen the Tivoli Gardens had long been a place of entertainment. I have not been able to establish who arranged the tour for Cunningham, but his links with Johan Adrian Jacobsen, the Norwegian colleague of Carl Hagenbeck, the recruiter of indigenous Greenlanders and 'Lapps' (Saami) for his German shows, suggest him as a possible candidate. Yet Cunningham made no acknowledgement to any agent in the Swedish edition of his pamphlet, which he updated in 1886 with quotes from English, Belgian, German and French papers – but not from Danish or Norwegian papers. Nevertheless, its existence suggests that he produced similar editions in the other Scandinavian countries, because the selling of the pamphlet was such an important feature of his presentation, and it was relatively simple to translate and produce.[3]

After the death of Bob in Chemnitz, Billy was the only surviving Biyaygirri man, and although he always commanded respect within the group as a senior and as a medicine man, he had deferred to Toby, who, as the eldest Manbarra man, and as a husband and father, was the natural leader. After the latter's death, the once 'reticent' Billy took on the leadership role. As the man of the party, he was ready to discuss 'their position and prospects in a lively manner with visitors'. Regrettably, the reporter did not share these views with the readers, but Billy's attitude confirms that he and his companions were active agents in the decision to continue touring. Assisted by Jenny's son – who was now ten years old – their performances continued to include their dances. Billy also devised a new routine in boomerang-throwing by 'discharging half-a-dozen boomerangs fast after one another, so that they all circled in the air like so many birds' (*Glasgow Evening Times*, 16 Feb. 1886). This became a much admired feature of their show, and later he made lighter, smaller boomerangs for the boy to use. There were other changes for the boy after his father's death, he could no longer use the name they had shared, because of the prohibition on naming the dead.[4] At first he was called Tom, but later he became known as Denny or Benny. It follows that Cunningham must have complied with Aboriginal custom when talking to the press, and he also omitted the list of Aboriginal names from the Swedish edition of the pamphlet – probably more because he did not wish to disclose how many of the group had died.

Apart from Jenny's grief for her husband, she and Billy were said not to like each other, though that most probably was for cultural rather than personal reasons – it suggests that a relationship between them was inappropriate because, although they came from different language groups, they shared the same kinship system which regulated the marriage rules. In Copenhagen the *Dags-Avisen* reporter (1 May) perceives the tension between them, noting that although Jenny was 'charming', she didn't 'seem to tolerate the man easily', addressing him 'in terms less than flattering to this Don Juan'. At the same time, Billy tells him 'he is looking for a wife. As soon as he sees a young girl he says "you and me. Me and you." But as yet no one has been tempted by his offer.'

Another reporter, however, fantasises that perhaps there is a 'free relationship' that precedes Jenny's husband's death, and 'who is to know that they did not agree to kill the man and eat him together. Like that, one can evade easily all consequences of later investigation.' And he draws a parallel with 'modern marriage dramas' where 'the court orders the disinterment of the deceased in order to investigate the presence of phosphate of arsenic or similar less tasty substances.' But his fantasies are undermined by the further observation that 'neither the man or woman can be called well grown or well fed' and that 'in reality she keeps herself away from him' except when he acquires some money, when 'she is soon enough ready to take it from him to put it into the family safe-keeping box, represented by a purse' (*Dagbladet*, 27 Apr.). The question of the nature of the relationship between Billy and Jenny also disturbs *Politiken*'s reporter, Jim, whose uninformed observations on 20 April cause him to suggest 'it would be surely more appropriate if the man and woman were to marry, because all three of them are lodged in one room.' On the other hand, he commends them for their daily 'soap-wash', comparing them favourably with the Sioux Indians, who 'were really pigs'!

Regardless of these inadequacies of personal hygiene, the Sioux Indians had recently attracted 3,000 visitors on their first day, whereas only 900 people attended the North Queenslanders' first show in Copenhagen. As a consequence, the liberal paper *Politiken* urged that 'these nice people deserve the attention of the public'. Mr Belly (Billy), whose volatile nature was now revealed, was described as 'a great humorist' and the widow and her son as 'attractive' and 'affectionate and playful together'. They performed on a red platform in the glass hall of the Etablissement National, a

61 'Australian Cannibal Boomerang Throwers', a coloured lithograph poster printed in English, Berlin, 1884. Another colour poster based on the pamphlet cover (pl. 8) was printed at the same time. Both were used in Scandinavia and probably elsewhere. Copies of both are in the Historisches Museum Frankfurt am Main.

place of popular entertainment, and when the crowds lessened 'they crept to a corner window to lap up the sunshine.' Billy introduced other innovative features to attract attention. Denny spun a top and played a harmonica, and Billy himself 'learnt the melody of God Save the Queen' (the British national anthem), which he presented with 'visible pride and little voice'. But as he was not able to keep the words in his head he accompanied himself on a 'gummi elasticum' or elastic band, or actually singing the words 'gummi elasticum'. So pleased was he with the result that 'he earnestly requested his impresario to tell a journalist, so that his talent could be known to a wider audience' (*Politiken*, 4 May; *Dags-Avisen*, 4 May).

For his part, the conservative *Dagbladet's* reporter writes on 27 April with mock disapproval of the garish red and yellow poster in the windows of the Etablissement National, 'that depicted with all the grotesque imagination of Anglo-American book-printing a whole assembly of cannibals . . . who position themselves threateningly' while others 'prepare a small human dinner à la carte'; especially as on arrival at the performance he found 'that were it not for their skin colour and other minor differences, one was in the company of civilised people'. The writer explained further that 'other things show how European the guests of the National have become.' For instance, when Billy, who sat elegantly smoking his cigar in a cigar-holder, offered another from the box in front of him to a bystander, he would only have become 'half-European . . . if he did not also know he should be paid for it'. When he was given a Norwegian 25 öre coin instead of the Danish equivalent he appealed to Cunningham 'to assure him it is real', and on another occasion he watched anxiously while a potential customer went off with a cigar in hand to find change of a krona (crown). The *Dags-Avisen* reporter, who wrote under the pseudonym 'Robinson Crusoe', also commented on Billy's aggressive sales techniques (1 May), saying that 'he wags a finger at you' for failing to buy his photo or the pamphlet, and how one day 'when a man pulled at his nosebone' he hit his arm several times with his wooden weapon, 'and furiously grabbed a sword shouting "I will kill you".' The man ran away, but 'Billy became so enraged that he was locked up for half-an-hour until he had calmed down.' Young Denny, who Jim of *Politiken* described as an 'unusually sweet child, happy and friendly', was equally able to defend himself. When youngsters of his own age pressed too close to him at a boomerang-throwing display on Northern Fields, he kicked out at them and 'induced a minor verbal salute in good Copenhagen style' (*Socialdemokraten*, 28 Apr.). The 'wild yells of the assembled youths' disquieted the performers, and 'rumour has it that the lady cannibal bit the finger of a female urchin who came to close' (*Dags-Avisen*, 28 Apr.).

It is plain that the Scandanavian reporting is different from anything encountered so far, except occasionally in provincial Germany. The lack of public concern for their own indigenous minorities, and their countries' colonial links are too tenuous either to induce a sense of colonial guilt or to require justification of colonial aggression.[5] Consequently, the constant reiteration of Cunningham's story of the Aborigines' capture, escape and recapture, and the emphasis on their physical attributes as signs of savagery and inferiority, so prevalent in the news reports throughout America and much of Europe, have been largely replaced in Scandinavia by observations about Billy, Jenny and her son which, if sometimes mocking and intrusive, at least see them as individuals, and are informative about their interaction with the public.

A cannibal scene, Copenhagen

When it comes to attributing cannibal practices to them, however, the Danes are sceptical – especially as Danish ideas of cannibalism appear limited to the ingestion of one's own kind for sustenance, or as an attribute of a belligerent nature. They make no inquiries – or assumptions – about other possible motives for the practice. 'Jim' writes for *Politiken* (20 Apr.) that 'Belli (Billy) himself asserts he has eaten humans, but seems altogether kind' – suggesting that they thought the combination incompatible. And he records a small conversation between Cunningham, the 'curious' showman, and an onlooker which suggests that the average fellow citizen shares his disbelief in the attribution of cannibalism to the Australian visitors.

> Onlooker: These people have surely never eaten humans?
> Showman: You cannot state such a thing.
> Onlooker: Why not?
> Showman: One may not affirm what one does not know!
> Onlooker: But can you prove that they *have* eaten humans?
> Showman: No.
> Onlooker: Well, then *you* can't affirm it.

'Jim' concludes ambiguously: 'Whether or not Billy has eaten people, one thing is sure, he himself is the real thing.' He does not propose that he stands for all 'savages'. Rather, the presence of the Aboriginal performers – and others like the Sioux – in their midst provided a stronger sense of the exotic difference than their own resident others, the Lapps (Saami) of Scandinavia and the 'Eskimo' of Greenland, and contributed to a textural change in their perception of the larger world. Further, the presence of these 'rare guests' in their city caused them to pose the question, who are the cannibals? While none of the reporters brought the intellectual curiosity or philosophical discipline of a Montaigne to seeking elucidation from their visitors, in Copenhagen satirical reflections in the radical press on cannibal appetites that consume the body politic disclosed the appeal of the cannibal metaphor in the popular political discourse of the period.

On Sunday 25 April 1886, the Danish left-wing satirical weekly, *Ravnen* (The Raven), published a cartoon in which three conservative Danish

62   'Cannibals from New Provisional-Land', cartoon from radical satirical weekly *Ravnen* (*The Raven*) 25 April 1886, Copenhagen, Denmark, representing three Danish reactionary politicians as Billy, Jenny and Benny (Toby).

politicians were represented as Jenny, her son and Billy (pl. 62). Under the heading 'Cannibals from New Provisional-Land', the cartoon reflected a period of conflict in Danish parliamentary and social history. Although in 1884 the left had gained eighty seats in the Folketing, the Danish lower house – two of which were held by the first Social Democrats ever to be elected – a right coalition dominated the Landsting (the upper house, representing business and landowner interests), led by J. S. B. Estrup, Prime Minister. In 1885, when the left-dominated lower house rejected the budget over the issue of making large appropriations for defence, Estrup persuaded the king to declare a provisional budget, thus enabling the right to maintain themselves in power. For several years, the country had provisional budgets until in 1887 the right regained political and parliamentary ascendancy. The period, which was seen as an Estrup dictatorship, was referred to as 'Provisorietiden' (time of provisional budgets). To maintain social order, Estrup kept close links with the military and introduced a paramilitary corps, called the gendarmerie-corps, stationed in major Danish towns. These were troubled times, and for the first six months of 1886 the Speaker of the Folketing was in prison.

Given these brief background details, the cartoon makes a powerful and immediately readable visual statement. The forces of conservatism are represented by Jenny on the left and Billy on the right, and Jenny's arm rests affectionately on the shoulders of her son, who is gnawing on a human bone. The boy is also wearing pants somewhat ambiguously labelled 'Arbetarbørn' (working-class kids). Behind, on the ground, lies a skull, wearing the cap of the paramilitary force. At the same time, the cartoon is accompanied by a caption that identifies the personalities and hints at double meanings, and a more complex reading.

> In the back-rooms of the *Ravnen*, today and for the following days, we exhibit: Cannibals from New Provisional Land. The family consists of three people: the man, Lars Di-Nesen, also called heart-breaker, his wife, Matzenia, and their son, Fy-Frederic. With regard to the lifestyle of these remarkable savages it is said that even if it is pure delight for them to flay Westerners alive, and even if most of all they would prefer to swallow socialists – skin, hair and all – they actually live on 'Conservatives', a tribe which therefore diminishes every day, and finally must become extinct, as in the long run it cannot satisfy the greedy Provisionalists, who will finally have no choice other than to eat one another right down to the last one. *Ravnen* has therefore hastened to arrange an exhibition while there are still a few prime examples of this remarkable race to be found. (N.B. If you want to be in good standing with Fy-Frederic, you need only call him 'Newspaperman' and 'Fyren' will be as happy as Ferslew when his puppet shouts 'Your Honour!')

Now for some explanations: Billy is recognisable from a photograph as Lars Dinesen, member of the Folketinget, who in his youth was left of centre in politics but for ten years had been intent on building the right-wing coalition. Dinesen is also a common Danish name, but hyphenated

'Di-Nesen' it could be rendered Mr Nose. Matzenia (Jenny) is identifiable as Henning Matzen, Professor of Constitutional Law and Member of Parliament, efficient organiser of Højre, the political right. The boy Fy-Frederic is a more ambiguous figure, but because it is suggested he might also be called 'Newspaperman', he may represent Jean Christian Ferslaw, the right-wing newspaper magnate, and supporter of the coalition. The reference to his sycophantic 'puppet' alludes to his power and the honours he has received. The prefix to his name, 'Fy', is like the English 'Fie', and suggests he is being reproached. As he is gnawing on a bone, perhaps he is being scolded for consuming his own kind 'right down to the last one'.[6]

Cannibal narratives are deeply embedded in all European cultures, but from the sixteenth century, and the linked beginnings of colonialism and capitalism that followed Europe's 'discovery' of the Americas – 'a moment crucial not just for the development of European colonialism but for that of capitalist modernity itself', when the civilised European self became defined by its savage/cannibal other – cannibal narratives have played an important ideological role in underwriting the colonial destruction and dispossession of indigenous people.[7] At the same time, throughout the development of European capitalism, cannibal narratives have also provided a metaphorical language of discourse about the nature of capitalist appetites – of which one of the earliest, Montaigne's observations that 'it is more barbarous to eat a man alive than to eat him dead', is most frequently invoked. By the mid-nineteenth century, Karl Marx held a more sophisticated view than the mere equation of cannibal consumption and capitalism. For him, 'the capitalist's "voracious appetite" for surplus value (and hence, surplus labour) is characteristic of capital as a mode of production', and emergent industrial capitalism had to learn to limit its appetites. Thus Marx's metaphors more often imply agents of limitation: the vampire, the werewolf and the parasite, that feed but do not totally consume.[8]

The Danish satirical cartoon – and its accompanying text – takes the argument in the direction of metaphorical excess in order to make a political point: the point being that their political opponents, the 'greedy provisionalists', are so vicious that they will not only consume the socialists but also their conservative allies, so that they will end by eating 'one another right down to the last one'. The publishers of *Ravnen* have seized an opportune moment to disseminate their cannibal narrative, for every Copenhagen newspaper, conservative and radical, is writing about the cannibal guests, and the whole town is agog to see them. A *Ravnen* writer works the metaphor even further in another item in the same issue, called 'Visiting the Cannibals', where he tells his timid companion, 'they won't eat you! We have, praise be to Estrup, laws that prohibit cannibals from eating Christians in Copenhagen.' Instead he suggests they ask 'Mr Cannibal' 'what parts of a human are the most tasty', and speculates about various prominent Danish citizens as suppliers of body parts.

What do Billy and his companions make of the cartoon when it is shown to them? (As it surely was, because there is a copy of it in Cunningham's own cuttings book.) Does it confirm their suspicions that there are cannibals among the white people too? As for Billy, the budding capitalist, accumulating his 25 öre coins, piece by piece, he has learnt the financial advantage of declaring himself to be a cannibal, and of playing the role of frightening the white people. But as an itinerant performer, what real connections can he make with the communities they pass through? Do the new skills he has acquired have any value outside the show-space? Or, for that matter, would he survive outside the partnership established between himself and Cunningham, the entrepreneurial show-man for whom Billy and his companions represent both labour and reserve capital? Surely he suspects by now that just as his companions have been consumed, the same fate awaits him.

Having exhibited considerable curiosity about the living arrangements of their visitors, and having attended their show 'in great numbers', the Danes seem to have established an affectionate familiarity with their Australian visitors and, as the time for their departure approached, another reporter (*Dags-Avisen*, 4 May) referred to Cunningham and his troupe as 'Kragelund and the gnomes', as it were incorporating them into Danish folklore. Their Scandinavian saga continued through Denmark and Norway, until Billy and his companions arrived in Stockholm as midsummer approached, with its long hours of daylight. There they performed at the Alhambra, a restaurant and place of entertainment on the edge of Djurgården, the great royal park that is a summer playground for the people of Stockholm. And there they would have seen the Swedes celebrating Midsummer Eve, dancing round the maypole in costume to the tune of fiddles and accordion players.

The Stockholmers seem to have taken to their hearts these cigar-smoking, boomerang-throwing southern visitors, who had found their way 'right up to the very North'. The nearby Djurgården is an ideal place for boomerang-throwing, and on June 19 (according to *Dagens Nyheter*) 'a cortège of three cabs' set out, with Billy 'in the first cab amidst his boomerangs – but looking quite peaceful, puffing away at a cigar' – until 'a perfect meadow tempted the son of Queensland to his martial sport. Then Mr Cannibal removed his cigar, let out a loud war-cry a few times and started his throws.' The boomerangs 'hovered around like monstrous birds, sometimes several at a time in the flight'. The Swedish reader was asked to imagine the scene 'in the midst of green Djurgården' and its effect on Billy's 'cannibal heart'. For it seems that he became so absorbed in his martial sport that Cunningham found it hard to get him to stop. 'Finally, resigned, he lit a new cigar and returned with us back to culture and punch at the Alhambra.'

Although the *Ny Illustrerad Tidning* (26 June) expressed more orthodox opinions about Billy and his companions, which were supplied by their impresario, an accompanying illustration by the artist Ernst Ljungh has caught the animated mood of their performance in a delightful silhouette of the three (pl. 63). Jenny, now bearing the title of 'Princess of North Queensland', is perched with her legs on a chair, smoking a cigar in a long holder, while Billy – also smoking a cigar – and 'the youngster' prance about 'dressed only in ostrich feathers'. At this time, the three frequently abandon their cowhide show clothes, using any accessories they fancy, and Jenny is particularly addicted to wearing large quantities of necklaces and bangles. Often they appear in ordinary western clothes, particularly when performing outdoors. Cunningham seems to have sidestepped the moral implications of the man and woman being unrelated, because they are now referred to as the Benny (Jenny?) 'family'. Perhaps this is also indicative of the more dominant role Jenny has assumed.

In an article headed 'Australian Guests' (9 July), a *Dagens Nyheter* reporter also notes the credibility gap between their actual appearance and 'Mr Cunningham's way of recommending his "artists" . . . calling them "truly bloodthirsty monsters in appalling ugly human shape".' (He is, of course, quoting from the pamphlet.) He concludes that even if they are not beautiful and their hairdos are incredible:

> During the exhibition Mr and Mrs Cannibal behaved peacefully and very obviously controlled their bloodthirstiness, because the bravest of the onlookers were without restraint allowed to touch their tattooed bodies, lift their hairy wigs and handle them in nearly whatever way they liked, given all due consideration and respect a civilised person

63   'Australnegrerna i Stockholm': Jenny, Billy and young Benny (Toby), engraving of cut-out or silhouette drawing by Ernst Ljungh, *Ny Illustrerad Tidning*, 26 June 1886.

from Stockholm will always show such far-travelled and rare guests as from the south seas.

Again, the ironic tone is reserved for his own society rather than the visitors, who, he observes, were 'unconcerned by the curious Stockholmers . . . as they sang and danced and pranced about among the audience'. In spite of the occasional minor incident, such as Billy's reaction to the attempt, in Copenhagen, to remove his nose ornament, the 'Benny family' have shown themselves to be remarkably disciplined and interactive performers, able to work an audience. Cunningham may be the manager – and without him there would have been no tour – but they are setting the pace, and they are enjoying themselves. So the tour continues through Helsingfors (Helsinki) and at Arkadia in St Petersburg, until their arrival in Moscow in late summer (26 August, according to the Julian calendar – 8 September in Western Europe). In Moscow the troupe performed at the zoo, twice daily at 2 pm and 9 pm, on an open stage – except that when it rained they were shown indoors. Entrance fee 50 kopek. And they also took regular 'walks' among the crowds. The engagement was a short one as the summer season at the zoo closed at the end of the month.

A cannibal scene, Moscow

A few days after their arrival the *Moscow Paper* published a short piece under the heading, 'The Man-Eaters have Come'.

64   (*facing page*)
Anthropological
Laboratory, Museum of
the Institute of
Anthropology
and Ethnology,
University of Moscow,
in background the casts
of the two Tasmanians,
Truganinni and
Woureddi. *Izvetstiia
Imperatorskago
Obshchestva*, 4, pt. 2.
Photogravure:
S. Herer and Nabgol'ts
& Co.

A little scene: Workmen are reading a newspaper in a café. One of them says that the man-eaters have come. Somebody asks where they are from, and he is told that they are from Australia . . . the man-eaters' country, that is not far from America. And they wondered how the directors of the zoo allow them to be shown to the public. One of the men says that during the day, the man-eaters have locks on their mouths, and during the night they are put on a chain. The man says that otherwise they might attack people, and you'll leave the show without one arm, having paid for the entrance.

Then they decide that the reason why the man-eaters didn't eat their keeper was that he was too thin. Next they wonder how the Aborigines are going to eat living people in front of the public. One of the workers is ready to bet 500 roubles that the man-eaters won't manage to cope with his mother-in-law. The others agree, and they decide that it is a lie that the Australians are man-eaters. Still they would like their boss to be eaten by the man-eaters. One man decides to take his wife to the show in order to scare her so that she will stop arguing with him. Others say that the man-eaters wear tight circus clothes and have green faces. Then they decide to leave the café because their bosses – their own man-eaters – have come.

The writer does not say who these literate workers were – builders' labourers or market workers, skilled or unskilled – or indeed whether their conversation was real or invented. Either way, he knew his readers. It was clearly evident that the presence of so-called cannibals in Moscow would stir the workers' reflections on their own social relations. Russia was undergoing rapid economic change, and as Crystal Bartolovich suggests, 'preoccupation with cannibals is one of the morbid symptoms of a capitalist appetite in crisis'.[9] The 1880s had begun with the assassination of Emperor Alexander II, and the slow and troubled emergence of industrial capitalism in Russia, matched by a strengthening revolutionary movement, was to culminate in the 1905 revolution, when, incidentally, the bitter fighting took place in the Zoological Gardens, destroying them utterly.[10]

In the late nineteenth century, Russian anthropologists in both St Petersburg and Moscow were very active participants in the European community of anthropologists, exchanging skeletal material, photographs

and artefacts with colleagues like Virchow in Berlin and with fraternal societies in Britain and France; the voyages of I. Krustenstern and O. Kotzebue and others contributed to the great ethnographic collections, especially from the Pacific, that were assembled in the nineteenth century. While the troupe was in Moscow, Cunningham obtained yet one more letter of authentication, and Billy, Jenny and her son also attended the Anthropological Laboratory of the Museum of the Institute of Anthropology and Ethnology, where once again they were surrounded by the skulls, skeletons and weapons of other indigenous people, and where

65   News item on the Australian Aboriginal performers in Arabic script. From Cunningham's cuttings book.

they would have seen casts of two Tasmanians, Truganinni and Woureddi (pl. 64). These were copies, made by the sculptor Sevriugin, from modelled heads exhibited in the Paris exposition of 1874.[11]

After Moscow, why did Cunningham and his troupe extend their journey? For the showman, the lure was fairly obvious – to Constantinople and back! Besides, it would hardly have been profitable to retrace their steps across northern Europe, and perhaps inadvisable because it was already autumn, but they could have returned by train to central Europe. R. A. had a small but good troupe of performers, willing to travel with him, and the journey itself seems to have become more important than any financial returns he might expect. For Billy, Jenny and Benny it had become the only way of life they knew. They took the railway south via Kiev to Odessa, and then crossed the Black Sea by steamer to Constantinople. By the end of October 1886 their presence in Constantinople was greeted in the Greek, Turkish, English and French language presses. They appeared at the Café Apollo on the Grand Rue de Galata and performed for 'His Imperial Majesty the Sultan, who, with His usual liberality, made Mr Cunningham a present of fifty pounds; and rewarded the two interpreters with ten pounds each' (*Levant Herald*, 18 Nov.).

By late January 1887 they were in Rome, where Professor G. Sergi wrote in contradictory terms, describing 'these affable people' and their ability to speak English, while at the same time reiterating the prevailing anthropological opinion about the cannibal nature of this 'near to disappearing' race.

A month later, in Vienna, the Countess Pauline Metternich was one of the first to visit the 'Australian guests', 'who were obviously pleased when the countess addressed them in English'. But when Cunningham gave his talk about them in English the 'huge audience' began to protest, and he became nervous. One young Austrian shouted that it was no problem for the upper classes to use a foreign language 'but at the people's school we didn't learn African' (*Wiener Tagblatt*, 14 Feb. 1887).

Looking back on the remarkable eighteen-month journey of Billy and his companions through towns and cities of northern Europe, where they

are addressed as 'rare strangers' or 'rare guests' – reflecting a cultural attitude to difference that is more curious and less fearful and hostile than
in many other places they have visited – an interaction with their public
takes place not achieved elsewhere. (Or, if occasionally achieved, was not
reported on.) Certainly the greater intimacy of the show-space has been a
contributory factor. Their reception has encouraged them to break free of
the frame of Cunningham's presentation of them as cannibal/savages and
their show has developed a more hybrid aspect, expressed through their
dress and jewellery and adopted musical instruments. Even Cunningham's
tongue-in-cheek cannibal presentation is exposed as a promotional device
to attract the crowds, for the success of his enterprise depends on their
attractiveness and their skills as entertainers. And, as is frequently said,
they are too attractive to be cannibals. In turn, the reporters who give
expression to scepticism and curiosity are not leaders of opinion but
reflectors of their own society. The trope of cannibalism is deeply embedded in all European cultures – even those without colonial connections –
in their mythologies and folk-tales about consuming gods and ogres like
Baba Yoga, the Russian version of the German 'kinderfresser' or child-
guzzler, and in great European literature such as Dante's *Divine Comedy*.
The presence of Billy and his companions seems to have touched a cord,
and to have stimulated cannibal fantasies applicable to each audience's
social and cultural circumstances.[12]

London and after

Back in London towards the end of April 1887, Cunningham shifts the
emphasis away from cannibalism in his promotional literature and offers
the 'Anthropological Wonders of the World, to Proprietors of Aquariums
and First-class Entertainment Halls &c., in the United Kingdom', in
an advertisement that detailed 'the highly successful tour' of his troupe of
Australian Aborigines 'through the Principal Continental Cities of
Europe'.[13] But the times were changing and there was serious competition
from much larger, better-capitalised enterprises. In May, Buffalo Bill
opened at the American Exhibition at Earl's Court, at about the same
time as Cunningham's troupe opened in the King's Rooms at the Royal
Pavilion in Brighton. There the ever inventive Billy cleverly illustrated
the use of the boomerang by shaping several examples from pieces of

cardboard, so that when 'he flung them round the room they fell at his feet or in his hand!' (*Brighton Examiner*, 13 May 1887). Earlier, Billy had given a similar performance with his 'mimic weapons' at a meeting of the Royal Anthropological Institute on 26 April,[14] where Cunningham himself had made the presentation. Although the audience included a missionary, the Reverend William Wyatt Gill, who said that he was familiar with both Cardwell and Palm Island, their home places, the brief report did not mention any conversation between them: it merely indicated that Gill thought they were 'fairly typical specimens of the race'. In other words, their authenticity was established, but it was as if those present thought there was nothing more to learn from the Aboriginal visitors.

Looking back on the encounters between Billy and his companions and the European anthropologists, only Houzé and Jacques in Brussels attempted an ethnographic account of their meeting that reflected its interactive nature. Rudolf Vichow's report excluded most references that could be considered anecdotal and relied on his own (unreliable) physiognomic observations (pp. 131–3 above), while Paul Topinard drew only negative conclusions from the living people in his presence. Yet something of an Aboriginal voice emerged against the grain of each of these accounts. As for the British encounter in 1887, if any cross-cultural communication took place it went unrecorded, presumably because it was considered to be of no scientific relevance. From our present perspective, the sterility of this anthropological gathering is stunning. Apparently no attention at all was paid to the individuals presented to them. At a point where we would most like to have recovered some indication of their state of mind at the end of the long continental journey, there is a silence. We shall never know, but it may even be that the encounter with Reverend Gill made Billy, Jenny and her son homesick, and perhaps hastened Cunningham's decision to bring the tour to an end, for it is at about this time, after surviving the loss of their companions and family, and after years of successful touring, when they are at their most professional, that their trail grows cold and the narrative falters .

Did illness or another death caused Cunningham to move the survivors on again precipitately? Or, having failed to secure other worthwhile engagements in England from mid-1887, did Cunningham return with them to New York? There is a Cunningham family story to the effect that 'they' stayed in New York with the showman in his sister's house, and it is Jenny, particularly, who is remembered. And although 'they' apparently did not want to return to Australia, the showman was determined they should do so. It is hard to believe that Cunningham did not tour his very experienced performers anywhere for the next six months, but I have not traced them during this period in England, New York or California, in spite of a news cutting in Cunningham's album that places him in California on 26 February 1888.[15] But a search finds R. A. Cunningham listed as a passenger departing from San Francisco on 10 March on HMS *Alameda.* He arrived in Sydney on 4 April. There is no doubt about his destination, because he is listed on the coastal steamer *Warrego*, departing Brisbane for Townsville on 14 April (corroborated by another dated newspaper cutting in his album), and arriving there on 18 April. Six persons are also listed as travelling steerage on that sailing, but there is no indication either in press reports or in official shipping lists that Billy, Jenny and her son are among them. Then, a week later, on 25 April Cunningham rejoins the *Warrego* on its return voyage to Sydney.[16] It seems R. A. has made this journey specifically to return his performers home; surely an unspoken commentary on the bond that has developed between them, yet again there is silence.

Several months later, on 23 August, in Melbourne, Cunningham gave an interview to *Melbourne Punch* in which he stated he had returned 'them' – though he does not say who, how many or when. He praised their linguistic abilities and said that they were now 'civilised to such an extent that they might enter Parliament'. The account went on to detail the much told story, as outlined in his pamphlet, of their capture and removal and, passing over their worldwide travels, it concluded with the reporter's unconvincing comments that 'on arrival of Cunningham and the blacks in North Queensland, the ruling passion was so strong in the aborigines that they at once made for their former haunts.'[17] The implication was that under the civilised veneer, acquired during many years of travel, they had remained savages, but it is hard to believe that when they returned to North Queensland their new personae would have gone unremarked, and enough was remembered for Dick Palm Island to mention the story of an ancestor going to America for a show to Tindale in 1938.[18]

Throughout the journey, Jenny had the strong motive of caring for her son to keep her going, but both mother and son had tuberculosis and it is

66   Billy, Paris, 1885.
Photograph: Prince
Roland Bonaparte.

not realistic to think of them surviving many more severe winters abroad, or under bad living conditions at home. Billy had always shown resistance to the disease, so that I have always rated him the ultimate survivor. The copy of the *Townsville Bulletin* of 18 April that listed Cunningham's arrival also reported hunger among the Aborigines, and that the tableland 'niggers' are stealing corn 'and leaving clothing or a dilly bag by way of exchange'. A week later the *Townsville Herald* announced that 'the annual distribution of blankets to the descendants of the original possessors of this portion of Australia will take place at the court house Tuesday next, the 1st of May.' A century of dependency was beginning. As I search the lists of personal names in the Aboriginal records of these North Queensland communities over the succeeding years, the anonymity is compounded because the names I search for, Jenny and Billy, are not unusual and are shared with the two survivors of the second group, exactly a decade later (chapter 10).

At the chance intersection of time and space, in Brighton, where I lost trace of Billy and his companions there is 'only a breath between there, and not there'[19] – and all that remains is a haunting. As Freud suggests, the sense of the uncanny – a haunting – represents the return of the repressed. Billy's haunting is a reminder that 'ghosts bring the past into our midst, that we might recognise it', that the history I have been trying to uncover is a repressed history; it is a 'countermemory' with which to prize open a fracture in a European linear history, to break with the negativity of a history of dispossession and deprivation and to allow the hidden stories to emerge.[20] Billy's absent presence is also a manifestation of my lack of preparedness to let go. It is a reminder that the story is unfinished – that although many incidents have been uncovered, the narrative woven from the traces of their story can never be anything but incomplete. Entanglement in the web of human actions belonging to the stories of others has muffled their voices, so that only echoes and whispers remain.

9   Absent Presence: 'Billy – Australien' at the Paris Exposition, 1889

But it was reserved for the Exposition Universelle of 1889 to make the grand display in regard to anthropology and its kindred sciences.

Thomas Wilson, *Anthropology at the Paris Exposition in 1889*, 1890

The key to comprehending the origin and diffusion of expositions, as well as their form, content, and function, turns on the understanding that international expositions complemented efforts by powerful groups within industrialized and industrializing nations to consolidate their political and economic authority at home, along with their imperial gains overseas.

R. W. Rydell, *Book of the Fairs*, 1992

Billy and his companions have gone from the European stage, along with the many other indigenous performers whose journeys intersected with theirs – the 'Bushmen', Tierra del Fuegians, Sioux, Labrador 'Eskimos' (Inuit) and others, but not without leaving their afterimages. For traces of many of these indigenous travellers remain in European anthropological journals and in photographs archived and exchanged between scientific colleagues, and over subsequent years they have been frequently recycled in popular geographical journals, where they are reduced to the anonymity of being unnamed examples of a *type*. Sometimes their bones and preserved body parts also left a more troubling presence in museum collections. While their own narratives remained fragmentary and elusive, they became absent presences in the narratives that Western scientists told themselves about humankind's origins and developmental history. And much of the data for the anthropologists' classificatory project underpinning their theorising was made possible by the symbiotic relationship that had developed between the showmen and the scientists within the show-spaces of Europe and America – the theatres, entertainment halls, restaurants, circuses and museums.

As the nineteenth century advanced, however, a new site of spectacle was developed that also had its roots in the much older associations between market places and fairs, and was linked with the phenomenal growth of cities – and here aspects of commerce, entertainment and education became inextricably mixed in the processes of presentation. Britain's Great Exhibition of the Industry of All Nations in 1851 – within its specially constructed Crystal Palace – marked the beginning of nationally promoted world fairs or international exhibitions that were a defining feature of European, American and European-settler colonial life throughout the latter part of the nineteenth century, dedicated as they were to epitomising and propagating the idea of social and economic progress based on advancements in all branches of science, technology, industry and the arts. These new and complex show-spaces, harnessing all the techniques of architectural enframing, exhibitionary presentation and performative entertainment, provided more structured surroundings for the display of a diversity of indigenous people from the colonial margins of each nation's empire than did the older commercially oriented circuses and show places. Indeed, the indigenous people as 'others' became indispensable living object lessons, the signifiers of a vanishing world of savagery against which the march of progress towards civilisation was measured. Further, the organising principles or 'controlling vision' that underpinned both the selection of contents and the forms of presentation of the great exhibitions drew on the rhetoric of the new anthropological science. They reflected a construction of human development in hierarchical terms, a supposed progression from inferior to superior that ideologically accommodated both the domination of the colonised by the colonisers and the rivalries between the imperial powers.

At the Crystal Palace exhibition in 1851, with the exception of the display of two San children, Flora and Martinas, described as of the 'earthman tribe' from South Africa,[1] a great variety of human 'types' were represented in still tableaux of modelled figures together with stuffed animals, and when these 'figures of savage tribes' were destroyed in the Crystal Palace fire of 1866, their loss was declared to be great 'in an educational sense'. For the function of such inert displays was to demonstrate the prehistory of the present, rather than the lives of contemporary people. The organisers thought them more manageable than living people, who were regarded as introducing a disorderly element reminiscent of popular fairs, vaudeville and circuses, which would undermine the educational intention. Nevertheless, the 1876 Centennial Exposition in Philadelphia, and the Paris Exposition of 1878 both included sections dedicated to anthropology. In Philadelphia, a 'centennial city' of popular 'attractions of wonder', including exotic examples of humanity, also mushroomed – until the city fathers decided that the chaotic message it generated subverted the high ideals directed towards nation-building, and had it demolished. In Europe, the Colonial Exhibition in Amsterdam in 1883 was more successful in formally integrating displays of representative groups of colonial peoples. On a visit from Paris, Prince Roland Bonaparte hailed their presence there as an 'advantage' because they enabled him to observe how people lived without having to travel (I paraphrase); and as an outcome he produced and published a great collection of photographs, *Les Habitants du Suriname à Amsterdam* (1884). With the Paris Exposition of 1889 – as Robert Rydell has proposed – 'a new synthesis emerged as French fair officials organised a colonial village of nonwhites'.[2] These new installations, which became known as 'ethnological villages', became a feature of subsequent international exhibitions. More than that, the Paris Exposition powerfully visualised the idea of progress through its formal construction as well as in its presentation.[3]

In the course of my continuing search for what happened to Billy, Jenny and her son, Toby, I turned to the Universal Exposition of 1889 in Paris.

In an elegant essay on the Eiffel Tower Roland Barthes wrote: 'The tower looks at Paris' in such a way that it transforms it into a 'kind of nature' – 'a new nature that is human space . . . a passive overview' which offers itself for decipherment.[4] He suggested that each onlooker imagines a history as they look. Among the histories Barthes considered, he surprisingly neglected the world of spectacle that filled the show-space at the tower's base on the occasion of its inauguration in 1889. The mix of peoples and cultures to be found there, and their commodification, prefigured the new brew of the twentieth century that found expression in urban modernity. One of the entrances to this world of spectacle was by the electrically propelled moving pathway that transported the visitors into a realm of Palaces, Pavilions and Galleries dedicated to Science and the Arts, Manufacture and Industry. On either side of the central gardens, immediately behind the Eiffel Tower, stood the twin palaces of the Fine Arts and the Liberal Arts; and at a point furthest from the River Seine, the great

Gallery of Machines, which stretched the width of the grounds, gave concrete expression to the conjunction of knowledge and power. These were the new cathedrals dedicated to progress. The great exhibitions played an important part in the consolidation of a bourgeois hegemony. They were openly didactic in purpose, and their promoters frequently referred to them as 'world's universities'.[5] For instance, throughout the summer months, the London Polytechnic took parties of eighty men and thirty women on weekly tours of the Paris exposition.[6] The eagerness of the participating crowds had its own self-regulatory function. In the great exhibitions the disciplinary function of the spectacle was exerted by the visitors' self-awareness of their position both inside and outside the spectacle.

So multilayered is the symbolism embedded in the constructed world of the Paris Exposition – the layout of which is well documented in catalogues, plans and photographs – that there are several possible starting points for unravelling its meaning.[7] The relevant one in the context of this discussion is the Palace of the Liberal Arts that contained four pavilions devoted to anthropology and related subjects, for anthropology, which was claimed as the modern French science, was a main focus of the exhibition. Here many of the intellectual ideas that underscored the whole event were presented in charts, tables, photographs, modelled figures, instruments and artefacts, bones and body parts. A popular account in the *Pall Mall Gazette* contrasted these 'severely instructive' contents of the Palace with the life in the surrounding streets where these ideas found their echoes in reconstructions of North African and Far Eastern colonial towns. There 'in the back settlement behind all the gorgeous finery of the pagodas and the palaces of the Further East the ingenious French have established colonies of savages whom they are attempting to civilise. They are the genuine article and no mistake, living and working and amusing themselves as they and their kinsfolk do in their own country.'[8] In the colonial quarter there were 'night fêtes' and parades of Cambodian dancers, Senegalese drummers, Arab horsemen, and Chinese dragons, and after the show the performers and onlookers drifted away together.[9]

If one entered the Palace of the Liberal Arts from the direction of the Seine, one came first to the gigantic gilt Buddha of Nara, from Japan, which was situated in front of the pavilion entirely devoted to anthropology, and was apparently the meeting point for anthropologists while the exposition was in progress. To the left of the Buddha were the casts (front and back view) of the Bushman, N'Ko, aged about twenty-two years, one of six Khoisan who had been presented as 'The Pigmy Earthmen' at the London Aquarium in 1884 (pl. 44) and subsequently on the continent. They had been examined by Virchow in Berlin, and Topinard in Paris while at the Folies Bergère. N'Ko – who was described as 'the hunter' – had died one month after being presented to the Société d'Anthropologie in Paris in October 1886, and Prince Roland Bonaparte had photographed the remaining five of the group.[10] Remains of some of the dead of other visiting indigenous groups, whose stories I have referred to, were among the casts, skulls and other skeletal material and body parts, submitted for display by the leading European and American anthropologists. So too were collections made in the colonies or acquired by exchange. Among these were five Australian skulls collected by Carl Lumholtz, two of which

67   Dr Paul Topinard, director of the anthropological laboratory stands among the collections displayed in the upper galleries of the Anthropological section, Universal Exposition, Paris, 1889. The photographs on the far wall include those of the Australian Aborigines and the 'Bushmen' by Bonaparte and others.

were from the Herbert River region, North Queensland, bordering on Billy's clan lands.

Collections were submitted on an individual basis rather than as national contributions. Professor Virchow presented a great chart of the colour of the eyes and skin of two million German schoolchildren, and Dr John Beddoe contributed similar classificatory charts for Britain. Each scientist represented his own specialisation, Francis Galton his attempt to represent type by composite photographs, H. H. Risley from Darjeeling his survey of Indian types, Professor Lombroso from Turin his preoccupations with the anthropology of 'criminal types', and Alphonse Bertillon the measuring instruments used in crime detection by the Paris police department.[11]

The displays of the pavilion were arranged on two floors around an open central court. A series of tableaux of modelled figures depicting makers of stone tools, grain growers, the first builders, Aztec paper-makers, and the first metalworkers were arranged around central tableaux of an encampment of Samoyed, Arctic hunter-gatherers and reindeer-breeders. This visualisation, lending authority to a conjectural history of civilisation, apparently 'attracted large crowds of people'. On the upper gallery were to be found 'a perfect arsenal of anthropological instruments devised or used by Dr. Topinard',[12] where the professor himself was in attendance daily to answer questions from the public (pl. 67). The cabinet opposite housed the collection of Prince Roland Bonaparte's Lapp (Saami) skulls, and the skull of Charlotte Corday (the murderer of Marat). At the end of the gallery, among photographs, full-face and profile, of more than 700 people from Bonaparte's extensive collection of portraits of visiting indigenous groups, were those of Billy and his companions.[13]

The eight entrances to these diverse internal spaces of the pavilion were each framed by pairs of decorative panels, painted by the artist Charles Toché, depicting a selection of racial types, one pair of which represented Esther the Hottentot and Billy the Australian. The latter was based on Bonaparte's photographs taken in 1885, although the European pug-dog had been transformed into an Australian dingo. The figure of Esther was attributed to a photograph by Paul Topinard. Esther was one of yet another group of thirteen Khoisan exhibited at the Jardin d'Acclimatation, Paris, in 1888–9. Wife of Jacob, the leader of the group, she was about thirty-five years old.[14] As a photograph (pl. 68) of the entrance framed by these two panels shows, just within the chamber, on either side of the central figure

68 Esther the Hottentot (l) and Billy the Australian (r), frame the entrance to the Anthropological section, Palace of the Liberal Arts, Universal Exposition Paris 1889, on the decorative panels painted by Charles Toché. Within the doorway, on either side of the figure of western man with his muscalature and nervous system exposed, stood the skeletons of a gorilla and an orang-utang, the whole forming a visualisation of contemporary evolutionary ideas.

of European man with his musculature and nervous system exposed, stood skeletons of a gorilla and an orang-utang, the whole forming a visu-alisation of contemporary evolutionary notions.[15] It seems the panels themselves no longer exist; thus the faded photographic record survives as the end-point of a series of representations, each more lifeless than the preceding one, and Esther and Billy's containment within them is analo-gous to their entrapment in Western anthropological discourse. They are gone and only their fugitive images remain.

On a panel above this same entrance, which led to the main display area for anthropology, was inscribed the names of scientists whom the French designated as the founding fathers of the 'Natural History of Man' – 'Buffon, Blumenbach, Cuvier, Saint-Hilaire, Retzius, de Baer, Lucae, Broca and Darwin'. Below them Esther and Billy represented one of the foundation narratives of the sociocultural evolutionary paradigm – the attempt to read the past through the bodies of particular 'racial types'. Beginning with Saartjie Baartman, early in the century, European scientists – and their American colleagues – had sought out the bodies of Hottentot/Bushman (Khoisan), particularly those of women, for examination and dissection, because the characteristics of the external female genital organs and their steatopygia (enlarged buttocks) were considered to be physical signs of their 'brutish nature', and hence of their place in the scale of human development. Khoisan women, perhaps more than the members of any other visiting indigenous group, were subject simultaneously to both the intense anthropological gaze and the prurient gaze of the public. One of the most extraordinary pieces of what would then have been regarded as empirical data was the publication of a chart comparing the outline profiles of the buttocks of the women in Esther's group.[16] And Fauvelle (1999b) has traced the development and consolidation of this foundation narrative through the processes of knowledge exchange over the century, as members of the different Khoisan groups removed from South Africa for display were subjected to these stigmatising processes in the anthropological laboratories of Europe and America. Considering the scientists' eagerness to make comparative examinations and dissections of other groups such as the Tierra del Fuegians and the Australian Aborigines, it is the more remarkable that Billy and his companions were able to resist some of the pressures of anthropological investigation and seem to have escaped the ultimate fate of dissection.

With the advantage of hindsight, something of the difference in the experiences of

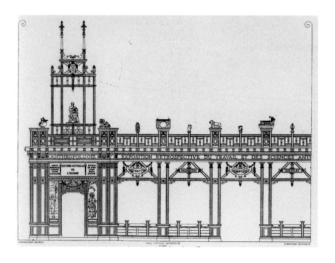

69   Plan drawing of exterior of anthropological galleries, Palace of the Liberal Arts, showing the entrance framed by Esther the Hottentot and Billy the Australian From *L'Exposition universelle internationale de 1889 à Paris*, Paris Ministère du Commerce et de l'Industrie.

the Hottentot and Australian groups is reflected in the way Esther and Billy are represented on Toché's panels. Esther, who is shown in profile, is stripped bare, whereas Billy, who is depicted frontally, is dressed in his show clothes – and not even the scarifications on his chest have been reproduced. Given the prominence of the panels, perhaps it was considered less offensive to the public tastes of the day to represent only the woman as naked and the man as clothed, but, given the anatomical nature of so many of the related displays, it is surprising. Bonaparte made a photograph (pl. 59) of Billy's torso in profile that would have served as a model for the artist, but perhaps as a rather indifferent artist, Toché did not have the skill to use it. Either way, the representation of Billy clothed is a reminder of the resistance he and his companions had to being stripped below the waist for examination. Neither Houzé and Jacques nor Virchow succeeded in carrying out the physical examinations they would have liked, although the Belgians claimed that 'one of them' had managed to briefly observe Jenny's external genitals undetected. Similarly, Virchow admitted having access only to the nude photographs taken by Carl Günther – and these did not yield anatomically explicit data. Only the portrait of Sussy, with her arm raised behind her head in a classic nude pose, suggests that flattery may have been the key to gaining consent to photograph her without clothes.

On the decorative panel, Billy's clothed image also reminds us of the dearth of information about sex-related matters in any of the documentation about the group, anthropological or otherwise. Although there was seldom mention of sexual relations within the group, these seem to have been carried out according to their own kinship rules. After Tambo's death, his widow, Sussy, formed a relationship with Jimmy,[17] and when, in turn, he died, Sussy was referred to as *his* widow. Only in Copenhagen, where Danish speculation about the relationship between Billy and Jenny triggered comments about Billy's discontent in not having a wife, do we learn anything about his sexual preferences or frustrations. Given the exposure of the details of the sex lives of the Fuegian women and of their intimacy with their 'keepers', for example,[18] one can only observe once again that the Australian group apparently exerted more control over the treatment they received than some indigenous groups, and that they were able to do so because, to a certain extent, they received support and protection from their impresario, Cunningham. Billy dressed in his performance clothes subverts the foundational narrative inscribed in the structure of the anthropological displays.

Otis T. Mason and Thomas Wilson from the Smithsonian Institution, Washington, were part of the US delegation to the International Congress of Anthropology, Archaeology and Prehistory that took place during the Exposition, and both reported with enthusiasm on the prominence given to anthropology, and the relationship between the formal scientific displays and the popular ethnological villages, seeing it as a conceptual model for the World's Columbian Exposition planned for Chicago in 1893.[19] The exposition was also visited by another American, Sol Bloom, 'an entrepreneur of popular culture of the city streets',[20] who was later hired to organise the entertainment strip, the Midway Plaisance, at the World's Columbian Exposition, Chicago. Not only did he gain some of his inspiration from Paris 1889, but he also hired some of the same North African performers. In due course, Robert Cunningham, too, was to see an opening for his enterprise in the Chicago fair.

Cunningham's Samoan interlude

Meanwhile, in spite of Cunningham's dalliance with the Australian hairless horse he had acquired for Barnum, he had not forsaken the touring of indigenous groups, and 1889 found him in Samoa.

During this period Samoan life was being shattered by foreign intervention and the accompanying internal strife. The Samoans hit the headlines early 1889 when six of the seven warships of the rival Western powers, Germany and the USA, were wrecked by a great hurricane in the Bay of Apia, off the island of Upolu, and the Samoans saved many lives. Cunningham arrived there in June with the aim of recruiting a group to perform their famous dances. In spite of the opposition of 'King' Mata'afa and other Samoan chiefs he succeeded in picking up a group of nine from the nearby island of Tutuila (one of the islands in the American zone of influence) and shipping them on SS *Alameda*, bound for San Francisco (*San Francisco Chronicle*, 19 Aug. 1889). The showman negotiated a three-year contact in which he undertook to pay their expenses, to supply them with necessary clothing, to pay each $12.50 per month, and to return them home on the expiration of their contract. After they had performed their Siva dances to great acclaim in San Francisco and California, Cunningham removed his 'Samoan Warriors' to New York, where on 18 October 1889 they opened for a short season at Koster and Bail's Theatre, before being transferred to Europe. As part of his complimentary package to New York newspaper editors, he issued a copy of his pamphlet about the Samoans and a set of photographs with the tickets.[21] Again, this American edition formed the basis of later German and Swedish editions and, as with the 1884 pamphlet about the North Queenslanders, provided Cunningham's own account of the Samoans' narrative of capture.[22]

According to the *New York Clipper* (26 Oct. 1889) only eight 'warriors' performed at Koster and Bail's Theatre, led by Atafu (Atofau), so that one of the party may have been already dead – 'Princess' Silaulii. Although the European versions of the pamphlet continued to depict a troupe of nine on the back cover, only seven men were named in the texts: Chief Manogi, Leasusu, Mua, Letuugaifo, Lealofi (poet and composer of songs), Foi and Tasita. The cover of the German version depicts a young warrior,[23] while the Swedish version depicts a young woman, probably 'Princess' Silaulii. According to a later account (*Samoan Times*, 15 Aug. 1891), all gradually succumbed to pulmonary diseases because they were compelled to dance 'clad only in native costumes' whatever the weather, during the American winter season. As a consequence, Atofau died in Belgium in April 1890, followed a few days later by Tu in Köln, Germany. In Berlin the survivors performed at Castan's Panoptikum and were presented by Professor Virchow to the Berlin Anthropological Society. The professor mentions a troupe of seven, but gives the body measurements of six men only.[24]

There were also dramatic developments in Berlin in July when Leasusu and Lealofi were induced to desert the troupe by the wife of a wealthy retired merchant named Max Hauke, who was said to be worth ten million marks. The lady scandalised the Charlottenburg neighbourhood by having the two Samoans accompany her in her carriage, dressed in fashionable European style. Ten days later Herr Hauke died suddenly and an autopsy was ordered. Apparently even an American paper ran the headline 'It May be Murder'. Frau Hauke soon tired of her Samoan escorts and paid for their passage home on SS *Lubeck* – and Cunningham sued her for 100,000 marks for the loss of 'his savages' (*Samoan Times*, 18 Oct. 1890). It is not known if the showman received any compensation, but shortly afterwards he returned to New York with the remaining five of the troupe. There he transferred them to an agent named Marshall, allegedly saying 'I've got all out of them that I could. Now you take them and see what you can do.' It was also asserted that Cunningham had paid them less than the sums due under their contract, and that he had even 'borrowed' $41 from each of them, all that they had on their return to America (as reported in *Samoan Times*, 15 Aug. 1891).

Marshall toured the Samoans through the fall and winter season of 1890–1, and Latuugaifo died of consumption in Denver, where his body was embalmed by the local undertaker and placed on display in a pine box. The inescapable assumption is that Marshall knew about the earlier fate of the embalmed Tambo in Cleveland Ohio.[25] The *Samoan Times* reporter commented that 'Latuugaifo was a brave man, and his fate is a sad one.' Finally, ill and in 'a deplorable condition', Manogi, Tasita, Mua and Foi were abandoned in New York where they were found by a journalist of the *New York World*, a Mr Jones. His reports about their plight compelled the government to take action, and the Secretary to the Treasury appointed Jones to escort the Samoans home – the expenses to be shared by the state and the *New York World*. Manogi was now very ill, and in spite of being carried in a private Pullman Palace railway car and nursed throughout the journey he died as the train passed through the Rocky Mountains. Mr Jones had him buried in Rawlins, Wyoming, with a headstone to mark his grave. Only Tasita, Mua and Foi survived to reached Tutuila.

R. A. Cunningham's involvement in the Samoans' exploitation added to his unsavoury reputation, although by the time of the 1891 incidents he was already in Germany, working as Advance Director for William Foote & Co., touring 'the principal theatres of Europe' with a troupe of 'genuine African American artists' who were billed as 'Savage, Slave, Soldier and Citizen'. Their plans to tour until 1893 brought Cunningham into contact again with Hagenbeck's firm and his circle of associates, including Adrian Jacobsen. In June, Hagenbeck's nephew, Heinrich Umlauff, wrote to Jacobsen about Cunningham and the show: 'I myself have not yet seen the Humbug but as much as I hear of it, it should be a real Negro Tingle Tangle [minstrel show] . . . and of course they are also making a great Poster campaign à la Buffalo Bill.' Apparently Umlauff was considering booking them for the "Land and People" exhibition in 1891, because he 'still had some confidence in Cunningham's people'. So he hoped 'there will be good business transacted with the Humbug' because people were interested in minstrel shows. The following month, however, Hagenbeck himself wrote to Jacobsen: 'That Cunningham is a great scoundrel; one cannot entrust anything to such a man, and you should not rely on anything he says.'[26]

Among 'Cunningham's people' was Colonel James Dodd, who was treasurer of William Foote & Co., and probably senior to R. A. in the firm. According to a letter of 30 August 1891 from Dodd to Adrian Jacobsen (bearing greetings from Cunningham), things were not going well. Although the show had good crowds in Koblenz and nearby towns, competition from a circus in Strasbourg had reduced their takings and the weather in Frankfurt am Main was too hot for people to sit in a crowded hall. But the Scandinavian part of the tour had been secured – presumably by Cunningham, for whom this was familiar territory. Dodd wrote again on 8 September, in reply to a telegram from Jacobsen. It is not clear what Jacobsen had offered, but Dodd's reply was a firm refusal: 'We can do better in small towns' than in a large-scale booking where 'we pay all the expenses.' And anyway, he told Jacobsen, they were about to embark on the Scandinavian leg of their tour. The prospects for Umlauff and Hagenbeck of doing 'good business' with the Humbug had faded, probably because Cunningham's past experience and contacts allowed the Americans to set up their own tour.[27]

It is difficult to arrive at conclusions from a fragmentary correspondence. As I have suggested earlier, there was already a difference in approach between Cunningham and Hagenbeck as to what constituted authenticity. It seems to me that there is more than a whiff of business rivalry in this exchange between American and German showmen, and that the latter were criticising Cunningham for his sharp business practices rather than his treatment of indigenous touring groups. Taking into account the Hagenbeck firm's treatment of the Tierra del Fuegians and Jacobsen's treatment of Tobias, the Labrador Inuit, it would have been a case of the pot calling the kettle black (see chapter 5). At the same time, the whole sequence of events does give some idea of the precariousness of the life of an itinerant showman. It seems the tour of the 'African American' entertainers was not to be for as long as planned, and once Cunningham had completed the touring arrangements for Foote & Co. his services may have been expendable, or maybe his colleagues had not found him to be the asset they had expected. Either way, they parted company and by mid-1892 Cunningham was in Australia ready to start on his next enterprise, that of recruiting an Aboriginal group for the World's Columbian Exposition, Chicago, the following year.

10   King Bill and Company: The Story of the Second Group

After arriving in Australia, Mr Cunningham found that [although the Aborigines] were only intended for the Chicago World's Fair . . . if they were not immediately gotten away . . . it would be impossible to secure them. Within ten days from the signing of the agreement they were forced on board one of the Pacific Mail steamers and brought to San Francisco.
                    Daily Courier (San Bernardino, California), 3 March 1893

In following the trail of Billy and his companions, details of their lives and experiences have been elusive. It has proved even harder to track the course of the travels of King Bill and his company a decade later through the increasingly commercialised world of spectacle, where they were exposed to ever more ruthless exploitation. The continuity between these two narratives is provided by the person of R. A. Cunningham, who was a creature of the boundary, preying on the displaced indigenous owners of the land. The showman's mobility triggered their mobility; the travels of both groups exposed the binding connections that flowed through ideas and actions, linking the colonial and metropolitan spaces. So let's return to North Queensland where the story of King Bill and his company also begins.

Mungalla

In May 1996, Walter Palm Island and I were driving along the highway north of Townsville towards the prosperous small town of Ingham, on the Herbert River, centre of the surrounding sugar-growing district. Walter turned off the highway onto a dirt road that ran very straight, enclosed by fields of tall green cane. The air was still and very hot. He knew the back-roads of the area because he had worked in the cane fields in his youth.

Turning sharp left at the end of a cane field we came again onto tarmac, and soon arrived at the entrance to the homestead of Mungalla, surrounded by lush green pastures. Situated on the flood-plain of the Herbert River, bordering on Halifax Bay, the property is traversed by Palm Creek and a network of other watercourses and swamplands, teaming with wildfowl. Mungalla, which is the heartland of the Nyawaygi-speaking clans, had been acquired by James Cassady in 1882, and the local people who – according to Cassady – then numbered no more than two hundred, predominantly women, were encouraged to stay and to pursue their hunter-gatherer lifestyle (pp. 26 and 55). Even before Cassady came to Mungalla his sympathies towards Aboriginal people made his properties something of a haven, compared with those of his neighbours.[1] In the time of Cassady and his son, Frank, there were three camps for the families of the mixed Aboriginal and South Sea Islander (kanaka) workforce employed in both the cane fields and pastoral work. Today these camp sites and nearby burial grounds of the ancestors,[2] shaded by mango trees and coconut palms, are sites of significance for the Nyawaygi, to whom ownership of Mungalla has recently been returned (January 1999).

It seems that the Aborigines who left Townsville with Robert Cunningham in 1892 were 'taken from Mungalla and other parts of the colony'. Quite how this came about is uncertain, but we have Cassady's own word for it when in 1896 he wrote to his local Member of Parliament, A. S. Crowley, asking him to investigate their non-return.[3] While the group was touring California they were usually described as coming from Townsville, and sometimes as having been 'picked up from a cattle station' (*San Francisco Examiner*, 5 Sept.). Occasionally a more persistent journalist established that they were from Ingham. In 1892 casual visitors would not have found Mungalla easily accessible from Townsville, so it is unlikely that Cassady would have entertained Robert Cunningham there. Possibly the two men met in Townsville, but it is hard to imagine that Cassady, even under convivial circumstances, would have been so naïve as to allow some of his best workers to be taken abroad. It could, of course, have been done in his absence, and this scenario would fit with reports that haste was involved. Alternatively, Aboriginal 'business' may have brought the group together in one of the Townsville fringe camps, and, as with the first group, the showman may have picked them up there.

Table 10.1 The names of King Bill and company, 1892–1898, by source (numbered 1 to 5 from the left).

San Francisco Chronicle, 3 Sept. 1892 From left to right as in Elite Studios photograph of the EIGHT (p. 70)	Barnum and Bailey *Route Book*, 1894 FIVE present	New York Journal, 19 July 1896 Spokesman: King Bill – all mentioned but only FOUR present	Virchow, Berlin, 17 Oct. 1896 Only THREE reach Europe	London shipping records 1898 TWO return
William 1 (reclining)	W. Ditehurogoo or W. Nitoo	b. William		
William 2 (standing)	W. Ditehurogoo or W. Nitoo	b. Billy	William (Maturra)	Willy
Tottie (Dottie), wife of William 2	[dead]	Taddy [dead]		
William 3 (King Bill)	King Dilagroo	b. King Bill husband of Janny	Dilgorru (King Bell) husband of Jenny	
Jenny, wife of William 3	Jennie Nagorar	Janny (Tagara)	Dagorri (Jenny)	Jenny
Harry Mathews or Dick Elliot	[dead or deserted]	c. Dick Gally [gone]		
Tommy Landerson or Gilman (seated centre)	Tommy Warrabulan	b. Tommy [dead]		
Dick Elliot or Harry Mathews (reclining right)	[dead or deserted]	c. Harry Bushelman [gone]		

As is customary, the group were reluctant to tell their Aboriginal names. Nitoo, Ditehurogoo and Dilagroo in source 2 are given credence locally as possible Nyawaygi names. Warrabulan is a Nyawaygi place name. The Aboriginal origin of Nagorar/Tagara is more doubtful as it is suspiciously like Tagarah/Tagorah, the name first attributed to Sussy, of the first group. One reporter, *San Francisco Examiner*, 5 Sept. 1892, remarked on the Aboriginal performers' uncertainty as to their English surnames. I have included almost all the variations recorded. In California, 'Left-handed William', who was probably William 2, was also called Howe(s) occasionally.

King Bill identifies the other men as either his brothers or his cousins. Differentiated in column 3 by 'b' and 'c'. See pp. 205–7.

There are other unanswered questions. What did the Townsville settler society know about Cunningham's treatment of the first group he had removed? Why didn't he seek out these same skilled performers again – only four years later? On the other hand, what account did he give to Atkinson, the police magistrates or anybody else for the non-return of most of the first party of nine? If the matter was raised at all, presumably he had attributed their deaths to tuberculosis, and, given the times, this would have been considered an acceptable explanation. Fortunately for the showman, word does not seem to have reached Queensland about his treatment and desertion of the Samoans, which might have aroused other suspicions.

Although the mention of Mungalla in Cassady's letter does not imply that the entire group were Nyawaygi, it can be established that the majority of them were. Unlike the first group, they were not written about by skilled anthropological observers in the course of their travels, but there are four main sources (see table 10.1) that provide some evidence of who they were and where they were from. Here, I shall simply introduce them by the English names they were using when they first reached San Francisco (Source 1), and relate these to the photograph taken of them in the Elite Studio, Market Street, in that city (pl. 70). Matters are complicated by the fact that three of the men are called 'William', and I denote them by the numbers 1, 2 and 3. Even so, it is often impossible to tell which of the Williams is being referred to in the various news reports.

The central standing figure is King Bill (William 3), later also called King Dilagroo, whose wife Jenny (Janny) stands to his left. That she is his wife is confirmed by a report in the *New York Journal* in 1896 (source 3), where King Bill states that he is accompanied by his wife. By that time the smaller woman, Tottie (Dottie), on his right, had already died. Dottie is wife to William 2, standing on her right. (This is also confirmed by pl. 75, the photograph of the six, taken in New York, in which each wife is seated in front of her respective husband.) Reclining in front of him is William 1, and seated centrally is Tommy Landerson or Gilman. Together, these six represent the core group from Mungalla.

According to the *New York Journal* of 1896 (source 3), King Bill states that these four men call each other brother; that is to say they were classificatory brothers, if not biological brothers. William 2 and William 3, who seem to have been actual brothers, can be identified as Nyawaygi by their body marks: horizontal rows of paired short scarifications, visible in

70   Photograph of the eight North Queenslanders removed in 1892. King Bill stands in the centre with his wife, Jenny, on his left. On his right is Dottie and her husband William 2. Reclining in front of them is William 1, and seated centrally is Tommy. These four men call each other brother. On the extreme right of the photograph, standing and reclining, are the 'cousins' Harry Mathews and Dick Eliot, though who is Harry and who Dick is not known. Photograph: Elite Studios, San Francisco, 1892.

the photographs (pls 79 and 80) taken of then in Berlin in 1896, the only time their bare torsos are revealed. Although Tommy's body marks are not visible, he can be identified by his name, Warrabulan, as given in the Barnum and Bailey *Route Book* for 1894 (source 2). Warubulan is the name of an important cave on Waterview Creek in Nyawaygi territory.[4] He also called himself Landerson, and although I have not yet been able to establish an unbroken descent line, the names Anderson (Anderssen) and

Landers are all names with Nyawaygi associations. These three men are all Nyawaygi.

The two women may or may not be Nyawaygi. Indeed it is very probable that Jenny was Manbarra, because on her return in 1898 she was described as a Palm Islander, and this was in the days before Aborigines in the region were transferred to the Palm Island settlement as a matter of course. Manbarra and Nyawaygi share a kinship system, and intermarry. It is possible that William 1 is also a Manbarra, but the evidence is conflicting. Archibald Meston (see below), in speaking about the men taken by Cunningham after their departure, referred to one as a Palm Islander, and by a process of elimination William 1 should be this man.[5] But a newspaper source described him as having thick horizontal body scars across his abdomen, which were characteristically Biyaygirrigan not Manbarra.[6] However, visual confirmation of this has not been found.

King Bill addressed the two men, Harry Mathews and Dick Elliot, on the extreme right of the photograph as 'cousins' (column 3), indicating that they were not close kin – which suggests that they were the members of the group who were from 'other parts of the colony'.[7] Even so, Dick and Harry, who were apparently both good riders, may have worked for Cassady as stockmen. As they were only with the group for the six months tour of California, it has not been possible to establish which one in the photograph is Dick and which Harry. Their features and hair also suggest that they may have been of part European descent, though the photograph cannot be entirely relied on as evidence on this point. On the other hand, local people who have examined the photograph think that William 2 and William 3 appear to be of part South Sea Islander descent. Given their apparent maturity, this would only just be possible, as the first South Sea Islanders did not arrive in the district until 1863 (except for a few who worked in the fishing and pearling industries).[8] That several were of mixed descent would accord with Meston's statement that the group were 'ordinary tame town blacks who spoke English fluently'.[9] But, whatever the accuracy of this assertion, unlike the first group removed in the 1880s the members of the second group had all worked for settlers. The women, Jenny and Dottie, had apparently been domestic servants and the men had worked in the pastoral industry. William 2 was apparently a tracker in the Black Police for a time. Given their ages, the unaccompanied men probably had wives and families at home.

Removal

The plans for World's Columbian Exposition, due to open in Chicago on 1 May 1893, were reported worldwide, and the Australian colonies were among the places from which exhibits were being sought, particularly by Professor Frederic Ward Putman, the head of the ethnological section. In distant North Queensland the papers reported, regretfully, that the state government had not found the funds to support its own contribution to the Fair.[10] But this did not stop individual entrepreneurs from launching their own schemes. One of these was Brabazon Harry Purcell, a Brisbane stock and station agent, who was also a self-declared expert on Aborigines. Another was Archibald Meston, a past member of the Legislative Assembly of the state and sometime journalist and explorer, who rated himself an expert on the geography, natural history and Aborigines of Queensland. Within a few years his advocacy of segregation of Aborigines on reserves for 'their own good' was to under-write the introduction of the infamous Aboriginal protection legislation of 1897. And Meston himself was to be appointed Southern Protector, responsible for Queensland Aborigines south of the Tropic of Capricorn. Meanwhile he entertained the idea of forming a company of 'wild blacks', uncontaminated by the evils of civilisation, to perform interstate. Late in 1891, Meston and Purcell combined to seek financial backers for their scheme to assemble a troupe of Aborigines 'carefully selected from wild tribes, to tour through Europe and America' – including the Chicago Fair.[10]

Meston was no doubt upset to discover, mid-1892, that the American showman R. A. Cunningham, an old hand at recruiting indigenous people for show purposes, was back in the north looking for Aborigines to take to Chicago. Purcell was away in the north-west of the state in search of Aborigines with 'outstanding physique'. Meston himself had not finished his recruiting. Once he had, he would commence what he called 'drilling' to prepare these men from different tribes for the large-scale theatrical presentation of Aboriginal life he and his partner had in mind, including tableaux that illustrated such incidents as 'the murder of a bushman' and 'tracking of a murderer'. From a present perspective, the photographic representation of the performance (pl. 71) conveys the shock of double vision. A scene that at first sight suggests Aboriginal compliance with a

71   Tableaux of Mounted Black Police in action, arranged for Meston's show, *Wild Australia*, 1892. Photographed, probably on a Sydney beach, by Charles Kerry. From Reverend William Bennett's collection of lantern slides of Meston's *Wild Australia*.

white view of the incident could also reflect an Aboriginal re-enactment through performance of actual events in the black–white conflict – that Meston may even have witnessed. Today such a representation demands we probe its ambiguity. Shown as a lantern-slide by the Reverend Bennett, its influence extended beyond the stage performance. In what narrative did he use it?

As far as can be established, neither Meston nor his partner had sought official endorsement or backing from the organisers of the World's Columbian Exposition for their plans, although it was on offer. And there is only one mention of Cunningham having had any contact with the 'World's Fair Committee' (*Daily Courier*, San Bernardino, 3 Mar. 1893).

Robert Cunningham disembarked in Townsville from the coastal steamer *Aramac* on 7 June 1892. And this time the Queensland authorities were not to make things easy for him. As the *North Queensland Herald* was later to report (19 July 1893):

> When Mr Cunningham obtained leave to take away a dozen blacks from this neighbourhood, all sorts of formalities, including the completion of a bond for their due return, were insisted upon . . . [For] when it was thought that Mr Cunningham's band of aboriginals would precede those of Messrs Meston and Purcell to the World's Fair and secure the advantage of such a novelty, difficulties were put in his way, although, as we have said, he had previously proved himself to be a trustworthy personage in such matters.[12]

How Cunningham went about things in Townsville can be partially reconstructed by following the official correspondence relating to the above-mentioned bond. Already familiar with this busy northern seaport, from his recruiting visit of ten years earlier, the showman re-established old contacts. One of them was Joseph George Atkinson, partner in Atkinson and Powell, Chemists and Druggists, in Flinders Street,[13] who was to play a crucial role in the showman's plans. On the day of his arrival, Cunningham at once lodged a request, via the police magistrate, for permission to remove Aborigines (unspecified) for his travelling show. Twenty days later he lodged a more specific request, through the solicitors Roberts and Leu, to remove Aborigines for exhibition at the Chicago Fair.[14] No doubt there had been time enough in the interval to establish that he could pick up a suitable group from the Townsville fringe camps or properties in the district, and he required a ruling in principle before hiring.

On 7 July the Under Colonial Secretary, W. E. Parry-Okeden, replied that the showman was first required to give 'security to the extent of £500 to return the Aboriginals, or to account for their non-return, to the satisfaction of the Government. It must also be proved to the satisfaction of the Government that the Aboriginals so taken understand the nature of the agreement.'[15]

This was a tough demand. In the following three weeks before the departure of the next steamer for San Francisco, Cunningham had to find Aborigines who were willing to go with him, and a local person prepared to stand surety for such a large sum. He made several applications for Aborigines to the Townsville Bench that appear to have been set aside, and one to the Bowen Bench on 18 July which recommended the Aborigines 'be not allowed to go away'.[16] In spite of these setbacks, by the end of the month the showman had achieved his goal. The chemist Atkinson agreed to be guarantor, and both men signed a bond (two separate documents), probably on 29 July, the day before the departure of the coastal steamer *Peregrine* – with Cunningham and 'eight Aboriginals' aboard.[17] The exact date of the signing is uncertain, because the bond has not been located, but a letter of 3 August, from Parry-Okeden, acknowledged the receipt of the documents, dispatched by the associated Brisbane-based firm of Roberts and Roberts on the preceding day, and authorising the removal 'of the eight Aboriginal Queensland natives described in the bond' . . . 'subject to the stipulations set forth'.[18] It transpired later that one of the 'stipulations' was that the Aborigines should be returned 'within three years'.[19] That the bond is missing is a great loss, because, almost certainly, it would have confirmed the names, ages and place of origin of the second group.[20]

The *Peregrine* reached Sydney on 5 August, and two days later Cunningham and the eight Aborigines sailed on SS *Monowai* bound for San Francisco. Little did the showman realise his troubles were just beginning. Travelling cabin class with him were the delegates to the 'Pan-Presbyterian' Council in Toronto – the fifth General Council of the United Reform Church – including John G. Paton, renowned missionary, and Dr Benton and James L. Rentoul, both professors from Ormond Presbyterian College, Melbourne. The Presbyterian mission in Australia worked in Victoria and Queensland, and Rentoul was an active campaigner against the 'ugly fact' of the 'dispersal' of the 'blacks' in North Queensland (*North Queensland Herald*, 23 Sept. 1891). Also aboard were the Earl of Ranfurley and his daughter, and Monsignor Colletti, a papal delegate, returning to Rome via America. When his fellow passengers rebuked Cunningham for not supplying the Aborigines with adequate warm clothing, he 'practically admitted' it was the result of their having been 'got aboard in somewhat of a hurry'. There was also talk about his past bad treatment of the Samoans in New York, which was passed on to the journalists when the SS *Monowai* reached San Francisco. The steerage passengers (including a Hawaiian called Palani Paakiki, who was to play an active part in their story a few years later) befriended the Aboriginal travellers, giving them clothing and fruit, and at the same time telling them they would never survive in America.

When the steamer docked, the steerage passenger joined with some of the cabin passengers to petition the immigration authority, and the British Consul, Donohue, to have the Aborigines sent home. Owing to a smallpox scare, the passengers were not allowed to disembark until late on 3 September, after the ship had been fumigated. But 'the shivering natives', who, it was reported, wanted to go back, were retained aboard by order of the Commissioner of Immigration, R. C. McPherson, who feared they 'might become public charges' if allowed to enter the country. He 'notified the steamship company he would hold it liable in the sum of $1,000 for each of the blacks should any of them get away'.[21]

To counter the adverse publicity, Cunningham invited the press aboard, and 'the Aborigines gave a simply astounding impromptu display of their accomplishments', sending their boomerangs 'spinning in the air over the deck of the ship'. It inspired one reporter to contemplate the effect of a 'returning' baseball that would dispense 'with the necessity of a catcher altogether'. The Aborigines also danced, 'more like spirits than actual things of life. With their coal black hair, shining faces and queer movements they made a fantastic picture'(*San Francisco Examiner*, 5 Sept.). Although they were fearful about the effects of cold, 'when sun came out they squatted on the spar deck near the bow and enjoyed themselves in their simple way' – drinking beer (*Daily Morning Call*, 4 Sept.).

The San Francisco papers also reported that Cunningham had paid the Queensland government a bond of £2,000, and although this figure was a fourfold multiplication of the sum guaranteed – but not yet forfeited – he had been without a show for four, maybe five, months and had a considerable investment to recoup. As a person 'well known' in Californian theatrical circles, no doubt he used his connections to influence the authorities to reverse their decision. Quite how he achieved it isn't known, but it seems that Commissioner McPherson was absent when, at last, on 16 September, Inspector T. G. Phelps allowed the Aboriginal party to land.[22] The following day the *Daily Morning Call* reported that Cunningham had installed the group – men and women together – in a large room at the Cosmopolitan Hotel, furnished only with camp beds, where they sat around, smoking and longing for home.

In due course the news of Cunningham's troubles in San Francisco filtered back to North Queensland, and Meston, who had apparently met Cunningham during his stay, responded to the news by saying that he had presented the showman with sixteen boomerangs, because those that his group had were useless,[23] adding that

> He wrote a very kind letter from New Zealand, thanking me for every little kindness he had received. I am satisfied Mr Cunningham will be very kind to the blacks, but he will do no good with natives of that type. No man unacquainted with the habits and nature and some dialect of Australian Aboriginals can ever exercise beneficial control.

For Meston, 'control' was the operative word. He indicated he was about to show how it should be done, because 'his' *Wild Australia* was about to open at the Brisbane Opera House.[24] Later the show went on to play in Sydney, but by the time it reached Melbourne, mid-1893, the enterprise had begun to unravel. Recriminations and accusations of embezzlement were exchanged between Meston and Purcell and, abandoning the show, Meston returned to Queensland. The outcome was that some twenty-seven Aborigines and Torres Strait Islanders had to be returned home from Sydney at the Queensland state's expense.[25] The newspapers railed that the government had demanded a bond from the professional and responsible Mr Cunningham, while they had allowed Meston and Purcell to proceed without providing any guarantees for the welfare of the Aborigines or for their return home. Questions in the Legislative Assembly about the incident revealed that the government had always been aware of Robert Cunningham's intentions and a spokesman added that it was only early days, as Cunningham had three years before the Aborigines were to be returned.[26] Later however, in 1897, the Queensland Aboriginal protection legislation included a clause prohibiting 'the removal of Aboriginals from one district to another or beyond the colony'. Although in the debate it was stated that the object was 'to prevent kidnapping', the House was not so concerned about enterprises like Cunningham's, rather its purpose (and in the event its practical effect) was to exercise control over the movement, employment, and interracial mixing of Aborigines within the state.[27]

Although Meston's *Wild Australia* show failed as a business enterprise, while it was running it gave powerful expression to the prevailing colonial discourse on Aborigines. That Aboriginal participation – through performance in the show – was embedded in that discourse exposes the mechanisms of white/state power. It was of a piece with the self-surveillance implicit in the role played by the Native Mounted Police, which had been imposed by the state on Aboriginal people.[28] Also, Meston's personal involvement in both the exhibition of Aboriginal people and the formulation of the repressive legislation of 1897 strikingly draws attention to the disciplinary function of the discourse. Cunningham's show performed a similar disciplinary function in the transnational arena of the show-space, but because it was an extraterritorial space King Bill and his company appeared to have the possibility of more independent action than they would have had in North Queensland – or in reality did have abroad. It was an illusion that depended on the continued success of the show and a supportive management, that is to say, for as long as the interests of Cunningham and the Aboriginal performers coincided.

72   Photograph of King Bill, used repeatedly in the advertisements in Californian newspapers during the Californian tour, 1892–3. Photographer unknown.

California

After all the delays, Cunningham pursued his preparations for the show with urgency: special cowhide costumes were made in the same style as worn by the first group, and photographs were taken. Apart from the group photograph taken at Elite Studios, one image of King Bill with boomerang raised and another of the two women were much used in Californian advertisements for the show (pl. 72). Other more casual sketches of them, 'based on photographs', were used as news pictures. (pls 73a and b) Handbills were distributed and advertisements were placed for the first performances – outdoors in Central Park and indoors at the Orpheum. Long established as San Francisco's premier vaudeville theatre, the Orpheum seated 3,500, and for 'popular prices – 25 cents – reserved seats 50 cents' the public were presented each evening with:

GENUINE CANNIBAL, BLACK TRACKERS AND BOOMERANG
THROWERS
The famous FAMILY FOREPAUGH [circus performers]
ACROBATS, THE SNAKE MAN, and many others

During the afternoon, in Central Park, King Bill and his company gave spectacular demonstrations of their skill with the boomerang in sessions at half-hourly intervals until 5 pm, for 25 cents per adult and 10 cents a child. (Later in the tour, admission was raised to 50 cents for adults and 15, then 25 cents for children.) The reporter for the *San Francisco Chronicle* (25 Sept.) decided that although the Aborigines 'were savage and barbarous in every attribute . . . they did not look like it as they stood watching Cunningham and waiting for the cue to give their performance'. And all the papers gave column inches to debating the art and the science of boomerang-throwing, an operation that was performed 'contrary to the laws of gravitation'. The 'Inghams', as they were beginning to be called, were a success.

As Cunningham surmised, once King Bill and his kin had enjoyed the crowd's applause they lost their shyness and soon settled into the routine of performance. It seemed that Cunningham, the risk-taker, would do

73a and b   'A Wild Throw', and 'Ready to Throw', illustrate a news item about King Bill and company, *The Call San Francisco*, September 1982.

some good after all 'with natives of that type', whom Meston had dismissed as detribalised 'poor specimens'. Although their dances, particularly the Swan dance (a favourite story of human transformation told in their home district), were acclaimed as 'weird' and 'fantastic', the showman immediately recognised that the strength of the show lay in the outdoor boomerang-throwing. He embarked on a tour, at first in the San Francisco Bay area, and then of the principal towns of California, showing the company on baseball grounds, race-tracks, fairgrounds and agricultural show grounds. His performers frequently insisted on appearing, not in their show clothes, but in their normal street clothes, warmly wrapped up against the cold. Cunningham complied; he was waiting for the warmer weather, he said, before travelling north with them to Chicago. Although he continued to advertise 'King Bill and his quintette [*sic*] of boomerang throwers' as AUSTRALIAN CANNIBALS! (per Steamship *Monowai* en route to the World's Fair) who performed their DEADLY BOOMERANG THROWING! the public quickly realised 'the Queensland blacks' were 'more or less civilised from long service on sheep runs and cattle stations' (*Oakland Times*, 16 Oct. 1892).

By the time they reached Sacramento at the end of October, Cunningham had enlisted as his business manager Frank Frost – a man whose show business connections were as extensive as his own. Frank was a nephew of Hyatt Frost, owner of Van Amburgh Circus (1857–92). He had worked with Robinson's Circus, and the Forepaughs in California, and he had joined Sells Bros circus on their Australian tour in 1892. Frost travelled ahead of the party, acting as advance booking agent, arranging the publicity and setting up special deals for schoolchildren. Although he was later to claim he was involved in the recruitment of King Bill and his company, I could find no evidence of it. In due course, however, he was to take over the second group from Cunningham.

In California, R. A. concocted some variations on the cannibal tale, to hold the interest of the otherwise disbelieving public. King Bill, he said, had been expelled from his tribe because he 'abducted the daughter of a chief, and ate her up' (*Sacramento Bee*, 28 Oct.). No doubt Bill found the story amusing because its telling encouraged his 'cavernous smile'. But sometimes the effects of such tales were leavened by more informed stories. In Stockton, the 'Inghams' met a Mr H. E. Perley, who had spent over twenty years mining and following other pursuits in Queensland, including a spell as superintendent of a sugar plantation near Ingham . . . 'where the [Aboriginal] families, all told, numbered a hundred people'. (Could it have been Mungalla?) Left-handed William 2 and the 'old Stocktonian' recognised each other, and shook hands. Two others from Mungalla (William 3 and Tommy) also recognised him, but he could not remember their faces – saying that he remembered Left-handed William as an expert tracker for the police in Ingham. (The Black Police camp at Molonga was close by Mungalla.) Perley's views on tracking skills, and other Aboriginal customs, were conveyed in two rather garbled interviews about the employment of Chinese, 'Kanaka' and Aboriginal labour in North Queensland. He had another story about being trapped by the floodwaters of the Herbert River on a mound, with a group of miners. About half a mile away was another mound on which were marooned a group of Aborigines, who swam the distance between to bring food to them in exchange for tobacco. The performances went particularly well in Stockton, and much amusement was caused when the band 'picked up the tune of the natives' song in the corrobrie [*sic*] dance and played it after the savages had finished'.[29]

Much other reporting was routinely derogatory. In the course of the tour, when considering the Aborigines' prowess with the boomerang, some pondered how 'these strange creatures . . . [belonging] to about the lowest order of humanity – not even excepting the Digger Indians' of California could possess such skills (*Sacramento Daily Record-Union*, 28 Oct.). The context for such views was provided by other reports in Californian papers about the Native Americans, whose 'blood . . . is as different and distinct from our own as can possibly be imagined. . . . They have never changed and never will' (*Berkeley Daily Advocate*, 11 Oct.). And a Stockton reporter, in the *Evening Mail* (11 Nov.), had similar difficulty in explaining the tracking abilities of the Sioux. There were also reports of the importation of 'crowds of negroes' as 'cheap labor', to replace 'the many Chinese in the gardens and kitchens' around Stockton (*Evening Mail*, 18 Nov.). The similarities between Californian and Queensland white prejudices were many. And they were fostered by Frost's customary presentation, when he lined up the Aborigines to 'point out their physical peculiarities' and discuss their cannibal propensities (*Fresno Weekly Republican*, 23 Dec.).

In Los Angeles, Cunningham was hailed as 'that veteran freak-hunter'. The tour was well in its stride, and the seasoned Aboriginal travellers were patently enjoying themselves. About that time, Cunningham wrote to his Townsville friend, Atkinson:

> I have not made much money out of the venture yet on account of the rainy weather. The blacks are well and happy as they ought to be, seeing that they stop at fine hotels and do the block dressed like dudes. They are as jolly as clams in high water and you would smile to see them cruising round the city in the height of fashion, with polished patent leather boots on and big cigars stuck in their mouths.[30]

In Santa Barbara Baseball Park, 'King Bill played a little joke . . . which made [the crowd] scatter. He threw his boomerang at the clubhouse, but it sailed the other way into the crowd. As it fell it struck a man and knocked his derby into the shape of a pie'; 'They enjoy the sport . . . and are greatly amused that the white people marvel at their powers' (*Santa Barbara Daily Press*, 27 and 28 Jan. 1893). By the time they reached San Diego they had perfected the feat of throwing small boomerangs around a crowded hall (*San Diego Union*, 13 Feb. 1893), and were also drawing huge crowds, in spite of fierce storms, to the baseball park at University Heights. Then, a few days later, King Bill and his company began a season at the grand Hotel del Coronado, across San Diego Bay, favoured by 'Princes, Presidents and Captains of Industry'. They performed before some three hundred guests in the theatre, and afterwards they mingled with the audience. One 'prominent guest' asked King Bill how many wives were customary among his tribe. 'His laconic reply was that "one gave them quite trouble enough".' Indulging too freely in cocktails, in such fashionable company, led to trouble. King Bill and his brother 'engaged in a fight' in front of the high-class hotel, Horton House, where they were staying, and they spent the night in San Diego gaol. Next morning they 'were released on $10 bail each, forfeited the money . . . and proceeded with the show, via the Southern California railway to San Bernardino'.[31]

As with the first group, it is difficult to arrive at any details of the economics of the show. Before they left San Francisco, the *Daily Morning Call* reporter (3 Sept.) had tried to find out what Cunningham had contracted to pay the North Queenslanders. The figure they told him, with some uncertainty, was ten shillings a week plus board – which he reckoned to be $2.50, that is, 31 cents each! The showman himself refused to discuss the matter. Later King Bill was to say that they had been promised thirty shillings a week each, plus expenses but had been paid only five dollars a week each in California.[32] As was customary, performers were only paid when they performed, and once the tour began it is evident from the news reports that King Bill and his company had money for their own disposal. Cunningham enjoyed touring a successful company and staying with them at the best hotels, and by 'putting in the winter' in California, he was trying to avoid any of them becoming ill. Being a pragmatist, Cunningham also planned the tour to match the talents his performers possessed, but, as he wrote to Atkinson, he did have some regrets:

> I used to show my previous crowd as wild men, but this mob are a lot too civilised, and are, therefore, not half so good a show. What I should like would be some regular myalls with big woolly heads and sticks through their noses. These niggers I have now go into the best barber's shops and get their hair cut and are shaved.[33]

The Californian tour seems to have ended at San Bernardino. The weather was appalling; the boomerang-throwing at Coles Race-Track had to be abandoned, and the show was not advertised beyond 12 March.

The Southern California railway company was advertising 'Go East to the World's Fair [via] the only line with its own tracks from California to St Louis and Chicago' and 'no change of cars'. As Cunningham and his company were on the railroad route, it seems they followed this advice. At any rate, I have not found evidence of them in California after San Bernardino. Later reports indicate that Dick Elliot died and Harry Mathews went off with another showman in California. Considering the closeness of the pair, it seems very probably that Harry stayed behind on account of the actual or approaching death of his close kin. One source also suggested, erroneously, that Dottie died in California, but she was still alive towards the end of 1893 in New York. In spite of their fears about the climate, while they were in California the company were well and their physical fitness was remarked on. The wet weather does not seem to have been a factor until late in the tour, so Dick's death was probably sudden and unexpected. Perhaps Cunningham adopted the strategy he followed with the first group a decade earlier, and moved on quickly when a death occurred.[34]

From Chicago to New York

'The World's Columbian Exhibition was one vast anthropological revelation', claimed Otis T. Mason. 'Not all mankind was there, but either in persons or pictures their representatives were.'[35] The Native Americans and other indigenous groups were represented formally in the Anthropology Building, and in displays such as the Smithsonian Institution's in the US Government Building. On the mile-long strip of land known as the Midway Plaisance, the Samoan, Javanese, Dahomeyan and other 'native villages', and the installations of many nations, provided popular entertainment. The arrangement of this 'living museum', stretching from the European villages at one end to the representatives of the 'savage races' at the other, reflected the hierarchical character of prevailing social evolutionary ideas. The contrast between the diversity, colour, clamour and aroma of the Midway Plaisance and the whiteness and lightness of the complex of neoclassical buildings, known as the White City, gave symbolic expression to the theme that dominated the fair: the idea of progress. Planned to be 'an exhibition of ideas rather than objects', the fair aimed to present America's material and national progress. A progress in which

74   'An opening on the
Plaisance', cartoon in
the journal *Puck* during
the Columbian World's
Fair, Chicago, 1893.

African-Americans were not only denied any part, but also discriminated
against during its construction, and during the fair itself – reflecting the
increased discrimination against them during this decade, and the general
hardening of attitudes based on notions of race (pl. 74).[36]

The commercial success of the Midway Plaisance was essential to the
economy of the fair. Although Sol Bloom, the organiser of the entertainment strip, hired some of the most popular attractions such as the North
African dancers, other concessions were leased either to various nations or
to approved independent entrepreneurs. Over six months, the fair attracted
27 million people, and many impresarios came to Chicago hoping to share
in the anticipated bonanza. Those whose shows were not accommodated
along the Midway Plaisance were to be found in the dime museums and
other places of entertainment in the surrounding city. R. A. Cunningham's
company of boomerang-throwers seems to have come into this category.
Soon after the opening, an informal gathering of 'all Nations' was arranged
on the Midway Plaisance, free to the public, in which performers who were
on exhibition within the official grounds and on the Midway Plaisance
were joined by outside attractions, and the Australian Bushmen were
listed as taking part with the Sioux and the Samoans, the 'Eskimos', the
Irish, the Swiss, and many others (*Chicago Tribune*, 17 May). But
Cunningham had to find an outdoor show place for his boomerang-

throwers, and in July the 'Wild Australian Bushmen and Human Flesh Eaters' were advertised as performing in Lakeside Park, 'Rain or Shine'. By September, they had moved on to Cincinnati, where the past exploits of their impresario, 'Uncle Bob', were given more column inches than their performance.

By late November, when King Bill and his brothers were throwing boomerangs at the Polo Ground in Brooklyn, the showman told the press it would probably be the last time they performed there. 'They need lots of room to show what they can do,' he said, and as the New York winter was too severe for the outdoor display of their skills, he expected to sail with his company for Europe the following week. For this purpose he had new photographs taken of the six in Frank Wendt's studio on the Bowery, Lower East Side. That year, Wendt had taken over the studio of Charles Eisenmann and, like him, he specialised in photographing circus performers such as Zip, the dog-faced boy, the tattooed lady, the elastic-skinned man, the Wild Men of Borneo and a roll call of Circassian beauties.

Cunningham's announcement is almost certainly a response to his company's complaints of the intense cold they were experiencing for the first time. In the photograph heavy undergarments are visible beneath their show clothes as they look unsmilingly at the camera. The brothers stand: from left to right they are Tommy, King Bill, William 2 and William 1. The two women, Jennie and Dottie, are seated in front of their respective husbands (pl. 75) In the same November article, Jenny is now called 'Tagara, daughter of the King of the North Queensland blacks', a name and story recycled from the first group. She is also referred to as the 'one lady cannibal'. It seems that Dottie is not performing. Two weeks later, King Bill and his brothers are still at the polo ground and, only a few days before Christmas, they are still in New York. 'Whoop La!' headlines the *New York World*, 'the greatest living freak finder has his six Australians ... at the Bryant Park Hotel.' The reporters goad the showman. This is 'the same man', they declare, 'who brought the nine Samoans to this country in 1889' and deserted them. Now they are informed that Cunningham is ill-treating the Australians, and that he does not give them any money.

'Money?' replies Cunningham. 'I guess not, not unless I have to. Why you don't know these bushmen. As soon as they get a little money they go out and spend it. They get cheated right and left. They can't make change,

75 Six of the second group; standing (l to r), Tommy, King Bill, William 2 and William 1; seated (l to r), Jenny and Dottie, each in front of her husband. Photograph: Frank Wendt, New York, 1893.

and they don't know the value of anything, and I have to buy everything for them.' He adds that they are 'a nice lot of savages' except when they drink whiskey. For instance, his manager, Frost, had given them money two days earlier; they had gone drinking and the police had nearly got them.

The showman's aggressive replies betrayed his anxieties. He did not want a repeat of the adverse publicity that accompanied his desertion of the Samoans. If he could not move on with the Aborigines to Europe – perhaps because Dottie was already ill and they were unwilling to go – he would part company with them, leaving them to the management of Frank Frost. Dottie died in New York, some time between the end of December and spring, when the five survivors, with Frost as manager, joined Barnum and Bailey's circus for the touring season of 1894.

By that time, the pattern of Cunningham's response to a crisis with his performers was well established. If possible, he moved them on. If they lost their appeal or became too difficult to manage, or too ill and weak, he discarded or deserted them, as he had done with the Samoans. In the vast and anonymous city of New York, such an action might pass unnoticed unless the press took an interest. The exploitative nature of show business as practised by itinerants like Cunningham was undeniable. In his case, however, when times were good, he had proved himself expansive, not mean. His strategy was to dominate and control by kindness, and to 'treat' his performers. He looked after their health as much out of self-interest as out of real concern for them and, as Professor Landois had said of his treatment of Billy and his companions in Europe, in the final analysis his performers were expendable. But Cunningham was becoming aware that in show business he was subject to the same laws of expendability as were his charges. 'Old Bob', as he was beginning to be called, began to experience their effect too, in the much more organised and commercialised business of shows of indigenous people in the 1890s.

Although Barnum was now dead, for the touring season of 1894 the company of Barnum and Bailey revived the *Ethnological Congress of Savage Tribes*, this time recruiting many of the groups who had spent 1893 on the Midway Plaisance, at the Chicago World's Fair. There were 'Armenians, Australians, Burmese, Cossacks, Dahomians, Egyptians, Esquimaux, Javanese, Klings, Malays, Nepaulese, Sikhs, Singahalese, Siamese, and Soudanese'. In spite of times being depressed, the season proved the most profitable for a decade. The route was extended to thirteen states, including Alabama and Tennessee. Frank Frost was one of two 'lecturers' employed to present the *Ethnological Congress*, and to shepherd the participants. Apart from a mention of a special demonstration of boomerang-throwing, given at Manhattan Field for the benefit of the New York press in early April, King Bill and his brothers attracted nothing like the press attention Billy and his companions had received a decade earlier. Then, according to the 1894 Barnum and Bailey *Route Book*, on 27 August, in Minneapolis, Minnesota, Tom was removed to hospital with pneumonia. Although he survived to rejoin the company at Rock Island, Illinois, the following month, he was the next to die, in New York, during the winter.[37]

The four survivors, Jenny and the three Williams, were to remain with Frank Frost, and together with him joined Pawnee Bill's Historical Wild West Show for its 1895 tour of the United States. Pawnee Bill (otherwise Major Gordon W. Lillie) was a man of many parts – plains scout, buffalo hunter, White Chief of the Pawnees, showman, oilman and banker – whose show quickly rivalled, then surpassed Buffalo Bill's Wild West Show. It was famous for its painted wagons, particularly the bandwagon that led the Grand Parade. Along with the cowboys, Mexicans and Sioux and Mohave villages, the show for that year included a 'Wild West Annex' of sideshows, including Sitting Bull's widow, Koko, a Snake Enchantress, Clio, the Tiger Lilies or spotted girls, and the Australian Cannibal Aborigines, William, Billie, Bill and Jennie. The Wild West Concert, which mainly consisted of plantation songs to the accompaniment of the banjo, concluded with the 'world renowned boomerang throwing by the three Australia Bushmen'. Frank Frost was credited as orator and press agent (Pawnee Bill's *Official Route Book* for 1894 and 1895). The North Queensland stockmen no doubt found this a more compatible company than the more diverse Barnum's circus.

At the season's end, however, the group was left to their own resources, and it seems that in both the winter of 1894–5 and 1895–6 they were based in New York. Like other itinerant show workers they had to fend for themselves in the winter months, staying in cheap boarding houses, and possibly doing casual work at the lower-class dime museums in the vicinity of the Bowery, Lower East Side.[38] In February 1895 the three brothers had a chance encounter with a fellow Australian, Joe Wilson, an architect from Melbourne, who had stayed on in America after visiting the Chicago fair. He had himself photographed with them (pl. 76) They stand cheerfully behind him, well wrapped in heavy overcoats, smoking pipes. A Wilson family story has it that Joe supplied both the warm coats and the tobacco and pipes. Yet, in spite of hardship, apparently they did not ask for assistance to go home.[39] In January 1896, Frank Frost reported to New York police headquarters that William (either 1 or 2) – said to be thirty-eight years old – had gone missing. He had gone with King Bill and Jenny to 'a

76   'Australian Natives, Black and White, New York, February 1895.' Standing (l to r): King Bill, William 1 and William 2; seated: Joe Wilson.

museum' (presumably to perform) and on the way home to 115 East Twenty-Seventh Street the others had been charged with being intoxicated and gaoled for the night.[40] In due course he turned up, and in May, when the season opened, Frank Frost installed King Bill and his brothers in a sideshow on the Bowery, Coney Island.

Meanwhile, in North Queensland, James Cassady, supported by his member of parliament A. S. Crowley, had set in train enquiries about the non-return of the Aborigines removed from Mungalla, and on 20 May 1896 the Colonial Secretary's office sought answers from J. G. Atkinson, only to learn that he had died recently, and that his estate was worthless, so that the bond could no longer be recovered. Meston reported that all he knew of Cunningham was that he was in America.[41]

Coney Island

> *Then the gaze is met by the sight of dazzling, magnificent Coney Island*
> *. . . The visitor is stunned; his consciousness is withered by the intense*
> *gleam; his thoughts are routed from his mind; he becomes a particle in the*
> *crowd.*
>
> Maxim Gorky, 1907

Just as the temporary plaster constructions of the idealised White City of Chicago's fair influenced later American urban architecture, the tawdry razzmatazz of the Midway Plaisance flowed into new sites of mass entertainment that were spawned in all the great American cities in the last decade of the century, and New York's Coney Island was the undisputed capital of them all. It attracted all classes, but by 1895 the pleasure grounds were only a five cents trolley ride away from the city, and for another dime each, the clerks, secretaries, shop assistants and tradesmen and women who serviced the great city came in their thousands, shedding their inhibitions on the beaches and in the fairgrounds. For a largely immigrant population who were already attuned to change, the experience of amusements costing little (many of which, like the Ferris wheel, were mechanised), available in an atmosphere free from social constraints, had great attraction. John Kasson has argued that the lines between the spectator and the performer blurred in the amusement parks established at Coney Island,[42] but what was true of funfairs that involved participation as well as spectatorship was not applicable to the sideshows along main promenades like the Midway and the Bowery. There, the living exhibits were presented as object lessons – just as they had been in earlier years, in the circus and dime museums.

When the barker enticed the public into the tent to contrast the 'freaks' and 'savages' on view with normal and familiar social beings like themselves, how did it affect those who became objects of this fleeting attention? Daily, King Bill and his kinfolk listened as the showman talked up their 'ugliness', their 'cannibalism' and their 'inferiority' for ten cents a time. They gave a few minutes of meaningless performance, inviting laughter and disbelief as they attempted to display their prowess with the boomerang within the confines of a tent. Imagine the cycle of lacklustre performance, despair, and escape into alcoholic stupor. Noting how the bored indifference of the Coney Island spectators gave way to cruelty, Maxim Gorky described how he witnessed 'white-skinned savages, men and women in straw hats and hats with feathers' prodding a mother monkey and her baby with umbrellas and sticks.[43] King Bill and his kin would have been similarly regarded as part of nature rather than culture. Without the encouragement of applause, without the pleasure of exercising their skills and displaying their own culture in any meaningful way, they were further isolated. Already part of the fringe society of itinerant entertainers, as their appeal lessened they slipped into the lower depths of society itself – living in cheap boarding houses in the city's slums.

These were the circumstances of their lives when Palani L. Paakiki, a Hawaiian, found them at Coney Island in June 1896 and mounted a rescue campaign. He had been involved in the earlier attempt in 1892 to have the eight North Queenslanders sent home when the SS *Monowai* docked in San Francisco. He wrote at once to the British Ambassador, Sir Julian Pauncefote, in Washington, describing his past involvement and the present plight of the four survivors, at the hands of the 'unprincipled scoundrel', Cunningham, who had 'turned [them] over to a man called Frost who pays them nothing'; judging by other attractions, he said, 'they should be paid at least $12 to $15 a week.' He claimed four had already died of 'neglect and exposure' and 'one is now sick'. He suggested that, as Aborigines are 'wards of the Government, and are treated as such in every colony in Australia', something should be done by the Consul General to recover their back wages – 'which would materially assist them' – and that a check should be made to establish whether or not a bond had been lodged with the consul in San Francisco, which 'is surely forfeit by this time'. He concluded:

> I am truly sorry to trouble you but feeling my own inability to assist these unfortunate people I have addressed myself to you, knowing that the representative of Imperial Power will assist the most humble of its subjects. I am also a British Subject. Your Obd. Servant.[44]

In spite of this declaration, Mr Paakiki was not entirely confident of imperial largesse. He also contacted the press. The outcome was a report in the *New York Journal* on 19 July, headed 'Held in Slavery on Coney

PRINCESS TAGARA.

77   Princess Tagara, 'Held in Slavery', Coney Island, New York *Journal*, 19 July 1896.

Island', in which the reporter told how he had been introduced to 'King Bill and his little band' by a 'much-travelled man' (unnamed) who spoke many languages, who had been greeted 'with tears' by the Aborigines. Surely this was Palani Paakiki whom they remembered from SS *Monowai* as a fellow passenger.

'We are not savages,' King Bill declared with some feeling, 'although we are natives of a wild country' – and he continued with the story of their travels that I have drawn on in the above account. He said that they had complained many times about their pay and board and had asked to be sent back, 'but [Mr Frost] gave us no hope'. He pointed to the four sausages that had been sent to the Bushmen's tent for their supper, and he claimed they were forbidden to go out, and were watched when strangers tried to speak to them. The 'proprietor', Frost (here erroneously called Trask), dismissed the charges, saying 'they're nothing but a race of cannibals!' And he made the usual excuse that they did not 'know the use of money', and if given it, used it to 'get drunk' and 'get into trouble'. Finally he made the familiar claim: 'they fear and love me at the same time.' And that was how he exercised control over them.

The article displays a cynical ambivalence. While purporting to expose the murkier levels of the entertainment industry, and decrying the enslavement of the Aboriginal performers, it is accompanied by a large illustration caricaturing 'Princess Tagara' (Jenny) with her hand resting on a large knobbly club (pl. 77).[45]

Meanwhile, the Ambassador had asked the British Consul in New York, Percy Sanderson, to investigate the affair and to find a philanthropic society willing to take care of the Aboriginal performers. A representative of the Consulate General visited Coney Island and talked with Jenny, whose account – unlike Bill's – stated that 'they were not badly treated but were desirous of returning to their homes.' Although 'they did not complain of not having received wages', Mr Paakiki had informed him that they had been contracted to receive £1 a week each, but unfortunately 'they were unable to produce a copy of the contract.'[46] Their manager, Mr Frost, denied this, saying that the arrangement was 'to receive food and clothing and such money as he chose to give them'. Sanderson had also asked the St George' Society and the Charity Organisation Society to take an interest, but when they 'refused to do anything' he handed the case to Mr Fox, an attorney, in the hope that 'doubtless he will see justice is done them'. It was 28 July and the Consul General seems to have departed for Newport, Rhode Island, for the August summer recess. Although references to the Coney Island case disappear from the consular records by early August,[47] according to another *New York Journal* report of 24 August, the Consulate General was still involved.

The reporter was told by one of Frost's employees that the 'Boss' had beaten Billy, 'who kept crying like a fool'. But when he spoke to the brothers at their boarding house they denied they had been beaten. When interviewed, the Vice-Consul said he was reluctant to take legal action against Frost in case he turned the Aborigines into the street and they became a charge on the United States. 'We have no funds to pay for their passage,' he said, 'and if we advanced any money for that purpose we are not sure that the Townsville government will refund it.' When the reporter wanted to know what the British would do if the *New York Journal* found a passage for them, he was told they would sue Frost for their wages and passage back to Australia. As the matter had already gone on for two months without action being taken, this seemed unlikely. Perhaps, because of the continuing publicity, Frost decided it wasn't worth further risk. The usual solution was taken and King Bill, Jenny and William 2 were moved out of New York, to Europe, leaving William 1 behind, supposedly near death.

Again the issue of the Aboriginal performers' compliance in spite of the treatment meted out to them suggests a conditioning that began even before they left North Queensland, and was reinforced constantly by economic deprivation and a manipulative brutality that undermined their sense of self-worth. Despairingly, they saw themselves through the white man's eyes.

Although Palani Paakiki's tenacious endeavours to achieve justice for King Bill and his company were subverted by a combination of dilatory officials and wily showmen, the incident remains a wonderfully positive moment in the grim story of the abuse of these people. Although humane in tone, Palani Paakiki's letter is primarily concerned with justice. It is a very succinct presentation of the case, based on careful discussions with the Aboriginal performers. Paakiki is knowledgeable about US immigrant regulations and the legal procedures of repatriation; and he is practical – and politically astute – in recommending that recovery of their unpaid wages would allow them to reach London, 'where the Agent General of Queensland would provide for them'. His familiarity with the Australian colonies suggests either that he had long been involved with British–Hawaiian affairs, or that he knew the history of the project for a Pacific Island confederation to be led by Hawaii, advocated by the Australian Charles St Julian.[48] He also addressed the British Ambassador with assured authority.

Who was Palani Paakiki?

As far as I have been able to establish, Palani Paakiki was not part of the delegation to the Pan-Presbyterian Council aboard the SS *Monowai* in 1892. He was probably among the nine steerage passengers who joined the ship in Honolulu. At the time, native Hawaiian royalists were directing civil unrest against the *haole* (white) dominated government. But by the end of January 1893 the unrest was overcome and a *haole*-dominated provisional protectorate was proclaimed. The ultimate outcome would be the annexation of Hawaii by the United States in 1898. Throughout these troubled years, the royalists sought British support for their cause, while the British, for their part, followed a policy of arm's length support. They were for an independent Hawaii, but ultimately not prepared to oppose the United States.[49] Hawaiian agents were therefore active abroad, lobbying their cause, or even employed directly by the British. As Britain's representative in Washington, Sir Julian Pauncefote was closely concerned with Hawaiian issues. Although Paakiki is a Hawaiian family name associated with the districts of Waimea, Hamuakua and south Kohala on the island of Hawaii, it is also possible that it was a pseudonym, or the name of a part-Hawaiian who was entitled to claim British nationality.[50]

Either way, the concluding lines to Palani Paakiki's letter suggest a political alignment with the royalists, and a familiarity with the British authorities. This much travelled and linguistically accomplished man wrote his letter to the British Embassy from 27 Pine Street, New York – a short street parallel to Wall Street, apparently a street of lodging houses favoured by government officials and lobbyists. His approach to the press revealed that he was not unworldly. Yet what is also important about Palani Paakiki's letter is that – more than any other contemporary commentator on the North Queenslanders' plight – he grasped the bigger picture, the reach of British imperial power, and sought to use this knowledge to attain justice for them. One more thought: according to the *Hawaiian Dictionary*, Pa'akiki means hard, tough, unyielding, obstinate . . .[51]

'Contentious Cannibals'

On the next stage in their journey King Bill, his wife, Jenny, and his brother William were drawn into a German colonial circuit, never seeming able to break free from entrapment in the show-space. For the preceding four years King Bill and his ever diminishing company had travelled only in America. Was alcohol used to persuade these three to leave New York without their kinsman? The most likely scenario is that when they boarded the ship they believed they were going home, and they also believed William 1 was dead (*North Queensland Herald*, 19 Dec. 1898). Instead, within a matter of weeks, they were advertised to appear at Castan's Panoptikum, Berlin: 'AUSTRALIER (KANNIBALEN) NEU! NEU! NEU! NEU!' (*Vossische Zeitung*, 18 Oct. 1896). And like their compatriots of a decade earlier, they were examined by Professor Rudolf Virchow. Their impresario, Herr Maass, told him that they were the same people who had been toured by R. A. Cunningham ten years earlier. Virchow's physical measurements of them, particularly of their heads, established this was not so. His report was very brief – after all, he had already established the type in 1884 – and he now wrote: 'Without any doubt, all three are authentic Australians'[52] (see table 10.1, Source 4).

In Berlin, King Bill and his kinsfolk were also photographed by Wilhelm Scharmann. These photographs were not anthropometric or even anthropological studies, they were studio portraits set against a background of rocks and live palms. In one, Jenny stands proud and tall, her shoulders bare, her torso draped in a fur cloak that touches the floor. She holds a

78   Jenny, Berlin, 1896.
Photograph: Wilhelm Scharmann.

spear diagonally, and clubs and boomerangs are arranged artistically on the floor around her (pl. 78).

In another she has a raised pineapple-knob club in her hand, and stands between her husband, King Bill, on her right, and his brother, William, on her left. There is another of them seated, and also a close head and shoulders portrait of all three (pl. 79). The men are clad only in woollen trunks, their torsos are bare and their body marks are visible. They wear nose-bones, not shown in the photographs taken of them in America. There is also a tableaux of the two brothers engaged in a stylised fight (pl. 80). The atmosphere is fin de siècle, and the effect is theatrical: the return of the Noble Savage. All three look fit and appear to be enjoying the photographer's attention.[53]

In Jenny's later account of the tour through Germany and Scandanavia, however, she refers to the showman, not as Maass, but as Manuel (also German), and says that he exhibited them in a small tent, 'only showing their tattoo marks'. Although Manuel was 'kinder to them than anyone else they were with',[54] their show was low key and the advertisements were

79   (L to r) William 2,
Jenny and King Bill.
Photograph: Wilhelm
Scharmann, Berlin,
1896.

80   Tableaux of men
fighting (l to r): King
Bill and William 2.
Photograph: Wilhelm
Scharmann, Berlin,
1896.

mostly a line or two in the entertainments column, so it is difficult to track their itinerary. But 'the three cannibals' were in Copenhagen in April 1897, 'when a threatening storm accumulated above their curly heads'. According to a Danish report,

> Mr Cunningham happens to have arrived in town, and wants to show in Court that he is the true owner of the Cannibal Number, that he once made a deposit of around 40,000 crowns, in order to be allowed to put them on display, and that the present Showman, his former assistant, in a false and devious manner some time ago had enticed the Blacks from Berlin by giving them whiskey and cigars, two stimulants wild people just cannot resist. Mr Cunningham has already presented his papers to the police, who however thought it might be difficult for him to have his claim upheld. The next few days will show who the cannibals belong to, and who has the right to display them.[55]

Apart from announcing Cunningham's reappearance on the scene, and apparent financial claims (if not continued interest in the group), the incident of the 'Contentious Cannibals' – as the headline put it – appears to have remained unresolved. The group moved on. In June they were advertised as on display in Christiania, Norway.[56] By late November, the showman was in Canada, visiting his mother, from whence he wrote to 'Friend Jacobsen' about acquiring some 'Greenland Esquamaios' (Inuit), and incidentally asked him 'not to forget to remember me to all the ladies that was so kind to assist me the time the Thief stole my Australians . . . Please write me all you know about the <u>Thief</u> and the Australians.'[57]

Was Frank Frost 'the former assistant' referred to and was he the 'thief'? Or was it Maass or Manuel? It is not clear. According to Jenny's later account, they were handed over next to a man called Hayman, 'who was no good' (*North Queensland Herald*, 19 Dec. 1898). Hayman was a name associated with American show business, and Cunningham may well have either employed him or subcontracted to him. By that time, King Bill had died – it is not clear where – and only his wife, Jenny, and his brother William 2 remained. According to the same report, 'Jenny and William left [Hayman] on their own account in Germany, [and] paid their own fares to London.' The report concluded: 'these blacks positively state that Cunningham is living in America in a large house, and has plenty of money, which they think he made at their expense.'[58]

But the *British Australasian* (22 Sept. 1898) told the story differently, say-ing that Cunningham had deserted them in Stockholm, 'after having paid their fares to England'.[59] They landed in London Docks from a Swedish ship, 'in good health but quite destitute', and were taken to Sir Horace Tozer, the Queensland Agent-General in London. There followed an inter-view in which Tozer (pompously) claimed he 'submitted [Jenny and William] to a searching examination', out of which they came with 'flying colours'. It seems he tested them by singing a 'corrobboree [*sic*] refrain' to them, which 'the woman took up . . . with accuracy.' This, he said, enabled him to establish they were the survivors of Cunningham's party whose whereabouts he had sought to discover from time to time. After much dif-ficulty Tozer persuaded the Salvation Army to give them temporary shel-ter[60] – the police, the workhouse and other charitable institutions having refused assistance. Finally they were 'sent back to Queensland at the expense of the Government as deck passengers' on the *Duke of Portland*, sailing on 30 September, via the Torres Straits route to Townsville. On the passenger list, where they were described as Willie, aged 46, and Jenny, aged 40, 'natives', their entries were the only ones written in red ink (table 10.1, source 5).[61] Apparently their experiences had aged them.

Home at last, the 'Palm Island Travellers' – as Jenny and William were called – were met by the Townsville police.[62] They came at once under the new legislation and, like the others in Queensland's Aboriginal communi-ties, their lives would be controlled henceforth by the operation of the Aboriginals Protection and Prevention of the Sale of Opium Act of 1897. If it was sometimes hard to track King Bill and his company on their jour-ney, it has been even more difficult to distinguish the many men called Old Man Bill, Willie, William, Bill, and the several women called Jenny, one from the other, in the departmental lists of movements of Aboriginal peo-ple, back and forth between Hull River Mission, Clump Point, Palm Island and other North Queensland Aboriginal reserves, in the ensuing years.

In London, although William had been described as not very commu-nicative, Jenny had been eager to tell their story, but who was prepared to listen to her tales of railway journeys and sea voyages, and of the Coronado Hotel, the vastness of New York, the dazzling lights of Coney Island, or to listen to the snatches of other languages she had picked up along the way? The *British Australasian* reporter deferred to Tozer, whose only concern had been to establish that he was the expert on matters

Aboriginal, based on his supposition that theirs was a simple culture, and she was a simple person who would have nothing to tell. Back home in Queensland, who among their own people would have had the experience to sustain an interest in the detail of her stories? It was enough to mourn the lost ones, those kinsmen and women who had gone abroad with Cunningham and died there.

'Called on his old Cannibal friend'

In the changing world of the 1890s touring shows of indigenous performers were still drawing huge crowds, particularly in France and Germany, but the emphasis was on ever more spectacular dance groups or exotic 'native villages' where the presentation was scripted to climax with staged combat and/or celebratory festivals. The French posters of the Dahomeyans or the Senegalese, say, showed scenes of colonial warfare as well as dancing. In their presentation, the shows were more directly linked with colonial narratives, the exploits of conquest in different imperial domains. Two Australian Aborigines displaying their body scarifications in a tent could hardly compete.

Unlike Farini, Cunningham did not make the transition to the management of a larger company and, although he tried, he failed to diversify his activities outside show business. Both men came from remarkably similar backgrounds in rural Canada and were the same age. Farini (William Leonard Hunt) grew up in southern Ontario, in a restrictive Protestant society, and Robert Cunningham in southern Quebec. They had the same urge to get out. Farini made his show business debut as a performer on the high wire, while Cunningham's musical talent provided his entrée. Farini had great success with Krao, the 'Zulus' and the 'Bushmen', but he then moved on to part ownership of a circus with W. C. Coup and later married into a wealthy German family[63]. Whereas R. A. was described as having 'drifted into show business', handling everything from 'pigs with seven legs' to 'prima donnas' and 'strange people from foreign lands'. The motivation he gave for constant travel was: 'If you want to have a good time, go where the English language isn't spoken.'[64]

In November 1897, a few months after Cunningham's encounter with King Bill and his small company in Copenhagen, he was back in Canada, and it seems it was time for reflection. He was sixty years old, and he had been home 'very little for more than forty years'. He wrote to 'Friend

Jacobsen' in Germany: 'My mother lives here. She is well to do has got a beautiful house etc. I am stopping here for a while to see what turns up.' He had been to see a group of six 'Greenland Esquamaios' (Inuit) on display in the American Museum of Natural History[65] – 'very intelligent little people' – and what he hoped would turn up was an agreement that he should procure some for Jacobsen. Three years later he wrote again to Jacobsen from San Francisco. He had just returned from Alaska for the second time. This time he proposed he should 'fetch' some Hawaiians – say, six girls and two men. Their 'Hula hula dance is startling and novel,' he wrote, and 'it would take about $3,000 to get them from the islands and land them in Europe . . . if you will furnish the money, I will go after them.' Once Jacobsen had recovered his costs, Cunningham suggested, they should each have a 'half interest in them'. He was, of course, prepared to have Jacobsen's authorised agent join him in the procurement. He hoped for a 'wire' or 'an answer by return'.[66]

Instead, with the passage of time, 'Old Bob' Cunningham, 'one of the most famous of globe-trotters', worked as a 'spieler' with a megaphone, hustling the crowds at Bostock's Animal Show, Manhattan Beach. Or 'the tall old man was to be seen selling tickets at the door of the opium den in Bluffton, Indiana. After 'fifty years on the road' he had a number of scrapbooks completely filled with lurid accounts of what he had done.'[67] Then, on 18 June 1902, Cunningham walked into Hogan's undertaking rooms in Cleveland, Ohio. According to the *Cleveland Press* reporter, he had come to call on 'his old Cannibal friend', Tambo. Hogan walked with him across to Western Reserve Medical College where he found the mummified body, still perfectly preserved. He studied the body a moment and said 'poor old Tambo!'

He retold the story of Tambo's traumatic death and the attempts of his kin to bury him in the traditional manner. Then he lapsed into *his* story of the capture of the group, and how he had tempted them with 'candy and gaudy garments', concluding:

> I am too old to go after freaks now, I went after Eskimos two years ago and froze my legs from the knees down. I am not well now and won't be for some time. But I'll never forget Tambo and his Cannibal friends. They'd steal knives from the table and fight among themselves or with strangers. Once in a while they'd go after me. They are like cattle. They followed one around, ate what was given them, and never showed delight except when they had fish, candy or ice cream.[68]

Touring Toby, Billy, Tambo and their companions had been the high point of Cunningham's career; caught in a time warp with the mummified Tambo, he might seem a man without insight or compassion, but I am unsure about relying on this single piece of casual reporting to probe Cunningham's moral ambiguities. Did he never wonder what had happened to the performers he had abandoned along the way, because they were either too ill to go on or had become disaffected? Yet this was the man who also undertook the long journey to return Jenny and possibly Billy to Townsville in 1888. Perhaps he had grown used to suppressing what was inconvenient to remember?

In 1993 I searched New York's Records of Death for Tommy, Dottie and William 1 – particularly William – because August or September 1896 when he supposedly died seemed the date most likely to be accurate. I searched under all possible family names, listed in the table above, plus Cunningham, and under the personal names. But New York was in the grip of a heatwave in August that year and many deaths of anonymous black men were recorded. I reconciled myself to not finding out. Then, in the *Official Route Book* of the Pawnee Bill's Wild West Show for 1899, listed among the attractions, I came across a 'Group of Australian Boomerang Throwers', named King Bill, John, Tom and William. On the opposite page, a photograph of the smiling Colonel Frank Frost (now a 'Press Representative') was reproduced. In the *Official Route Book* for 1900 and 1901, the troupe members were named as King Bill, John, Tom and Phillip. a Pawnee Bill's Courier for 1901 shows a small representation of an Australian night-time camp scene, with kangaroos cooking. The accompanying text features a large inset piece on the Black Trackers, in the abhorrent language already familiar to us: 'The lowest order of human kingdom', 'no object of worship, no marriage ceremony' and so on. Another undated example shows a graphic of Aborigines wearing the familiar skin costumes. In Pawnee Bill's *Herald* of 1902 a representation based on the photograph of the original eight of King Bill's company is used to publicise 'a native village of cannibals, costing over $25,000 to transport from their faraway Australian home'. And in Pawnee Bill's Wild West Show *Courier* for 1904, the photograph of Jenny, her son, Toby, and Billy, taken by Negretti and Zambra in 1885, has been recycled. (In reality, if still alive, by 1904 young Toby would have been a man of about twenty-seven.) The 1905 *Herald* had only a brief two-line mention of the

81 Portrait of Aboriginal performer in Pawnee Bill's Wild West show, 1899 to *c.* 1905, identified as William 1. Photograph: Harry Bock.

Boomerang Throwers 'in the concert', alongside 'Colored Nashville Students'.[69]

Frank Frost, the manager of the Boomerang Throwers for Pawnee Bill, provides a link between these performers and the earlier shows. Is it possible that any of these people could be survivors of either group? Or are they Frost's invention? At least for one of them there is some evidence. Between 1900 and 1905, Harry Bock, or 'Buckskin Harry', a member of the Pawnee Bill Company, photographed the show, and among the 150 images that have survived is one of an Australian Aborigine, 'King Bill'. Looking at the photograph, I see that he is not the 'King Bill', husband to Jenny, who went on to Germany, but the renamed William 1 who was left behind in New York. After all, every troupe of boomerang-throwers had to have a King Bill.[70]

In the photograph, the old man kneels and, smiling, he reaches out to play with his dog (pl. 81). Although his face is in shade, I am convinced it is William 1. His nose is broader and different in shape from the noses of either of the other two Williams, and his beard is full and bushy. (And the other two Williams are positively identified, anyway, in the photographs taken of them in Berlin.) Nor can he be Billy of the first group – who was characterised by a wispy beard.

Who, then, were John, Tom and Phillip? Were they surviving members of the second group, King Bill and company? Were Dick and Harry now called John and Phillip? Did Frank Frost reunite William and Tommy with Dick and Harry? Or did William teach three black Americans to throw the boomerang?

As I study the photograph of the old man, and strive for a sense of the existential dimension of his life, I am reminded again of the archivist in the famous New York Library who, over a decade ago, had treated my enquiries about Australian Aborigines in the circus with scepticism, assuring me that 'they were fakes – these people shown in the circus.'

11   *Welcome Home Tambo*

You already know enough. So do I. It is not knowledge we lack. What is missing is the courage to understand what we know and to draw conclusions.

Sven Lindqvist, 'Exterminate All the Brutes', 1997

Tambo's 'return' was a singular event in which the past and present collided and tilted into the future, precipitating meanings.[1] Within the family and community it activated processes of cultural renewal that found important expression through the performance of the ceremony to release Tambo's spirit, and through the funeral, in both their private and public aspects. Although there were some Palm Islanders who were troubled by Tambo's return in February 1994, for the majority the mourning and the memorialisation also embraced the symbolic return of other 'lost ones' who had been removed during the period when Aboriginal lives were controlled under the Protection Act introduced in Queensland in 1897. The fear of removal looms large in the social memory of present-day Palm Islanders, as it does for other Indigenous Australians, because it was the main punitive instrument used against the Islanders under the Act. After the Palm Island Settlement was established in 1918, it became, in effect, a penal establishment – though recalcitrant Aborigines could be removed from the Island as well as to it. For generations, removal under the Act robbed this and other Aboriginal communities of their emerging leaders. Consequently the community's response to the repatriation of Tambo's embalmed remains and his burial on Palm Island derived considerable spiritual strength from the shared experience of removal. The concern was for more than a recovery of history; it was a matter of spiritual reincorporation of the lost one.

Tambo's body was not a replication, it was the real thing, and as such it was the focus for these proceedings. When I spoke to Walter Palm Island by phone that day in October 1993 when news of the discovery of Tambo's embalmed body was released, we did not have a lot to say; we both knew the important thing was that Tambo would be going home. By the time I reached Cleveland a couple of days later the Australian authorities had set the process in motion.

While in Cleveland I also learnt that the actual inquest into Tambo's death had taken place some weeks earlier. On 18 August 1993 the coroner, Dr Balraj, had pronounced the official cause of death as 'probable pneumonia', recapitulating the details of the original Record of Death of 23 February 1884. She noted Tambo's subsequent embalmment, and that he had been for some years in the basement of C. J. Smith's funeral home,[2] until its closure and the sale of the property. (For Tambo's death see p. 105.) She had conducted an external non-invasive autopsy, and included the sad detail that Tambo now weighed only 35 lb. Under American law the body of the deceased can only be handed over to living relatives, and apparently it was thought unlikely that Australian Aboriginal kin could be found. After some weeks, a concerned citizen of Cleveland who was aware of the discovery and identification of the body informed the Australian Embassy in Washington of Tambo's existence, and they requested that the coroner forward the documentation. Several more weeks passed, and another concerned citizen, disturbed by the lack of action, broke the story to the Cleveland media – who by chance made contact with me in San Antonio.[3]

It was remarkable that Tambo had escaped either being consigned to a pauper's grave or having his bones deposited in a museum. There is a core Aboriginal belief that the return of the spirits of the dead to their dreaming sites is vital to the harmonious ordering of the universe, and to the preservation of spiritual well-being of kin and community. The ritual disposal of the dead plays a significant part in ensuring this. In 1884, Tambo's kin had begun the ritual and, although they were interrupted, the embalmment of the body had not ended the process; it had merely suspended it. Such a situation can be accommodated within Aboriginal belief systems and practices, because sometimes in the past a considerable time elapsed between initial funerary ceremonies and the final disposal of the bones or other remains.[4] Nevertheless, Tambo's special circumstances required new forms of ritual both for the release of his spirit, which took place in Cleveland, and for the funeral ceremony on Palm Island. Tambo's embalmed body was seen as an anchor for his spirit; wherever the body was, the spirit was somewhere about. Thus it was essential to enlist the assistance of a Native American of the Seneca nation – within whose tribal domain Cleveland was situated.[5]

One of the things that bothered me was that I had not yet found a photograph of Tambo that would provide a likeness. On arrival in Cleveland, however, I found that the television news reports of the event had transmitted a photograph of the shrunken, mummified figure of the diminutive Tambo in his display box. Taken in 1945 to publicise a visit of Frank Drew, the dime museum proprietor who had been the instigator of the embalmment, the photograph also shows two nubile young women standing on either side of the box, pointing at the embalmed figure.

It is a photograph of witness, as powerful as a holocaust photograph. If Tambo's embalmed body had not survived, it would be the only evidence – apart from contemporary newspaper reports – of the careless inhumanity underlying the display of Tambo over many years. The inclusion of the two girls heightens the sense of desecration. At the same time, the accompanying report indicates that, apart from Drew's annual viewings, Tambo had 'disappeared from public notice', having been consigned to the basement of the funeral home, together with other mummified corpses. The reason, it seems, was that the proprietor, Murray Smith, would 'permit no clowning with the mummy of Tambo-Tambo', adding that his father had taught him 'the dead should be treated with respect. That applies also to a primitive from Australia.' The implication was that Smith disapproved of Drew's behaviour, although he felt he could not refuse him access.

Because of the events that took place in Cleveland, both at the time of Tambo's discovery and the later performance of the ceremony of the release of his spirit, circulation of this photograph in a public context needs further examination. To put it plainly the use the media made of it in America, to stress the macabre circumstances of the discovery of the body, reanimated the atmosphere of a nineteenth-century 'freak' show. Such a disrespectful use would have provoked an outcry if it had been a holocaust photograph; thus it exposed the racism that continues to pervade attitudes to indigenous people such as the Australian Aborigines. At the press conference called by the coroner, Dr Balraj, in an attempt to defuse the photograph's dehumanising power, I explained that the descendants were offended by the sensational manner of its display. The reply was that as the photo was already in circulation it would be difficult to restrict its use, but an apology, and an explanation of the issues, was transmitted during the next TV news item on Tambo by at least one TV station.[6]

As evidence of a dreadful inhumanity, it is important the photograph is not suppressed. But to show or not to show it is, I consider, a decision for the Manbarra descendants, who are entitled to decide for each context anew the appropriateness of the inclusion or not of the photograph – a difficult matter to monitor outside national boundaries.[7]

Although the young man's name was given as Tambo in the official documentation, the media's doubling of it as Tambo-tambo also added a twentieth-century contribution to the 'freak' factor. Nevertheless, the Palm Island family decided that Tambo's show name was so closely identified with his story that it should continue to be used as his public name.

Releasing the spirit

Tambo's repatriation was secured under Australian Commonwealth legislation of the 1980s by which financial responsibility was assumed for assisting in the identification, notification and negotiations associated with the return from overseas of significant Aboriginal cultural property, including skeletal and other remains. The policy is administered mainly through the Aboriginal and Torres Strait Islander Commission (ATSIC). Specifically, Aboriginal remains are to be dealt with in accordance with any reasonable directions of the kin and community involved.[8] Thus the funding was provided by ATSIC and the Queensland state government for the Palm Island delegation to bring their deceased ancestor home. The Palm Island community also raised a further $10,000 towards the burial and the funeral expenses.

In Townsville, it was agreed that the delegation should consist of the two senior Manbarra elders, Walter and his brother Reg, and the respected Bwgaman elder, Kitchener Bligh, a Nyawaygi-speaker, who had been separated from his family as a young boy, and removed from his own territory to Palm Island.[9] Thus the delegation represented both the traditional owners and the 'historical' people transferred to Palm Island after the establishment of the settlement in 1918. Even before then, as near neighbours, the Manbarra and Nyawaygi had kinship ties and there was a close linguistic affinity. Manbarra was no longer spoken, and

82   (L to r): Reg and Walter Palm Island and Kitchener Bligh perform the release of Tambo's spirit in front of his coffin, Cleveland Ohio.

Walter and Reg knew only a few phrases, so it was important that Tambo's spirit be addressed in a language he would recognise as from his homeland.

In the meantime (thanks to Tambo) I continued with my now extended research time, knowing that I would be returning to Cleveland for the ceremony. On a cold day in early December, we met the Palm Island travellers in the Cleveland airport lounge; three tired men, clad in thin cotton shirts, who were making their first journey outside Queensland. As the hotel on Water Street where Tambo had died no longer existed, and the street itself was transformed, it was not possible to make a meaningful visit to the site.[10] Instead, that evening, to prepare themselves for the following day's ceremony, the three men chose to use the photograph of the embalmed Tambo as a focus for their mourning. As Walter later said: 'we stood in silence and opened his photograph. His presence was with us then.'[11] In spite of its distressing content, the photograph performed a private function.[12]

For the ceremony, Tambo's casket was draped with the red, black and gold Aboriginal flag.[13] Clayton Logan, an elder of the Seneca nation, participated in the brief, completely private part of the ceremony. Then Walter, Reg and Kitchener performed the public part of the ceremony, repeating their call to the ancestor to join them. Walter spoke the words of the Lord's Prayer in the language of his ancestors, then his brother Reg rendered this version of the prayer back into English (see p. 34). Afterwards, at the press conference, Kitchener Bligh spoke quietly about his own removal to Palm Island as a boy, seventy years earlier; he said that the experience, shared with most Palm Islanders, reinforced the significance of Tambo's return for them all – as well as for the descendants, the traditional owners. The *Plain Dealer* reported (8 Dec. 1993) that Dr Balraj spoke for all present when she said how deeply moved she was that 'a family of someone who died more than a 100 years ago comes all this way here . . . and with the greatest reverence, to take their ancestor back home to be buried'.[14] Although the media were specially asked not to use the photograph of the mummified Tambo, when it came to the evening news, all but one of the four TV stations used the image. Indeed, one used it as a small logo in the top right-hand corner throughout the item.[15] But Walter, Reg and Kitchener had decided not to look at the television news. Instead, they had slept. They had done what they came to do, and they were pleased to be taking their ancestor home, knowing that his spirit was with them.

Final journey

Tambo's repatriation took place during the period of intense public debate in Australia that followed the 1992 High Court decision – known as the Mabo decision – that overturned forever the legal fiction of Australia's foundation on *terra nullius*, unoccupied land, and acknowledged the principle of Native Title in lands and waters where it had not yet been extinguished.[16] This debate about Indigenous Land Rights overlapped with another, relating to reconciliation. The Council for Aboriginal Reconciliation, involving Indigenous and non-Indigenous participation, had been set up under an Act of 1991, as a recommendation of the Royal Commission into Aboriginal Deaths in Custody. It was seen by the federal Labor government of the time as a way of meeting Aboriginal aspirations, as well as marshalling public responses to issues of Aboriginal disadvantage relating to 'land, housing, law and justice, cultural heritage, education, and employment, health, infrastructure and economic development' – not

83   Cover of *Townsville Bulletin* Supplement, 27 June 1998, to mark the tour of *Captive Lives* exhibition in their city (portrait of Walter Palm Island superimposed on a photo of Cunningham, Billy and Jenny).

through imposed social policies, but by a shared reformulation of the social contract between Indigenous and non-Indigenous Australians that would provide a new foundation for policy making. The objective was for consensus to be achieved by the centenary of Australian federation in 2001. Thus, at the time of Tambo's return there were discrepant forces at work. Some of the media dwelt on the macabre aspects of the event, drawing on the discriminatory language of difference that reinforced old stereotypes. For those committed to reconciliation, however, Tambo's repatriation provided an occasion for affirmative speech and action. For some others, disturbed by the implications of the Mabo decision, and doubting the effectiveness of reconciliation as a political strategy, his return was nonetheless seen as the resolution of a terrible story. Experiences of displacement are also embedded in the personal and social memories of other communities within Australia, and are anyway within reach of the imagination of all. Here was an event with which many in the wider

Australian society could empathise, and for which they could express sorrow.[17]

In the community, the return of the deceased ancestor was experienced at a more personal level; the Palm Islanders were reclaiming one of their own lost ones. Tambo's return activated the processes of cultural renewal that take place 'as people live their lives, make decisions, and act with ineluctable reference to their culture and therefore their past, whether or not they are conscious of this'.[18] Oral expression was, of course, central to the processes of cultural transmission and transformation embedded in the performance of the culminating ceremonies: the release of the spirit and the funeral – including the funeral feast. But from early in the preparations, imagery also played a dynamic part in how the deceased ancestor was imagined both outside and within the community. In the absence of a photographic likeness, the media usually represented the ancestor symbolically by cutting out the closely cropped head of Billy from the Bonaparte group portrait (pl. 60), sometimes combining it in a montage of photographs to illustrate a particular aspect of the story or ceremony that was being represented (pl. 85). Within the community, however, as the fragmentary story intersected with real Aboriginal needs to strengthen continuities with their past, some chose to commemorate their ancestor in visual narrative form. An image of a brooding Aboriginal face, merged with the outline of Great Palm Island, came to symbolise the returned ancestor. It was one of the designs printed on the shirts for the male pall-bearers and guards of honour, and on the aprons worn by the women who served at the funeral feast (pl. 84). A painting by Alan Palm Island, incorporating the same composite design, surrounded by a representation of the principal creative being, the Carpet Snake, was used as the logo on the Invitation to the Celebrations, the Order of Service for the funeral, and on the Tambo committee's stationery. The commonplace and the ceremonial were bound together by a graphic imagery that represented a spiritual presence.

Josephine Geia (later chairperson of the Palm Island Council) explained to me how the image had come about. Several years earlier, she had had some success with a sarong fabric design that incorporated a map of the island. She decided to repeat it, and enlisted the talents of her uncle, James McAvoy (who was a mural-painter), to add 'something of Aboriginality' to the design. When she saw the face emerging from the

84   Representation of Tambo
printed on aprons worn by the
servers at Tambo's funeral feast.
Designed by James McAvoy.

island she was very moved because 'it was out of the ordinary, this face
of a man, and not knowing that anything was coming . . . long before
anything ever came up about Tambo.' Looking back, Josephine and others
spoke of it as a sign.[19]

Executed in a Western figurative style, the surrounding emblems of
turtle, dolphin and drum may appear to non-Aboriginal eyes to be
merely decorative, but they refer both to site-specific myths and to
historical associations with Torres Strait Islanders (Josephine's kin)
who were removed to Palm Island early in the twentieth century. The
composite image marks the persistence of graphic imaging as an
Aboriginal mode of expression and transmission of ideas. At the same
time, through its iconic form, the design was accessible to both Aboriginal
and non-Aboriginal viewers. It reflects the Palm Islanders' simultaneous
accommodation of, and resistance to, the pressures of the dominant
culture. As for the central mythic image, the ancestral figure *is* the island.
Such a visualisation of Aboriginal space signals the resilience of core
beliefs that celebrate the spiritual connections with the land – in spite of
their coexistence with the Christian beliefs strongly held by most of the

PART of the 4000-strong funeral procession to honour Tambo Tambo, an Aborigine who was abducted from his homeland in north Queensland and died overseas 110 years ago.

Funeral rain – hero happy at last

By BEN ROBERTSON
on Palm Island

THE heavens opened yesterday as Tambo's tribal "mother" embraced the spirit of her Aboriginal son for the first time in 110 years.

Tambo's great-great-great-nephew Walter Palm Island, 55, his closest living relative, stood proudly in his suit beside the grave as the rain tumbled down, and smiled.

"It is a good sign. I'd say Tambo is happy for the first time," he said.

"After all that he has been through, it is a great relief to know that he is at peace.

"He left Palm Island a slave but he has returned a hero."

About 4000 people, including United States Ambassador Edward Perkins and Federal Aboriginal and Torres Strait Islander Affairs Minister Robert Tickner, attended Tambo's funeral yesterday on the anniversary of his death in 1884.

Tambo's mummified remains were found in the basement of a US funeral home in Cleveland, Ohio, last October.

He was one of nine Aborigines abducted from two north Queensland islands in 1883.

The nine captives were exhibited as "savages" and performed boomerang and spear throwing and traditional dancing during a North American tour with Barnum, Bailey and Hutchison's Greatest Show on Earth.

Tambo, wife Sussy and five others were members of the Manbara tribe from Palm Island, off Townsville. The other two were Biyaygiri people from Hinchinbrook Island, north of Townsville.

Hospital records show Tambo died of pneumonia aged 23 in a hotel in Cleveland on February 23, a year after he was captured by circus agent Robert Cunningham.

Walter Palm Island, his brother Reg, 32, and Bwgcolman elder Kitchener Bligh, 81, went to America in December last year to retrieve the body.

North American Indians from the Seneca tribe performed a sacred "smoking ceremony" on December 7 in Cleveland to release Tambo's spirit from their land.

Tambo's body was placed in a Townsville funeral home and was taken by boat to Palm Island yesterday.

A traditional Aboriginal burial ceremony was held at the grave site followed by an ecumenical Christian memorial service.

Mr Perkins said he considered it a special privilege to have witnessed the event.

"I just can't imagine the national psyche of the American people being complete unless the American Government had facilitated in helping these remains get home," he said.

Mr Tickner said Palm Islanders saw yesterday's service as a celebration rather than a day of great sorrow.

BILLY, one of the captured Aboriginal circus performers.

WALTER Palm Island beside the grave of his great-great-great-uncle . . . 'a great relief to know that he is at peace'.

US Ambassador Edward Perkins.

85   Page from *Townsville Bulletin*, February 1994, reporting Tambo's funeral.

islanders. Consequently, the face merged with the island articulated a narrative of identity that was reanimated by the deceased ancestor's return. Its integration into ordinary, everyday things signalled its cultural significance. Although there was no photographic likeness available at the time, in retrospect, I wonder if a likeness would have been as effective a motive force as the mythic image in the experiential revaluation of the Islanders' past.[20]

The funeral was organised by the Manbarra-Bwgaman Tribal Elders Council and the Justice Group, chaired by Josephine Geia, rather than the Palm Island Council,[21] because traditional authority was considered more appropriate for the occasion. Tambo had reanimated a connection with the past for all Palm Islanders and the elders saw the conduct of the proper funerary ceremonial and the accompanying celebration of Tambo's return before assembled guests and the media as having a unifying function: a public affirmation of the kinship that had grown over the years between the traditional Manbarra owners and the Bwgaman, or people who had been removed to the island in historical times.

On the day, over 2,000 people gathered along the foreshores of Great Palm Island, as Tambo's coffin, draped in the Aboriginal flag, was carried ashore attended by the chief mourners and honoured guests, including US Ambassador, Edward Perkins, and the federal Minister for Aboriginal and Torres Strait Islander Affairs, Robert Tickner. Again, the ceremony moved from the public domain to a reserved, ritual space of mourning by the grave-site, where the traditional burial was followed by a Christian service. Heavy rain began to fall – as was apparently to be expected at the funeral of an important elder. Later, in the public space, the celebration of Tambo's return provided an opportunity for expressions of reconciliation, particularly in the reading of a letter to this effect from the then Prime Minister, Paul Keating.[22]

For the closely involved, particularly Walter, his brothers and their extended families, Tambo's return certainly strengthened their sense of identity and of belonging. Meanwhile, I had located a likeness of Tambo, and on a subsequent visit in 1996 I brought a framed photograph of the group of nine, including Tambo, and another of his wife, Sussy, to hang in Walter's living room in Townsville. There, in that domestic space, they have become familiar objects and the subject of discussions about family likenesses. Reintegrated into family history, the ancestors have been repossessed in conversation and in memory.

On the occasion of Tambo's return, the public's response to a powerfully symbolic event signalled the possibility of a change in relations between the Indigenous minority and the dominant society, but the wounds of the past are not healed so easily. For the possibility to be sustained, real social and economic needs must be addressed. On Palm Island in the 1990s unemployment was still over 80 per cent, with all the attendant social malaise that flows from a long history of economic deprivation. Some ten years earlier, Kitchener Bligh, together with six other elderly Palm Islanders, had commenced an action before the Human Rights and Equal Opportunity Commission against the Queensland Government for the proportion of their wages illegally withheld during the 1970s. The 1996 hearing, held on Palm Island, established that 'the government had deliberately, intentionally and knowingly, discriminated against these workers because of their race.' For its part, the state government remained in denial until a renewed action in a federal court was threatened, and only then did it capitulate. In April 1997 a public apology was made to the complainants, and each was paid $7,000.[23] Although the action related to the recent past, the root causes extend back over almost a century of mismanagement, muddle and misappropriation that characterised Queensland state policy towards Indigenous Australians. Kitchener Bligh's story reminded me of the earlier experiences of another Nyawaygi man, King Bill.

'Give them money? I guess not, not unless I have to'

The words that R. A. Cunningham used to justify his exploitation of King Bill and his company could have applied equally well to the experiences of King Bill's kinsfolk and neighbours who remained at home in North Queensland. A hundred years later, the Queensland government might also have spoken the same words to justify the administration of Aboriginal Affairs in that state.

According to the showman, Aborigines were children, who did not understand money, or the value of things. They would spend it on trinkets, alcohol and other vices. But he looked after them because 'they were a nice lot of savages.' He did not add that when they were no longer useful to him, he abandoned them. Both Billy and his companions in the 1880s, and King Bill and his company a decade later, shared these experiences of working for the white man. Except for the occasional do-gooder whose attempts to rescue them were easily thwarted by the showmen, as itinerant performers they were on their own. Back in North Queensland, the protective policies introduced by the 1897 legislation institutionalised the same nineteenth-century practices and attitudes as those experienced abroad by the Aboriginal travellers. The same coupling of discriminatory attitudes and economic exploitation prevailed as the labour of Aboriginal men, women and children increasingly became part of the economy of the missions and government settlements, and Aborigines were contracted out to rural industries such as the pastoral, cane and fishing industries. With few exceptions, Aborigines became wards of the state, subjected to a harsh regime of control and surveillance, throughout most of the twentieth century, the object being the regulation of 'social, sexual and labour relations between the Aboriginal and colonial populations'[24].

Although enforced confinement of Aborigines on Queensland reserves ceased from 1971, the more immediate sordid history of underdevelopment and enforced economic dependency continued, as Aboriginal workers continued to be paid at the illegal rate of 72 per cent of the minimum state wage.[25] Make no mistake, the $7,000 Kitchener Bligh and the others received (only months before Kitchener's death) was not a handout, or compensation for the years of deprivation: it was a delayed part-payment of wages that had been illegally withheld, and without any additional compensation. This is unfinished business: further actions are in process and the state government continues to try to close down all litigation on the issue.[26]

By the year 2000, the reconciliation debate had also stalled, with the federal government's failure to bring the formal process to fruition by acknowledging the institutionalised discrimination against Indigenous Australians. In spite of this there have been some pluses. For the Palm Islanders, there has been a landmark agreement signed in 1998 between Palm Island's native title-holders, the Manbarra, and Bwgaman Palm Islanders, outlining the mutual rights and responsibilities of both groups (see *Townsville Bulletin*, 25 Mar. 1998). The following year the Nyawaygi recovered their dreaming sites at Mungalla, on Halifax Bay. As the property was freehold, native title had been extinguished, so the purchase was made on behalf of the Nyawaygi people by the Indigenous Land Fund, and in mid-July 2000 a new era began for them when Kitchener Bligh's son, Maurice Bligh, and others took part in the handover ceremony.[27]

Very early in my search for what happened to the Aboriginal travellers, the manner of Tambo's resurfacing – a 'flash' from the past, 'blasted out of the continuum of history'[28] – caught the public imagination. Within Australia, this response (together with the response to other events in the 1990s)[29] held the promise of a realignment of Indigenous and non-Indigenous histories, through the emergence of new narratives that acknowledged the history of Aboriginal dispossession and continuing disadvantage. Although the stories of Billy and his companions and King Bill and his company remain incomplete, Tambo's return establishes the relevance of the whole narrative for the present. What happened to the Aboriginal travellers abroad and what happened to their kin in the contact zone at home were interdependent, linked through related colonial structures. But, as Walter Benjamin cautioned, the 'flash' of history must be seized: the present economic and social injustices endured by Aborigines that have their roots in that past must be addressed. Only then will the symbolically charged event of Tambo's return stand confidently as a redemptive moment in Indigenous and non-Indigenous relations.

Abbreviations

AIATSIS	Australian Institute of Aboriginal and Torres Strait Islander Studies
ATSIC	Australian and Torres Strait Islander Commission
BM	British Museum
NAA	National Archives Australia
NARA	National Archives and Records Administration (USA)
NLA	National Library of Australia
NSW	New South Wales
NSWA	New South Wales Archives
PRO	Public Record Office, London
QPD (LA)	Queensland Parliamentary Debates (Legislative Assembly)
QSA	Queensland State Archives
SOAS	School of Oriental and African Studies, University of London
V&P QLA	Votes and Proceedings, Queensland Legislative Assembly

Notes

The epigraph to the book is from the address by Sir William Deane, the then Governor-General of the Commonwealth of Australia at the opening of the *Captive Lives* exhibition, Canberra.

Introduction: The Journey

1 Houzé and Jacques 1884.

2 For the introduction to Walter, I am indebted to anthropologist Nicolaas Heijm, who had worked with the Palm Island community for several years. I had already made my first attempt at piecing together the fragmentary story (Poignant 1993) and when other commitments allowed I was pursuing a research project which I was beginning to call *Captive Lives*.

3 Genealogical Sheet 63, Palm Island, Queensland, 28 Oct. 1938. N. B. Tindale's papers, Museum of South Australia. Dick Palm Island, born *circa* 1880, would have been only two when Tambo and the others left, so that he must have been told the story later. See below, pp. 18 – 24, for identification by appearance body marks and language group.

4 Tonkin 1992, 12. A useful distinction borrowed from oral history is that between history-as-lived and history-as-represented.

5 The consultative aspect was funded by AIATSIS (The Australian Institute of Aboriginal and Torres Strait Islander Studies). The exhibition toured throughout Australia from November 1997 to mid-2000, and is now a permanent installation in Townsville, Queensland.

6 Father and son were both called Toby and apparently 'little' was used as an affectionate diminutive.

Because nowadays it has demeaning connotations I shall be restrained in my use of it.

7 Although I first saw these Bonaparte photographs in the collection of the Royal Anthropological Institute, the negatives (housed in Musée de l'Homme, Paris) show a larger area than the print, so that the wall behind the backdrop is visible. Bonaparte photographed the 'Bushmen' against the same background.

8 At this point in their journey, although Cunningham must have needed new photographs of his much-reduced group, it is unlikely that the anthropological photographer, Bonaparte, made them available. To date, prints of these photographs have only been found in institutional collections.

9 A record or a 'quotation' from experience (Berger and Mohr 1982, 96): the idea of quotation acknowledges the frame, and raises questions about life outside the frame (absence) as well as about what is within it (presence); thus it assists the interrogatory process.

10 My attempt here to read – cross-culturally – the fleeting expression of emotions and subtle nuances, as they have been arrested by the mechanics of the camera, is obviously a subjective exercise, but the reading of body language and facial expressions is something we all do as part of living and surviving. This cognitive process (Zeki 1999, 179) is to be distinguished from the extremes of nineteenth-century systemised practices of physiognomy and phrenology that played such an important part in racial stereotyping.

11 I note that my first published analysis of this image in these terms was made before the rediscovery of

Tambo's embalmed body. Ethnographically, death and embalmment were appropriate associations to make, given the obvious dislocation of these North Queensland Aborigines.

12 According to Walter Benjamin, such representations, which he referred to as dialectical images, 'are the concrete "small particular moments" in which the "total historical event" was to be discovered' (Benjamin in Buck-Morss 1989, 70).

13 Pseudo-scientific language pervaded show publicity, see chapter 4.

14 Bakhtin 1981, 84, 250–3; Clifford 1988, 236.

15 See Appadurai 1991, 193; Marcus 1995, 35–55. Marcus discusses montage as a way of rendering 'a description of a cultural process in trans-cultural space'.

16 For instance, see Corby 1993.

17 Presumably Virchow also asked the Aborigines, but he was establishing the matter 'scientifically'.

18 *Ota Benga, the Pygmy in the Zoo* by Phillips Verner Bradford and Harvey Blume (1992); *Give me my Father's Body: The Life of Mimik, the New York Eskimo,* by Kenn Harper (1989); Gabi Eissenberger, *Entefürt, verspottet und gestorben: latinamerikanische Völkerschauen in deutschen Zoos* (1996); Hilke Thode-Arora, 'Abraham's diary' (2002).

19 For a discussion on nation and narrative in the Australian context see Attwood 1996, 100.

20 As Hayden White writes (1980, 9): 'far from being a problem, then, narrative might well be considered a solution to a problem of general human concerns, namely, the problem of how to translate *knowing* into *telling* . . . the problem of fashioning human experience into a form assimilable to structures of meaning that are generally human rather than culture-specific.'

21 Collectively, the colonial discourse, the representational processes through which the colonial subject is constructed.

22 Brayshaw (1990, 53) reviews the historical sources. There are few records of either ritual cannibalism or what she refers to as gustatory cannibalism, i.e. human flesh eaten with relish.

23 For discussion on the process of transference involved see Kilgour 1990, 17; Taussig 1986, 105–7; and in the context of the Australian contact zone, Schaffer 1995, 106–27.

24 Nicholas Thomas (1994) cautions us about regarding either colonialism or the cultures of the different colonialisms as unitary. *Cannibalism and the Colonial World* (Barker, Hulme and Iversen 1998) provides an introduction to the ongoing debate about 'the reality of cannibalism as a social practice' in indigenous societies, and about the significance – and persistence – of the cannibal trope in nineteenth-century American and European cultures, particularly in their representations of indigenous other.

25 I am mainly using 'anthropology' throughout this book in the continental sense, to mean what the English called physical anthropology; see Stocking 1987, 9. In this period, phrenology (begun by Franz Joseph Gall in 1796 and developed by Johanne Gaspar Spurzheim) and physiognomy (Johan Caspar Lavater (in essays 1775–8)), now considered pseudo-sciences, had equal status with anthropology. Both attempted to systematise techniques of interpreting inner mental attributes by 'reading' outer bodily signs.

26 In September 1992, I attended the handover of Aboriginal skeletal remains from the Anatomy Museum, University of Edinburgh, see Poignant 1992. See also Fforde, Hubert and Turnbull 2002.

27 Hulme 1986, 12.

28 Unsourced news item from the cuttings book, no date.

29 The figure presented by Baudelaire, and familiarised by Walter Benjamin, as the strolling interpreter of the 'modern' urban experience, later seen by Benjamin as the loiterer with intent who produces news/literature/ads for the purpose of information/entertainment/persuasion; Buck-Morss 1989, 306.

30 From the Cunningham cuttings book: a translation of an extract from the *Mescheder Zeitung,* Aug.

8, 1885, is one of the few reports he seems to have kept in translation.

31   Houzé and Jacques (1884, 99) noted this expression of 'fear and submission', see p. 125.

32   The identification of hostage with the captor, as noted in recent times, is a related response.

1   Meet the Travellers

1   I have located references to the American edition but not yet a copy of it. Cunningham continued to print and update other language editions in the course of their tour. To date I have located Belgian, German, Swedish and Norwegian editions.

2   Seven prints from five negatives; two are enlargements from two of the negatives.

3   The copy in Bibliothèque Nationale, Paris, is accompanied by an identifying sketch – unattributed.

4   News reports indicate that both photographs and the pamphlet were sold to dime museum audiences.

5   Tambo's mummified body showed no horizontal scarring across his abdomen or any other scarring in 1993. Cunningham in 1902 (*Cleveland Press*, 18 June) spoke as if Tambo had some scarring. Perhaps not an entirely reliable observation after almost twenty years. But he may have had light scarring similar to Toby's. Jimmy, who was about the same age, and also Manbarra, only had vertical scars on one upper arm. The photograph of the nine is not clear enough to verify the point. In 1902 Cunningham was speaking about the practice of scarring as a process.

6   Cassady in Curr 1886–7 vol. 2, 425; Lumholtz 1979, 303.

7   For Tambo, *Cleveland Herald*, 27 Feb. 1884.

8   Other variations on the island's name found in the sources are Burkuman (taped interview with Reg Palm Island by Noel Loos in 1972), today called Burrguman. Bwgcolman or Bwgaman, with variant spellings, is used today to distinguish the 'historical peoples', introduced to the island over the last century, from the traditional owners, the Manbarra. More recent linguistic work done by Nicolaas Heijm and Walter Palm Island (1997) on the language of the Manbarra has clarified the linguistic picture.

9   Dixon and Blake 1983, 434.

10   James Cassady in Curr 1886–7 vol. 2, 424.

11   Brayshaw 1990; Johnstone (1903) in Johnstone-Need 1984, 103. The close affinity of these three groups, noted by Sub-Inspector Johnstone, is confirmed by R. M. W. Dixon's linguistic studies. He designates the three dialects as of the Warrgamay language group (Dixon and Blake 1979).

12   Here it is not appropriate to do more than sketch in the character of these communities pre-invasion. For those who would care to pursue the matter in more detail both Brayshaw (1990) and R. M. W. Dixon (1983) and their bibliographies are good access points to other earlier sources. For additional linguistic information I have drawn on the work of Nicolaas Heijm and Walter Palm Island. Linguistic and boundary issues are still current.

13   The shield and wooden sword according to Carl Lumholtz, were 'necessary' companions in this area (1979:131). According to Houzé and Jacques, the shield was 80 cm long and 35 cm wide. Light in weight and kidney-shaped, a pattern of chevrons painted in alternate red and white ochre radiated from a nodal point on its slightly convex outer surface. Its shape, size and decoration were characteristic of shields that were made in the Cardwell-Rockingham Bay area, and it closely resembles others from the same area to be found in several Australian and British collections (see Brayshaw 1990, 63, 249–58). A rainforest shield in type, it was made from the flanged buttress of the fig tree. In plate 4, and in four group photographs taken of the seven to reach Europe – two by Negretti and Zambra in London, and two by Carl Günther in Germany – the shield is only ever held by the Biyaygirri men. Bob holds it in plate 5, but as Billy holds it in the other instances it was probably his shield.

The sword had the same distribution as the rain-forest shield. Made from hardwood, one end was carved into a short handle, which was coated with gum and wrapped with twine to provide a better grip when it was swung, using only one hand. The average length of surviving specimens from this area is about one and a half metres. By comparison, the sword taken overseas, best seen in pl. 51, was only about a metre long and 12 cm at its widest point (Houzé and Jacques 1884, 135). Swords of a similar length were more characteristic of the area around the town of Mackay, further south. Surviving specimens of swords from Palm Island are rare, but as it happens, there is a sword in the collection of the South Australian Museum made by Walter Palm Island's grandfather (and collected by the anthropologist Tindale in 1938) that is 92 cm × 8.5 cm, which corresponds in length with the sword carried by the group (pl. 1). Although Billy held the sword in most of the photographs, in others it is held by one or other of the Manbarra men, Toby or Jimmy. Therefore it is quite possible that it was a Palm Island sword. In most of the photographs Bob held a different kind of fighting stick or club, common throughout the area. About 70 cm long and slightly bulbous at its more pointed end, it is probably best seen in pl. 3, where it rests against the backdrop to the right of Jenny. Although it is not unlike a woman's yam digging stick, the photographs show only men holding it.

14 Wittke 1930, 140–2.

15 Although I would have preferred confirmation from an additional source, the context in which it is mentioned is very convincing.

16 Native Mounted Police, variously referred to as Native Police and Black Native Troopers, were recruited outside an area (see Kennedy 1902; Loos 1982, 25). Toby may have worked as a tracker or guide for them on a particular occasion or on a casual basis.

17 Lumholtz 1997, 91, 251, 303. Carl Lumholtz was half way through a stay, which had begun in August 1882.

18 Reported in *Townsville Bulletin*, 2 Mar. 1998. Based on a series of key letters and documents: QSA. Hom/J200, 2118/1913; I am grateful to Nicolaas Heijm for sharing this file with me and transcrib-

ing a letter signed Dick Palm Island, dated 3 June 1913.

19 I have explored this theme at greater length in Poignant 2003.

20 The information that capes and belts of whole skins of the small Tullah possum were sometimes worn was volunteered by an elderly, reliable informant from a small Aboriginal community a little north of Cardwell – before I showed her the photographs (Bessy Jerry, taped interview with the author). I have checked in museum collections in Australia and Europe without finding examples or photographic records.

21 Brilliant 1997, 57.

2 'Now Enough'

Epigraphs: Although McNab was arguing for a new state-wide policy for Aborigines, it was at the time of what were described as 'the present hostilities in the North' – that are part of our story. (Letter in V & P QLA, 8, 1876.) Mark Twain visited Australia in the late 1890s and his comment is a response to stories he heard from the North Queensland frontier.

1 Dalrymple's report, 1864, quoted in Bowen (Governor of Queensland) 1865.

2 'Diary of Thomas Henry Huxley, aboard HMS *Rattlesnake* 1849': Huxley 1935, 108.

3 Observed in 1860 by G. E. Dalrymple and J. W. Smith RN on the *Spitfire* Expedition, discussed in Brayshaw 1990, 31. We cannot know if these were Birri clans from the south side of the bay, Wulguru clans, or a mix.

4 Recollections of an early settler, C. S. Rowe, in 'Rowe's diary', May 1931, *Cummins and Campbell's Monthly Magazine*.

5 Translation authorised by Walter Palm Island in a Press Release in December 1993, associated with Tambo's return. Queensland Aboriginal dialects, RCMS 291, Royal Commonwealth Society Collections, Cambridge University Library.

6 Houzé and Jacques 1884, 133–9.

7 Brayshaw 1990, 41–3, reviews the sources that asso-

ciate body scarification and wearing of a nose-bone with initiated men, though it was not necessarily part of the actual ceremony among these clans.

8   Murrell (Morrill) 1863; Lumholtz 1979, 139; Meston 1898; Roth Bulletin 4: 1902, 15.

9   'A fragment of a description of a bora at Mt Milbir-raman', *Science of Man 6.1* (1898): 10–11, reported by Archibald Meston, who in the 1890s was to become first Protector of Aborigines in South Queensland.

10   Allingham 1977, 174.

11   *The Way We Civilise*, a pamphlet reprinting the newspaper's correspondence on these issues 1880, 28.

12   Letter to Governor Bowen, 1864.

13   See, for instance, Carrington 1871; Eden 1872b; Finch-Hatten 1885.

14   The argument developed here and below owes much to analyses of earlier Australian frontiers by B. Morris 1992, 86, and of the Putomayo of South America by Taussig 1986 and 1992. Both Governor Macquarie in New South Wales and Governor Arthur in Tasmania invoked 'terror' as a legitimate strategy.

15   Nevernever, writing to the *Queenslander*, 8 May 1880, 28, began his exploration of this idea with: 'We are all savages; look beneath the thin veneer of our civilisation and we are very identical with the blacks . . .'

16   See particularly Loos 1982; Evans, Saunders and Cronin 1975; Reynolds 1989.

17   Murrell's account first published as Morrill, J. 'Journal of an Expedition to Rockingham Bay', *Port Denison Times*, 26 March, 2 April 1864, and later edited, by Edmund Gregory, 1896, see Morrill 1896, 24–6, 30.

18   Dalrymple's report, 1864, in Bowen 1865.

19   Analysis of the workings of the Black Police is bedevilled by lack of documentation, so this is a rare survival of an exchange of letters disclosing policy relating to the Native Mounted Police and the Aborigines, QSA, Col/A64, 65/352. A detachment of NMP usually consisted of four to six black

troopers, led by a European lieutenant and/or sub-inspector, and a camp sergeant.

20   Davidson did not call his place Bellenden Plains until after Dec. 1866, when he at last registered his claim with the Land Commissioners; the name was chosen because 'it is the nearest station to Bellenden Ker', the highest peak in the district.

21   The regulations under the new Lands Act permitted an applicant for a sugar lease to select a block within ten miles of the coast or on a navigable river (between 320 and 1,280 acres) and on proof of having cultivated a tenth of the land within three years he was relieved of the obligation of residence (Eden 1872, 282). To secure the lease Davidson had only to 'mention a fixed point' 'for protection to be granted until the land was surveyed.

22   Typescript of John Ewen Davidson's transcribed 'Journal – 1865 to 1868'. I am very grateful to Ron Store, then Librarian, James Cook University, Townsville, for locating this for me. The following quotes are from diary entries on 7 Jan., 30 Mar., 24 June, 4, 22 and 31 July and 2 Nov. 1866 and 12 June 1867.

23   Eden 1872a, 55.

24   Windshuttle (2000), in his denial of the degree of slaughter of the Aborigines in the nineteenth century, argues that it would have been abhorrent to Christians.

25   From entries in Davidson's diary for 24 June, 22 July and 31 July 1866.

26   BM accession records: the shield 7696, the sword 7697, necklace 7706, pear-shaped bag 7701, bicor-nual basket 7700 and cylindrical fish-trap 7702. See also references in Brayshaw 1990, 256, 262, 307, 300, 296.

27   Johnstone-Need 1984, 55, 64, 141.

28   Memoir by Korah Wills, transcribed by Heather Frankland. OM 75–75, John Oxley Library, State Library of Queensland.

29   Eden 1872a. Eden, who also wrote about Bellenden Plains in *My Wife and I in Queensland* (1872b), showed a familiarity with John Ewen Davidson's

30 Bakhtin 1981, 158.

31 In *My Wife and I in Queensland*, Eden creates another character, Emma, who has made a similar adjustment – and that within four years of the establishment of Cardwell.

32 Bowen 1865.

33 The incident has continued to be written about in that vein ever since; my concern here is to examine its consequences for the local clans.

34 This was the view of Gowlland in the official report of 1872, 3. His unpublished journal of the search conveys a tremendous sense of immediacy, but can only be drawn on briefly in this account.

35 Moresby's published account (1876, 41–50), drawn on here, is brief. Lieutenant Hayter's unpublished log (1872–3) supplies some details of time and place of incidents. Although Gowlland (1872) deals only with events from 15 March, he provides the most reliable figures for the survivors and the dead. Contemporary news reports are inconsistent. They included *Port Denison Times*, 28 Mar. 1872 which published a report of official enquiry of 16 March, *Marlborough Chronicle*, 21 Mar. 1872, *Brisbane Courier*, 11 and 22 Mar. 1872, and *Town and Country*, 9 March 1872. Johnstone's retrospective account of 1903 in *Spinifex and Wattle*, compiled by J. W. Johnstone-Need (1984, 18–45) incorporated accounts of survivors of the larger raft, Thomas Ingham and W. J. Forster, that Johnstone challenges.

36 As told by an Aboriginal survivor to an early settler Chris Wildsoet, see Colliver and Woolston [1998]; see also Jones 1961, 171.

37 Johnstone later wrote that he scoured '*all the black's camps*' from the Murray River (near Tam O'Shanter Point) north to Point Cooper, beyond the river that was later named Johnstone (Johnstone-Need, 1984, 45).

38 QPD, vol. 45, 323–4.

39 Heydon may have been related to one of the rescued whose name was variously spelt as Haydon and Hayden.

40 'Alleged outrages committed on the Aborigines in Queensland by the Native Mounted Police', V & P QLA, *1875*, 621–8.

41 Reports in the *Brisbane Courier*, 11 Mar., 27 Aug. and 19 Sept. 1874, in Collinson papers, John Oxley Library.

42 Report on Pearl-Shell Fisheries of Torres Strait, 1879, in V&P QLA, 1880; see also Prideaux 1988.

43 Loos 1982, 138.

44 QSA, Col/A306, 5,664/1880, 29 Sept. Sub-Insp. Johnstone to C. P. Seymour and enclosure; 26 Oct. C. P. Seymour to Col. Sec.

45 QSA, Col/A333, three letters, 1385/1882 B. Fahey, Coll. Customs, Cooktown to Coll. Customs, Brisbane, 2.3.1882; 1304/1882 H. FitzGerald, Inspector Police Cooktown to Seymour, Commissioner of Police, Brisbane, 2.3.1882; 1225/1882 Howard St George, Police Magistrate to Colonial Secretary, 13.3.1882. In spite of the incident having taken place on shore, apparently the only legislation applicable was an Imperial Slave Act.

46 QSA, HAR 13/1, Seaman's Engagement Book, 1874–92; Col/A353, 460/83 Steve Barry to Col. Sec. 22.01.1883. Name lists are seldom useful as identification. Very often they go: Dick 1, Dick 2, Dick 3 . . .

47 QSA, Col/A340, 3552/1882, Report and Depositions re the imprisonment of Aborigines (deserters from the *Prompt*).

48 '[Mr Thompson] contended that this warfare – for it was nothing less – was accompanied by cases of cruelty which were a disgrace to white men. The whole thing was a history of horrors', 22 Oct. 1880, QPD, vol. 7.

49 See Lumholtz 1979.

50 *Queenslander*, 4 Sept. 1880; both letters were reprinted in the pamphlet, *The Way We Civilise*, 1880, 43, 51–6.

51 Thanks to Robert Ørsted Jensen, who drew my attention to this later letter, not republished in the pamphlet.

52   For the exchange of letters see *The Way We Civilise*, 1880, 51–3. According to a report in the *Brisbane Courier*, 24 Apr. 1875, the murder was committed by ' blacks from various tribes' who were using Hinchinbrook as a refuge.

53   *Queenslander*, 2 Dec. 1876, p. 19. Johnstone later described how he trapped and 'dispersed' them by scraping the bark bottoms of their six canoes to a thin layer so that they sank when they tried to embark, (Johnstone-Need 1984, 58–9).

54   Reserves for Aboriginals, Cardwell District, V& P QLA, 1877, vol. 2. 1245.

55   James Cassady and William Craig both figure in the story of the second group removed by Cunningham in 1892 (see pp. 203–4 and 227). Their stories, and the stories of other sympathetic settlers like Heydon, are almost as elusive as that of Billy and his companions.

56   *The Way We Civilise*, 1880, 56.

57   Armit also rebuked those white men who cohabited with Aboriginal women, which given his personal antagonism to Cassady is interesting.

58   Evans Saunders and Cronin 1975, 58–66.

59   Letter from Armit to *Queenslander*, published 4 Sept. 1880.

60   Brayshaw 1990; Dixon 1983.

61   QPD (LA), 1876: 1453.

62   The visit of James Tyson, a southern entrepreneur, was reported: news cutting, A. Meston papers, OM 64–17, Box 2, envelope 5, John Oxley Library.

63   Letter, Craig to Commissioner of Police, Parry-Okenden, 26 Jan. 1898, in Dixon 1983, 8.

64   Neighbours but not friends: in 1874 Cassady had been forced to retract his allegation that a trooper called Sam – a deserter – had been shot on Johnstone's orders. The story was dismissed as hearsay, although it was admitted that Sam had disappeared and no one knew 'whether he was alive or dead'. Sworn affidavit and letter: QSA, Col/A202, 23 Oct. 1874.

65   Curr 1886–7, vol 2, 424 and 426. I have not found confirmation for Johnstone's 'reasons' regarding

these first years in any other sources. Later, yes, disease, alcohol and opium played their part.

66   Johnstone-Need 1984, 90.

67   V&P QLA 1884 vol 2, 951.

68   B. Smith 1980, 17.

69   Lane-Poole 1889, 214.

70   Hull 1886, vol 1, 104–5.

71   See Hulme 1990, 18–34, where he argues the links between Enlightenment ideas and colonial practices.

3   Colonial Circuits

1   Cooper and Stoler 1997, 34.

2   *New York Clipper*, Oct. 1882. For Gaylord/Cunningham connections: *Figaro* (San Francisco), 26 Apr. 1883, *Canterbury Times*, Christchurch, Dec. 1883, discussed below. J. B. Gaylord also exemplified the crossover in management personnel that existed between the circus and minstrelsy, see Waterhouse 1990, 88.

3   According to St Leon's *Index of Australian Show Movements*, in Queensland, Brisbane, Rockhampton, Bowen, Charters Towers, Ravenswood, Townsville and Cooktown were visited as early as 1876 by the Watkins and Bungaroo Great Asiatic troupe; and in 1877 Ashton's Circus performed in Bowen and Charters Towers. The goldfields were profitable venues. It was Barnum and Coup's Greatest Show on Earth that Cunningham and his troupe were to join in 1883.

4   Documents relating to payment of personnel and other tour expenses are housed in the McCaddon Collection, Princeton University Library. Joseph T. McCaddon was the company's business manager and James A. Bailey's brother-in-law.

5   In 1893, two Sioux Indians, Eagle Elk and American Bear, were deported. They had come to Australia with a circus and stayed on. I have not established yet if they came with Cole's a decade earlier. Consular records, Australia, Record Group 84, Roll 15, NARA Washington.

6   St Leon 1992, 61–2. In spite of changes in name and

ownership, the relationships between these circuses can be tracked in the news cuttings kept by Cunningham by following the principal acts, the Great Valhalla Brothers (acrobats) and Professor Barlow and his 'Fairy Ponies' and 'School of Educated Dogs and Monkeys'.

7   Cunningham's Australian itinerary is reconstructed from news items from his cuttings book: although often undated, they have either been traced in the relevant newspapers or cross-checked with St Leon's *Index of Australian Show Movements*, 1992.

8   St Leon 1992, iv.

9   Waterhouse 1990, 16.

10 *St Louis Daily Globe-Democrat*, 1 June 1883. See Bogdan 1988, 74 on the showman's role in the amusement industry.

11 *Sacramento Daily Record*, 28 Oct. 1892; *Santa Barbara News*, 28 Jan. 1893.

12 Cunningham family records. Also Cunningham records, Family History Centre (Mormon) Microfilm roll no. 1992245, frame 25.

13 *Miners' and Business Men's Directory for year January 1st 1856*, section on Columbia, Tuolumne County; and *History of Tuolumne County*, 1882 (repr. 1973).

14 The Olympic Circus, based in San Francisco in 1849, was one of the earliest in the west (Wilmeth 1982).

15 Quoted in Caughey and Caughey 1962, 22; see Heizer 1978; also S. Cook 1976.

16 The main Californian records for Cunningham are *Miners and Business Men's Directory for the year 1856*: *History of Tuolumne County*, 1882: J. Carlyle Parker, *A Personal Name Index to Orton's Records of California men in the War of Rebellion, 1861 to 1867*, c.1978. The latter is a facsimile of Richard H. Orton's compilation of Californian Civil War Records, 1890. Checked against original microfilm roles in NARA San Bruno, California. San Francisco directories began in 1871, and those consulted include *Bishop's* and the *Langley Director*. San Francisco census records checked for 1870 (reel 79, p.106), 1880 and 1900. There are none for

1890. I have found no indication of Cunningham's marital status.

17 Quoted in Truettner, William H., The West as America 1820–1920 Smithsonian Institution, Washington 1991, 39.

18 Taylor, 1980, 12.

19 Barnum's Advance Courier, 1884, 10.

20 In other accounts said to have been eight.

21 Account reconstructed from *Pittsburg Critic*, Feb. 1884; *Northern Territory Government Gazette*; A5938 Northern Territory Government, South Australian Archives; Cunningham 1884; shipping lists: NAA (Brisbane Branch) BP 159/27, vol. 2, ships reports out coastwise, and BP 159/13 Ships reports in, interstate and overseas.

22 QSA, Col/A353/335 of 1883: Police Magistrate Thursday Island to Col. Sec., 23 Dec. 1882.

23 NAA (Brisbane Branch) BP 159/27, vol. 2; NSWA, Roll 453, Coastals from North Queensland, has arrival of *Quiraing* 28 Jan. with Cunningham and eight Aborigines. Maybe 'Little' Toby was not counted.

24 See Lumholtz 1979, 366.

25 *Figaro*, 26 Apr. 1883. The account below is also based on reports in *Sydney Morning Herald*, 19–24 Feb. 1883, *Sydney Evening Echo*, 20 Feb. 1883, *Sydney Evening News*, 22 Feb. 1883, *Sydney Bulletin*, *Queenslander*, 3 Mar. 1883. See also NSW *Parliamentary Debates*: Legislative Council, 1883, 551–2. No Police Department records seem to have survived in either state, except for the Darlinghurst Gaol Entrance Book, Feb. 1883 (1439 Jimmy, 1440 Billy), R2346 5/1920, NSWA.

26 George Thornton (1819–1901), a founding member of Aboriginal Protection Association, NSW, 1880, and Chairman of the Aboriginal Protection Board in 1883.

27 *Sydney Morning Herald*, 23 Feb. 1883, *Argus* (Melbourne), 26 Feb. 1883, *Age* (Melbourne), 10 Mar. 1883.

28 *Auckland Evening Star*, 20–2 Mar. 1883.

29 Houzé and Jacques may have been confused because both men, Tambo and the other of uncertain name, had died in America and following cus-

tom, in talking about them the group would not have referred to either of them directly by name but by some such euphemism as 'that man who died in America'.

30 Tuttle was known for having installed the first hydaulic lift in Sydney. Various parts of the Columbia goldfields carried his family name: Tuttletown, Tuttle Creek and so on.

31 McCaddon Collection of the Barnum and Bailey Circus, Manuscripts Division. Department of Rare Books Special Collections. Princeton University Library.

32 From the album of Dr R. Neuhauss, 1884, Ethnologisches Museum, Berlin. Regrettably, it is not reproduced here.

33 Edwards 2001, 13.

34 See also the seminal essay by I. Kopytoff: 'The cultural biography of things' in Appaduria 1986.

35 Houzé and Jacques 1884, 142–5.

36 *Canterbury Times* (Christchurch), 1 Dec. 1883. Both the *Canterbury Times* item and the *Figaro* item are from Cunningham's own press cuttings book.

4   American Spectacle

1 The source or accuracy of Barnum's figures is not the issue; it is their use to confirm a pre-existent opinion. For instance the 780 refers only to those Aborigines living on reserves in Victoria.

2 As described in the 1883 *Route Book*; other accounts say three rings plus an elevated stage.

3 One is overwhelmed by statistics in the circus literature. These come from various Advance Couriers and P. T. Barnum's Statement, 16 Oct. 1882, in the *New York Clipper*, enclosed as a cutting with correspondence to Professor Baird of the Smithsonian Institution, Permanent Administrative Files, Smithsonian Institution Archives. Saxon (1989, 310) quotes a different figure of $6,000 for daily running costs from *New York Sun*, 13 Jan. 1884. See further discussion on Barnum's figures below footnote 36.

4 *St Louis Daily Globe-Democrat*, 28 May 1883.

5 See Cronin 1992. There is a correspondence: the route books give the population of each place and the number of days allocated.

6 P. T. Barnum's Advance Courier 4, 1875, quoted in Adams 1997, 109.

7 B. Parkinson n.d., 4–5; Flint 1983, 209.

8 'A sheet' was a printer's unit of measurement, 44 × 28 inches. Typical sizes for circus posters were 3, 6, 8, 16 sheet sizes (Tom Parkinson 1978, 42).

9 Barnum 1883; T. Parkinson 1978, 42; *Penny Press* (Cleveland), 13 Aug. 1883.

10 Saxon 1989, 68–76; Reiss 2001.

11 Barnum 1871.

12 See Riess 2001, 208. Saxon (1989, 21) asserts that Barnum never 'owned' Heth, only 'the right to exhibit her'. Bluford Adams (1997) examines the degree of Heth's complicity. Reiss (2001) explores the Barnum–Heth relationship in a number of insightful ways that cannot be pursued here.

13 A hardening of attitudes to Black Americans increased in the last decades of the century, see p. 220.

14 Odell (1927–49) quoted an advertisement which implied a living person was to be shown (vol. 4, 1928, 584). Later a cast of Vendovi's skull was exhibited.

15 Wilkes 1845, 127, 143.

16 *American Journal* 44: 393–4. See Joyce 2001 on the links between the Wilkes expedition and anthropology; for Vendovi's story see also Poesch 1961, and for Vendovi's skull, Stewart 1978, 204–8, and Viola and Margolis 1985.

17 Lyons (2001, 126–38) explores how anticipatory fears shaped both observations and accounts in this incident.

18 These reports, which spoke of eating human flesh 'from habit and taste', were a source for John Crawfurd's 1866 article for the journal of the Ethnological Society of London, of which he was president 1863–8. Crawfurd was a doctor and colonial administrator, and his polygenist views discomforted those members of the Ethnological

19 Rosemarie Garland Thomson, 'Introduction', in Thomson 1996, 10.

20 For life histories (and commentaries on them) of marginalised people who were exhibited in the American circus, both those called 'freaks' and exotic imports, see Bogdan 1988, Odell 1927–49 and P. T. Barnum's *Struggles and Triumphs* of 1869 (Barnum 1871), his own revised edition of his first autobiography *The Life of P. T. Barnum, Written by Himself*, 1855.

21 The presentation of the exotic 'other' in association with the anomalous 'other' appears to have been much more marked in America than Europe.

22 The Fijians' story became an often repeated tale. I am grateful to Lila Fourhman-Shaull, of the Historical Society of York County, for copies of *York Daily*, 15–16 May 1872, *York Dispatch*, 3 and 9 Apr. 1897, 25 May 1903, 25 Oct. 1929 (very comprehensive review of earlier reports), and *York Gazette and Public Advertiser*, Nov.–Dec. 1993. Other sources: Gardenhire 1871; Barnum 1873; Barnum's Advance Courier, 1872; Shettel 1929; Hubley 1987; Shultz 1992; and Mathew Brady's photograph in the National Portrait Gallery, Smithsonian Institution. News reports (*Chicago Tribune*, 30 May and 1 June 1883) expressing fear of grave robbing and dissection were typical.

23 Barnum had established links with the new national museums in New York and Washington over the preceding decade, particularly as a donor of animal skeletons as well as animals 'in the flesh', see Correspondence Remington-Kellog to Betts in Smithsonian Institution Archives, Permanent Administrative Files.

24 Barnum's letter to agents, 9 Aug. 1882, and Barnum to Baird, 25 Oct. 1882, are in the Smithsonian Institution Archives, Permanent Administrative Files, and the reply, Baird to Barnum, 31 Oct. 1882, is in the Bridgeport Public Library.

25 They were white men, Hiram and Barney Davis, the former born two years before his parents emigrated from England. Given their stage names, Waino and Plutano, by Lyman Warner, they were managed by him and then by his son, Hanford, touring the shows of America and Europe for more than fifty years.

26 According to Blumenbach, all five of the racial divisions were descended from 'a single primeval Caucasian type': Stocking 1987, 26. White, primal and pure! For a discussion about the show type, see Frost 1996, 248.

27 Bogdan 1988.

28 Schivelbusch (1986) analyses the cultural transformations wrought by the railway journey, including 'the fear always implicit in the snorting beast'. The 'Bushman' N'co N'qui (N/Kon N/Qui), when shown at the Royal Aquarium, London, gave a graphic account of his railway and steamship experiences simply with the aid of natural gestures and sounds that vividly conjure up pictures of locomotives, tunnels, and the animation on board a vessel getting out of harbour' (unidentified newspaper report, 20 Sept 1884), in John Johnson Collection, Bodleian Library.

29 From accounts in *Baltimore Morning Herald*, 7 and 8 May; *Baltimore American and Commercial Advertiser*, 8 May 1883; and Barnum's *My Diary or Route Book* for 1883.

30 According to Houzé and Jacques, the boomerangs they had averaged between 60 and 65 cm in length and were carved from plain wood, not from a curved branch or root such as mangrove. Although the men also made boomerangs in the course of the tour these were probably for sale rather than their own use (see pp. 135–6).

31 Christopher Pinney (1997, 16–20) traces the emergence of the graphic stereotype of the Toda from early accounts such as Captain Henry Harkness's *A description of a Singular Aboriginal race in the Blue Mountains of Coimbatoor in the Southern Peninsula of India*.

32 This is not a search I embarked on; looking for the origins of one group has been enough.

33 I have not been able to establish whether this particular block originated with Barnum's organisation or the newspaper.

34   I have traced the relationship between representational processes and mechanical processes of reproduction in more detail in Poignant 2003. The development of the stereotype as a method of replication was among the processes that advanced the industrialisation of printing from the beginning of the nineteenth century. In simplest terms, metal stereotype plates were made by first taking an impression of the original set-up of type or woodblock in a mould of papier-mâché or similar material, which was then cast in metal. Although he was not the inventor, Firmin Didot named the process stereotype circa 1794. The cultural meaning of stereotype dates from 1804 (O.E.D.).

35   *Pittsburg Critic*, Feb. 1884. Newscutting, Cunningham's cuttings book.

36   Ibid, both quotes. Several accounts also suggested they feared R. A.

37   'A chat with Barnum', *St Louis Daily Globe-Democrat*, 1 June 1883. I am, of course, haunted by an as yet undiscovered report.

38   Paraphrased accounts from the *Wheeling Daily Intelligencer*, 15 May 1883, *Chicago Tribune*, 5 and 6 June 1883, and from Barnum's *My Diary or Route Book*, 1883.

39   'Cultural work' (Thomson 1996, 10) is a useful way of referring to the effects of representational processes.

40   Figures of takings are from Barnum's *My Diary or Route Book*, 1883, and for overwintering from *New York Clipper*, 16 Oct., 1882. The set of figures kept by business manager Joseph T. McCaddon from 1881 to 1897 are reproduced and discussed in Saxon 1989, 310–11. Expenses for 1883 were $850,159, and for 1884, $948,253.

41   *New York Clipper*, vol. 3, 1884, 767.

42   'Curiosities of nature', *Penny Press* (Cleveland), 23 Feb. 1884.

43   Catalogue, no date, in Chicago Historical Society.

44   *Chicago Daily Tribune*, 16 Feb. 1926, among newspaper clippings, Chicago Historical Society.

45   These performers were listed as under Barnum's control for that season. Such contracts were not necessarily long-term. Earnings are from 'Curiosities of nature', in *Penny Press*, 23 Feb. 1884. The source of earnings equivalents, as reported in a lecture by Bram Stoker, 'Impressions of America', *Daily Express* (Dublin), 30 Dec. 1885, gives a female servant £40–50 per annum (equivalent at the time to $194.4–243), a policeman £240 per annum ($1,166.40).

46   *Cleveland Herald*, 27 Feb. 1884.

47   *Cleveland Leader*, 25 Feb. 1884.

48   *Baltimore American and Commercial Advertiser*, 11 Dec., 1883.

49   *Pittsburg Critic*, Feb. 1884, from Cunningham's cuttings book.

50   *Cleveland Leader*, 25 Feb. 1884.

51   Almost identical versions in *Elberfelder Zeitung*, no. 173, 25 June 1885, and *Barmen Zeitung*, 26 June 1885, and similar versions in unsourced papers in Cunningham's cuttings book from Berlin, 14 July 1884, and Weisbaden, 1 June 1885. I have chosen the German versions as the most feasible because of the consistency of the reports. In a French language version in Houzé and Jacques (1884, 139), the child is said to be not Toby but another guest in the hotel – a version that can be attributed either to Cunningham's invention or to a misunderstanding across languages.

52   Houzé and Jacques 1884, 139.

53   Brayshaw 1990, 47; Roth 1907, 26–31.

54   From the *Cleveland Leader*, 25 and 28 Feb. and 3 Mar. 1884; *Penny Press*, 23, 25, 26 Feb. and 1 Mar. 1884; *Cleveland Evening News*, 26 Feb. 1884; *Cleveland Herald*, 27 Feb. 1884; *Cleveland Plain Dealer*, 25, 27, 28 Feb. and 1 and 6 Mar. 1884. There were unsympathetic headings like *Plain Dealer*'s 'Tambo turned up his toes'.

55   This excluded his weapons, which were passed to kin. By the time Billy was the sole male survivor, photographs show him with an excess of boomerangs. Drew recognised the plastering with mud as a form of embalmment, which may have given him the idea of having the body embalmed,

although he does not explicitly say so. Unsourced, undated interview with Drew, 'List to the tale of Tambo', copy held by author.

56 I acquired copies of all the relevant documentation when I visited Cleveland after Tambo's body was discovered. See chapter 11.

57 'List to the tale of Tambo', typescript of unsourced interview with Frank Drew *c.*1945, copy held by author.

58 The most bizarre suggestion was that each had a sharp stick with a hook at the end, 'used for carving human steaks from the backs of their captive enemies' (*Plain Dealer*, 28 Feb. 1884).

59 The medical condition of Tambo and the others who died after him will be discussed later in the light of more informed European accounts.

60 I have seen a copy dated as late as August 1884. The same image was also used as a small vignette on the final page of the composite route book for the years 1881 to 1885.

61 *Illustrirte Zeitung*, no. 2169, 1885, mentions and illustrates the same three Zulu men, two women and child as in pl. 34. For the Sioux see ibid., 2 Feb., 1884.

62 Lindfors 1996; Bogdan 1988, 187.

5   European Spectacle

1 See Rothfels 1996; Semonin 1996.

2 Johann Friedrich Blumenbach (1752–1840), Professor of Medicine at Göttingen, arrived at a fivefold division of the human family: Caucasian, Mongolian, American, African and Malayan ('On the natural variety of mankind', 1795), a system of classification that continued to have currency in the nineteenth century. A copy of the broadsheet is now in the National Library of Australia, Canberra, and several German collections.

3 Dickens 1853, 168; Bernth Lindfors, 'Charles Dickens and the Zulus', in Lindfors 1999. In his analysis, Lindfors asserts that Dickens set out to puncture the concept of the Noble Savage, rather than to advocate extermination of the living exam-

ples, whereas Dickens made clear his indifference to their survival.

4 Brand 1991, 2–5.

5 Barsley 1966.

6 Ohmann, 1996, 36.

7 Jobling and Crowley 1996; Poignant 2003.

8 Hagenbeck 1909, 20. See Thode-Arora 1989, 168–71, for tables setting out some of the Völkerschauen (shows of indigenous people) taken on tour in Germany both by Hagenbeck's firm and independently from 1870s to 1930s, with sizes of some of the audiences.

9 The Jardin was established in 1859 for the presentation of both botanical and zoological specimens from all parts of the world. The inclusion of human exhibits simply added another dimension. See Schneider 1982 for a full analysis of attendance figures etc.

10 Schneider 1982, 136.

11 Thode-Arora 2002, 2–17; 1991, 87–115; 1989, 153–8; J. G. Taylor 1981, 43.

12 The group have been identified as Kaweshkar from Dawson Island near the Magellan Straits (Eissenberger 1996).

13 Hagenbeck, 2 Dec. 1881, in Eissenberger 1996, 150.

14 Hagenbeck, 17 Mar. 1882, in ibid., 169–75.

15 Virchow 1889 (tr. Bleismer *c.* 1889, 564); see epigraph to chapter 6. There is a copy of the Bleismer translation (pp. 550–70) in Box 39, folded into note book 552, Otis T. Mason note books A. M. N. H., Smithsonian Institution.

16 Eissenberger 1996, 177–82.

17 Massin 1996; Proctor 1988.

18 Edwards 2001, 13–16, 27–49.

19 Eissenberger 1996, 141–3, 194. The 'Eskimo woman' (a Labrador Inuit) referred to was shortly to die of smallpox (see next chapter).

20 A collection of translations of letters Cunningham received from European anthropologists is at Galton papers [R. A. Cunningham] 227/6, University College, London. See also p. 148, 168, chapter 7.

21 Lackinger (1983) has produced an interesting but incomplete list for 1870 to 1885.

6   Palaces of Illusion and Scientific Discipline

1   The Crystal Palace, built for the great exhibition of 1851, was removed a few years later from Kensington to Norwood, South London. It was the most extensive show-space in the metropolis.

2   *Guide to the Crystal Palace and Park*, 1884.

3   Ibid.

4   Where Central Hall stands today, just off Parliament Square.

5   Farini previously presented a group of Zulu warriors at St James's Hall, Piccadilly, in 1879. The interest of the British public had first been aroused by the stunning defeat of British troops at Isandhlwana by the Zulu leader, Cetshwayo, in early 1879, and then the Zulus' defeat. Farini followed it with other successful Zulu shows in London and with Barnum's circus in America. By 1884 Farini managed thirty-three Zulu, in three different troupes (Peacock 1999, 93). For his later exploits in Africa, see Clement 1967.

6   Rothfels 1996, et al.

7   Houzé and Jacques 1884, 99.

8   Ibid., 100.

9   Roth 1901–6, Bulletin 5, 19.

10 Although taken in 'poor conditions of clarity', several were used in the report, but I have not managed to locate the originals.

11 Houzé and Jacques 1884, 63.

12 Ibid., 123.

13 Ibid, 146.

14 While the English utilitarian philosopher Jeremy Bentham did not coin the word *panopticon*, he used it in 1787 for his concept of a prison with a central observation tower surrounded by a circular arrangement of cells in a design that allowed total unobserved surveillance. This gave the word a wide currency (Oetterman 1997, 40–4), for it described a universal optical 'machine' that could be applied to other situations – the hospital, asylum, factory and so on. By the end of the century its use in a more generalised sense, as in Castan's Panoptikum, points to the complementary relationship between surveillance and spectacle – and the disciplinary function of spectacle. See Martin Jay (1994, 381–434) for a discussion of 'the complementary apparatuses of surveillance and spectacle so central to the maintenance of disciplinary or repressive power in the modern world' (at 383).

15 It seems that it was only in Köln that the block for the 'cannibal' cover was also used as an advertisement. Elsewhere most of the ads were text only. Copies of German edition of the pamphlet are to be found in Historisches Museum, Frankfurt am Main, and Museum für Völkerkunde, Hamburg (Jacobsen-Archiv).

16 *Kölnische Zeitung* noted two of the group had died in America, but got the sexes wrong, saying they were women.

17 Warner 1995, 187.

18 Eissenberger 1996, 129. Pichocho's wax figure is still exhibited as an 'ethnographic treasure' in Berlin's Nachfolge-Panoptikum, a successor establishment to Castan's.

19 Warner 1995, 195.

20 Foucault in Jay 1994, 410.

21 The following account of the Australians in Virchow's laboratory is based on Virchow 1884, 407–18.

22 See Cowling 1989. As the cities were places of strangers, the practice of physiognomic observation became a process of detection/interpretation. See Brand 1991 on the detective as interpreter of the city, Edgar Allan Poe and the detective novel.

23 Virchow 1884, 413.

24 Ibid. 414.

25 Ibid. 417.

26 Massin (1996, 95) provides an example of Virchow's joking reference to the advantages of Germany's new imperialism for obtaining African heads as a consequence of a fight 'between two tribes'.

27 Ibid., 119–20. These ideological changes were paralleled in the 1880s by the rise in German anti-Semitism, to which Virchow was vigorously opposed.

28 Alternatively, the spears in the photograph may have been borrowed from a museum collection.

29 *Norddeutsche Allgemeine Zeitung*, 23 Oct. 1881, in Eissenberger 1996.

30 Eissenberger 1996, 149–75.

31 J. G. Taylor 1981, 41; Thode-Arora 1991 and 2002.

32 See Roth 1907, 20. (This was also the reason for the restriction on naming the dead.) I have not traced the origin of this mummified body but according to Brayshaw (1990, 43), smoking (desiccation and mummification) seems to have been practised a little further north of Rockingham Bay on the Johnstone River.

7 'Rare Strangers'

1 Maximilian Carl August Flinzer, 25 Jan. 1832–12 July 1889; a son was also Maximilian.

2 Eissenberger (1996, 192–4), provides examples of resistance to Virchow making measurements by an 'Eskimo' woman (Labrador Inuit) in 1880, and the Fuegian women in 1881.

3 I had first enquired by correspondence for this document in 1991, without success.

4 I later collected a copy from Chemnitz Standesamt, stamped on the reverse, affirming that 'it is approved that this document conforms to the main register.'

5 According to Ziemssen's *Cyclopaedia of the practice of medicine* (1875–), vol. 19, 460, dealing with Germany, the average time for complete dissolution of the body was between twelve and forty years depending on the disease, the coffin and the nature of the soil.

6 I continued to pursue this matter by correspondence after my visit.

7 Weindling 1994, 119–31

8 Bailey 1896; Lassek 1958.

9 Burdett 1893 vol. 3

10 This most useful detail is from entry 'Vaccination' in *Encylopaedia Britannica*, 1894, found for me by the indefatigable Christine Winter, Australian National University.

11 Eissenberger 1996, 162–5, 171

12 Lassek 1958; Walton 1982, 389.

13 The note accompanying the list states that 'the items that are not part of this catalogue are either stolen or not identifiable', so the list is thorough but not absolutely definitive.

14 The news cutting, from Cunningham's own collection, is from *Hallesches Tagblatt*, 21 Feb. 1885, with a Nordhausen byline. Nordhausen is 50 kilometres from Halle, and the item was possibly only printed because of the illustrious professor's presence there. It has not been possible to newspaper search these small towns.

15 I looked particularly at textile manufacturing (Kiesewetter 1981, 253) but even there 'insight into the situation of workers in different regions ... remains partial and inadequate'. Apart from regional variations, it is difficult to differentiate according to skill, age, sex and working time.

16 According to Professor Landois, the group kept the proceeds of selling photographs and booklets and also begged (*Mescheder Zeitung*, 8 Aug. 1885).

17 FO 255/16 in the PRO London. In fact, the British Consulate was notified on 24 June 1885 by 'Président du Conseil & Ministre de la Maison et des Affaires Étrangères de son Altesse Royale, Le Grand Duc de Hesse'.

18 Personal communication from Dr Thode-Arora, who has researched Johan Adrian Jacobsen and his family connections.

19 The Rheinischen Missionsgesellschaft was established in Barmen in 1828, and worked in South West Africa from the 1860s. The only German colonies established by 1884 were South West Africa (later Namibia), Togo and the Cameroons, followed by East Africa (in 1885), Rwanda and German New Guinea. The Micronesian and Samoan colonies in the Pacific came later (Junker 1912, 1–9).

20 'Authentication' is an issue throughout the tour; alert to it, Cunningham supplies the documentation to the press.

21 Sussy's admission to a children's hospital is not explained, but the tone of the report suggests that it was where the best care was available.

22 By way of confirmation of the church records, I also searched for the official registration of death

in the City Registry Office without success. The combination of the newspaper reports and the church records is very convincing.

23   This paper's mention of three boomerang-throwers would suggest that Toby was still alive, and died after the 14th. But Topinard (1885) places the death before the boomerang demonstration and says that only Billy performed. According to the first scenario there are only five intensive days of performance, anthropological investigation and photography; according to the second there are ten. The oppressive pressures would have been equally great in either case.

24   Topinard, 'Présentation de trois Australiens vivants' (1885), from which the account of the interview is drawn.

25   Apart from mnemonic devices such as the message stick and counting procedure, in the Cardwell district special terms were used to count the days between successive performances of regular ceremonies (Roth, 1908–10, 79).

26   English translation of a letter from Topinard, 25 Nov. 1885, presumably done at the time for Cunningham. In Galton papers [R. A. Cunningham] 227/6, University College London.

8   To Constantinople and Back

1   Glaister 1886: the usual physical measurements, body markings and languages spoken are covered and, quoting James Dawson's *Australian Aborigines*, 1881, ritual cannibalism is mentioned as part of a solemn funerary rite in North Queensland. The *Glasgow Herald* and *Glasgow Evening News* report the performances through February into March 1886.

2   Kirshenblatt-Gimlett 1991, 401.

3   There is also a Norwegian word in the Swedish edition that suggests its genealogy.

4   Dread of mentioning the name of a deceased is linked with a spirit of the dead being a cause of illness or death (Roth 1901–6, Bulletin no. 5, Item 72, 20).

5   Although there must have been an awareness of the slave uprising in 1879 in the Danish Crown colonies in the West Indies, where Danish interests had begun with the Danish West Indian company from 1671 to 1754.

6   For unravelling this political puzzle, I am very indebted to Terry Carlbom and his Danish colleague, Niels Barfoed.

7   Hulme 1998, 5, 6.

8   Bartolovich 1998, 212–24.

9   Ibid. 234.

10   This chance piece of information was given to me as an explanation for the lack of zoo archives before that date.

11   As established from the computerised catalogue of the Museum of the Institute of Anthropology and Ethnology, University of Moscow. The casts have recently been restored and are still on display in the museum.

12   I make no claim to my sample, used for developing these ideas, being exhaustive, but it is extensive.

13   A cutting from Cunningham's cuttings book, no source or date.

14   *Journal of the Anthropological Institute* 17: 83–4.

15   I have not been able to do an extensive search of Californian papers for 1887–8, but a careful search covering Cunningham's six-month tour of California with the second group in 1892–3, found no mention of a visit by an earlier group.

16   There is a gap in the incoming and coastal shipping records for this period, but Cunningham's movements can be traced from newspaper shipping lists for 1888: *San Francisco Chronicle*, 10 and 11 Mar., *Sydney Morning Herald*, 5 Apr., *Brisbane Courier*, 17 Apr. *Townsville Bulletin*, 18 Apr., (confirmed *Townsville Herald*, 21 Apr.), *Sydney Morning Herald*, 30 Apr. (arrival and departure Brisbane on return journey confirmed in *Queenslander*, 5 May).

17   At the time of the Melbourne interview, Cunningham was on the point of departure for America. Always in search of new curiosities, it seems that the showman had obtained a hairless horse for Barnum's menagerie while in Australia.

According to the newspaper shipping lists, he embarked with it on the SS *Alameda*, arriving in San Francisco on 30 September 1888.

18   See introduction above. The hazards are many in searching Queensland newspapers: unreadable microfilms, missing pages and editions.

19   In the words of the poet Paul Celan in *No Man's Rose* (1963), trans. M. Hamburger (1996).

20   Huggan (1998, 128–9) examines the function of the ghost in indigenous West Indian literature, and draws on Foucault's idea of countermemory, of 'tracing a genealogy of breaks, fissures, disruptions' (1998, 128–9, 269 n. 3).

9   Absent Presence

1   'Earthman' and 'Bushman' were European designations of various San people. These children were brought from 'somewhere along the Orange river'. Flora lived until 1864, when she was twenty-two, and her body went to the Royal College of Surgeons for dissection; see A. G. Morris 1996: 70. There is a sketch of them in the *Illustrated Magazine of Art* of 1853, p. 445. See also Fauvelle 1999b, 448.

2   Rydell 1992, 4.

3   My rather narrow focus on indigenous visitors and anthropology in relation to great exhibitions ignores much else of importance, such as the attitudes to women, and, in America, attitudes to Black and Native Americans.

4   Barthes 1983, 241.

5   Rydell, 1992, 2.

6   *Pall Mall Gazette, Extra*, no. 49, 1889.

7   *L'Exposition universelle internationale de 1889 à Paris. Catalogue général officiel. Exposition rétrospective du travail et des sciences anthropologiques* (1889), section 1: 'Anthropologie – Ethnographie' the catalogue combined with the plans and photographs is invaluable for reconstructing the appearance of the exhibition; Alphand 1892.

8   'Paris and its Exposition', *Pall Mall Gazette, Extra*, no. 49, 1889.

9   *Illustrée* (1889), no. 27: 213. *Illustrée* published a partwork, 'L'Exposition de Paris 1889', throughout the year, with covers and centrefold frequently dedicated to the exotic performers from the colonies.

10   Following Virchow and Topinard, their names were – N/Kon N/Qui, N/Arkar, N/Arbessi, N/Fim N/Fon, N/Ko, N/Dissi. Some documents that partly establish the European itinerary of the Khoisan group led by N/Kon N/Qui are Royal Aquarium programme, 11 Oct. 1884; Virchow 1886; Topinard 1887. Bonaparte's photograph appears in Fauvelle-Aymar 1999a. The casts of N'Ko and his death is also discussed in Wilson 1890, 643. See also Fauvelle 1999b, 459.

11   *Catalogue général officiel*, 1889; *Illustrée* (1889), no. 27: 243; Wilson 1890, 641–8.

12   Athenaeum 17 August, 1889.

13   *L'Exposition universelle. Catalogue général officiel*, p. 63. Not all of these were taken by Bonaparte. For instance, the display included those taken in Berlin in 1884 by Carl Günther, and collected by the Prince.

14   The same photograph was used in an article by J. Deniker in *Revue d'Anthropologie* (1889), which attributes the photograph to the 'collection' of Prince Roland Bonaparte. See also Fauvelle-Aymar 1999a, Fig. 4.

15   *L'Exposition universelle. Catalogue général officiel*, p. 37.

16   Deniker in *Revue d'Anthropologie* Series 3, 4: 1–27 (1889): 16. Almost certainly derived from comparison of photographs.

17   Houzé and Jacques 1884.

18   Eissenberger 1996, 166–71.

19   Wilson 1890; Rydell 1984, 54–6.

20   Gilbert 1991, 42.

21   A copy of Cunningham's letter, 17 Oct. 1889, accompanying his press release and complimentary tickets exists in his news cutting album.

22   See Cunningham 1890 in the bibliography for details. I have not located an American edition. But I found the Swedish edition in the Royal Library,

Stockholm. Copies of the German edition are in the Jacobsen Archiv, Museum für Völkerkunde Hamburg.

23 I am grateful to Peter Mesenhöller for directing my attention to the photograph on which this lithograph is based, in the collection of Commander A. Ekström, Etnografiska Museum, Stockholm; and for sharing with me the *Samoan Times* references and the reports of the deaths of Tu and Atofau in the Köln press. This is the only source for the name 'Tu'. I have followed the *Samoan Times* for the spelling of their names except for Tu; the variations in the other sources are only slight.

24 Virchow 1890, 387–92 & p. IV. Names recorded by Virchow and Cunningham are recognisably of the same people.

25 Peter Messenhöller has attempted to trace what happened to Latuugaifo's mummified body without success.

26 Extracts from letter 26 June 1891 from Heinrich Umlauff to Jacobsen, and 15 July 1891 from Carl Hagenbeck to Jacobsen, Jacobsen Archiv, Museum für Völkerkunde Hamburg, quoted in Thode-Arora 1989, 41–2, 180. This exchange of letters led Dr Thode-Arora to conclude that Cunningham was 'without reservations a prototype of a bad impresario of these indigenous shows' (1989, 41). I hope that my chapters 9–11 suggest a more complex analysis.

27 Letters in Jacobsen Archiv, Museum für Völkerkunde Hamburg. I am very grateful to Dr Thode-Arora for sharing copies with me.

10 King Bill and Company

1 James Cassady was born in County Antrim, Ireland, in 1837 and brought to Australia by his parents in 1848. He was said to be the first white man to cross the River Burdekin in 1861 (in the squatters' rush to take up land in the Kennedy district). Before taking up Mungalla he held other properties in the surrounding area, such as Rosella Plains and Fairview. Widowed in 1867, he did not remarry and he brought up his only son, Frank. He died in 1902.

2 Richard Wallace, resident at Mungalla in 1996, provided rough sketches of the sites.

3 QSA Col/G110 Acc.48/2040 96/4761, Under Colonial Secretary to Hon. A. S. Crowley.

4 Dixon 1983, 510.

5 A. Meston papers, OM 64-17, Box 2, envelope 5; an undated news cutting, John Oxley Library.

6 *Evening News* (Stockton), 11 Nov. 1892.

7 Bearing in mind the link between European place names and adopted European names, it is worth noting that Mt Elliot lies just south of Townsville.

8 In fact, I was referred to the Dennis family, and the resemblance is striking. As they trace their descent from Billy Cassady (part South Sea Islander), born 1886, the evidence of the link with the two Williams is strong, if not yet conclusive.

9 A. Meston papers. John Oxley Library.

10 *North Queensland Herald*, 13 Apr. 1892. Later, in October, there was another attempt. 'About five hundred Aboriginals from various parts of the world have been already arranged for,' wrote James Harding, the Official Agent for the Polynesian Commission for the Fair. But, in Queensland, the Colonial Secretary, S. W. Griffith, was not persuaded to support an Aboriginal addition to the Polynesian contingent. (QSA Col/714, 1892/13108).

11 For biographical notes on Meston see Lack 1951, and A.D.B. QSA, Col/A752 1893/12837 traces the development and collapse of Meston and Purcell's show. See also numerous newspaper reports: *North Queensland Herald*, 9 Dec. 1891, 10 Aug. 1892, 19 July 1893.

12 This is the only reference I have found to Cunningham's 1882 visit and removal of the first group. It suggests he gave an acceptable answer as to their fate.

13 Atkinson (who arrived in 1881) was not related to the prominent pioneering Atkinson family of the same district (Aldine *History of Queensland*, vol. 2, iv), who later bought Mungalla from the Cassadys.

14 Request of June 7 and 27 June 1892: QSA Col/B32 register of incoming letters to Colonial Secretary/7334 Bench T and 7919 R. For Roberts and Leu, see A. Smith 1986.

15 QSA Col/G74 letter 92/3922 Under Colonial Secretary to Roberts and Leu.

16 QSA Col/B32 /8290 Bench T and 8602 Bench B.

17 NSWA Coastal In 1892 5 Aug. *Peregrine*; NAA, Brisbane branch BP 159/27 Townsville interstate out 1891–4.

18 QSA. Col/G75 Letter 4477 and Q.S.A. Col/G76 Letter 92/4954, both Under Colonial Secretary to Messrs Roberts and Roberts. This was not the end of the process, which continued after Cunningham's departure. The documents were returned to the solicitors for stamping on 26 August, and were to be returned again to the Colonial Secretary's office, and that is where they should have survived. I, and others, have searched long and hard for them without success.

19 V&P QLA, 1893, vol. 1: 59, 4 July.

20 A later bond (QSA, Hom/A7 letters 1897/1380 1 Feb. 1897 to 1897/4450 5 Apr. 1897) regarding the removal of two girls gave such details. It was not granted, however, because 'previous cases have turned out very unsatisfactory'.

21 San Francisco papers *Daily Morning Call* and *Evening Bulletin* for 2, 3, 4, 5 and 6 Sept. 1892.

22 Congress passed the first federal law controlling immigration in 1882, which was supervised by the Department of the Treasury until March 1891, when a bureau was established with responsibility for administering alien contract laws. I attempted to trace the story both in American immigration records at NARA (Washington) and in correspondence with British consuls without success. In same month, the entry of exhibitors and their workers for the Chinese village, Chicago Fair, was documented. Donohue was on leave from 2 Sept. to 1 Oct. 1892: PRO FO 115/929 Correspondence from Consuls; FO/964 Regulation of Immigration (U.S.).

23 According to the *Los Angeles Times*, 5 Jan. 1893, the men had discarded a 'number of new sticks' (presumably Meston's gift) and 'used their old and tried pieces which were thrown with accuracy and ease'. When I showed the Elite Studio photograph (pl. 70) of the group to local people, it was generally agreed that the boomerangs they held were not from the coastal plain where the Nyawaygi lived, but from the rainforest. The man standing on the extreme right in the photograph holds two pineapple clubs, so-called because of the toothed knob. Clubs like these, which in length averaged 70 cm, had widespread distribution along the coast of the Herbert-Burdekin region (Brayshaw: 85, 275–8), within which lay Nyawaygi territory.

24 *North Queensland Herald* reports from 2 Nov. 1892 and through the month, and A. Meston papers. John Oxley Library. The $1,000 penalty imposed by McPherson was converted as £200.

25 QSA Col/A752 bundle 1893/12837 letters: 1893/5901 to 1893/12837 and telegram 4 July 1893; *The Observer*, 15 July 1893.

26 *North Queensland Herald*, 19 July and 22 Nov. 1893; V&P QLA, 4 July 1893. Cunningham (and by extension, Atkinson) also had to account for 'the failure to return any one or more [unless] by some cause for which [he] could not be held responsible', QSA Col/G108 Acc. 48/2038 96/3185, Under Col. Sec. to J. G. Atkinson.

27 QPD (LA), 1897: 1632.

28 Meston supported the abolition of the Native Mounted Police, but it was replaced by the more insidious self-policing system within Aboriginal reserves. See discussion in King and McHoul 1986.

29 From accounts in the *Evening Mail*, Stockton, 14 and 18 Nov. 1892.

30 'Townsville Blacks in America. A letter from Mr Cunningham', *Evening Star* (Townsville), 8 Mar. 1893. Cunningham's motive was probably to reassure his guarantor. Publication of the letter is not surprising: the travels of prominent citizens routinely received press attention and in 1890s Cunningham was a 'celebrity'.

31 The relevant court and gaol records for San Diego have not survived.

32 *New York Journal*, 19 July 1896 (source 3 in table above).

33 *Evening Star* (Townsville), 8 Mar. 1893.

34 I searched the death records in San Bernardino without success. The account in the *New York*

Journal, 19 July 1896 (source for source 3 of the table above), is very garbled, giving variant names such as Dick Gally and Harry Bushelman, and mentioning another unidentifiable man, Jack Ruel. The report of 19 December 1898 in the *North Queensland Herald* summarises four deaths in America, one in California, and three in New York; these are Dick in California and Tottie, Tommy and William 1 in New York. It seems the latter's kin did not realise that he lived on, see below.

35   Otis T. Mason was among those instrumental in achieving the emphasis on anthropology at the fair. See Rydell (1984, 55) for discussion on the role of anthropology and the social evolutionary concepts underpinning the prevailing ideology represented in the fair. See also Gilbert 1991.

36   See Rydell 1984 for extensive references, both contemporary and recent commentary.

37   According to the Barnum and Bailey *Route Book* of 1894, the circus also visited Cleveland Ohio, 16 July, for one day only, but it is unlikely that King Bill and his company even heard about the mummified Tambo, let alone saw him.

38   Although there is no direct evidence of this, the story was an all too familiar one; for example, Fiji Jim and his wife struggled to survive in show business in New York for some sixteen years.

39   I am grateful to Norman Wilson, Joe's grandnephew, for the photograph. No other relevant papers survived.

40   A news cutting from Cunningham's scrapbook, hand-inscribed, *New York World*, 15 Jan. 1896, indicates he was still informed about them although they were no longer with him.

41   QSA Col/B 36 Register in letters, 96/67 24 C, Cassady to Col. Sec, the actual letter has not survived. QSA: Col/G108 96/3186, A. S. Crowley to Under Colonial Secretary; Col/G110 Acc. 48/2040 96/4761, Under Colonial Secretary to A. S. Crowley; Col/G108 Acc. 48/2038 96/3185 Under Colonial Secretary to J. G. Atkinson; Col/B 36, 10300 Pol and Hom/A1 10607/Pol. 1896 'merely notes that Late Mr Atkinson is "worthless".' Supreme Court of Q/d

Northern (Townsville) Registry Ecclesiastical files 6/1897 Death Cert. 9815.

42   Kasson 1978, 65. The enclosed amusement parks only began to be established from 1895 on, Luna Park not until 1903.

43   Gorky 1907, 317.

44   PRO FO 115/1037 To Consuls. Fortunately Palani Paakiki's letter of 28 June 1896 survived as an enclosure with a draft of a letter of 3 July from Pauncefote to Sanderson.

45   The report was originally found in the first of two undated news cuttings from the *New York Journal*, preserved between the leaves of high quality paper of incoming letter 3 July, British Consulate General New York, PRO FO 281/31; the dates were later established in Library of Congress newspaper archives. In the articles (19 July and 24 Aug.) the 'Boss' is variously called Trask or Fross, but the diplomatic correspondence establishes that he was Frank Frost.

46   This figures differs from the newspaper reports that mention thirty shillings.

47   PRO: FO 281/36; FO 115/1036; FO 115/1050.

48   Kuykendall, III: 1967, 305.

49   Andrade 1990.

50   Biographical searches: McKenzie n.d.; *Hawaiian Directory*, 1890–1 and 1891–2; *McKenny's Hawaiian Directory*, 1894; *Polk Directory*, 1898; in the Hawaii State Archives, Dept of Interior Booklets 22, 23, 29, 36, 39, 42, 71, 72 and 81 all had references to Paakiki as a family name but direct connection was not established; *Hawaiian Annual*, index for 1875–1932; Latter Day Saints Genealogical Index, Hawaii.

51   Mary Kawena Pukui and Samuel H. Elbert.

52   Virchow, 1896.

53   Only the pineapple clubs and the boomerangs were brought with the group from North Queensland. The fur cloak was probably borrowed from the museum's collection and the nose-bones, shield and spears were acquired or manufactured along the way. The oblong shape of the shield conforms in size and decoration to a type referred to as a club shield by Brayshaw (79–81). It was

54   smaller than the rainforest shield and with a more southerly distribution, which included Nyawaygi territory.

54   *North Queensland Herald*, 19 Dec. 1898. The *British Australasian* (22 Sept. 1898) provides another interview with Jenny about the Northern European tour.

55   News cutting heading translates as 'Contentious cannibals', *Dannebrog*, 15 Apr. 1897 in an unidentified newspaper in Cunningham's cuttings book.

56   Dagbladet, 13 June 1897.

57   Letter is, R. A. Cunningham to A. Jacobsen 25 Nov. 1897, Jacobsen-Archiv, Museum für Völkerkunde Hamburg.

58   Cunningham's sister, not Cunningham, had a house in New York.

59   This seems to be the less reliable version. Apart from this reference to Stockholm, I have not found other evidence confirming where Cunningham was in 1898.

60   Unfortunately the Salvation Army's London records were destroyed by World War II bombing.

61   PRO BT 27/273 July–Sept. 1898, Passenger Lists outwards; QSA Imm/126 1883–1909, 625. M.F. no. 21967 lists 'Willie' (married) and 'Jennie' (Single), 'Aboriginals', among the arrivals, Townsville.

62   QSA Hom/B2 13995, 14232 and 15226 register correspondence about their return, but no actual letters survive between Home Secretary and Police, Townsville.

63   Peacock 1999.

64   This impression is built up from *Cincinnati Times-Star*, 4 Sept. 1893, and other unattributed cuttings in Cunningham's own cuttings book.

65   Refers to the six brought back by Robert E. Peary in 1896. The story of the attempts of Minik to recover the body of his father, Qisuk, from the museum is told in Harper 1989. Four skeletons were returned at last by the museum in 1993.

66   Letters Cunningham to Jacobsen, 27 Nov. 1897 and 13 Dec. 1900, Jacobsen-Archiv, Museum für Völkerkunde Hamburg. I am grateful to Dr Thode-Arora for sharing these letters with me.

67   Unidentified cuttings, Cunningham's scrapbook and *Evening Banner*, 24 July 1902, Bluffton, Indiana.

68   The unattributed cutting is inscribed by hand with the incorrect date of June 1891, but established as being *Cleveland Press*, 18 June 1902. Cunningham also recalled that Tambo had cast his boomerang around the steeple of the First Presbyterian Church. He must have done it during the earlier visit of Barnum's circus in 1883, because Tambo died on arrival in Cleveland, 23 February 1884.

69   For several of these years the route books and heralds also advertised another 'feature': 'Australian Wanno, Half Man, Half Monkey' together with 'What is it?'. These performers were 'show characters' whatever their nationality.

70   I am indebted to Meg Allen of Circus World Museum who introduced me to the Harry Bock Photographic Collection, and sent me a digitised copy of the photo. Farnum 1992 includes over half of the Bock photographs.

11   **Welcome Home Tambo**

1   Dening refers to such an event as an 'ethnographic moment' of encounter, the first product of which 'is interpretation, an understanding of what is new and unexperienced in the light of what is old and experienced'; it is a 'space between cultures filled by interpretation, occasions of metaphoric understanding and translation' (1996, 195–6).

2   The article 'Quiet anniversary held for Tambo', *Cleveland Plain Dealer*, August 1945, says Tambo was on public display at Hogan and Harris's ambulance station (apparently also undertakers) for some two dozen years. In 1902 when Cunningham visited him he was at the Western Reserve Medical College (see p. 237). I could find no other reference to him being there. It seems he was probably with Smith's funeral home for some seventy-five years, and during that time appears to have had very little public exposure. This conclusion is partly based on the interview I had with an elderly family member.

3   A sale of property was involved and inevitally saveral people became aware of the story.

4   For various reasons, the kin responsible for conducting the rite might be prevented from doing so, particularly in recent times: see the film *Waiting for Harry* by Lester Hiatt and Kim McKenzie where the funerary rites are delayed until the leader of the ceremonies arrives (Film Australia, 1980).

5   There were no longer Seneca in the vicinity of Cleveland and, with the assistance of Dr Esther Bockhoff, cultural anthropologist at the Natural History Museum, Cleveland, the Australian Embassy was put in contact with representatives of the Seneca nation across the border in New York State.

6   Sound recording (not video) held by me.

7   Issues relating to cultural protocols of this type are about paying due respect. They are not inflexible, because they are also about allowing Indigenous Australians the opportunity to respond to changing circumstances.

8   Under the Aboriginal and Torres Strait Islander Protection Act 1984 the Minister has the power to deal with human remains, if they are put into the Minister's charge. The Aboriginal and Torres Strait Islander Commission Act 1989 defines ATSIC's powers, but they are currently under revision.

9   It is an irony of the sort perceived by Frantz Fanon that the Indigenous often had to bear names that evoked their imperial masters.

10   The site of the dime museum on Superior Street remained, but Tambo had died before he could perform there.

11   As reported by John Camplin for Australian Associated Press at Townsville, on the return of the delegation on 10 Dec. 1993.

12   On this occasion, the images of the two girls were covered.

13   In the unpretentious surroundings of F. J. Corrigan funeral home.

14   The fulfilment of government policy was given a human face by Michael Williams, the First Secretary to the Consul General in Washington.

Mike handled the arrangements: the selection of a suitable funeral director, the liaison with the Seneca elder, the negotiations with the media, and so on, with a respect for the private nature of the relatives' ceremonial duties. When the delegation arrived in Cleveland, he quickly established an easy relationship with the three Palm Islanders that carried them through the brief, but emotionally strenuous, four days stay.

15   It was also use as a flash in part of the media presentation of Tambo's return within Australia, but it was given nothing like the exposure it received in America.

16   The outcome was the result of a successful Torres Strait Islander land claim brought by Eddie Koiki Mabo and others. Justices Deane and Gaudron maintained that unless the nation be diminished, the common law must be revised, i.e. morality came before legal precedent. See 'Mabo v. Queensland No. 2', *Australian Law Journal Reports* 66 (1992) and discussions in Rowse 1993 and Attwood 1996.

17   Morris-Suzuki (1998, 28) discusses this point in her comments on the *Captive Lives* exhibition.

18   Silverman and Gulliver 1992, 21.

19   Josephine Geia, taped interview with the author, 1996.

20   In the past, it was not only Aboriginal peoples who 'lost' the likeness of an ancestor on death, or diaspora. In the West, the widespread use of photographic likenesses as memento mori dates from c.1855 when the inexpensive carte-de-visite made possible photographic portraiture for the masses. The use of graphic, not necessarily figurative, means of imaging ancestors and prominent persons is probably a cultural universal.

21   The Justice Group is a community initiative (supported by Corrective Services) as an alternative to courts and prison for juvenile offenders. Miss Geia kindly allowed me access to minutes of planning meetings.

22   Copy of letter held courtesy of Walter Palm Island.

23 Kitchener Bligh was a skilled master painter. Dr Rosalind Kidd was the expert witness on the case. For a succinct account of Kitchener Bligh's story see Kidd, www.linksdisk.com/roskidd/dr4htm. Also Kidd 2000.

24 Kidd, 1997, 1.

25 The same policy applied to other Queensland Aboriginal communities, with variations in its application.

26 See Kidd 1997 and 2000. Keep up-to-date via www.eniar.org; Human Rights and Equal Opportunity Commission, www.humanrights.gov.au; Kidd, www.linksdisk.com/roskidd.

27 Indigenous Land Corporation newsletter, *Land Matters* 11 (2000), available at www.ilc.gov.au.

28 See Benjamin 1968, 255.

29 Many thousands of Australians indicated their commitment to reconciliation through the Sea of Hands, planted at particular sites across Australia. Millions signed 'Sorry' Books as an expression of their regret for the long history of removal of children from their families. Then, at the Sydney Olympics in 2000, there was the moment when Cathy Freeman held aloft the Olympic torch, and lit the Olympic flame. See speech to Australian Native Title and Reconciliation, at www.linksdisk.com/roskidd/site/speech13.htm.

Bibliography

References cited

Adams, Bluford 1997. *E pluribus Barnum: The Greatest Showman and the Making of US Popular Culture.* Minneapolis: University of Minnesota Press.

Aldine History of Queensland, Morrison, W. Frederic, 1888.

Allingham, A. 1977. *Taming the Wilderness.* Townsville: James Cook University of North Queensland.

Alphand, A. 1892. *L'Exposition universelle internationale de 1889 à Paris: Palais – Jardins – Constructions diverse – Installations générales.* Paris: Ministère du Commerce et de l'Industrie.

Altick, Richard. D. 1978. *The Shows of London.* Cambridge, Mass.: Belknap Press.

Anderson, Benedict 1991. *Imagined Communities* (rev. edn). London: Verso.

Anderson, Patricia 1991. *The Printed Image and the Transformation of Popular Culture.* Oxford: Oxford University Press.

Andrade, Ernest Jr 1990. 'Great Britain and the Hawaiian revolution and republic, 1893–1898', *Hawaiian Journal of History* 24: 91–116.

Appadurai, Arjun (ed.) 1986. *The Social Life of Things: Commodities in Cultural Perspective.* Cambridge: Cambridge University Press.

——1991. 'Global Ethnoscapes', in R. G. Fox (ed.), *Recapturing Anthropology.* Washington: School of American Research.

Arens, William 1998. 'Rethinking Anthropophagy', in Barker, Hulme and Iversen 1998.

Ariès, P. 1974. *Western Attitudes to Death.* London: Marion Boyars.

Atkinson, R. L. 1979. *Northern Pioneers.* Townsville: Atkinson.

Attwood, Bain (ed.) 1996. *In the Age of Mabo: History, Aborigines and Australia.* St Leonards, NSW: Allen & Unwin.

Bailey, J. B. 1896. *The Diary of a Resurrectionist from 1811 to 1812.* n.p.: Swan Sonnenschein.

Bakhtin, M. M. 1981. *The Dialogic Imagination*, ed. Michael Holquist. Austin: University of Texas Press.

Bancel, Nicolas et al. 2002. *Zoos humains de la Vénus hottentote aux reality shows.* Paris: La Découverte.

Banks, Joseph 1962. *The Endeavour Journals: 1768–1771*, ed. J. C. Beaglehole. Sydney: Angus & Robertson.

Barker, Francis, Hulme, Peter, and Iversen, Margaret (eds) 1998. *Cannibalism and the Colonial World.* Cambridge: Cambridge University Press.

Barnum, P. T. 1871. *Struggles and Triumphs, or Forty Years' Recollections* (1869). New York: American News.

Barsley, Michael 1966. *The Oriental Express.* London: Macdonald.

Barthes, Roland 1983. 'The Eiffel Tower', in *Selected Writings*, ed. Susan Sontag. London: Fontana/Collins.

Bartolovich, Crystal 1998. 'Consumerism and the cultural logic of late cannibalism', in Barker, Hulme and Iversen 1998.

Bates, H. W. (ed.) 1869–72. *Illustrated Travels: A Record of Discovery, Geography and Adventure* (serialised). London: Cassell, Petter & Galpin.

Baud, M. 1997. 'Imagining the other, Michael Taussig on mimesis, colonialism and identity', *Critique of Anthropology* 17.1.

Benjamin, Walter 1968. 'Theses on the Philosophy of History', in *Illuminations: Essays and Reflections*, ed. Hannah Arendt, trans. Harry Zohn. New York: Schocken Books.

Bennett, T. 1988. 'The exhibitionary complex', *New Formations*, 4 (Spring).

Berger, John, and Mohr, Jean 1982. *Another Way of Telling*. Cambridge: Granta.

Bhabha, Homi 1983. 'The other question – the stereotype and colonial discourse', *Screen* 24.6: 18–36.

Blanckaert, Claude 1988. 'On the origins of French ethnology', in George W. Stocking Jr (ed.), *Bones, Bodies, and Behaviour: Essays in Biological Anthropology*. Madison: University of Wisconsin.

Bogdan, Robert 1988. *Freak Show: Presenting Human Oddities for Amusement and Profit*. Chicago: University of Chicago Press.

Bonaparte, Prince Roland 1884. *Les Habitants du Suriname à Amsterdam*. Paris: D. A. Quantin.

Bowen, George Ferguson, Sir 1865. *On the new settlement in Rockingham Bay, and the advance of Colonization over North-Eastern Australia*, including J. [*sic*] E. Dalrymple's report on his journey from Rockingham Bay to the Valley of Lagoons. London: Colonial Office.

Bradford, Phillips V., and Blume, Harvey 1992. *Ota Benga, the Pygmy in the Zoo*. New York: St Martins Press.

Brand, Dana 1991. *The Spectator and the City in Nineteenth Century American Literature*. Cambridge: Cambridge University Press.

Brändle, Rea 1995. *Wildfremd, Hautnah, Völkerschauen und Schauplätze, Zürich 1880–1960, Bilden und Geschichten*. Zürich: Rotpunktverlag.

Bratlinger, P. 1988. *Rule of Darkness: British Literature and Imperialism, 1830–1914*. Ithaca: Cornell University Press.

Brayshaw, H. 1990. *Well Beaten Paths: Aborigines of the Herbert Burdekin District, North Queensland: An Ethnographic and Archaeological Study*. Townsville: James Cook University of North Queensland.

Bredt-Dehnen, Deitrich (ed.) 1989. *450 Jahre Evangelische Kirchengemeinde Sonnborn 1539–1989*. Sonnborn: Evangelische Kirchengemeinde.

Breslin, Bruce 1992. *Exterminate with pride: Aboriginal–European Relations in the Townsville-Bowen region to 1869*. Townsville: Department of History and Politics, James Cook University of North Queensland.

Bricka, C. F. (ed.) 1897. *Dansk Biografisk Lexikon*. Copenhagen.

Briggs, Asa 1993. *Victorian Cities* (1963). Berkeley: University of California Press.

Brilliant, R. 1997. *Portraiture*. London: Reaktion Books.

Brown, Julie K. 1993. *Contesting Images: Photography and the World's Columbian Exposition*. Tucson: University of Arizona Press.

Buck-Morss, Susan 1989. *The Dialectics of Seeing: Walter Benjamin and the Arcades Project*. Cambridge, Mass.: MIT Press.

Burdett, Henry C. 1893. *Hospitals and Asylums of the World*, vol. 3: *Hospital History and Administration*. London: Churchill.

Carlyle, J. P. 1978. 'A personal name index to *Richard H. Orton's Records of Californian Men in the War of Rebellion, 1861 to 1867*' (facsimile of 1890 original). Detroit: Gale Research.

Carrington, George 1871. *Colonial Adventures and Experiences by a University Man*. London: Bell & Daldy.

Carter, P. 1987. *The Road to Botany Bay: An Essay in Spatial History*. London: Faber and Faber.

Caughey, John, and Caughey, Laree 1962. *California Heritage: An Anthology of History and Literature*. Los Angeles: Ward Ritchie Press.

Chase, A., and Sutton, P. 1987. 'Australian Aborigines in a rich environment', in W. H. Edwards (ed.), *Traditional Aboriginal Society: A Reader*. South Melbourne: Macmillan.

Clement, A. J. 1967. *The Kalahari and its Lost City*. Johannesburg: Longmans.

Clifford, James 1988. *The Predicament of Culture: Twentieth-Century Ethnography, Literature, and Art*. Cambridge, Mass.: Harvard University Press.

Colliver, F. S., and Woolston, F. P. 1980. *The Rain Forest Sword and Shield in Queensland*, Occasional Papers in Anthropology 10 (July). St Lucia: Anthropology Museum, University of Queensland.

——[c. 1998]. 'The Wildsoet interview – some recollections of the Aborigines of the Tully area', in

Queensland Heritage, 11. Brisbane: Library Board of Queensland.

Cook, James W. 1996. 'Of men, missing links, and non-descripts: the strange career of P. T. Barnum's "What is It?" exhibition', in Thomson 1996.

Cook, Sherburne F. 1976. *The Population of California Indians 1769–1970*. Berkeley: University of California Press.

Coombes, Annie 1994. *Reinventing Africa: Museums, Material Culture and Popular Imagination*. London: Yale University Press.

Cooper, F., and Stoler, L. 1997. 'Between metropole and colony: rethinking a research agenda', in F. Cooper and L. Stoler (eds), *Tensions of Empire*. Berkeley: University of California Press.

Corby, R. 1993. 'Ethnographic showcases, 1870–1930', *Cultural Anthropology* 8.3: 338–69.

Cowling, Margaret 1989. *The Artist as Anthropologist: The Representation of Type and Character in Victorian Art*. Cambridge: Cambridge University Press.

Crawfurd, James 1866. 'Cannibalism in relation to ethnology', *Transactions of Ethnological Society of London*, new series, 4.

Creed, Barbara, and Hoorn, Jeanette (eds) 2001. *Body Trade: Captivity, Cannibalism and Colonialism in the Pacific*. Annandale: Pluto Press Australia.

Cronin, W. 1992. *Nature's Metropolis: Chicago and the Great West*. New York: W. W. Norton.

Cull, Richard 1853. 'A brief notice on the Aztec race, with a description of the so-called Aztec Children by Professor Richard Owen', *Journal of the Ethnological Society*.

Cunningham, R. A. 1884. *History of R. A. Cunningham's Australian Aborigines, Tattooed Cannibals, Black Trackers and Boomerang Throwers, Two Tribes, Men and Women*. London. For French (Belgian edition) updated as Histoire curieuse des Aborigenes d'Australie, Cannibales tatoues . . . Brussells, 1884. Also in German (update) as *Geschichte von R. A Cunningham's Austral-Ureinwohner, Tätowierte Kanibalen, Schwarze Pfadfinder und Bumerang-Schleuderer, 2 Stämen, Männer und Frauen*, Köln, 1884; in Swedish (updated again) as *Berättelse om K.* [*sic*] *A. Cunningham's Austral-Invånare, Tatuerade*

Kannibaler, Svarta Spårfinnare och Bumerangkastare, bestående af Två Stammar, Män och Qvinnor, Accidens Tryckeriet, Stockholm, 1886.

——1890. *Beskrifning öfver Herr R. A. Cunninghams Samoa-Krigare under anförande af sin Höfding Manogi*. Stockholm. Also in German as *Beschreibung der Samoa-Krieger des Herrn R. A. Cunningham unter Führung ihres Häuptlings Manogi, Auf ihrer Reise um die Welt*, printed by Adolph Friedländer, 1890.

Curr, E. M. 1886–7. *The Australian Race*. 4 vols, Melbourne: Farres.

Dahl-Engelstift (ed.) 1923. *Dansk Biografisk Haandslexikon*. Copenhagen.

Dalrymple, G. E., and Smith, J. W. 1860. *Report of the Proceedings of the Queensland government schooner Spitfire, in search of the mouth of the River Burdekin, on the north-eastern coast of Australia*. V&P QLA.

Deniker, J. 1889. 'Les Hottentots au jardin d'acclimatation.' *Revue d'Anthropolgie*, 4: 1–27.

Dening, G. 1996. *Performances*. Melbourne: Melbourne University Press.

Dexter, R. R. W. 1966. 'Putman's problems popularising anthropology', *American Scientist* 54.3.

Dickens, Charles 1853. 'The Noble Savage', *Household Words*, Saturday, 11 June.

Dixon, Robert 1995. *Writing the Colonial Adventure: Race, Gender and Nation in Anglo-Australian Popular Fiction 1875–1914*. Cambridge: Cambridge University Press.

Dixon, R. M. W. 1979. 'Wargamay', in Robert M. W. Dixon and Barry J. Blake (eds), *Handbook of Australian Languages*, vol. 1. Amsterdam: John Benjamins BV.

——1983. 'Nyawaygi', in *Handbook of Australia Languages* vol. 3.

Eden, Charles Henry 1872a. 'An Australian search party', in vol. 6 of Bates 1869–72.

——1872b. *My Wife and I in Queensland*. London: Longmans, Green.

Edwards, Elizabeth 2001. *Raw Histories: Photographs, Anthropology and Museums*. Oxford: Berg.

Eissenberger, Gabi 1996. *Entführt, verspottet und gestorben, Lateinamerikanische Völkerschauen in deutschen Zoos*. Frankfurt am Main: Iko.

Ellingson, T. 2001. *The Myth of the Noble Savage.* Berkeley: University of California Press.

Engels, Friedrich 1839. 'Letters from Wuppertal', *Telegraph für Deutschland*, nos. 49, 50, 51, 52, 57, 59. Also in Karl Marx and Friedrich Engels, *Collected Works*, vol. 2, London: Lawrence & Wishart, 1934.

Engels, Peter, and Eckhart, Franz G. 2000. *Kleine Darmstädter Festgeschichte.* Darmstadt.

Evans, R., Saunders, K., and Cronin, K. 1975. *Race Relations in Colonial Queensland: A History of Exclusion, Exploitation and Extermination.* St Lucia: University of Queensland Press.

Farnum, Allen L. 1992. *Pawnee Bill's Historic Wild West: A Photo Documentary of the 1900–1905 Show Tours.* Schiffer Publishing.

Fauvelle-Aymar, François-Xavier. 1999a. 'Des murs d'Augsbourg aux vitrines du Cap', *Cahiers d'Études Africaines*, 39: 539–61.

Fauvelle, François-Xavier. 1999b. 'Point d'histoire: Les Khoisan dans la littérature anthropologique du XIX siècle. Réseaux scientifiques et construction des savoirs au siècle de Darwin et de Barnum', *Bulletin et Mém. de Société d'Anthropologie de Paris*, new series, 11: 3–4, 425–71.

Fiedler, Uwe 1997. *Chronik mit Löchern.* Chemnitz: Schlossbergmuseum Chemnitz.

Finch-Hatton, H. 1885. *Advance Australia! An Account of Eight Years Wandering, and Amusement in Queensland, New South Wales, and Victoria.* London: Allen.

Flint, Richard W. 1977. 'The evolution of the circus in nineteenth-century America', in Myron Matlaw (ed.), *American Popular Entertainment: Papers and Proceedings of Conference on the History of American Popular Entertainment.* Westport: Greenwood Press.

——1983. 'The circus is the world's largest, grandest, best amusement institution'. *Quarterly Journal, Library of Congress* 40.3.

Fforde, C., Hubert, J., and Turnbull, Paul (eds) 2002. *The Dead and their Possesions. Repatriation in Principle, Policy and Practice*, London Routledge.

Foucault, Michel 1997. *The Birth of the Clinic* (1973). London: Routledge.

Fox, Matt. J. 1919–23. *The History of Queensland*, vols 1–3. Brisbane: Hussey & Gillingham.

Fretz, Eric 1996. 'P. T. Barnum's theatrical selfhood and the nineteenth-century culture of exhibition', in Thomson 1996.

Frost, Linda 1996. 'The Circassian beauty and the Circassian slave: gender, imperialism, and American popular entertainment', in Thomson 1996.

Gardenhire, W. C. 1871. *Fiji and the Fijians*, pamphlet. (Copy in Harvard Library.)

Geist, Johann F. 1997. *Die Kaisergalerie: Biographie der Berliner Passage.* München: Prestel.

Gibson-Wilde, Dorothy M. 1984. *Gateway to a Golden Land: Townsville to 1884.* Townsville: History Department, James Cook University of North Queensland.

Gibson-Wilde, D. and Gibson-Wilde, B. 1988. *Hotels of Queensland 1864–1914.* Townsville: History Department, James Cook University of North Queensland.

Gilbert, James 1991. *Perfect Cities: Chicago's Utopias 1893.* Chicago: University of Chicago Press.

Glaister, John 1886. 'Note on the Australian Aborigines being exhibited in Glasgow, March 1886', *Philosophical Society of Glasgow* 17: 182–91.

Gorky, Maxim 1907. 'Boredom', in *The Independent* 63, 8 Aug: 309–17. New York.

Gould, Stephen Jay 1981. *The Mismeasure of Man.* New York: W. W. Norton.

Greenwood, J. 1862. *Wild Sports of the World: A Boys' Book of Natural History and Adventure.* London: S. O. Beeton.

——1864. *Curiosities of Savage Life.* London: S. O. Beeton.

Gowlland, J. T. Lieutenant R. N. 1872. *New Guinea Expedition per Brig 'Maria' (correspondence respecting rescue and arrival of survivors of.)* Published report to New South Wales Government, six pages and map. (Copy from John Oxley Library.)

Guttstadt, A. 1900. *Krankenhaus-lexikon für das Deutsche Reich.* Berlin: Verlag von Georg Reimer.

Hagenbeck, Carl 1909. *Beasts and Men.* London: Longmans. An abridged translation of *Von*

Tieren und Menschen, Berlin: Vita Deutsches Verlagshaus.

Handy, Moses P. 1893. *The Official Directory of the World's Columbian Exposition*. Chicago: W. B. Gonkey.

Harper, K. 1989. *Give me my Father's Body: The Life of Minik, the New York Eskimo*. New York: Blackhead.

Heizer, R. F. (ed.) 1978. *Handbook of North American Indians*, vol. 8: *California*. Washington DC: Smithsonian Institution.

Herbert, Ulricht 1990. *A History of Foreign Labor in Germany 1880–1980*, trans. William Templer. Ann Arbor: University of Michigan Press.

Hobsbawm, Eric 1987. *The Age of Empire 1875–1914*. London: Weidenfeld & Nicolson.

Honour, Hugh 1989. *From the American Revolution to World War I*, vol. 4 of *The Image of the Black in Western Art*. Cambridge, Mass.: Harvard University Press.

Horn, Pierre L. (ed.) 1991. *Handbook of French Popular Culture*. Westport: Greenwood Press.

Houzé, E., and Jacques, V. 1884. 'Communication de MM. Houzé et Jacques sur les Australiens du Musée du Nord. Séance du 28 Mai, 1884', *Bulletin de la Société d'Anthropologie de Bruxelles* 3–4: 53–153.

Hubley, Patricia 1987. 'Disturbing the dead in York, PA', *Susquehanna Monthly Magazine*, 15–17 Apr.

Huggan, Graham 1998. 'Ghost stories, bone flutes, cannibal countermemory', in Barker, Hulme and Iversen 1998.

Hull, Alfred A. 1886. 'Queensland, as it was and as it is', *Journal of the Royal Geographical Society, Queensland Branch*, 1.

Hulme, Peter 1986. *Colonial Encounters: Europe and the Native Carribbean, 1492–1797*. London: Routledge.

——1990. 'The spontaneous hand of nature: savagery, colonialism and the Enlightenment', in P. Hulme and L. Jordanova, *The Enlightenment and its Shadows*. London: Routledge.

——1998. 'The cannibal scene', in Barker, Hulme and Iversen 1998.

Huxley, T. H. 1935. *T. H. Huxley's Diary of the Voyage of the H. M. S. Rattlesnake*, edited by Julian Huxley. London: Chatto & Windus.

Jay, Martin 1994. *Downcast Eyes: The Denigration of Vision in Twentieth-Century French Thought*. Berkeley: University of California Press.

Jobling, Paul and Crowley, David 1996. *Graphic Design: Reproduction and Representation since 1800*. Manchester: Manchester University Press.

Johnstone, Robert A. 1903, 'Spinifex and Wattle', A series of articles in The *Queenslander*, compiled and republished by J. W. Johnstone-Need, 1984, Cairns: Johnstone-Need.

Jones, Dorothy 1961. *Cardwellshire Story*. Brisbane: Jacaranda Press.

Joyce, Barry 2001. *The Shaping of American Ethnography: The Wilkes Exploring Expedition 1838–42*, Critical Studies in the History of Anthropology 2. Lincoln: University of Nebraska.

Jukes, J. Beete 1847. *Narrative of the Surveying voyage of HMS Fly, commanded by Captain F. P. Blackwood, R.N. . . . during the Years 1842–1846*. London.

Junker, Alois 1912. *Die Deutschen Kolonien*. München: Verlag de Jos.

Jütte, Robert 1996. *Institutions of Confinement: Hospitals, Asylums, and Prisons in Western Europe and North America, 1500–1950*. Washington DC: German Historical Institute and Cambridge University Press.

Kaeppler, Adrienne 1985. 'Anthropology and the US Exploring Expedition', in Viola and Margolis 1985.

Karasek, Erika and Neuland, Dagmar 1991. *Sensationen Sensationen Merk-Würdiges aus Museum und Panotpikum*. Berlin: Museum für Völkskunde.

Karasek, Erica et al. 1999. *Faszination Bild. Kultur Kontakte Europa*. Berlin: Museum Europäischer Kulturen.

Karp, Ivan, Kreamer, Christine Mullen, and Lavine, Steven D. (eds) 1992. *Museums and Communities: The Politics of Public Culture*. Washington DC: Smithsonian Institution Press.

Kasson, John F. 1978. *Amusing the Millions: Coney Island at the Turn of the Century*. New York: Hill & Wang.

Kennedy, E. B. 1902. *The Black Police of Queensland:*

Reminiscences of Official Work and Personal Adventures in the Early days of the Colony. London.

Kidd, Ros 1997. *The Way We Civilise: Aboriginal Affairs – the Untold Story.* St Lucia: University of Queensland Press.

—— 2000. *Black Lives, Government Lies.* St Lucia: University of Queensland Press.

Kiesewetter, Hubert 1981. 'Regional Disparity in Wages: the Cotton industry in nineteenth century Germany', in Bairoch P. and Levy-Leboyer M. (eds), *Disparities in Economic Development since the Industrial Revolution.* London: McMillan.

Kilgour, Maggie 1990. *From Communion to Cannibalism: An anatomy of the Metaphors of Incorporation.* New Jersey: Princeton University Press.

—— 1998. 'The function of cannibalism at the present time', in Barker, Hulme and Iversen 1998.

King, D. A., and McHoul, A. W. 1986. 'The discursive production of the Queensland Aborigines as subject: Meston's proposal 1895', *Social Analysis* 19.

King, Phillip Parker 1826. *Narrative of Survey of the Intertropical and Western Coasts Waters of Australia: performed between the years 1818 and 1822.* London: John Murray.

Kirshenblatt-Gimlett, Barbara 1991. 'Objects of ethnography', in Ivan Karp and Steven D. Levine (eds), *Exhibiting Cultures: The Poetics and Politics of Museum Display.* Washington DC: Smithsonian Institution Press.

Kiss, Ken n.d. 'Panorama', in *Crystal Palace Matters.* London: Crystal Palace Foundation.

Kopytoff, I. 1986. 'The cultural biography of things', in Appadurai 1986.

Kuykendall, Ralph S. 1967. *The Hawaiian Kingdom III: 1874–1893.* Honolulu: University of Hawaii Press.

Lack, C. 1951. 'A century of Brisbane journalism', *Queensland Historical Society Journal* 4.4.

Lackinger, Ingeborg Viktoria 1983. *Die Heilkunde in der 'Illustrirten Zeitung' 1870–1885.* Altrogge:Verlag Murken.

Lane-Poole, S. (ed.) 1889. *Thirty Years of Colonial Government: A Selection from the Dispatches and Letters of The Right Hon. Sir George Ferguson Bowen,* vol. 1. London: Longmans Green.

Lassek, A. M. 1958. *Human Dissection, its Drama and Struggle.* Springfield, Ill.: Charles Thomas.

Lattas, A. 1987. 'Savagery and civilisation: towards a genealogy of racism', *Social Analysis* 21 (Aug.).

Lavater, J. C. 1789. *Essays on Physiognomy, for the promotion of knowledge and the love of mankind* (1775–8), trans. Thomas Holcroft. 3 vols, London: G. G. J. and J. Robinson.

Lindfors, Bernth 1996. 'Ethnological show business: footlighting the dark continent', in Thomson 1996.

—— (ed.) 1999. *Africans on Stage: Studies in Ethnological Show Business.* Bloomington: Indiana University Press; Cape Town: David Philip.

Lindqvist, Sven 1997. *'Exterminate All the Brutes'.* London: Granta Books.

Loos, Noel 1982. *Invasion and Resistance: Aboriginal-European Relations on the North Queensland Frontier 1861–1897.* Canberra: Australian National University Press.

Lumholtz, C. S. 1979. *Among Cannibals* (repr. of 1888 edn). Firle, Sussex: Caliban Books.

Lyons, Paul 2001. 'Lines of fright: fear, perception and the "seen" of cannibalism in Charles Wilkes's "Narrative" and Herman Melville's "Typee"', in Creed and Hoorn 2001.

MacGillivray, J. 1852. *Narrative of the Voyage of H.M.S. Rattlesnake . . . 1846–1850.* London: T. and A. Boone.

McIntosh Ian S. 2000. 'When will we know we are reconciled?', *Anthropology Today* 16.5 (Oct.).

McKenzie, Edith Kawalohea n.d. *Hawaiian Genealogies extracted from Four Local Language Newspapers.* n.p.

Mackenzie, John M. (ed.) 1986. *Imperialism and Popular Culture.* Manchester: Manchester University Press.

McNiven, Ian J., Russell, Lynette, and Schaffer, Kay (eds) 1998. *Constructions of Colonialism: Perspectives on Eliza Fraser's Shipwreck.* London: Cassell/Leicester University Press.

Marcus, George 1995. 'The modernist sensibility in

recent ethnographic writing and the cinematic metaphor of montage', in L. Devereaux and R. Hillman (eds), *Fields of Vision: Essays in Film Studies, Visual Anthropology, and Photography*. Berkeley: University of California Press.

Massin, Benoit 1996. 'From Virchow to Fischer, physical anthropology and "modern race theories" in Wilhelmine Germany', in George W. Stocking Jr (ed.), *Volkgeist as Method and Ethic: Essays on Boasian Ethnography and the German Anthropological Tradition*. Madison: University of Wisconsin Press.

Meggs, Philip B. 1998. *A History of Graphic Design*, 3rd edn. New York: John Wiley.

Merivale, Herman 1841 (1839–41). *Lectures on Colonization and Colonies*, delivered before the University of Oxford (1838–41) London: Longman, Orme, Brown, Green, Longmans.

Meston, A. 1895. *Geography of Queensland*. Brisbane: Queensland Government Printer.

——1898. 'A fragment of a description of a bora at Mt Milbirraman', *Science of Man* 6.1: 10–11.

Mondière, A. T. 1886. 'Les Australiens exhibés à Paris', *Revue d'Anthropologie*, series 3, 9: 313–17.

Montaigne, Michel de 1958. 'On Cannibals', in *Essays*. London: Penguin Books.

Moresby, John 1876. *Discoveries and Surveys in New Guinea and the D'Entrecasteaux Islands . . . visits to the pearlshelling stations in the Torres Straits of* HMS *Basilisk*. London: John Murray.

Morrill, James, 1896. *Narrative of James Murrell's Seventeen Years Exile among the Wild Blacks of North Queensland*, edited by Edmund Gregory. Brisbane: Edmund Gregory.

Morris, Alan G. 1996. 'Trophy skulls, museums and the San', in Skotnes 1996.

Morris, B. 1992. 'Frontier colonialism as a culture of terror', in *Power, Knowledge and Aborigines*, special issue of *Journal of Australian Studies*, 35. Bundora: La Trobe University Press.

Morris-Suzuki, T. 1998. 'Unquiet graves: Kato Norihiro and the politics of mourning', *Japanese Studies* 18.1.

Morton, Samuel George 1839. *Crania Americana or a Comparative View of the Skulls of Various Aboriginal Nations of North and South America*. Philadelphia: J. Dobson; London: Simpkin and Marshall.

Nott, J. C., and Gliddon, G. 1857. *Indigenous of the Earth*. London: Lippincot.

Obeyesekere, Gananath 1998. 'Cannibal feasts in nineteenth-century Fiji: seaman's yarns and the ethnographic imagination', in Barker, Hulme and Iversen 1998.

Odell, George C. D. 1927–49. *Annals of the New York Stage*, vols 1–12. New York: Columbia University Press.

Oetterman, Stephen 1997. *The Panorama: History of a Mass Medium*. New York: Zone Books.

Ohmann, Richard 1996. *Selling Culture: Magazines, Markets and Class at the Turn of the Century*. London: Verso.

Parkinson, Bob n.d. 'The circus and the press', *Bandwagon* 7.2. (Copy in Chicago Historical Society.)

Parkinson, Tom, and Fox, Charles Philip 1978. *The Circus Moves by Rail*. Bouldar Colerado, Pruett Pub. Co.

Peacock, Shane 1999. 'Africa meets the Great Farini', in Lindfors 1999.

Phillips, Jerry 1998. 'Cannibalism qua capitalism: the metaphorics of accumulation in Marx, Conrad, Shakespeare and Marlowe', in Barker, Hulme and Iversen 1998.

Pickering, Charles 1848. *The Races of Man and their Geographical Distribution*, vol. 9 of *US Exploring Expedition 1838–1842*. Boston: Charles C. Little.

Pieterse, Jan Nederveen 1992. *White on Black: Images of Africa and Blacks in Western Popular Culture*. New Haven and London: Yale University Press.

Pinney, Christopher 1997. *Camera Indica: The Social Life of Indian Photographs*. London: Reaktion Books.

Poesch, Jessie 1961. *Titian Ramsay Peale 1799–1855 and his Journals of the Wilkes Expedition*. Philadelphia: American Philosophical Society Memoirs.

Poignant, R. 1992. 'The grid on contested ground', *Olive Pink Society Bulletin* 4.1.

——1993. 'Captive Aboriginal lives', in K. Darian-Smith (ed.), *Captive Lives: Australian Captivity Narratives*,

Working Papers in Australian Studies 85, 86 and 87. London: Menzies Centre for Australian Studies, University of London.

——1997. 'Looking for Tambo', *Olive Pink Society Bulletin* 9.1–2.

——2003. 'The making of "professional savages" from P. T. Barnum 1883 to *Sunday Times* 1998', in C. Pinney and N. Peterson (eds), *Photography's Other Histories*. Durham, N.C.: Duke University Press.

Prideaux, P. 1988. *From Spear to Pearl-shell*. Brisbane: Boolerong Press.

Proctor, Robert 1988. 'From Anthropologie to Rassenkunde in the German anthropological tradition', in George W. Stocking Jr (ed.), *Bones, Bodies, Behaviour: Essays on Biological Anthropology*, vol. 5 of *History of Anthropology*. Madison: University of Wisconsin.

Ralph, Julian 1896. 'Coney Island', *Scribner's Magazine* 22.1 (July).

Reed, David 1997. *The Popular Magazine in Britain and the United States 1880–1960*. London: British Library.

Reiss, Benjamin 2001. *The Showman and the Slave: Race, Death and Memory in Barnum's America*. Cambridge, Mass.: Harvard University Press.

Reynolds, H. 1981. *The Other Side of the Frontier*. Ringwood: Penguin Books Australia.

——1989. *Dispossession, Black Australians and White Invaders*. St Leonards, NSW: Allen & Unwin.

——1990. *With the White People*. Ringwood: Penguin Books Australia.

Roth: W.E. 1902. Games, Sports and Amusements. *North Queensland Ethography: Bulletin 4*. Department of Home Secretary, Brisbane.

Roth. W. E. 1903. 'Superstitions, magic and medicine', *North Queensland Ethnography: Bulletin 5*. Department of Home Secretary, Brisbane.

——1907. 'Burial ceremonies and disposal of the dead', North Queensland Ethography: Bulletin 9, *Records of the Australian Museum* 6.5.

——1909. 'Tabu and other forms of restriction; Counting and Enumeration; gesture language'. North Queensland Ethnography: Bulletin 11, *Records of the Australian Museum* 7.

——1910a. 'Decoration, deformation and clothing', North Queensland Ethnology: Bulletin 15, *Records of the Australian Museum* 8.

——1910b. 'Social and individual nomenclature', North Queensland Ethnology: Bulletin 18, *Records of the Australian Museum* 8.

Rothfels, Nigel 1996. 'Aztecs, Aborigines, and Ape-People: science and freaks in Germany, 1850–1900', in Thomson 1996.

Rowe, C. S. 1931. 'Rowe's diary', *Cummins and Campbell's Monthly Magazine* (Townsville), Apr., May, June.

Rowlands, M. J. 1996. 'Prehistorical archaeology of the Great Barrier Reef Province: retrospect and prospect', in P. Veth and P. Hiscock (eds), *Archaeology of Northern Australia, Tempus* vol. 4. St Lucia: Anthropology Museum, University of Queensland Press.

Rowse, Tim 1993. 'Mabo and moral anxiety', *Meanjin* 52: 2.

Russell, Lynette (ed.) 2001. *Colonial Frontiers: Indigenous–European Encounters in Settler Societies*. Manchester: Manchester University Press.

Rydell, Robert W. 1984. *'All the World's a Fair': Visions of Empire at American Expositions, 1876–1916*. Chicago: University of Chicago Press.

——1992. *Book of the Fairs: Materials about World's Fairs 1834–1916 in Smithsonian Institution's Libraries*. American Library Association.

St Leon, M. V. 1983. *Spangles and Sawdust: The Circus in Australia*. Richmond: Greenhouse.

——1992. *Index of Australian Show Movements, 1833–1956*. Glebe, NSW: St Leon.

Sahlins, Marshall 1983. 'Raw women, cooked men, and other "great things" of the Fiji Islands', in Donald Tuzin and Paula Brown (eds), *The Ethnography of Cannibalism*. Washington DC: Society for Psychological Anthropology.

Saxon, A. H. 1989. *P. T. Barnum: The Legend and the Man*. New York: Columbia University Press.

Schadow, Gottfried 1835. *National-Physiognomieen*. Berlin.

Schaffer, Kay 1995. *In the Wake of First Contact: The Eliza Fraser Stories*. Cambridge: Cambridge University Press.

Schivelbusch, Wolfgang 1986. *The Railway Journey: The Industrialization of Time and Space in the Nineteenth' Century*. NewYork: Berg. (German edn 1977.)

Schmidt-Linsen-Hoff, Viktoria, Wettengl, Kurt and Junker, Almut (eds) 1986. *Plakate 1880–1914: Inventarkatalog der Plakatsammlung des Historischen Museums Frankfurt*. Frankfurt am Main.

Schneider, William H. 1982. *An Empire for the Masses: The French Popular Image of Africa 1870–1900*. Westport: Greenwood Press.

Schubert, Gustav 1884. 'Die Sioux-Indianer im Berliner Panoptikim [*sic*]', *Illustrirte Zeitung*, no. 2118 (Feb.), pp. 91, 94, 96.

——1885. 'Die Zulukaffern im Berliner Panopticum [*sic*]', *Illustrirte Zeitung*, no. 2169 (Jan.), pp. 87, 89.

Segal D. A., and Handler, R. (eds) 1993. 'Introduction: nations, colonies and metropoles', *Social Analysis* 33 (Sept.).

Semonin, Paul 1996. 'Monsters in the marketplace: the exhibition of human oddities in early modern England', in Thomson 1996.

Sheringham, Michael (ed.) 1996. *Parisian Fields*. London: Reaktion Books.

Shettel, James W. 1929. 'Death of Barnum's cannibal', *The Circus Scrap Book* 1.4 (Oct.).

Shultz, Suzanne M. 1992. *Body Snatching: The Robbing of Graves for the Education of Physicians in Early Nineteenth Century America*. Jefferson, N.C.: McFarland.

Silverman, M., and Gulliver, P. H. 1992. *Approaching the Past: Historical Anthropology through Irish Case Studies*. New York: Columbia University Press.

Skotnes, Pippa (ed.) 1996. *Miscast: Negotiating Khoisan History and Material Culture*. Exhibition catalogue, South African National Gallery, Cape Town.

Smith, Anne 1986. *Roberts Leu and North, a Centennial History*. Townsville: James Cook University of North Queensland.

Smith, B. 1980. 'The spectre of Truganini', A.B.C. Boyer Lectures. Sydney: Australian Broadcasting Commission.

Staehelin, Balthasar 1993. *Völkerschauen im Zoologischen Garten Basel 1879–1935*. Basel: Basler Afrika Bibliographien.

Stewart, T. D. 1978. 'The skull of Vendovi: a contribution of the Wilkes expedition to the physical anthropology of Fiji', *Oceania*, vol. 13.

Stirling, A. W. 1884. *The Nevernever Land: A ride in North Queensland*. London: Samson, Low, Marston.

Stocking, George W. Jr 1987. *Victorian Anthropology*. New York: Maxwell Macmillan International.

——1995. *After Tylor: British Social Anthropology 1888–1951*. Madison: University of Wisconsin Press.

Strother, Z. S. 1999. 'Display of the Hottentot body', in Lindfors 1999.

Taussig, M. 1986. *Shamanism, Colonialism, and the Wild Man*. Chicago: University of Chicago Press.

——1992. 'Culture of terror – space of death', in N. B. Dirks (ed.), *Colonialism and Culture*. Ann Arbor: University of Michigan Press.

Taylor, H. J. 1980. *The History of Townsville Harbour, 1864–1979*. Brisbane: Boolarong.

Taylor, J. Garth 1981. 'An Eskimo abroad, 1880, his diary and death', *Canadian Geographic*, Oct–Nov.

Thode-Arora, Hilke 1989. *Für fünfzig Pfennig um die Welt. Die Hagenbeckschen Völkerschauen*. Frankfurt am Main: Campus Verlag.

——1991. 'Das Eskimo – Tagebuch von 1880. Eine Völkerschau aus der Sicht eines Teilnehmers', *Kea: Zeitschrift für Kulturwissenschaften* 2: 87–115.

——2002. 'Abraham's diary – a European ethnic show from an Inuk participant's viewpoint', *Journal of the Society for the Anthropology of Europe* (Fall/Winter 2002). English version of Thode-Arore 1991.

Thomas, Nicholas 1991. *Entangled Objects: Exchange, Material Culture and Colonialism in the Pacific*. Cambridge, Mass. Harvard University Press.

——1994. *Colonialism's Culture: Anthropology, Travel and Government*. Melbourne: Melbourne University Press.

Thomson, Rosemarie Garland (ed.) 1996. *Freakery*. New York: New York University Press.

Tindale, N. B., and Birdsell, J. B. 1941. 'Tasmanoid tribes in north Queensland: results of the Harvard–Adelaide Universities Anthropological Expedition 1938–39', *South Australian Museum Records* 7.1: 1–9.

Tonkin, E. 1992. *Narrating our Pasts: The Social Construction of Oral History*, Cambridge Studies in

Oral and Literate Culture 22. Cambridge: Cambridge University Press.

Toole-Stott, R. 1971. *Circus and Allied Arts, a World Bibliography.* Derby: Harper.

——1992. *Circus and Allied Arts, a World Bibliography*, vol. 5. London: Aardvark.

Topinard, Paul 1885. 'Présentation de trois Australiens vivants. Séance du 19 Novembre 1885', *Bulletin de la Société d'Anthropologie de Paris*, series 3, 8: 683–99.

——1887. 'Présentation de quatre Boshimans vivants par M. Topinard. Séance du 7 October 1886', *Bulletin de la Société d'Anthropologie de Paris*, series 3, 9: 530–78.

Truettner, William H. (ed.) 1991. *The West as America: Reinterpreting the Images of the Frontier 1820–1920.* Washington DC: Smithsonian Institution Press.

Twain, Mark 1989. *Following the Equator* (1907), reprint. New York: Dover.

Viola, Herman J., and Margolis, Cralyn (eds) 1985. *Magnificent Voyagers: The US Exploring Expedition 1838–42.* Washington DC: Smithsonian Institution Press.

Virchow, Rudolf 1883. 'Australier Bonny, Alfred and Susanne' (session of 17 Feb. 1883), *Zeitschrift für Anthropologie, Ethnologie und Urgeschichte* 15: 190–3.

——1884. 'Australier von Queensland' (session of 19 July 1884), *Zeitschrift für Anthropologie, Ethnologie und Urgeschichte* 16: 407–20.

——1886. 'Bushmanner', *Zeitschrift für Anthropologie, Ethnologie und Urgeschichte* 18: 221–39.

——1889. 'Anthropology in the last twenty years', pp. 550–70 trans. C. A. Bleismer from *Correspondenz-Blatt der deutschen Gesellschaft für Anthropologie, Ethnologie und Urgeschichte*, 20.9 (Sept.): 89–100.

——1890. 'Samoaner' (session of 21 June 1890), *Zietschrift für Anthropologie, Ethnologie und Urgeschichte* 22: 387–92 and pl. 4.

——1896. 'Drei Australier' (session of 17 Oct. 1896), *Zeitschrift für Anthropologie, Ethnologie und Urgeschichte* 28: 528–9.

Vogan, Arthur J. 1890. *The Black Police: A Story of Modern Australia.* London: Hutchinson.

Walton, G. I. 1982. 'The study of anatomy at Leipzig University', *Scientific Journal* 106.

Warner, Marina 1995. 'Waxworks and wonderland', in Lynne Cooke and Peter Wollen (eds), *Visual Display: Culture beyond Experience.* Seattle: Bay Press.

Waterhouse, R. 1990. *From Minstrel Show to Vaudeville.* Kensington: New South Wales University Press.

Waterson, D. B. 1972. *A Biographical Register of Queensland Parliament: 1860–1929.* Canberra: Australian National University Press.

Weindling, Paul 1994. 'Public health in Germany', in Dorothy Porter (ed.), *History of Public Health and the Modern State.* Amsterdam: Rodepi.

White, Hayden 1980. 'The value of narrativity in the representation of the real', *Critical Enquiry* 7.1: 5–27.

Wilkes, Charles 1845. *The Narrative of the United States Exploring Expedition*, vols 3 and 5. Philadelphia: Lea and Blanchard.

Wilmeth, Don B. 1982. *Variety Entertainment and Outdoor Amusement: A Reference Guide.* Westport: Greenwood Press.

Wilson, Thomas 1890. *Anthropology at the Paris Exposition in 1889.* Washington DC: Smithsonian Institution.

Windshuttle, K. 2000. 'The myths of frontier massacres in Australian history', *Quadrant* 44 (Oct.–Dec.).

Wittke C. 1930. *Tambo and Bones: A History of the American Minstrel Stage.* Durham, N.C.: Duke University Press.

Word, Willhelm Reginald 1992. *The Protestant Evangelical Awakening.* Cambridge: Cambridge University Press.

Zeki, Semir 1999. *An Exploration of Art and the Brain.* Oxford: Oxford University Press.

Ziemssen, H. von (ed.) 1875–. *Cyclopaedia of the Practice of Medicine*, vol. 19.

Articles without named authors, circus publications and popular ephemera etc.

'Archivo per l'anthropologia et la ethnologia Societa Italiana di Anthropologia', *Etnologia* 15 (1885): 195, and 16 (1886): 524.

'Die Australneger in Berlin', *Illustrirte Zeitung*, no. 2143, 26 July 1884, pp. 95–6.

Barnum's *Advance Courier*, 1872.

Barnum's *Advance Courier*, 1884.

'Barnum's American Museum', in *Gleason's Pictorial Drawing-Room Companion,* New York, 1853.

——1873. *History of Animals and Leading Curiosities contained in P. T. Barnum's World's Fair.* New York: Wynkoop and Hallenbeck. (Copy in Hertzberg Circus Collection.)

——1883. *My Diary or Route Book, Greatest Show on Earth.* (Copy in Hertzberg Circus Collection.)

——1884. *My Diary or Route Book, Greatest Show on Earth.* (Copy in Circus World Museum.)

——1881–5. *Route Book of P. T. Barnum's Greatest Show on Earth,* seasons of 1881, 1882, 1883, 1884, 1885.

Barnum and Bailey 1894. *Barnum and Bailey Route Book,* season of 1894.

Barnum, Bailey and Hutchinson *c.*1883. *History of Native Nubians imported by Barnum, Bailey and Hutchinson.*

Broadsheet of Krao. *John Johnson Collection Human Freaks 4,* Bodleian Library, University of Oxford.

Bowen Region to 1869. Townsville: James Cook University of North Queensland, 1992.

'Carl Lumholtz och hans forskningar i Australien' in *Ny Illustrerad Tidning* nr. 48.(Stockholm) 27 Nov. 1886.

'Echoes from the Fair', *The Argonaut* (San Francisco), 26 June 1893.

Elberfeld Zoo Report, 1901.

'Exhibition of Natives of Queensland, 26 April 1887', *Journal of the Anthropological Institute* 17 (1888): 83.

'Exposition of the Anthropological Sciences at Paris', *The Athenaeum,* no. 3225, 17 Aug. 1889.

'L'exposition de Paris 1889', *Illustrée* (partwork), Paris, 1889.

L'Exposition universelle internationale de 1889 à Paris. Catalogue général officiel. Exposition rétrospective du travail et des sciences anthropologiques. Lille: L. Danel, 1889.

'From Prince Roland Bonaparte a Collection of Photographs of New Caledonian and Australian Natives (Queensland), 8 Dec. 1885. For the Library 1885', *Journal of the Anthropological Institute* 15 (1886): 422.

Gemeindebrief: Evangelische Kirchengemeinde Wuppertal-Sonnborn, Aug–Sept. 2000.

Geschichte der Rheinischen Missionsgesellschaft, pamphlet, *c.*2000.

Guide to the Crystal Palace and Park, by authority of the Directors. London: Charles Dickens and Evans Crystal Palace Press, 1884.

Hawaiian Annual, index for the years 1875–1932.

Hawaiian Directory, 1890–1 and 1891–2.

Hill, Heinrich *c.*1830. *Indianischer* [*sic*] *Buschmenschen aus New Holland, eingeschisst in Botany Bay, und einer Afrikanerin, von der Kuste Angola* (broadsheet).

History of Tuolumne County, 1882, reprinted 1973. Los Angeles Public Library.

Izvetstiia Imperatorskago Obshchestva, vol. 49. Moscow University, 1886.

'Living Curiosities at Barnum's Museum', *Harper's,* 15 Dec. 1860.

'Mabo v. Queensland No. 2', *Australian Law Journal Reports* 66 (1992).

McKenny's Hawaiian Directory, 1894.

Midway Types, The People of the Midway Plaisance World's Fair 1893. Chicago: American Engraving Company, 1894.

Miners' and Business Men's Directory for year Jan 1st 1856, section on Columbia. Tuolumne County, 1856, reproduced 1976. Los Angeles Public Library.

Mixed illustrations from Carl Lumholtz's *Among Cannibals,* unidentified news cutting, after 1889.

'P. T. Barnum's The World in Contribution', *Harper's,* 29 Mar. 1873.

'Parade of All Nations', *The Graphic,* July–Dec. 1893, p. 192.

'Paris and its Exposition', *Pall Mall Gazette, Extra,* no. 49, 1889.

Pawnee Bill's *Herald,* 1902. (Copy in Circus World Museum.)

Pawnee Bill's *Herald,* undated cutting. (Copy in Milner Library, University of Illinois.)

Pawnee Bill's Historical Wild West Show, *Official Route Book, combined seasons 1894, 1895* and for seasons of 1899, 1900 and 1901. (Copies from Circus World Museum.)

Pawnee Bill's Wild West Show, *Courier*, 1901. (Copy in Milner Library, University of Illinois.)

Pawnee Bill's Wild West Show, *Courier*, 1904. (Copy in Circus World Museum.)

Pawnee Bill's Wild West Show, programme 1905. (Copy in Circus World Museum.)

The African 'Earthmen' at the Westminster Aquarium, 20 Sept. 1884. Unidentified newspaper illustration and article. *John Johnson Collection Human Freaks 4*, Bodleian Library, University of Oxford.

The Pigmy 'Earthmen': Royal Aquarium, London, 11 Oct. 1884. *John Johnson Collection: Human Freaks 4*, Bodleian Library, University of Oxford.

Politikens Danmarkshistorie, vol. 12, 1870–1913.

Rise and Progress of Queensland Industries, The Queensland Court, International Exhibition of 1880, Melbourne, pamphlet on pearl-shell and bêche de mer.

The Way We Civilise: A Series of Articles and Letters reprinted from The Queenslander Newspaper. Brisbane: The Queenslander, 1880.

'Vaccination', entry in *Encyclopaedia Britannica*, 1894.

Unpublished sources

Anon, 'When Ingham was young', typescript, *c*.1964. John Oxley Library, State Library of Queensland.

Baird, letter to P. T. Barnum, 31 Oct. 1882. Bridgeport Public Library.

Barnum, P. T., 'Know all men . . .', letter, 27 Oct. 1882. Hertzberg Circus Collection, San Antonio Public Library, Texas.

Barnum, P. T., letter to agents etc., 9 Aug. 1882. Permanent Administrative Files, Record Unit 192, Smithsonian Institution Archives.

Barnum, P. T., letter to Baird, 25 Oct. 1882. Permanent Administrative Files, Record Unit 192, Smithsonian Institution Archives.

Camplin, John, typescript of Australia Associated Press report on Tambo's return, 10 Dec. 1993.

Cunningham, R. A., *The following are copies of a few of the Certificates that have been granted by Professors of Anthropological Societies in the different parts of the World.* Privately printed in English after 26 Apr. 1887.

Davidson, John Ewin, 'Unpublished Journal 20 April 1865 to 29 January 1868', typescript. James Cook University Library.

Deane, Sir William, Address by Governor-General of Commonwealth Australia at opening of *Captive Lives* exhibition, Nov. 1997, Canberra. (Copy held by NLA.)

Embassy of Australia and Coroner's Office, Cleveland, correspondence, Oct. 1993.

Galton Papers [R. A. Cunningham] 227/6 University College, London University Library: letter 13 April 1887, R. A. Cunningham to President of Anthropological Institute, with enclosures.

Geia, Josephine, taped interview with the author, 1996.

Gowlland, J. T. Lieutenant R. N. 1872. Autograph MS: *Expedition in Search of the Missing Passengers of the Schooner 'Maria'*. John Oxley Library, State Library of Queensland.

Hayter, Francis, MRF 121, Microfilm of a logbook of Lieutenant F. Hayter 1871–3, HMS *Basilisk* New Guinea to Australia. National Maritime Museum, London.

Heijm, Nicolaas. 1997. *Document Records of Manbarra Oral Traditions, Transcriptions and Tables.* (For private distribution.) Anthropology and Sociology, University of Queensland.

Jerry, Bessy 1996. Taped interview with the author.

'List to the Tale of Tambo, Wherein Showman Drew Tells of Cleveland Museum Days', typescript of interview with Frank M. Drew, [*c*.1945?].

Meston, A., papers, OM 64-17, Box 2, envelope 5, John Oxley Library, State Library of Queensland.

Palm Island, Walter, taped interview with the author, 1996.

Price, Charles, 'Language of the Townsville area' ('Coonambela'). Formerly MS 330, 1885, Royal Commonwealth Society, London, now Queensland Aboriginal dialects, RCMS 291, Royal Commonwealth Society Collections, Cambridge University Library.

Remington-Kellog to Betts, correspondence, Permanent Administrative Files, Record Unit 192, Smithsonian Institution Archives.

Tindale, N. B. 1938. MS Harvard and Adelaide

Universities Anthropological an Expedition Journal, vol. 1: 575–768., Museum of South Australia.

Wills, Korah HaIcomb, 'Unpublished memoir, begun in 1895', typescript (transcribed by Heather Frankland), OM 75-75, John Oxley Library, State Library of Queensland.

Official records and other archives

Australia

Darlinghurst Gaol Register, Feb. 1883, R2346.5/1920, Reel E 8, NSWA

NAA, Brisbane Branch BP 159/27, vol. 2, Ships coastwise.

NAA, Brisbane Branch BP 159/13, Ships reports in, interstate and overseas.

NSW *Police Gazette* 1883, 1892.

NSW *Parliamentary Debates*: Legislative Council, 1883.

NSWA Coastal In 1892 5 Aug., *Peregrine*.

NSWA, Roll 453, Coastals from North Queensland.

QPD (LA), 1876: 1420–24. Enclosure 5, Rev. Duncan McNab to Ministry of Lands.

QPD (LA), 1880.

QPD (LA), 1897: 1632.

QSA, Col/A64, 65/352.

QSA, Col/A306, 5664/1880.

QSA, Col/A333, 1385/1882, 1304/1882, 1225/1882.

QSA, Col/A340, 3552/1882.

QSA, Col/A202/23.10.1874.

QSA, Col/A353/335 of 1883.

QSA, Col/B32 register of incoming letter to Col. Sec./7334 Bench T and 7919 R.

QSA, Col/B32/8290 Bench T and 8602 Bench B.

QSA Col/B36 register of incoming letters to Col. Sec. 96/6724C.

QSA Col/B36 register of incoming letters to Col. Sec. 100300 Pol.

QSA, Col/G74 letter 92/3922 Under Col. Sec. to Roberts and Leu.

QSA, Col/G108 96/3186 A. S. Crowley to Under Col. Sec.

QSA, Col/G110 Acc. 48/2040 96/4761 Under Col. Sec. to A. S. Crowley.

QSA, Col/G108 Acc. 48/2038 96/3185 Under Col.Sec. to J. G. Atkinson.

QSA, Col/G75 Letter 4477 Under Col. Sec. to Roberts and Roberts.

QSA, Col/G76 Letter 92/4954 Under Col. Sec. to Roberts and Roberts.

QSA, Col/714, 1892/13108.

QSA, Col/A752 1893/12837 letters; 1893/5901 to 1893/12837 and telegram, 4 July 1893.

QSA, Har 13/1.

QSA, Hom/A7 letters: 1897/1380 1 Feb. 1897 to 1897/4450 5 Apr. 1897.

QSA, Hom/B2 13995, 14232 and 15226 Register Correspondence Home Secretary and Police, Townsville.

QSA, Col/B36 10300 Pol. and Hom/A1 10607 Pol. 1896.

QSA, Imm/126 1883–1909 p. 625 M.F. no. 21967.

QSA, HOM/J200, 2118/1913.

QSA Supreme Court Qld Northern (Townsville) Registry, Ecclesiastical files 6/1897, cert. 9815.

V&P QLA, 1860–1901.

V&P QLA, 1875, 621–8 'Alleged outrages committed on the Aborigines in Queensland by the Native Mounted Police'.

V&P QLA, 1884, vol. 2: 951.

V&P QLA, 1893, vol. 1: 59, 4 July.

V&P QLA, 1877, vol. 2: 1245.

South Australian Archives A5938 Northern Territory Government.

Germany

'Bob': Record of Death (Sterberegister), item 3070, 8 Nov. 1884, Chemnitz Standesamt.

Index to deaths 1882–1970 and Register of the Deceased in the Evangelical Reformed Church (Verzeichnis der Gestorbenen in der evangelische-reformierten Gemeinde zu Sonnborn) from 1 Jan. 1884 to 1904, item 48, 'Susi Dakara'.

Jacobsen-Archiv, Museum für Völkerkunde Hamburg: letters R. A. Cunningham to A. Jacobsen, 25 Nov. 1897, 13 Dec. 1900; letters James Dodd of William Foote & Co. to A. Jacobsen, 30 Aug. and 8 Sept. 1891.

'Jimmy': Cemetery Records (Verzeichnis der Beerdigten), item 383, 3 June 1884.

United Kingdom

Australia G97/A, MSS Brit. Emp. S22, G97B/3A.P.S.: Aboriginal Protection Society Papers, Rhodes House Library, Oxford.
Council for World Missions Archives, SOAS.
Christian Missionary Society South Seas Archives, SOAS.
PRO FO 5/2159.
PRO FO 115/929 From Consuls.
PRO FO 115/1036.
PRO FO 115/1037 To Consuls.
PRO FO 115/1050.
PRO FO 255/16 XL/97576.
PRO FO 716.2 Register of deaths.
PRO FO 281/31 and enclosures.
PRO FO 281/36.
PRO Copyright 1/368/69–73.
PRO Copyright 1/669.
PRO BT 27/273 July–Sept. 1898.

United States

Abstract of Record of Death, supplied by physician, Herman Bock, Coroner. Cuyahoga County, Ohio.
Consular records, Australia, NARA, Record Group 84, Roll 15.
Coroner's Verdict, Office of Coroner, Cuyahoga County Ohio, 18 Aug. 1993.
Cunningham records, Family History Centre (Latter Day Saints), Microfilm roll no. 1992245, frame 25.
Hawaii State Archives, Department of Interior Booklets 22–81.
Immigration Files, RG 85, NARA.
Latter Day Saints Genealogical Index, Hawaii: Paakiki.
McCaddon Collection of the Barnum and Bailey Circus. Manuscripts Division. Department of Rare Books and Special Collections. Princeton University Library.
Report of autopsy, Office of Coroner, Cuyahoga County Ohio, 20 Aug. 1993.
San Francisco census records, 1870, 1880, 1900.

Newspapers consulted for the relevant periods

Australia, New Zealand and the Pacific

Age, Melbourne
Argus, Melbourne
Auckland Evening Star
Brisbane Courier
Canterbury Times
Cleveland Bay Express
Daily Bulletin
Daily Telegraph, Sydney
Evening News, Sydney, 1883
Evening Star, Townsville
The Friend, Honolulu
Marlborough Chronicle
North Queensland Herald, Townsville
Northern Territory Government Gazette
Port Denison Times
Melbourne Punch
Queenslander
Samoan Times
Sydney Bulletin
Sydney Evening Echo
Sydney Morning Herald
Town and Country
Townsville Bulletin
Townsville Herald

Austria (Vienna)

Illustrirtes Wiener Tagblatt
Neues Wiener Tagblatt
Wiener Tagblatt

Belgium

L'Étoile Belge

Denmark

Berlingske Politiske og *Avert et Tidende*
Dagbladet
Dagens Nyheder
Dags-Avisen, Copenhagen
Illustreret Tidende

Morgonbladet
Nationaltidende
Politiken
Ravnen
Socialdemokraten

England

Brighton Examiner
Brighton Guardian
British Australasian
Daily Albion, Liverpool
Daily Chronicle
Illustrated London News
London Standard
Norwood Review and Crystal Palace Reporter
Pictorial World

Finland

Hufvudstadsbladet

France

Du Cri du Peuple, Paris
Gil Blas, Paris
La Dépêche, Lille
L'Écho du Nord, Lille
Moniteur de l'Armée, Paris
La Nature
Le Tour du Monde
La Publicité Roubaix

Germany

Das Ausland
Barmen und Umgebung
Barmen Zeitung
Berliner Börsen-Courier
Berliner Tageblatt
Breslauer Morgen-Zeitung
Chemnitzer Tageblatt
Darmstädter Tagblatt
Elberfelder Zeitung
Frankfurter Zeitung
Hallesches Tagblatt
Illustrirte Zeitung

Kleine Press, Frankfurt
Kölnische Zeitung
Mescheder Zeitung
National-Zeitung, Berlin
Neueste Nachrichten für Elberfeld
Norddeutsche Allgemeine Zeitung
Täglicher Anzeiger für Berg und Mark
Über Land und Meer. Allgemeine Illustrirte Zeitung
Vossische Zeitung, Berlin
Wiesbadener Tagblatt

Greece, Turkey, Middle East (Constantinople)

Greek cutting no name, 31 Oct. 1886
Levant Herald
Turkish cutting no name, no date

Holland

Binnenlandsche Berichten
Schiedamsche Courant

Ireland

Belfast Evening Telegraph
Belfast Newsletter
Daily Express, Dublin
Freemason's Journal and Daily Commercial Advertiser, Dublin
Irish Times
Morning News and Examiner
Northern Whig

Italy (Rome)

Giornale la Tribuna, news cutting

North America including Canada

Baltimore American and Commercial Advertiser
Baltimore Morning Herald
Berkeley Daily Advocate
Chicago Tribune
Cincinnati Times-Star
Cleveland Evening News
Cleveland Herald
Cleveland Leader
Cleveland Plain Dealer

Cleveland Press
Daily Alta
Daily Courier, San Bernardino
Daily Morning Call, San Francisco
Evening Banner, Blufton, Indiana
Evening Bulletin, San Francisco
Evening Mail, Stockton
Evening News, Stockton
Figaro, San Francisco
Fresno Weekly Republican
Los Angeles Times
New York Clipper
New York Journal
New York World
Oakland Times
Penny Press, Cleveland
Pittsburg Critic
Pittsburg Leader
Pittsburgh Chronicle Telegraph
Sacramento Bee
Sacramento Daily Record-Union
San Diego Union
San Francisco Chronicle
San Francisco Examiner
Santa Barbara Daily Press
Santa Barbara News
St Louis Daily Globe-Democrat
Wheeling Daily Intelligencer
York Daily
York Dispatch
York Gazette and Public Advertiser

Norway

Aftenposten
Christiania Intelligentssedler
Christiania Nyheds og Advertissements Blad
Dagbladet

Russia

Moscow Bulletin
Moscow Paper
Petersburgskaia Gazeta

Scotland

Evening Citizen
Glasgow Evening News and Star
Glasgow Evening Times
Glasgow Herald
North British Daily Mail

Sweden

Dagens Nyheter
Göteborgs Handels-och Sjöfarts-Tidning
Göteborgs-Posten
Lunds Weckoblad
Ny Illustrerad Tidning
Skånska Dagbladet
Stockholms Dagblad
Svensksa Dagbladet

Websites

European Network for Indigenous Australian Rights
www.eniar.org
Human Rights and Equal Opportunity Commission
(Australia): www.humanrights.gov.au
Indigenous Land Corporation newsletter, *Land Matters*
11 (June 2000), at www.ilc.gov.au
Rosalind Kidd, www.linksdisk.com/roskidd, and
her speech to Australian Native Title and
Reconciliation (ANTaR), 27 May 2000, 'The
Reconciliation Debate – New Dimensions', at
www.linksdisk.com/roskidd/site/Speech13.htm

Index